cook smarter

get started

Cooking delicious dinners every night of the week takes planning and organization. This means keeping a well-stocked pantry (see pages 6–7), putting together a weekly meal plan, and giving careful thought to how dinner preparation fits into your schedule each day.

You might feel that you're too rushed to sit down and work out an entire week's worth of meals each weekend. However, the time you spend doing just this will actually save you time over the course of the week. With these simple strategies, you'll save hours in the kitchen and at the market, you'll waste less food and money, and you'll also avoid unhealthy take-out and fast-food choices.

Look at the whole week of meals During the weekend, take time to think about how many meals you need to prepare in the coming week. You'll want to keep your menus varied, such as a vibrant Asian stir-fry one night, a hearty pasta the next, and a savory roast pork loin the third night.

Match your menus to your schedule As you plan your week's meals, keep your own calendar in mind. Extra-busy evenings might call for a simple soup, sandwich, or salad that can be put together quickly, or a dish that can be assembled in the morning to braise all day in a slow cooker. Celebrations or even casual get-togethers with friends can be a good excuse for putting more festive dishes like braised pork chops or lamb stew on the menu.

Cook on the weekend When cooking dinner is not a harried chore, you can relax and take pleasure in it. If possible, prepare some or all of Monday night's meal over the weekend. Or, if you decide to roast a chicken or braise a brisket for dinner on the weekend, double the recipe, and you can save time preparing another delicious home-cooked meal later in the week. You can also cook a double batch of a dish that freezes well, such as a stew, curry, or soup, and store the leftovers in the freezer for future use (see page 12 for more information on freezing and reheating meals).

Get everyone involved Enlist kids and other family members to help plan menus for the coming week. When everyone gets involved, they'll be sure to enjoy each meal more.

make the most of your time

Once you've decided on your meals for the week, give some thought to how you will organize your time. The more you can do in advance, the more quickly and easily a meal will come together when you are ready to prepare and serve it.

Stock up Avoid last-minute shopping trips for missing ingredients by keeping your kitchen well stocked. Over the weekend, check the pantry and refrigerator for the staples you'll need during the week. Also, keep a good supply of basic, nonperishable ingredients on hand, so you can improvise simple main and side dishes when needed; see the Pantry Checklist on page 7 for suggestions.

Shop less If you've made a weekly meal plan and your pantry is well stocked, you should need to shop only a couple of times a week for highly perishable ingredients, such as fresh produce, meat, poultry, or seafood. If you know that you'll be really pressed for time during the week, purchase your meat and poultry on the weekend along with your pantry staples, and wrap and freeze what you won't be using within the next couple of days.

Cook smarter Before you begin, read the recipe carefully. Take note of any steps that could be done simultaneously, such as mixing the eggs for a frittata while the vegetable filling cooks, or seasoning and cooking shrimp (prawns) while the accompanying rice steams. Get out all the equipment required, so everything is ready when you need it. Finally, set out the serving dishes and utensils.

Prep ahead Use a food processor to make quick work of chopping vegetables. Double up the prep by chopping extra vegetables for one or two other recipes one night and then storing them in an airtight container in the refrigerator until you need them. Or, depending on your daily schedule, you may be able to get a jump on dinner earlier in the day by prepping the ingredients.

Ready your ingredients Assemble and measure all your ingredients before you begin cooking. That way, you won't need to dig through the pantry in search of ingredients at the last minute, and counters won't be cluttered with cartons and jars. Pick up a set of small nested bowls in graduated sizes for holding the ingredients.

CLEAN AS YOU GO

Keep your kitchen organized by cleaning up as you go. Start out with a clean kitchen and an empty dishwasher—and make sure you have clean dish towels on hand. Put away ingredients as you use them, wipe down your work surfaces frequently, and move used pans and bowls to the sink or dishwasher once you are done with them. Fill dirty pans with hot water to soak while you're eating; by the time you're back in the kitchen, any browned-on food will be easier to scrub off.

ASK FOR HELP

Smart cooks know how important it is to have help in the kitchen. Ask family members to assist in dinner preparations, such as washing salad greens, chopping vegetables, and setting the table. After the meal, ask for help clearing the table, washing the dishes, and cleaning up the kitchen.

shop smarter

Whether you're shopping at a supermarket or visiting multiple food shops, a well-organized shopping list will save you time and money. Using the freshest produce and other high-quality ingredients will help ensure great-tasting dinners and healthy eating.

SHOPPING TIPS

Fresh ingredients Seek out a butcher, fishmonger, produce store, and specialty-food shop that stock top-notch ingredients at reasonable prices, and patronize them regularly. If there is a farmers' market in your area, get in the habit of visiting it regularly.

International ingredients Although the recipes in this book call for items that you will find in most supermarkets, ethnic markets or other specialty stores will offer a wider (and often cheaper) selection of authentic foods. Another great source is online. You can shop when it's convenient and have specialty ingredients delivered right to your doorstep.

Wine Ask a wine merchant to recommend good everyday wines at reasonable prices. If you have a favorite wine, consider buying it by the case, so you always have a supply on hand; you often will get a discount for buying in quantity.

A good shopping list is the backbone of smart meal planning. Here's how to use a list to streamline your trip to the market.

Prepare in advance Always make a list of what you need to buy before you go to the market. You'll save time at the store, and you'll avoid the frustration of coming home without a key ingredient. Being focused will help you save money, too.

Make a template Create a shopping list template on your computer. At the beginning of each week, you can post a new list on the refrigerator, then fill it in during the week as you run out of ingredients or get ideas for next week's dinners.

Categorize your lists Use these simple categories to keep your shopping lists organized:

- PANTRY ITEMS Check the pantry before a trip to the market and note any items that need to be restocked to make the meals on your weekly plan. This category can include items to store in the freezer as well as in the cupboard.

- FRESH INGREDIENTS These are for immediate use and include produce, seafood, meats, and some cheeses. You might need to visit different stores or supermarket sections, so divide the list into subcategories, such as produce, meats, and cheese, to help make your shopping efficient.

- OCCASIONAL PURCHASES This is a revolving list of refrigerated items that keep for some time and are replaced as needed, such as butter and eggs.

Be flexible Being organized does not mean being rigid. Change your menus based on which ingredients at the market are freshest. You might not find the exact item you need, or you might see something different that appeals to you.

the pantry

The pantry is typically a closet or one or more cupboards in which you store ingredients that don't require refrigeration. Make sure that your pantry is relatively cool, dry, and dark when not in use and that it is situated away from the heat of the stove, which can hasten spoilage.

Follow these steps as a starting point in creating a well-stocked kitchen and becoming a smarter cook.

Clean Remove everything from the pantry. Clean the shelves and reline them with paper, if needed.

Restock Discard any item that has passed its expiration date or has a stale or otherwise questionable appearance. Reshelve the items, organizing them by type so that everything is easy to find. Keep staples you use often toward the front of the pantry. Place older packages in front of newer ones so the old ones are used first.

Take inventory Consult the Pantry Checklist on page 7 to make a list of items that you need to buy or replace. Then, shop for the items on your list and restock your pantry.

Label Using an indellible marker, write the purchase date on perishable items. Clearly label and date foods bought in bulk.

Organize herbs & spices Keep dried herbs and spices in labeled airtight containers, preferably in a separate spice or herb organizer, shelf, or drawer. Arranging them in alphabetical order will help you find them quickly when you are cooking.

stay organized

- As you plan your weekly meals and make a shopping list, always check your pantry to make sure that you have all the ingredients you'll need and that you don't buy something you already have.

- Rotate items as you remove them, moving the oldest ones to the front of the pantry so they will be used first. Be sure to discard any item that has passed its expiration date and replace it if needed.

- When you run out of an item, immediately note it on your shopping list so that you remember to replace it.

PANTRY STORAGE

Dried herbs & spices These seasonings start losing flavor after 6 months, so buy them in small quantities and replace them often.

Oils Store opened bottles at room temperature for up to 3 months or in the refrigerator for up to 6 months. If storing in the refrigerator, bring to room temperature before using.

Grains & pastas Keep grains in airtight containers for up to 3 months. The shelf life of most dried pastas is 1 year. Although safe to eat beyond then, the flavor may be compromised.

Pantry produce Check onions and potatoes occasionally for sprouting or soft spots. Don't put them near each other, as they both produce gases that hasten spoilage.

Canned foods Discard cans that show signs of expansion or buckling. Once a can is opened, transfer the unused contents to an airtight container and refrigerate.

pantry checklist

To help you stock and organize your pantry, the checklist below is divided into two parts: staples and bonus items. Using it as a starting point to create your own master pantry list, you can move ingredients from one part to another and add items for preparing your favorite dishes.

STAPLES

DRIED HERBS & SPICES
- ❑ bay leaves
- ❑ chili powder
- ❑ cinnamon
- ❑ garlic powder
- ❑ oregano
- ❑ paprika
- ❑ peppercorns, black
- ❑ red pepper flakes
- ❑ rosemary
- ❑ sage
- ❑ salt, kosher or sea salt

PASTAS & GRAINS
- ❑ rice, long-grain
- ❑ small pasta such as macaroni or penne
- ❑ strand pasta such as spaghetti or linguine

CANNED, BOTTLED & JARRED FOODS
- ❑ beans, black, white, and/or pinto
- ❑ broth
- ❑ jam or jelly
- ❑ ketchup
- ❑ mayonnaise
- ❑ mustard
- ❑ peanut butter
- ❑ soy sauce
- ❑ tomato paste
- ❑ tomatoes, canned

PANTRY PRODUCE
- ❑ garlic
- ❑ onions
- ❑ potatoes

OILS & VINEGARS
- ❑ oil, canola or corn
- ❑ oil, olive
- ❑ vinegar, balsamic
- ❑ vinegar, red wine
- ❑ vinegar, rice
- ❑ vinegar, white wine

WINE & SPIRITS
- ❑ red wine, dry
- ❑ white wine, dry

MISCELLANEOUS
- ❑ baking powder
- ❑ baking soda (bicarbonate of soda)
- ❑ bread crumbs, dried
- ❑ cornstarch (cornflour)
- ❑ flour, all-purpose
- ❑ sugar, brown
- ❑ sugar, granulated

BONUS ITEMS

DRIED HERBS & SPICES
- ❑ allspice, ground
- ❑ cayenne pepper
- ❑ cumin
- ❑ curry powder
- ❑ marjoram
- ❑ nutmeg
- ❑ pepper, white
- ❑ sesame seeds
- ❑ thyme

PASTAS & GRAINS
- ❑ couscous, instant
- ❑ grains such as barley, farro, or quinoa
- ❑ polenta, quick-cooking
- ❑ rice, Arborio
- ❑ rice noodles

CANNED, BOTTLED & JARRED FOODS
- ❑ anchovies, fillets or paste
- ❑ capers
- ❑ chickpeas (garbanzo beans)
- ❑ coconut milk, unsweetened
- ❑ curry paste
- ❑ honey
- ❑ molasses
- ❑ olives
- ❑ red bell peppers (capsicums), roasted
- ❑ tomatoes, oil-packed sun-dried
- ❑ tuna packed in olive oil
- ❑ Worcestershire sauce

PANTRY PRODUCE
- ❑ mushrooms, dried
- ❑ shallots

OILS & VINEGARS
- ❑ oil, Asian sesame
- ❑ oil, peanut
- ❑ vinegar, sherry

WINE & SPIRITS
- ❑ brandy
- ❑ sherry, dry

MISCELLANEOUS
- ❑ beans, dried
- ❑ lentils, dried
- ❑ sugar, powdered (icing)
- ❑ tortillas, corn or flour
- ❑ vanilla extract

the refrigerator & freezer

Once you have stocked and organized your pantry, you can apply the same principles to your refrigerator and freezer. Proper freezing will preserve most of the flavor and nutrients in fruits and vegetables and is an especially good way to store stocks, soups, and stews.

Clean Remove items and wash the refrigerator thoroughly with warm, soapy water, then rinse well with clean water. Wash the freezer at the same time, following the manufacturer's instructions.

Restock Check the expiration dates on items and discard any that have passed their time. Toss out any foods that look questionable. As you replace the items in the refrigerator and freezer, group similar items so that everything is easy to find. Place older items toward the front to encourage you to use them first.

Take inventory Make a list of items you want to buy or replace.

Label Use an indellible marker to label items that you plan to keep for more than a few weeks, writing the date directly on the package or on a piece of masking tape affixed to it.

stay organized

- As you plan your weekly meals and make a shopping list, check the contents of the refrigerator and freezer and see what ingredients should be used that week.

- When you use the last of an item, immediately note it on your shopping list so that you remember to replace it.

general storage tips

- Foods lose flavor under refrigeration, so proper storage and maintaining a temperature below 40°F (5°C) are important.

- Freeze foods at or below 0°F (-18°C) to retain color and flavor.

- Don't crowd foods in the refrigerator or freezer. Air should circulate freely to keep foods evenly cooled.

- If necessary, use a refrigerator or freezer thermometer to monitor the performance of your fridge and freezer.

FREEZER SHORTCUTS

» When freezing raw meat, poultry, or seafood, remove it from the original packaging and wrap it in one- or two-serving portions, which can be individually thawed as needed.

» Chop or grate fresh garlic and ginger and freeze in small amounts in an ice-cube tray. Transfer the frozen cubes to a resealable plastic bag and store for up to 1 month.

» When preparing recipes that call for marinating as a first step, double the amount of both the meat and the marinade, and then freeze them separately for a future meal.

» Freeze unused broth or coconut milk in resealable plastic freezer bags.

» Keep packages of presliced bell peppers (capsicums), peas, squashes, and green beans and bags of peeled shrimp (prawns) on hand in the freezer for preparing a balanced meal on short notice.

Wrap properly Use only moistureproof wrappings, such as aluminum foil, airtight plastic containers, and resealable freezer-weight plastic bags. Choose plastic containers that can be filled almost to the brim with liquids such as stock or soup; leave some room for expansion but not so much that the container holds excess air. Other foods should be enclosed in a double layer of wrapping, and as much air as possible should be expelled before sealing.

Label clearly Use a permanent marker to label all packages or containers with the contents and today's date before you put them in the freezer. You can also add a "use-by" date. Use the charts on pages 417–420 for specific timing.

Thaw safely To preserve the texture of frozen meat, poultry, and fish, and to prevent bacteria growth, always thaw these items in the refrigerator. Vegetables can be thawed at room temperature, if necessary. For safety reasons, do not add frozen or wet ingredients to very hot oil in order to avoid splattering and potential burns.

cold storage tips

Here are some general tips for storing cold items in the refrigerator. See the storage charts on pages 417–420 for specific storage times.

fresh herbs & vegetables

- Trim the stem ends of a bunch of fresh parsley, basil, or cilantro (fresh coriander), stand the bunch in a glass of water, drape a plastic bag loosely over the leaves, and refrigerate. Wrap other fresh herbs in a damp paper towel, slip into a plastic bag, and store in the refrigerator crisper. Rinse and stem all herbs just before using. Store tomatoes, eggplants (aubergines), and winter squashes at room temperature.

- Cut about ½ inch (12 mm) off the ends of asparagus spears, stand the spears, tips up, in a glass of cold water, and refrigerate, changing the water daily.

- Rinse leafy greens, dry in a salad spinner, wrap in damp paper towels, and store in a resealable plastic bag in the crisper.

- Transfer mushrooms to a paper bag and store in the refrigerator. Rinse or brush clean just before use.

- In general, store other vegetables, such as broccoli, cauliflower, carrots, and summer squashes, in resealable bags in the refrigerator's crisper and rinse just before using.

meat, poultry & seafood

- Place packaged meats on a plate in the coldest part of the refrigerator. Check the expiration date and use before that date arrives. If only part of a package is used, discard the original wrapping and enclose in fresh wrapping.

- Most seafood should be used the day of (or day after) purchasing.

cheese & dairy

- Wrap all cheeses well to prevent them from drying out. Hard cheeses, such as Parmesan, have a low moisture content, so they keep longer than fresh cheeses, such as fresh mozzarella or ricotta.

- Store dairy products in their original packaging. Check the expiration date and use before that date arrives.

the right tools

Some cooks like to acquire the very latest gadgets, but you don't need a lot of fancy equipment to prepare a great meal. Make sure that you have the basic tools and then consider adding such items as a food processor, a mandoline, or a slow cooker, if they suit your cooking style.

Blender With its sharp blades and tall glass container, the blender can perform some of the same tasks as the food processor (below), such as puréeing soups and sauces and chopping bread into crumbs.

Food processor This kitchen workhorse chops, grates, shreds, and purées vegetables, among many other tasks. A mini processor is useful for mincing a small amount of garlic or fresh herbs and for making pesto, sauces, and marinades.

Mandoline Consisting of a rectangular frame, a cutting blade with a plain and a serrated edge, and a guiding plate to control thickness, this tool uniformly slices vegetables and fruits with a sweep of the hand. French-fry and julienne blades are also available.

Rasp grater Available in various sizes and degrees of fineness, this handheld tool is used to quickly and easily grate hard cheese, citrus zest, fresh ginger, and even nutmeg.

Rice cooker The rice cooker is designed to cook rice conveniently and consistently. Some rice cookers allow custom settings for specific types of rice; others easily convert to steamers for cooking vegetables. If rice shows up often in your weekly meals, this cooking tool will be a welcome addition to your kitchen.

Salad spinner Since greens for salads should be crisp and dry, this implement is a handy one to have on hand. It has a pump, crank, or pull cord that is activated to rotate the rinsed greens in a perforated basket and eliminate residual moisture from the greens quickly.

Slow cooker Three essential components—an exterior metal casing with a heating element, a glazed stoneware insert for holding the food, and a tight-fitting lid—make up this appliance. Large cookers can hold a whole chicken or a large cut of meat. See page 23 for slow cooking tips, techniques, and a list of recipes.

KITCHEN BASICS

Cutting tools Good knives are indispensable to working efficiently in the kitchen. You'll want to have an 8-inch (20-cm) chef's knife, a paring knife, and a serrated bread knife, as well as a sharpener.

Kitchen shears Fresh herbs, dried mushrooms, and canned whole tomatoes are some of the ingredients that can be chopped quickly with kitchen shears. Heavy-duty shears are great for trimming firm vegetables and poultry bones.

Pans A frying pan, a roasting pan with a rack, and heavy saucepans in assorted sizes are all you need to prepare most recipes. A Dutch oven is handy for making braised dishes, and a stockpot is ideal for cooking soups and pasta.

Bowls Small bowls, graduated in size, are helpful for holding ingredients after you have prepared and measured them. You'll also need two or three larger bowls for mixing.

easy techniques

Nothing will speed your time in the kitchen more than familiarity with a handful of everyday cooking techniques that are used throughout this book. With a little practice, you'll gather confidence in your culinary abilities, and you'll shorten the time you spend at the stove.

COOK'S TRICKS

Slice meat For quick-cooking techniques like stir-frying, cut meat across the grain into very thin slices for both tenderness and quick cooking. To facilitate slicing, freeze the meat for about 30 minutes to firm it up. You can also ask your butcher to thinly slice the meat when you purchase it.

Cut vegetables Cut vegetables into uniform pieces so they cook evenly. Cut them into bite-sized pieces, taking into account that the denser a vegetable is, the more time it will take to cook through. Long, thin strips (known as a julienne) maximize surface area, reducing cooking time while adding visual appeal.

Preheat pans Be sure the pan and cooking fat are hot before adding seafood, poultry, meats, or vegetables. The flavor and texture of the finished dish will be better, and the cooking time will be shorter. Even roasting pans can be preheated for a few minutes.

Blanch This technique is useful for par-cooking ingredients or loosening the skins of fruits and vegetables before peeling. To blanch, plunge food into boiling water for a very short period of time (usually 30 seconds to 1 minute), then into ice water to stop the cooking.

Deglaze Some recipes call for deglazing the pan after browning meat or poultry. To do so, remove the meat from the pan, leaving behind the drippings and browned bits. Place the pan over medium-high heat and pour in broth, wine, or another liquid. As the liquid boils, stir, scraping up the browned bits from the pan bottom.

Grill Grilling over a gas or charcoal grill creates delicious main dishes in minutes. With practice, even setting up a charcoal grill can become a quick process. See page 21 for grilling tips and tricks.

Reduce Simmering or boiling a liquid, such as broth or wine, is a good way to enhance flavor. As you do so, the quantity of the liquid decreases, and the liquid thickens into a flavorful sauce.

Roast Roasting meats and poultry in an uncovered roasting pan in a hot oven intensifies their flavors. Because the oven does most of the work, this technique requires little hands-on cooking time. Before you start, line a heavy roasting pan with aluminum foil and brush the foil with a little olive oil to help prevent sticking.

Sauté Sautéed foods are cooked quickly, usually in a frying pan over medium or medium-high heat in a small amount of butter or oil. Be sure to dry any ingredients to be sautéed on paper towels before adding them to the pan, or they will steam rather then sear.

Stir-fry Stir-frying is very similar to sautéing, with two notable differences: stir-frying is done over high heat, and the foods are cut into uniformly small pieces that cook very quickly. Before you start, make sure that all the ingredients are prepared, measured, and placed by the stove, as you won't have time to stop cooking and chop.

make more to store

Preparing a double batch of a dish and saving the second helping to serve later is a smart way to reduce your time in the kitchen. You can also make such things as a tart dough, a tomato sauce, or a baked ham on the weekend and use them to make quick meals during the following week.

storing leftovers

- You can store most prepared main dishes in an airtight container in the refrigerator for up to 4 days or in the freezer for up to 4 months.

- Let food cool to room temperature before storing it in the refrigerator or freezer. Putting hot food in the refrigerator will warm up the other foods stored there and may encourage bacterial growth.

- Freeze soups and stews in small batches, which allows you to heat up just enough to serve one or two people.

- Thaw frozen foods in the refrigerator or in the microwave. To avoid bacterial contamination, never thaw them at room temperature.

- For master recipes (opposite page) and basic recipes (page 14), follow each recipe's instructions for storage methods. Some recipes, such as frozen sauces, are brought to room temperature rather than reheated. Others, such as frozen tart dough, need to thaw in the refrigerator overnight, so you'll need to build this time into your meal planning.

- To keep meals interesting, allow a few days before reheating and re-serving leftovers. Or, freeze them if they will keep.

reheating meals

- When reheating refrigerated or frozen leftovers in the oven, reheat them at the original cooking temperature; using a higher temperature could result in dry, overcooked foods.

- Always use a preheated oven for reheating. Transferring frozen food in a ceramic or glass baking dish directly from the freezer to an unheated oven could cause the dish to break.

- If reheating a dish in a microwave, use medium power. If reheated on high power, the edges of the food could overcook before the center is heated.

GOOD CANDIDATES FOR FREEZING

- Braised meats and meatballs
- Baked pasta dishes (if frozen before baking)
- Doughs
- French fries, mashed potatoes and onion rings
- Most stews, soups and curries
- Stocks and sauces

FOODS THAT DON'T FREEZE WELL

- Cooked eggs and custards
- Cooked strand pasta
- Dishes with cream cheese, cottage cheese, whipped cream, or buttermilk
- Potato salad or chunks of boiled potato
- Watery raw vegetables such as cucumbers, lettuces, and tomatoes

fundamental recipes

In the Basic Recipes chapter, you will find a selection of recipes that form the foundation for a variety of dishes throughout the book. These recipes, including stocks, sauces, and doughs, are easy to prepare in advance and can be easily stored for future use in the refrigerator or freezer. See page 14 for a list of basic recipes.

Scattered throughout this book are master recipes, such as roasted chicken and baked ham, that can stand alone as a single meal, but can also be doubled, and the extra used during the following week in dishes such as salads, pastas, sandwiches, and more. See below for a list of master recipes and the many other recipes in which they can be used. See page 15 for full month of Sunday and weeknight menu ideas for utilizing both basic and master recipes.

MASTER RECIPES

Summer Vegetable Kebabs (page 205)
- Vegetable Rigatoni with Goat Cheese (page 173)
- Vegetable Quesadillas (page 206)

Classic Roast Chicken (page 267)
- Chicken Cobb Salad (page 91)
- Chicken Salad Provençal (page 98)
- Chicken & Mango Salad (page 99)
- Chicken Tostada Salad (page 103)
- Chutney Chicken & Pistachio Salad (page 104)
- Vietnamese Chicken Salad (page 105)

- Chicken & Arugula Pesto Pasta (page 159)
- Chicken Couscous (page 189)
- Chicken & Spinach Quesadillas (page 268)
- Chicken-Pesto Panini with Mozzarella (page 278)
- Green Chicken Enchiladas (page 291)

Grilled Flank Steak (page 305)
- Steak, Arugula & Pecorino Salad (page 113)
- Steak & Tomato Sandwiches (page 306)
- Steak Tacos with Guacamole (page 307)

Braised Brisket (page 320)
- Pappardelle with Shredded Beef Ragù (page 167)

- Shepherd's Pie (page 321)
- BBQ Brisket Sandwiches (page 322)

Baked Ham with Green Beans (page 328)
- Black Bean Soup with Ham (page 133)
- Baked Croque Monsieurs (page 329)

Roast Pork Loin with Pan Sauce (page 333)
- Cuban Pork Sandwiches (page 336)
- Chipotle Pork Tacos (page 337)

Pound Cake (page 379)
- Cherry Trifle (page 380)
- Mixed Berry–Cream Cake (page 381)

BASIC RECIPES

Vegetable Stock (page 27)
- Miso Noodle Soup (page 122)
- Creamy Asparagus Soup (page 126)
- Spring Vegetable Soup (page 128)

Mushroom Stock (page 28)
- Creamy Mushroom Bisque (page 142)
- Mushroom & Broccoli Rice Pilaf (page 221)

Chicken Stock (page 29)
- Chicken-Tortilla Soup (page 120)
- Chicken Noodle Soup (page 125)

Beef Stock (page 30)
- French Onion Soup (page 121)
- Tortellini in Broth (page 137)
- Beef & Barley Soup (page 149)

Tomato-Basil Sauce (page 31)
- Baked Chicken Parmesan (page 274)
- Spaghetti & Meatballs (page 172)
- Sausage Lasagna (page 180)

Bolognese Sauce (page 32)
- Stuffed Cannelloni (page 176)
- Roasted Eggplant Lasagna (page 225)

Roasted Tomato Sauce (page 33)
- Baked Rigatoni with Ricotta & Sausage (page 181)
- Meatball Sandwiches (page 313)

Basil Pesto (page 34)
- Minestrone with Pesto (page 127)
- Ziti with Pesto & Potatoes (page 175)
- Chicken-Pesto Panini with Mozzarella (page 278)

Romesco Sauce (page 35)
- Roasted Vegetables with Romesco (page 207)
- Grilled Pork Chops with Romesco (page 346)

White Beans (page 36)
- Seared Tuna with White Beans (page 245)
- Sausages with White Beans (page 343)
- Quick Cassoulet (page 347)
- Lamb Chops with Garlic & Rosemary (page 352)

Green Lentils (page 37)
- Lentil, Bacon & Frisée Salad (page 110)
- Lentil, Potato & Spinach Curry (page 211)

Flaky Pastry Dough (page 38)
- Rhubarb Pie (page 387)
- Pumpkin Pie (page 388)
- Berry Galette (page 397)

Sweet Tart Dough (page 39)
- Pecan Tart (page 390)
- Pear Custard Tart (page 391)

- Chocolate-Raspberry Tartlets (page 395)
- Strawberry–Cream Cheese Tart (page 398)

Savory Tart Dough (page 40)
- Ham & Spinach Quiches (page 60)
- Beef Empanadas (page 76)

Cream Cheese Dough (page 41)
- Spinach & Goat Cheese Tartlets (page 61)
- Mushroom Tart (page 220)

Yeast Dough (page 42)
- Rosemary Focaccia (page 70)
- Cherry Tomato & Pesto Pizza (page 71)
- Olive & Onion Flatbread (page 73)

Chocolate Cookie Dough (page 43)
- Chocolate Star Cookies (page 370)
- Ice Cream Sandwiches (page 371)
- Mocha Sandwich Cookies (page 372)

Butter Cookie Dough (page 44)
- Chocolate-Dipped Butter Cookies (page 373)
- Key Lime Tart (page 396)
- Lemon Tart with Raspberries (page 399)

a month of menus

Each weekly menu begins with a leisurely Sunday night supper and is followed by suggestions for dinners tailored to busy weeknights. You may need to double a recipe or two on Sunday so that you have leftovers for use in a quickly assembled dish a few days later.

WEEK 1	WEEK 2	WEEK 3	WEEK 4
Sunday Classic Roast Chicken (page 267) Summer Vegetable Kebabs (page 205) rice pilaf	**Sunday** Braised Brisket (page 320) Potato & Gruyère Tartlets (page 215) braised greens	**Sunday** Roast Pork Loin with Pan Sauce (page 333) Roasted Vegetables with Sage Butter (page 212) creamy polenta	**Sunday** Minestrone with Pesto (page 127) Rosemary Focaccia (page 70) green salad with balsamic vinaigrette
Monday Farfalle with Salsa Cruda (page 163)	**Monday** Mushroom Risotto (page 190)	**Monday** Red Pepper & Goat Cheese Frittata (page 227)	**Monday** Indian Vegetable Curry (page 209)
Tuesday Chicken Couscous (page 189) (use leftover chicken)	**Tuesday** Pappardelle with Shredded Beef Ragù (page 167) (use leftover brisket)	**Tuesday** Chipotle Pork Tacos (page 337) (use leftover pork)	**Tuesday** Cherry Tomato & Pesto Pizza (page 71) (use leftover yeast dough & basil pesto)
Wednesday Vegetable Quesadillas (page 206) (use leftover vegetable kebabs)	**Wednesday** Sesame Chicken Stir-Fry (page 281)	**Wednesday** Creamy Mushroom Stroganoff (page 179)	**Wednesday** Apricot-Glazed Chicken (page 275)
Thursday Braised Pork Chops with Cherry Sauce (page 341)	**Thursday** Creamy Polenta with Asparagus (page 184)	**Thursday** Balsamic Chicken & Peppers (page 297)	**Thursday** Shrimp Pad Thai (page 183)
Friday Miso-Marinated Salmon (page 241)	**Friday** Moroccan Lamb Burgers (page 354)	**Friday** Sea Bass with Ginger (page 233)	**Friday** Steaks with Herb Butter (page 303)

bulk it up

Once you have chosen the centerpiece of your meal, a quick bread, pasta, or grain side dish will give the meal substance. Garlic bread or crostini pair well with soups, salads, and pastas. Rice, couscous, polenta, and other grains are good partners for meat and poultry.

BREAD, PASTA & GRAINS

Bread Warm a crusty French or Italian loaf and serve it with room-temperature butter or olive oil. To make garlic bread, mix melted butter with minced garlic to taste. Halve a baguette horizontally and brush with the garlic butter. Wrap in aluminum foil and place in a 300°F (150°C) oven until the bread is crisp and heated through. Accompany Mediterranean salads with warm pita wedges. Serve Latin-inspired dishes with fresh tortillas, warmed by wrapping them in a clean kitchen towel and microwaving them for 30 seconds.

Corn bread Warm slices of purchased corn bread in the oven or toaster oven. Or, make your own using a mix; add frozen corn kernels for texture and flavor. Serve alongside braised meats or a bowl of chili.

Couscous Precooked dried couscous, sometimes called instant or quick-cooking couscous, requires only rehydrating in boiling water before serving. Typically served hot, it is also good cold:

toss it with minced green (spring) onions and chopped fresh tomato and drizzle with a light vinaigrette. Or, add raisins, currants, toasted nuts, or fresh herbs and mix well.

Crostini Spread toasted baguette rounds with store-bought spreads, such as tapenade, hummus, or roasted red pepper (capsicum) spread. Serve as a starter or with soups or stews.

Egg noodles Egg noodles are a natural match for many slow-cooked dishes. You can save time by purchasing fresh egg noodles, such as fettuccine, which take only 2–3 minutes to cook.

Noodle salad Boil soba or egg noodles and toss with bottled sesame or peanut dressing. Sprinkle with chopped green (spring) onion or fresh cilantro (fresh coriander).

Polenta Quick-cooking polenta is ready to serve in less than 10 minutes. Make a double batch, add some Parmesan cheese, and

serve half at one meal. Pour the remainder into a lightly oiled baking dish, let cool, cover, and refrigerate. Cut the polenta into triangles or squares and broil (grill) or pan-fry until browned on both sides. Serve at a second meal.

Rice Cook aromatic white or nutty brown rice, cool to room temperature, and refrigerate in resealable plastic bags. For coconut rice, substitute unsweetened coconut milk for one-fourth of the cooking liquid. For herbed rice, stir chopped fresh Thai basil, mint, or cilantro (fresh coriander) into the hot rice before serving.

Whole grains Amaranth, quinoa, farro, millet, kasha, and other whole grains make robust, nutritious side dishes. Sauté the grains with a little canola oil or butter. Add simmering water or vegetable broth, cover tightly, and simmer until just tender. Remove from the heat, fluff with a fork, and let steam, covered, for a few minutes to finish cooking.

round it out

Vegetables make both versatile and healthful side dishes. Whatever the month, you can find produce that can be sautéed, roasted, or steamed, or served fresh with seasonings. If your main dish needs a protein complement, offer a selection of cheeses or deli meats.

VEGETABLES & PROTEINS

Cooked greens Buy packaged, prewashed greens, such as Swiss chard, spinach, beet greens, or mixed braising greens, and sauté them in olive oil. Shred or chop tougher greens, such as kale and collards; add a small amount of broth, cover, and cook, stirring often, until tender.

Cucumbers Toss sliced cucumbers with vinaigrette and chopped fresh herbs as an accompaniment to fish. Or, dress the slices with rice vinegar, Asian sesame oil, a pinch of sugar, and a sprinkle of toasted sesame seeds to serve alongside Asian dishes.

Mashed potatoes Fluffy mashed potatoes are perfect for soaking up the juices of slow-cooked meats. See page 243 for an all-purpose mashed potato recipe. Mix in chopped fresh herbs for variety.

Roasted vegetables In the time it takes to put together the main dish, you can also roast vegetables such as broccoli and cauliflower florets, asparagus spears, or small fingerling or creamer potatoes.

Toss cut vegetables in a little olive oil, salt and pepper, and herbs or spices, if desired, and roast on a baking sheet in a single layer at 425°F (220°C) for 10–20 minutes (depending on the vegetable), tossing occasionally. Cubed root vegetables such as butternut squash or sweet potatoes can be roasted at 350°F (180°C).

Salad To save time, look for packaged, prewashed greens. Choose salad ingredients that complement the main dish: a salad with lettuce, cucumbers, and an Asian-style dressing to accompany a curry, or an arugula (rocket) salad with a balsamic vinaigrette and shaved Parmesan cheese to pair with an Italian-style pasta.

Soy-glazed vegetables Sauté diced winter squash, cubed eggplant (aubergine), or sliced mushrooms in olive oil with some minced fresh ginger until golden. Mix equal parts soy sauce, brown sugar, and rice vinegar. Stir the mixture into the vegetables and reduce to a glaze.

Steamed vegetables You can steam or blanch many vegetables a day ahead, and then reheat them in a frying pan with a drizzle of olive oil or a pat of butter at dinnertime. Or, mix them with slivered almonds or fresh herbs, toss them with olive oil and lemon juice or a vinaigrette, or sprinkle with grated Parmesan cheese, and serve them at room temperature.

Tomatoes Arrange fresh, ripe tomato slices on a platter. Sprinkle with sea salt and pepper and drizzle with olive oil. Top with fresh basil and sliced fresh mozzarella. Or, use crumbled feta cheese and chopped fresh herbs such as thyme or flat-leaf (Italian) parsley.

Cheeses Just before you begin preparing dinner, set out two or three cheeses so they can come to room temperature. Serve with baguette rounds or crackers.

Sliced meats Assemble an assortment of sliced deli meats on a large plate or platter and serve with bread or breadsticks on the side.

keep it healthy

Preparing food at home is one of the most healthy choices you can make. Most take-out and ready-made meals are designed to taste appealing but may not be wholesome. When you cook for yourself and your family, you have final say about what goes into the pot and onto the plate.

Balance your menus The idea of eating right is often cast as deprivation. Here is a better way to approach it: instead of concentrating on consuming less fat or less refined sugar, prepare more whole grains, vegetables, and fruits. These foods should fill most of your plate. Then, you can round out your meals with reasonable portions of dairy, poultry, meat, and fish. Take a break from meat and other foods with saturated fats every so often by serving a hearty meatless meal—you'll find many options in this book.

Shop for freshness and variety At most supermarkets, the center aisles contain processed and prepared foods, and the perimeter is lined with fresh produce, dairy products, and seafood, poultry, and meat. Try to keep most of your purchases from along the perimeter. Think of each shopping trip as an opportunity to try something new, whether a vegetable that's in season or a whole grain from the bulk bin.

Check ingredients When you buy a prepared item, read the ingredients on the label. If the list is excessively long and full of additives, look for a simpler, purer version of the same item. Remember that the ingredients appear on the label according to the amount used. Make sure that the first listed ingredients are those you expect and want, not corn syrup or another item lacking in nutritional substance.

Make healthy substitutes You can make small adjustments to any recipe to make it more nutritious. To thicken soups and sauces, in place of cream, use puréed or shredded potato, or puréed cooked dried beans. Citrus juice or a flavored vinegar can stand in for most of the oil in a marinade. You can also forgo butter-rich sauces on vegetables and add a sprinkling of lemon, lime, or orange zest or a scattering of chopped toasted nuts. Low-fat or non-fat yogurt is often a great substitute for sour cream, and buttermilk for cream when baking. Instead of a butter-rich pastry pie crust, try a graham cracker or gingersnap cookie crust, or a meringue shell.

HEALTHY MENUS

Vietnamese Chicken Salad
(page 105)

cooked rice vermicelli noodles

———

Greek Bulgur Salad
(page 188)

hummus, plain yogurt, and pita

———

Vegetable & Tofu Stir-Fry
(page 208)

brown jasmine rice

———

Miso-Marinated Salmon
(page 241)

green salad with
citrus dressing

———

Balsamic Chicken & Peppers
(page 297)

baby spinach salad with
mustard vinaigrette

———

**Chile-Rubbed Pork with Corn
Salsa (page 345)**

roasted sweet potatoes

cook with the seasons

When vegetables and fruits are in season, they not only taste great but also have the best color and texture. These qualities will enhance every dish you prepare. Use these lists of seasonal produce as a guide to planning your menus and shopping for ingredients.

SPRING	SUMMER	FALL	WINTER
• artichokes	• avocados	• apples	• Belgian endive (chicory/witloof)
• asparagus	• bell peppers (capsicums)	• broccoli	• cabbage
• beets	• berries such as blackberries, blueberries and raspberries	• Brussels sprouts	• Chinese broccoli
• carrots (young)	• chiles	• cauliflower	• citrus fruits such as lemons, oranges, and tangerines
• fava (broad) beans	• corn	• chestnuts	• escarole (Batavian endive)
• fennel	• cucumbers	• cranberries	• fennel
• green garlic	• eggplants (aubergines)	• grapes	• hearty greens such as kale and Swiss chard
• green (spring) onions	• figs	• hearty greens such as kale and Swiss chard	• herbs such as rosemary and sage
• herbs such as chives, cilantro (fresh coriander), dill, mint, and parsley	• green beans	• herbs such as bay leaves, rosemary, and sage	• mushrooms (cultivated and wild)
• leeks (young)	• greens such as arugula (rocket) and spinach	• mushrooms such as chanterelle and porcini	• pomegranates
• lettuces (young)	• herbs such as basil, mint, and parsley	• onions	• radicchio
• mushrooms	• melons	• pears	• root vegetables such as celery root (celeriac), beets, parsnips, and turnips
• new potatoes	• tomatoes	• persimmons	• watercress
• peas and sugar snap peas	• stone fruits such as apricots, cherries, nectarines, plums, and peaches	• root vegetables such as beets, carrots, parsnips, potatoes, turnips, and yams	• winter squashes
• radishes	• squashes such as zucchini (courgettes)	• squashes such as acorn, butternut, and pumpkin	
• rhubarb			
• strawberries			

spring & summer menus

Cooks look forward to the arrival of spring asparagus and juicy strawberries in markets, followed soon by the succulent corn and sweet tomatoes of summer. The menus here showcase produce of both seasons in dishes that range from light soups to classic desserts.

SPRING	SUMMER	FIT FOR COMPANY
Smoked Salmon Pinwheels (page 66)	**Summer Vegetable Kebabs (page 205)**	**Crab & Lemon Risotto (page 191)**
young lettuce and herb salad	orzo pasta with lemon	butter lettuce salad with shaved fennel and goat cheese
Artichokes with Lemon Aioli (page 198)		**Strawberry Shortcakes (page 361)**
	Spicy Gazpacho (page 141)	
Spring Vegetable Soup (page 128)	mixed salumi plate	**Creamy Polenta with Asparagus (page 184)**
frittata with ham	garlic-rubbed grilled bread	**Classic Roast Chicken (page 267)**
crusty French bread		**Rhubarb Pie (page 387)**
	Italian Burgers with Peppers & Onions (page 315)	
Grilled Asparagus & Prosciutto Salad (page 84)	tomato and basil salad	**Veal Chops with Tomato Vinaigrette (page 325)**
Capellini with Lemon, Garlic & Parsley (page 161)		grilled zucchini (courgettes)
	Edamame, Corn & Tomato Salad (page 83)	sliced tomatoes with sea salt
Chicken & Leek Pie (page 273)	grilled turkey sausages	**Apricot Clafoutis (page 358)**
mixed baby greens salad with radishes and green onions		
	Tilapia with Sweet Peppers (page 248)	**Prosciutto-Wrapped Peaches (page 58)**
Grilled Pork Chops with Romesco (page 346)	sautéed green beans	**Grilled Summer Vegetable Salad (page 87)**
grilled leeks	arugula (rocket) salad with corn	crostini with pesto spread
roasted new potatoes		**Melon Granita (page 404)**
	Eggplant with Spicy Chile Sauce (page 199)	
	pickled cucumber salad	

featured technique: grilling

Cooking on an outdoor grill can become a regular part of your meal planning from the first warm days of spring all the way through summer. Here are some helpful tips to make any meal you prepare on the grill a delicious success.

Prepare in the morning On days that you plan to use the grill for dinner, check your supplies, marinate and season the food, and get the grill ready for use.

Clean and oil the rack Use a wire grill brush with a scraping tool to clean the grill rack twice: once before you begin cooking, to remove any accumulated debris, and once after cooking, while the rack is still hot and is easier to clean. Just before putting the food on the grill, grasp a wadded-up paper towel with tongs, dip it into vegetable oil, and use it to lightly coat the grill rack with oil.

Start the fire Gas grills should be preheated for at least 15 minutes, following the manufacturer's directions. Set one burner on high and the other(s) on low to create hot and cool zones. When using a charcoal grill, it's best to use a chimney starter to light coals quickly and efficiently without the need for lighter fluid, which can give foods an "off" flavor. Once the coals are lit, arrange them on one side of the fire bed to create hot and cool zones. The food can be seared over the hotter area and then moved to the cooler area to finish cooking.

Use the right type of heat Direct-heat grilling is the method most grilling cooks know best, with small pieces of food like burgers or chicken parts cooked directly over high heat in 20 minutes or less. Indirect heat cooks foods by reflected heat, much like roasting in an oven. This method is used for cooking larger pieces of food, like a pork loin or whole chicken.

Avoid flare-ups Flare-ups, which occur when fat drips from the food onto the fire, can give food an unpleasant taste and appearance. If they occur, move food to a cooler area of the grill, and cover.

Give it a rest Allow grilled foods to stand briefly before serving, usually about 5 minutes for meat and poultry and about 3 minutes for seafood. This gives the juices time to redistribute themselves throughout the food, producing a more evenly moist result.

fall & winter menus

Summer's offerings might still appear in markets in early autumn, but soon produce bins are full of root vegetables, sturdy greens, pears, and apples. With the change in weather and the coming of winter, consider making the substantial fare in the menus below.

FALL	WINTER	FIT FOR COMPANY
Potato-Cheddar Soup (page 136)	Indian Vegetable Curry (page 209)	Pork Chops with Apple-Sage Stuffing (page 338)
baby spinach salad with apples and blue cheese	steamed basmati rice	sautéed spinach with pine nuts and currants
crusty wheat bread	purchased samosas	Pear Custard Tart (page 391)
Pasta with Roasted Squash & Bacon (page 166)	Endive & Radicchio Gratin (page 224)	Turkey Cutlets with Herbed Pan Gravy (page 300)
sautéed Brussels sprouts	Italian Meatloaf (page 314)	mashed sweet potatoes
		roasted broccoli
Braised Chicken with Mushrooms (page 282)	BBQ Beef Sandwiches (page 309)	Pumpkin Pie (page 388)
mixed greens salad with persimmons	cabbage coleslaw	
	orange slices	Citrus-Marinated Olives (page 45)
Seared Salmon with Mashed Potatoes (page 243)	Roasted Root Vegetable Soup (page 148)	Shepherd's Pie (page 321)
steamed broccoli	garlic bread	spinach salad with goat cheese and pomegranate seeds
	radicchio salad with pears and walnuts	Cranberry Upside-Down Cake (page 384)
Pasta Shells with Cauliflower (page 174)		
sautéed chard	Lentil, Bacon & Frisée Salad (page 110)	Roasted Squash with Spiced Couscous (page 201)
roasted garlic and sliced baguette	Beef & Barley Soup (page 149)	Roast Pork Loin with Pan Sauce (page 333)
	crusty bread	Gingerbread Cake (page 376)

Electric slow-cookers have been around for decades, but each generation rediscovers them as a great convenience. You can prep in the morning, leave your food to cook all day, and come home to a delicious stew, roast, or braise. Most slow-cooker models automatically switch to the warm setting once the cooking time is over.

SLOW-COOKED DISHES

If you own a slow cooker, put it to work with these recipes:

featured technique: slow cooking

Although practical the year-round, slowly simmering foods on the stove top or in a slow cooker is ideal for autumn and winter, seasons that call for making satisfying stews and braising meats and poultry. Here are some general slow-cooking tips to keep in mind for ensuring perfectly braised meals.

Brown meat or poultry Taking the time to quickly brown meat or poultry before combining it with other ingredients in a slow-cooked stew or braise will impart a richer flavor to the finished dish. Never crowd the pan or the food won't brown properly, and use tongs or a slotted spoon to transfer the food to a plate until you are ready to combine it and any accumulated juices with the other ingredients.

Skim fat When slow cooking fatty meats such as short ribs, you'll notice pools of fat on the surface of the cooking liquid. A large, shallow spoon or ladle is the ideal tool for skimming the fat away before the dish is served. You can also drape paper towels across the surface to soak up small amounts of fat.

Cook in advance These dishes are great candidates to make ahead of time and reheat, as their flavor improves after standing for a day or two. Before serving, add a garnish to liven up the dish: a sprinkle of fresh herbs, a squeeze of citrus, or a dollop of sour cream.

use a slow cooker with success

- SELECT THE TIMING Each recipe in this book that has a slow cooker option provides two choices for cooking times. If you plan to start the slow cooker and leave for the day, the low-temperature setting is recommended. Generally, this setting, which produces a gentle simmer, also results in more tender food and concentrated flavor. To cook the food faster, choose the high-heat setting.

- AVOID OVERFILLING For the best results, fill the slow cooker no more than one-half to two-thirds full.

- UNCOVER WITH CARE It is sometimes necessary to lift the lid on the slow cooker, such as when adding ingredients or checking for doneness. Avoid doing this too often, as it lowers the cooking temperature inside the pot.

planning for company

Hosting friends, family, or colleagues need not be intimidating, even during a busy workweek. If you plan the menu ahead of time, choose simple and delicious recipes, shop strategically, and make some dishes in advance, you'll be able to cook and entertain with confidence.

Plan ahead When you are planning a get-together, take the time to shop several days in advance. Write down your menu ideas before you head to the store and you'll be able to stock your kitchen with much of what you'll need.

Cook on the weekend Take time on the weekend to prepare dishes that will keep for a few days, like dips and sauces. Have your refrigerator stocked with tasty basics that can be easily put together for quick appetizers and simple first courses.

Make batches Prepare a double batch of your favorite dishes and those you think will be popular with guests. Have the extras arranged on plates in the refrigerator and easily accessible, so you can replenish your platters when they start to empty.

Be creative Lemon slices, lettuce leaves, and cucumber slices all make appealing garnishes or food-friendly beds for appetizer platters. Think of new ways to serve your appetizers. For instance, serve chilled soups in slim cordial or shot glasses and hot soups in demitasse or espresso cups.

Circulate new dishes Bring out new dishes one or two at a time throughout the party. It will boost interest and keep items from wilting or drying out before they are eaten.

Keep it fresh Use small serving plates and replenish them frequently. They are more appealing than a single large platter.

Leave space Crowded platters can be awkward to navigate. Make sure there's enough room on the platter for guests to easily remove what they want.

Set out extras Put out small bowls of foods that are good for nibbling: nuts, such as cashews, almonds, pistachios, and candied walnuts; dried fruits, such as apricots; and good-quality olives.

WINE & SPIRITS

Always keep a supply of good-quality wines, spirits, and mixers on hand, so you don't have to run to the store when friends arrive unexpectedly. For serving, arrange the wines and spirits on a table or counter and include a few traditional mixers, a selection of glasses, some ice cubes, and a stack of coasters. If serving white wine, keep it cool in an ice bucket.

THE BASIC BAR

Wines
- Champagne or prosecco
- Selection of white wines
- Selection of red wines

Spirits
- Rum
- Vodka and/or Gin
- Whisky

Mixers
- Cola
- Cranberry and orange juices
- Soda water and tonic water

menus for simple get-togethers

Whether you are inviting an intimate group or a large crowd, one of the best ways to entertain casually is to set out a variety of dishes for guests to serve themselves. The menus here include recipes that can be made ahead and recipes that can easily be doubled or tripled.

FRENCH GARDEN PARTY

Radishes with Butter & Sea Salt
(page 49)

Ham & Spinach Quiches
(page 60)

Potato & Gruyère Tartlets
(page 215)

frisée salad with mustard
vinaigrette

Berry Galette (page 397)

TO DRINK: Kir, Côtes du Rhône

HOLIDAY OPEN HOUSE

Spiced Roasted Nuts (page 46)

Bacon-Wrapped Dates
(page 53)

Steak Crostini with Creamy
Horseradish (page 63)

sliced oranges with fresh mint

Ginger-Molasses Cookies
(page 374)

TO DRINK: Champagne,
mulled cider, microbrewed ales

ALFRESCO IN TUSCANY

Crostini with Ricotta
& Prosciutto (page 47)

Fried Chickpeas (page 52)

Antipasto Platter
(page 54)

Red Pepper & Goat Cheese
Frittata (page 227)

Italian Affogato (page 406)

TO DRINK: Prosecco,
Pinot Grigio, Italian sodas

LATIN FIESTA

Guacamole & Sweet Potato Chips
(page 55)

Beef Empanadas (page 76)

Chile-Rubbed Pork with Corn
Salsa (page 345)

black beans and rice

jicama salad with lime vinaigrette

TO DRINK: Mexican beer,
margaritas, watermelon
aguas frescas

BOOK CLUB NIGHT

Crostini with Lemony Chicken
Salad (page 67)

Pear Compote with Cheese
(page 77)

Classic Crab Cakes (page 262)

shaved fennel salad with
lemon vinaigrette

Lemon-Buttermilk Bars
(page 360)

TO DRINK: Sauvignon Blanc,
Pinot Noir, sparkling water

BIG GAME PARTY

Glazed Chicken Wings (page 57)

Cherry Tomato & Pesto Pizza
(page 71)

Cuban Pork Sandwiches
(page 336)

tortilla chips with guacamole
and salsa

Chocolate-Raspberry Brownies
(page 369)

TO DRINK: fresh lemonade
or limeade, microbrewed beer

pairing food & wine

Throwing a party is a great opportunity to try out new wine varieties. Here is an overview of wine styles and corresponding varietals or regional bottlings, plus examples of foods they pair well with. Stop by a trusted wine shop for advice about what to drink with a particular dish.

WINE STYLES	VARIETALS		PAIR WITH
Sparkling			
• crisp and light	• Champagne	• Prosecco or cava	• oysters and other seafood
Crisp whites			
• fresh aromas • "green" flavors • high acidity	• Albariño • Chablis • Pinot Grigio	• Sauvignon Blanc • Soave • White Rioja	• light pasta dishes • lean white fish • pork tenderloin
Soft whites			
• floral aromas • stone fruit flavors • a backbone of acidity	• Chenin Blanc • Gewürztraminer • Grüner Veltliner	• Pinot Blanc • Pinot Gris • Riesling	• spicy Asian dishes • caramelized vegetables • pork paired with fruit
Rich whites			
• full aromas and flavors • creamy, buttery texture	• Chardonnay • Marsanne	• Semillon • Viognier	• rich seafood dishes • chicken with cream sauces
Pink wines			
• cherry aromas and flavors	• Dry rosés made from many varietals		• seared tuna
Juicy reds			
• berry aromas • juicy flavors • food friendly	• Barbera • Beaujolais/Gamay • Cabernet Franc	• Dolcetto • Grenache • Pinot Noir	• turkey with gravy • tomato-based pasta dishes • rich salmon dishes
Smooth reds			
• earthy, herbal, or spicy aromas and flavors • balanced acidity	• Grenache • Malbec • Merlot	• Pinot Noir • Sangiovese • Tempranillo	• beef stew • braised chicken or pork • duck breast
Bold reds			
• earthy, musky aromas • big, hearty flavors • full-bodied texture	• Cabernet Sauvignon • Mourvèdre • Nebbiolo	• Petite Sirah • Syrah • Zinfandel	• grilled steak • braised short ribs • hearty lamb dishes

basic recipes

vegetable stock

Trim, halve, and rinse the leeks, then cut into chunks. In a stockpot, combine the leeks, onions, carrots, celery, parsley, mushrooms, and peppercorns. Add 5 qt (5 l) water and bring to a boil over high heat. Reduce the heat to medium-low, cover partially, and simmer until the vegetables are very soft and the flavors have blended, about 1 hour. Season to taste with salt. Pour the contents of the pot through a fine-mesh sieve into a large bowl. Press down on the solids to extract all the liquid, and discard the solids.

storage tip Let the stock cool, then transfer to airtight containers. Refrigerate for up to 3 days or freeze for up to 3 months. For ease of use, you can store the stock in 1-cup (8–fl oz/250-ml) or 1-qt (1-l) plastic containers, in ice cube trays, or in heavy-duty resealable bags.

Leeks, 5 large

Yellow onions,
5, quartered

Carrots, 8, coarsely
chopped

Celery, 6 stalks, coarsely
chopped

**Fresh flat-leaf (Italian)
parsley,** 6 sprigs

Button mushrooms,
½ lb (250 g), halved

Peppercorns, 10

Salt

**MAKES ABOUT 5 QT
(5 L) STOCK**

use for

Miso Noodle Soup
(page 122)

Creamy Asparagus Soup
(page 126)

Spring Vegetable Soup
(page 128)

mushroom stock

Olive oil, 2 tablespoons

Yellow onions, 2 large, chopped

Button mushrooms, 1½ lb (750 g), sliced

Dried shiitake or porcini mushrooms, ½ oz (15 g)

Celery, 4 stalks, chopped

Peppercorns, 1 teaspoon

Salt

MAKES ABOUT 1.75 QT (1.75 L) STOCK

use for

Creamy Mushroom Bisque (page 142)

Mushroom & Broccoli Rice Pilaf (page 221)

In a large saucepan over medium-high heat, warm the oil. Add the onions and sauté until lightly browned, about 15 minutes. Add the fresh and dried mushrooms, celery, and peppercorns along with 2½ qt (2.5 l) water. Bring to a boil, reduce the heat to medium-low, and simmer, uncovered, for 40 minutes. Season to taste with salt. Remove from the heat and let stand for 1 hour. Pour the contents of the pan through a fine-mesh sieve into a large bowl. Press down lightly on the solids to extract all the liquid, and discard the solids.

storage tip Let the stock cool completely, then transfer to airtight containers. Store in the refrigerator for up to 3 days or in the freezer for up to 2 months.

chicken stock

Put the chicken in a stockpot. Add water to cover by 1½ inches (4 cm). Bring to a simmer over medium-high heat and skim any foam from the surface. Add the onions, leeks, carrots, celery, parsley, thyme, peppercorns, and 2 teaspoons salt. Return to a boil. Reduce the heat to low and simmer gently, uncovered, until the chicken is cooked through, about 1 hour.

Transfer the chicken to a platter, let cool slightly, then remove the meat from the carcass, reserving the skin and bones. Reserve the meat for another recipe. Return the skin and bones to the pot and continue to simmer, uncovered, for about 1 hour. Pour the contents of the pot through a fine-mesh sieve into a large bowl. Press down on the solids to extract all the liquid, and discard the solids.

storage tip Let the stock cool completely, cover, and refrigerate for several hours or overnight. Before using the stock, skim the solidified fat from the surface. The stock will keep in airtight containers in the refrigerator for up to 3 days or in the freezer for up to 3 months. The chicken meat will keep in the refrigerator for up to 3 days.

Whole chicken, 1, about 4 lb (2 kg), quartered

Yellow onions, 2, quartered

Leeks, 2 small, white and pale green parts, halved, rinsed, and chopped

Carrots, 4, quartered

Celery, 4 stalks, quartered

Fresh flat-leaf (Italian) parsley, 6 sprigs

Fresh thyme, 6 sprigs

Peppercorns, 10

Salt

MAKES ABOUT 4½ QT (4.5 L) STOCK

use for

Chicken-Tortilla Soup (page 120)

Chicken Noodle Soup (page 125)

beef stock

Beef and veal soup bones, 6 lb (3 kg)

Carrots, 3, cut into thick slices

Yellow onions, 3, cut into thick slices

Salt and freshly ground pepper

Celery, 3 stalks, chopped

Leeks, 2, white and pale green parts, halved, rinsed, and chopped

Garlic, 1 clove

MAKES ABOUT 5 QT (5 L) STOCK

use for

French Onion Soup (page 121)

Tortellini in Broth (page 137)

Beef & Barley Soup (page 149)

Preheat the oven to 400°F (200°C). Arrange the bones in a single layer in a roasting pan. Add the carrot and onion slices. Roast until the bones are browned, 45–60 minutes. Transfer the bones and vegetables to a Dutch oven or stockpot.

Add 8 qt (8 l) water, 1 tablespoon salt, and 2 teaspoons pepper to the pot. Bring to a boil over medium heat. Skim any foam from the surface and then add the celery, leeks, and garlic. Reduce the heat to low, cover partially, and simmer for 4–5 hours, skimming any foam from the surface. Remove the bones from the pot and discard. Pour the contents of the pot through a fine-mesh sieve into a large bowl. Press down on the solids to extract all the liquid, and discard the solids.

storage tip Let the stock cool completely. Cover and refrigerate for several hours or overnight. Before using the stock, skim the solidified fat from the surface. The stock will keep in airtight containers in the refrigerator for up to 3 days or in the freezer for up to 3 months.

tomato-basil sauce

In a large saucepan over medium-low heat, warm the oil. Add the garlic and sauté until lightly golden, about 3 minutes. Stir in the tomato paste, chopped tomatoes, basil leaves, and ½ teaspoon salt. Bring to a simmer and cook, stirring occasionally, until the tomatoes break down, about 15 minutes. Remove from the heat and let cool slightly. Using a food processor or blender, process the sauce until smooth. Or, position a food mill with the fine grinding disk over a large saucepan and pass the sauce through it. Season with salt and pepper.

cook's tip For a quick meal, cook 1 lb (500 g) fusilli, penne, or other medium-sized pasta until al dente, according to the package directions. Place 2 cups (16 fl oz/500 ml) of the sauce in a warmed serving bowl. Drain the pasta and toss with the sauce. Serve, passing freshly grated Parmesan at the table.

storage tip The sauce can be stored in airtight containers in the refrigerator for up to 3 days or in the freezer for up to 3 months. When reheating the sauce, stir in an additional 1–2 tablespoons olive oil.

Olive oil, ¼ cup
(2 fl oz/60 ml)

Garlic, 4 large cloves, minced

Tomato paste, ½ cup
(4 oz/125 g)

Canned whole plum (Roma) tomatoes, 8 cups
(64 fl oz/2 l), chopped, with juice

Fresh basil, 10–12 leaves

Salt and freshly ground pepper

**MAKES ABOUT 8 CUPS
(64 FL OZ/2 L) SAUCE**

use for

Spaghetti & Meatballs
(page 172)

Sausage Lasagna
(page 180)

Baked Chicken Parmesan
(page 274)

bolognese sauce

Olive oil, 2 tablespoons

Pancetta, 2 oz (60 g), chopped

Yellow onions, 2, minced

Carrots, 2, minced

Celery, 1 stalk, minced

Ground (minced) beef, 3 lb (1.5 kg)

Beef broth, 2 cups (16 fl oz/500 ml)

Dry red wine, 1½ cups (12 fl oz/375 ml)

Crushed plum (Roma) tomatoes, 1 can (28 oz/875 g)

Milk, ½ cup (4 fl oz/125 ml)

Salt and freshly ground pepper

MAKES ABOUT 3 QT (3 L) SAUCE

use for

Stuffed Cannelloni (page 176)

Roasted Eggplant Lasagna (page 225)

In a large frying pan over medium-high heat, warm the oil. Add the pancetta and sauté for about 1 minute. Add the onions, carrots, and celery and sauté until the onions are translucent, about 5 minutes. Add the beef and cook, breaking up the meat, until it is no longer red, about 7 minutes. Transfer to a Dutch oven or slow cooker. Add the broth and wine to the frying pan and raise the heat to high. Bring to a boil and deglaze the pan, stirring to scrape up the browned bits on the pan bottom. Pour the liquid over the meat and stir in the tomatoes.

If using a Dutch oven, bring to a boil over medium-high heat. Reduce the heat to low, partially cover, and simmer, stirring occasionally, until the sauce has thickened, about 1½ hours. (If using a slow cooker, cover and cook on the high-heat setting for 4 hours or the low-heat setting for 8 hours.) Add the milk and stir to combine. Cover and continue to cook for 20 minutes longer. Season with salt and pepper.

storage tip Store the cooled sauce in airtight containers in the refrigerator for up to 3 days or in the freezer for up to 3 months.

roasted tomato sauce

Preheat the oven to 450°F (230°C). Place the peppers, onions, tomatoes, and garlic on 2 rimmed baking sheets. Toss the vegetables with the oil, season with salt and pepper, and spread in an even layer. Roast until tender, about 30 minutes. Let cool until easy to handle, then remove and discard the skins from the tomatoes and peppers and transfer the flesh to a bowl. Squeeze the roasted garlic from the cloves into the bowl and add the roasted onions and basil. Pulse the vegetable mixture in a food processor until coarsely chopped. Season with salt and pepper.

cook's tip For a quick meal, cook 1 lb (500 g) fusilli, penne, or other medium-sized pasta until al dente, according to the package directions. Place 2 cups (16 fl oz/500 ml) of the sauce in a warmed serving bowl. Drain the pasta and toss with the sauce. Serve, passing freshly grated Parmesan at the table.

storage tip The sauce can be stored in airtight containers in the refrigerator for up to 3 days or in the freezer for up to 3 months. When reheating the sauce, stir in an additional 1–2 tablespoons olive oil.

Red bell peppers (capsicums), 2, seeded and quartered

Yellow onions, 2, cut into wedges

Plum (Roma) tomatoes, 3 lb (1.5 kg), halved lengthwise and seeded

Garlic, 2 heads, halved crosswise

Olive oil, ¼ cup (2 fl oz/60 ml)

Salt and freshly ground pepper

Fresh basil, 1 cup (1½ oz/45 g) chopped

MAKES ABOUT 8 CUPS (64 FL OZ/2 L) SAUCE

use for

Baked Rigatoni with Ricotta & Sausage (page 181)

Meatball Sandwiches (page 313)

basil pesto

Fresh basil, 4 cups
(4 oz/125 g) tightly
packed leaves

Garlic, 4 cloves

Olive oil, 1 cup
(8 fl oz/250 ml)

Pine nuts, ⅔ cup
(3 oz/90 g), toasted

**Salt and freshly ground
pepper**

Parmesan cheese,
1½ cups (6 oz/180 g)
freshly grated

Unsalted butter,
4 tablespoons (2 oz/60 g),
at room temperature

**MAKES ABOUT 5 CUPS
(40 FL OZ/1.25 L) PESTO**

use for

Minestrone with Pesto
(page 127)

Ziti with Pesto & Potatoes
(page 175)

Chicken-Pesto Panini with
Mozzarella (page 278)

In a food processor, combine the basil,
garlic, oil, pine nuts, 1 teaspoon salt, and
several grindings of pepper. Process until
a coarse paste forms, stopping occasionally
to scrape down the sides of the bowl with
a rubber spatula. Transfer to a bowl and
stir in the cheese and butter.

cook's tip For a quick meal, cook
1 lb (500 g) bucatini, spaghetti, or
other strand pasta until al dente,
according to the package directions.
Drain the pasta, reserving about
½ cup (4 fl oz/125 ml) of the cooking
water. In a large serving bowl, mix
2 tablespoons of the cooking water
with 1 cup (8 fl oz/125 ml) of the
pesto. Add the drained pasta and
toss to combine. Add as much of the
remaining cooking water as needed
to achieve a nice sauce consistency.
Serve with freshly grated Parmesan.

storage tip The pesto can be
stored in an airtight container in the
refrigerator for up to 2 days or in
the freezer for up to 2 months. Press
a piece of plastic wrap on the surface
of the pesto to prevent discoloring.

romesco sauce

In a food processor, finely chop the garlic. Add the almonds and pulse until finely chopped. Add the roasted peppers, vinegar, and paprika and process until smooth. With the motor running, gradually add the oil. Season with salt and pepper.

storage tip The romesco sauce can be stored in airtight containers in the refrigerator for up to 1 month. Drizzle a thin layer of olive oil over the surface before covering with the lid. Bring to room temperature and stir well before serving.

Garlic, 2 cloves

Slivered almonds, 1 cup (4½ oz/140 g), toasted

Roasted red bell peppers (capsicums), 2 jars (12 oz/375 g each), drained

Sherry vinegar, 4 teaspoons

Smoked paprika, 2 teaspoons

Olive oil, 6 tablespoons (3 fl oz/90 ml)

Salt and freshly ground pepper

MAKES ABOUT 2½ CUPS (20 FL OZ/625 ML) SAUCE

use for

Roasted Vegetables with Romesco (page 207)

Grilled Pork Chops with Romesco (page 346)

white beans

Dried small white beans such as cannellini or navy, 2 lb (1 kg), picked over and rinsed

Olive oil, 2 tablespoons

Yellow onion, 1, chopped

Garlic, 4 cloves

Salt and freshly ground pepper

MAKES ABOUT 10 CUPS (4 LB/2 KG) COOKED BEANS

use for

Seared Tuna with White Beans (page 245)

Sausages with White Beans (page 343)

Quick Cassoulet (page 347)

Lamb Chops with Garlic & Rosemary (page 352)

Put the beans in a large pot, add cold water to cover, and bring to a boil. Drain the beans and transfer to a Dutch oven or slow cooker. In a frying pan over medium-high heat, warm the oil. Add the onion and garlic and sauté until the onion is soft, about 4 minutes. Add the onion-garlic mixture and 1½ tablespoons salt to the beans and stir to combine. Add cold water to cover the beans by 2 inches (5 cm).

If using a Dutch oven, bring to a boil over medium-high heat. Reduce the heat to low, partially cover, and simmer until the beans are tender, 1½–2 hours. (If using a slow cooker, cover and cook on the high-heat setting for 4 hours or the low-heat setting for 8 hours.) Season to taste with salt and pepper.

storage tip Store the cooled beans in airtight containers in the refrigerator for up to 3 days or in the freezer for up to 1 month.

green lentils

In a large saucepan, combine the lentils, carrot, celery, onion, parsley, and 8 cups (64 fl oz/2 l) water. Bring to a boil over medium-high heat, then reduce the heat to medium-low, cover, and simmer until the lentils are tender and the liquid has been absorbed, 30–35 minutes. Remove and discard the vegetables.

storage tip Store the cooled lentils in an airtight container in the refrigerator for up to 3 days. Lentils do not freeze well.

Green lentils, 1 lb (500 g), picked over and rinsed

Carrot, 1, halved

Celery, 1 stalk, cut into 3 pieces

Yellow onion, 1, halved

Fresh flat-leaf (Italian) parsley, 5 sprigs

MAKES ABOUT 6 CUPS (42 OZ/1.3 KG) COOKED LENTILS

use for

Lentil, Bacon & Frisée Salad (page 110)

Lentil, Potato & Spinach Curry (page 211)

flaky pastry dough

Flour, 4 cups (1¼ lb/
625 g)

Salt, 1 teaspoon

Unsalted butter,
1½ cups (12 oz/375 g)
plus 3 tablespoons,
cold, cut into cubes

Ice water, ¾ cup
(6 fl oz/180 ml)

MAKES 3 DOUGH DISKS

use for

Rhubarb Pie (page 387)

Pumpkin Pie (page 388)

Berry Galette (page 397)

In a food processor, combine the flour
and salt and pulse briefly to mix. Scatter
the butter over the flour mixture and pulse
just until the mixture forms coarse crumbs
about the size of peas. Drizzle the ice
water over the flour mixture and pulse just
until the dough starts to come together.
Transfer to a lightly floured work surface,
divide into 3 equal portions, and press
each into a flat disk. Wrap each dough
disk in plastic wrap and refrigerate for
30 minutes before using.

storage tip Store the wrapped
dough disks in the refrigerator for
up to 3 days or in the freezer for up
to 1 month. If freezing the disks,
place the wrapped disks in heavy-
duty resealable plastic bags. Thaw
disks overnight in the refrigerator
before using.

sweet tart dough

In a food processor, combine the flour, sugar, and butter. Pulse just until the mixture forms coarse crumbs about the size of peas. Drizzle the ice water over the flour mixture and process just until fine crumbs form. Transfer to a lightly floured work surface, divide into 3 equal portions, and press each into a disk. Wrap each dough disk in plastic wrap and refrigerate for 30 minutes before using.

storage tip Store the wrapped dough disks in the refrigerator for up to 3 days or in the freezer for up to 1 month. If freezing the disks, place the wrapped disks in heavy-duty resealable plastic bags. Thaw disks overnight in the refrigerator before using. Or, roll out the dough and line a tart pan. Place the pan in a heavy-duty resealable plastic bag and refrigerate or freeze until needed.

Flour, 3 cups (15 oz/470 g)

Powdered (icing) sugar, ⅓ cup (1½ oz/45 g)

Unsalted butter, 1½ cups (12 oz/375 g), cold, cut into cubes

Ice water, ⅓ cup (3 fl oz/80 ml)

MAKES 3 DOUGH DISKS

use for

Pecan Tart (page 390)

Pear Custard Tart (page 391)

Chocolate-Raspberry Tartlets (page 395)

Strawberry–Cream Cheese Tart (page 398)

savory tart dough

Flour, 3½ cups
(17½ oz/545 g)

Salt, ½ teaspoon

Unsalted butter, 1 cup
(8 oz/250 g), cold, cut
into cubes

Eggs, 2, lightly beaten

Lemon juice,
1 tablespoon

Ice water, ¼ cup
(2 fl oz/60 ml), or more
if needed

MAKES 2 DOUGH DISKS

use for

Ham & Spinach Quiches
(page 60)

Beef Empanadas
(page 76)

In a food processor, combine the flour, salt, and butter. Pulse just until the mixture forms coarse crumbs about the size of peas. In a small bowl, whisk together the eggs, lemon juice, and ¼ cup ice water. With the motor running, quickly add the egg mixture to the flour mixture and process just until the dough comes together, adding more ice water if the dough seems too dry. Transfer to a lightly floured work surface, divide in half, and press each half into a thick disk. Wrap each disk in plastic wrap and refrigerate for 30 minutes before using.

storage tip Store the wrapped dough disks in the refrigerator for up to 3 days or in the freezer for up to 1 month. If freezing the disks, place the wrapped disks in heavy-duty resealable plastic bags. Thaw disks overnight in the refrigerator before using.

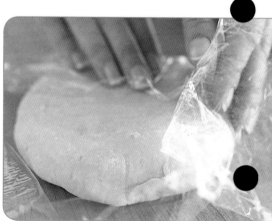

cream cheese dough

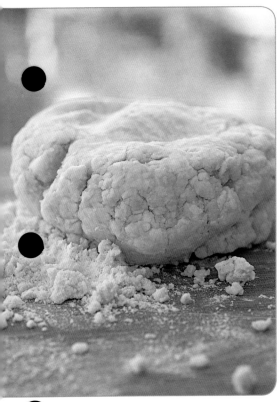

In a food processor, combine the flour and salt and pulse briefly to mix. Scatter the butter and cream cheese over the flour mixture and pulse just until the dough starts to come together. Transfer to a lightly floured work surface, divide in half, and press each half into a flat disk. Wrap each disk in plastic wrap and refrigerate for 30 minutes before using.

storage tip Store the wrapped dough disks in the refrigerator for up to 3 days or in the freezer for up to 1 month. If freezing the disks, place the wrapped disks in a heavy-duty resealable plastic bag. Thaw disks overnight in the refrigerator before using.

Flour, 2 cups (10 oz/ 315 g)

Salt, 1 teaspoon

Unsalted butter, 1 cup (8 oz/250 g), cold, cut into cubes

Cream cheese, 8 oz (250 g), at room temperature, cut into cubes

MAKES 2 DOUGH DISKS

use for

Spinach & Goat Cheese Tartlets (page 61)

Mushroom Tart (page 220)

yeast dough

Flour, 3½ cups
(17½ oz/545 g)

Instant yeast,
2¼ teaspoons (1 packet)

Sugar, 1 tablespoon

Salt, 1 tablespoon

Warm water (110°F/43°C),
1¼ cups (10 fl oz/310 ml)

Olive oil, 2 tablespoons

MAKES 2 DOUGH BALLS

use for

Rosemary Focaccia
(page 70)

Cherry Tomato & Pesto
Pizza (page 71)

Olive & Onion Flatbread
(page 73)

In a food processor, combine the flour, yeast, sugar, and salt and pulse to blend. Add the water and olive oil and pulse just until the dough comes together. Transfer to a lightly floured work surface. Knead the dough for 1–2 minutes to form a smooth ball. Place in an oiled large bowl, turn to coat the dough with the oil, and cover with plastic wrap. Let the dough rise in a warm place until doubled in bulk and very spongy, about 1½ hours.

Turn the dough out onto a lightly floured work surface, punch down, and knead into a smooth cylinder. Divide in half and knead each half to form 2 smooth balls, dusting with flour if sticking. Cover with a kitchen towel and let rest for 10 minutes.

storage tip Place each ball in a resealable plastic bag and refrigerate until ready to use, up to overnight. Return to room temperature before proceeding with the recipe. To freeze the dough, wrap in plastic wrap before placing in the bags and freeze for up to 2 months. To thaw, unwrap the dough, place on a plate, and let stand until it reaches room temperature and begins to rise again, about 3 hours.

chocolate cookie dough

In a large bowl, using an electric mixer on medium speed, beat the butter and brown sugar until creamy. Add the eggs and vanilla and beat until smooth. In another bowl, stir together the flour, cocoa powder, baking soda, cream of tartar, and salt. Add the dry ingredients to the wet ingredients and mix on low speed until blended. Turn out the dough onto a lightly floured work surface. Divide into 3 equal portions, pat each into a flat disk, and wrap each in plastic wrap.

storage tip The wrapped dough disks can be stored in the refrigerator for up to 3 days or in the freezer for up to 1 month. If freezing the disks, place the wrapped disks in heavy-duty resealable plastic bags. Thaw disks overnight in the refrigerator before using.

Unsalted butter, 1½ cups (12 oz/375 g), at room temperature

Light brown sugar, 3 cups (21 oz/655 g) firmly packed

Eggs, 3

Pure vanilla extract, 1 tablespoon

Flour, 3½ cups (17½ oz/545 g)

Unsweetened cocoa powder, 1 cup (3 oz/ 90 g) plus 2 tablespoons

Baking soda (bicarbonate of soda), 1½ teaspoons

Cream of tartar, 1½ teaspoons

Salt, ¾ teaspoon

MAKES 3 DOUGH DISKS

use for

Chocolate Star Cookies (page 370)

Ice Cream Sandwiches (page 371)

Mocha Sandwich Cookies (page 372)

butter cookie dough

All-purpose (plain) flour,
3 cups (15 oz/470 g)

Cake (soft-wheat) flour,
2¼ cups (9 oz/280 g)

Salt, 1½ teaspoons

Unsalted butter,
2¼ cups (18 oz/560 g),
at room temperature

Powdered (icing) sugar,
1½ cups (6 oz/185 g)

Pure vanilla extract,
1 tablespoon

MAKES 3 DOUGH DISKS

use for

Chocolate-Dipped Butter
Cookies (page 373)

Key Lime Tart (page 396)

Lemon Tart with
Raspberries (page 399)

Sift together the all-purpose and cake flours and the salt into a bowl. In a large bowl, using an electric mixer on low speed, beat the butter, sugar, and vanilla until smooth, about 1 minute. Add the flour mixture and mix just until a moist dough forms. Turn out the dough onto a lightly floured work surface. Divide into 3 equal portions, pat each into a flat disk, and wrap each in plastic wrap.

storage tip The wrapped dough disks can be stored in the refrigerator for up to 2 days or in the freezer for up to 1 month. If freezing the disks, place the wrapped disks in heavy-duty resealable plastic bags. Thaw disks in the refrigerator overnight and soften at room temperature. Or, roll out the dough and line a tart pan. Cover tightly with plastic wrap, and refrigerate overnight, or freeze for up to 1 month. The crust can go directly from the freezer to the oven.

appetizers

citrus-marinated olives

1 Marinate the olives
In a clean 3-cup (24–fl oz/750-ml) jar, combine the olives, fennel seeds, orange zest and juice, garlic, pepper flakes, peppercorns, and oil. Cover the jar and shake to compact the ingredients. The contents should reach within about 1 inch (2.5 cm) of the rim. Uncover and add water until the ingredients are just covered. Shake the jar to release any air bubbles. Cover and let marinate for at least 15 minutes. The oil will rise to the top.

2 Serve the olives
Using a slotted spoon, transfer the olives to a bowl, discarding the liquid in the jar. Serve the olives alongside a small bowl to collect the pits.

cook's tip Store the marinated olives in the jar or an airtight container in the refrigerator for up to 1 month. The longer the olives marinate the better, as the flavors will continue to develop over time.

Brine-cured green olives such as Manzanillo, 1 lb (500 g), drained

Fennel seeds, 2 tablespoons

Finely grated zest and juice from 1 orange

Garlic, 2 cloves, thinly sliced

Red pepper flakes, ½ teaspoon

Peppercorns, 10

Olive oil, 3 tablespoons

MAKES ABOUT 3 CUPS (1 LB/500 G) OLIVES

spiced roasted nuts

Unsalted butter,
4 tablespoons (2 oz/60 g)

Curry powder,
1 tablespoon

Salt

Ground cinnamon,
½ teaspoon

Ground cumin,
½ teaspoon

Cayenne pepper,
1 teaspoon

Brown sugar,
1 tablespoon packed

Pecans or mixed nuts,
1 lb (500 g)

**MAKES ABOUT 4 CUPS
(1 LB/500 G) NUTS**

1 Prepare the seasonings
Preheat the oven to 350°F (180°C).
Line a rimmed baking sheet with aluminum
foil. In a large saucepan over medium
heat, combine the butter, curry powder,
2 teaspoons salt, cinnamon, cumin,
cayenne, and brown sugar. Cook, stirring
occasionally, just until the butter is melted
and the flavors are released, 2–3 minutes.

2 Roast the nuts
Add the nuts to the spice mixture
and toss until evenly coated. Spread the
nuts in a single layer on the prepared
baking sheet. Bake until deep golden
brown, about 15 minutes. Slide the foil
and nuts onto a wire rack and let cool
completely before serving.

cook's tip Once completely cool,
the nuts can be stored in an airtight
container or a heavy-duty resealable
plastic bag at room temperature for
up to 2 days. Or, refrigerate them
for up to 2 weeks. Remember to
bring the nuts to room temperature
before serving.

crostini with ricotta & prosciutto

1 Toast the bread
Preheat the oven to 350°F (180°C).
Arrange the baguette slices on a baking
sheet and brush lightly with the oil. Bake
until crisp and golden, 10–15 minutes.
Transfer to a platter.

2 Assemble the crostini
Spread each bread slice with about
2 teaspoons of the fig jam, then top with
some cheese and a piece of prosciutto.
Season with pepper and serve.

> cook's tip Some types of fig
> preserves or jam use whole figs,
> making it too chunky to spread.
> To solve this problem, place in
> a food processor and pulse once
> or twice until the figs are broken
> down and the jam is spreadable.

**French or sourdough
baguette,** 24 slices, each
about ½ inch (12 mm)
thick

Olive oil, 2 tablespoons

Fig jam or preserves,
1 cup (10 oz/315 g)

**Whole-milk ricotta
cheese,** 1¼ cups
(10 oz/315 g)

Prosciutto, 6 thin slices,
each cut into 4 pieces

Freshly ground pepper

MAKES 24 CROSTINI

crab salad bites

Fennel bulb, ½, trimmed, quartered lengthwise, and finely chopped

Fresh lump crabmeat, ½ lb (250 g), picked over for shell fragments and squeezed to remove excess liquid

Shallot, 1, finely chopped

Fresh chives, 1 tablespoon finely snipped, plus more for garnish

Fresh flat-leaf (Italian) parsley, 1 tablespoon minced

Mayonnaise, 2 tablespoons

Crème fraîche or sour cream, 1 tablespoon

Lemon juice, from 1 lemon

Salt and freshly ground white pepper

Belgian endive (chicory/witloof), 6 large heads

MAKES 6–8 SERVINGS

1 Prepare the crab salad
In a bowl, stir together the fennel, crabmeat, shallot, 1 tablespoon chives, parsley, mayonnaise, crème fraîche, lemon juice, ¼ teaspoon salt, and ¼ teaspoon pepper. Taste and adjust the seasonings.

2 Assemble the salad
Trim the root ends from the endive heads and separate into spears. Arrange 24 of the largest spears on a platter. Spoon a generous amount of crab salad onto the wide end of each spear. Garnish with the remaining chives and serve.

radishes with butter & sea salt

1 **Prepare the butter and radishes**
Place the butter in a small bowl. Using a fork, whip the butter until light and fluffy. Trim the stems and root ends from the radishes, leaving some small stems and leaves intact, if desired, as a garnish.

2 **Assemble the platter**
Transfer the butter to a ramekin or a small serving bowl for dipping or spreading. Arrange the radishes on a large platter or serving tray and place the ramekin of butter alongside. Pour a mound of 2–3 tablespoons sea salt on the platter or in a small bowl for sprinkling and serve. »

Unsalted butter, ½ cup (4 oz/125 g), at room temperature

Radishes, 32, from 3–4 bunches, chilled

Sea salt

MAKES 32 SMALL BITES

radishes with butter & sea salt
continued

cook's tip

To vary the flavor, choose from the large array of different sea salts available today—from pink Himalayan salt, to black Hawaiian salt harvested from lava beds, to hand-harvested, intensely flavored *fleur de sel* (flower of salt) from France.

caprese skewers

1 **Assemble the skewers**
Thread 1 mozzarella ball half, 1 tomato half, and 1 basil leaf half on a wooden toothpick. Repeat to create the remaining skewers.

2 **Arrange on a platter**
Place the caprese skewers on a platter and drizzle with the oil. Season generously with salt and pepper and serve. (The skewers may be covered and refrigerated for up to 2 hours; serve chilled or at room temperature.)

Fresh mozzarella cheese balls (*bocconcini*), 12, halved

Cherry tomatoes, 12, halved lengthwise

Fresh basil, 12 large leaves, torn in half

Olive oil, for drizzling

Salt and freshly ground pepper

MAKES 24 SKEWERS

cook's tip If you cannot find *bocconcini* (small mozzarella cheese balls) at your local market, you can substitute full-sized balls of fresh mozzarella cheese. Using a sharp chef's knife, cut the cheese into ½-inch (12-mm) cubes.

fried chickpeas

Chickpeas (garbanzo beans), 2 cans (15 oz/470 g each), rinsed and drained

Olive oil and canola oil for frying

Coarse salt and freshly ground pepper

Smoked paprika, ½ teaspoon

MAKES ABOUT 2 CUPS (12 OZ/375 G) CHICKPEAS

1 **Dry the chickpeas and heat the oil**
Preheat the oven to 200°F (95°C). Arrange a double layer of paper towels on a rimmed baking sheet and place in the oven. On another layer of paper towels, spread the drained chickpeas and gently roll to dry them. Set a heavy frying pan over high heat. Add equal amounts of olive oil and canola oil to reach about ¾ inch (2 cm) up the sides of the pan. Heat the oil until it reaches 350°F (180°C) on a deep-frying thermometer.

2 **Fry the chickpeas**
Add half of the chickpeas to the hot oil and fry, stirring occasionally, until golden and crisp, 2–3 minutes. Adjust the heat to maintain the oil at about 350°F. Using a slotted spoon, transfer the chickpeas to the prepared baking sheet. Season with salt and pepper, and keep warm in the oven. Repeat with the remaining chickpeas. Sprinkle the fried chickpeas with the paprika and toss well. Taste and adjust the seasonings and serve.

cook's tip The best varieties of smoked paprika are from Spain, where the spice is known as *pimentón*. If it is unavailable, substitute hot Hungarian paprika.

bacon-wrapped dates

1 **Prepare the filling**
Preheat the oven to 400°F (200°C) and place a baking sheet in the oven to heat. In a small bowl, combine the Parmesan cheese and cream cheese and mix until smooth.

2 **Fill the dates**
Slice each date along one side to make a pocket and insert 1–2 teaspoons of the cheese filling. Wrap a piece of bacon around each stuffed date. The bacon should cover the opening in the date and overlap slightly. Secure the dates with small wooden toothpicks. (The dates may be refrigerated overnight; return to room temperature for about 15 minutes before roasting.)

3 **Cook the dates**
Using tongs, place the dates on the hot baking sheet. Roast until the bacon is brown and crisp, 15–20 minutes. Transfer to a platter and serve.

> **cook's tip** Using pitted dates speeds the preparation. If they are unavailable, use a small, sharp knife to make a slit along the side of each date and pull out the pit. The bacon will help seal the date so the filling does not leak out, and it will also cover any ragged edges.

Parmesan cheese, ¼ lb (125 g), coarsely grated

Cream cheese, 2 tablespoons, at room temperature

Pitted dates, preferably Medjool, 18

Lean bacon, 6 slices, each cut crosswise into 3 pieces

MAKES 18 DATES

antipasto platter

Zucchini (courgettes),
4 small, cut lengthwise
into thick slices

**Asian eggplants
(slender aubergines),**
3, cut lengthwise into
thick slices

Olive oil, ¼ cup
(2 fl oz/60 ml), plus
1 tablespoon

Garlic, 2 cloves, minced

**Salt and freshly ground
pepper**

**Assorted brine-cured
olives,** ½ lb (250 g)

Ripe tomatoes, 4 small,
thickly sliced

**Fresh mozzarella
cheese,** ½ lb (250 g),
thickly sliced

Fresh basil,
2 tablespoons finely
shredded

Dry salami or *coppa*,
¼ lb (125 g), sliced

Prosciutto, ¼ lb (125 g),
thinly sliced

**Roasted red bell
peppers (capsicums),**
2, cut into strips

MAKES 4–6 SERVINGS

1 Cook the vegetables

Prepare a gas or charcoal grill for
direct-heat grilling over high heat, or
preheat the broiler (grill). In a shallow dish,
combine the zucchini and eggplant slices,
¼ cup oil, and garlic. Toss to coat and
season generously with salt and pepper.
Place the zucchini and eggplant on the
grill rack and cook, turning once, until
tender and golden, about 3 minutes per
side. (Or, arrange the slices on a rimmed
baking sheet and broil/grill, turning
once, for about 3 minutes per side.)

2 Assemble the platter

Place the olives in a small bowl
and set on a large platter. Cut the grilled
vegetables crosswise into bite-sized pieces
and arrange on the platter. Arrange the
tomato and cheese slices on the platter,
overlapping them, then sprinkle with
the basil and drizzle with the remaining
1 tablespoon oil. Fan out the salami and
prosciutto slices on the platter. Arrange
the peppers alongside, and serve.

guacamole & sweet potato chips

1 Make the sweet potato chips
Preheat the oven to 500°F (260°C). Lightly oil 2 baking sheets. Arrange the sweet potato slices in a single layer on the prepared sheets and drizzle with the oil. Bake until the slices are golden and crisp, about 10 minutes. Turn the slices, rotate the pans, and cook until the slices are golden and crisp on the second side, about 10 minutes longer. Transfer to paper towels to drain. Season with salt and let stand at room temperature for 5 minutes. Transfer to a platter and set aside.

2 Prepare the guacamole and serve
Meanwhile, scoop the flesh from the avocado halves and place in a bowl. Mash with a fork. Add the onion, minced cilantro, chile, lime juice, and ½ teaspoon salt. Stir to combine. Garnish with the shallot and cilantro leaves and serve with the chips. »

Sweet potatoes, 1 lb (500 g), peeled, halved lengthwise, and cut crosswise into very thin slices

Olive oil, 2 tablespoons

Salt

Hass avocados, 2, halved and pitted

White onion, 2 tablespoons minced

Fresh cilantro (fresh coriander), ¼ cup (⅓ oz/10 g) minced, plus leaves for garnish

Serrano chile, ½ small, seeded and minced

Lime juice, from 1 lime

Shallot, 2 tablespoons finely chopped

MAKES 4–6 SERVINGS

guacamole & chips variation

cook's tip

Instead of making sweet potato chips cut 8-inch (20-cm) corn tortillas into wedges. Stack the tortillas, and, using a sharp knife, cut the stack in half. Then cut each half into 8 wedges. Cook as directed for sweet potatoes in Step 1. Or, you can substitute purchased tortilla chips.

glazed chicken wings

1 **Glaze the chicken wings**
In a large glass or ceramic bowl, toss the wings with ¾ teaspoon salt and ¼ teaspoon pepper. In a large frying pan over medium-low heat, warm the oil. Add the garlic and cook, stirring, until translucent, about 2 minutes. Remove from the heat, add the tamarind paste and vinegar, and whisk until smooth. Set aside ¼ cup (2 fl oz/60 ml) of the glaze for basting. Add the wings to the pan and toss to coat with the remaining glaze.

2 **Cook the chicken**
Preheat the oven to 400°F (200°C). Place the chicken on a baking sheet in a single layer, discarding the glaze in the pan. Roast, turning occasionally, for 10 minutes. Stir the honey into the reserved glaze. Continue to roast, basting the chicken with the honey-infused glaze and turning occasionally, until firm and golden, about 15 minutes longer. Transfer to a platter, garnish with the green onions, and serve.

> **cook's tip** For a stronger, more concentrated flavor, place the glaze-coated wings in a resealable plastic bag or in a tightly covered dish and marinate overnight. Bring to room temperature before roasting.

Chicken wings or drumettes, 24, patted dry

Salt and freshly ground pepper

Canola oil, ¼ cup (2 fl oz/60 ml)

Garlic, 4 large cloves, minced

Tamarind paste or concentrate, 3 tablespoons

Red wine vinegar, 3 tablespoons

Honey, 3 tablespoons

Green (spring) onions, 4, white and pale green parts, minced

MAKES 24 WINGS

prosciutto-wrapped peaches

Yellow or white peaches, 3, peeled if desired

Prosciutto, 8 thin slices

Fresh mint, 24 leaves

MAKES 24 PIECES

1 Cut the peaches and prosciutto
Halve each peach and remove the pit. Cut each peach half into 4 equal wedges. Then, cut each prosciutto slice lengthwise into 3 strips.

2 Assemble the appetizers
Place a mint leaf on each peach wedge and wrap with a strip of the prosciutto. If desired, secure with a toothpick. Transfer to a platter and serve.

cook's tip Peaches are often peeled by blanching them and removing the skin with your fingers. If you don't have the time to blanch the peaches, halve them lengthwise, and, using a vegetable peeler or a sharp paring knife, carefully remove the skin in long strips.

shrimp & basil skewers

1 **Make the basil oil**
Place 28 short bamboo skewers in water to soak for 20 minutes. Bring a small saucepan of water to a boil. Stir in the basil and cook for 45 seconds. Drain and rinse under cold running water to stop the cooking. Squeeze the basil leaves in a paper towel to extract as much water as possible. In a mini food processor, combine the basil and the oil. Pulse until blended, scraping down the sides of the container.

2 **Cook the shrimp**
Preheat the broiler (grill). Place a footed wire rack on a baking sheet. Thread 2 shrimp onto each skewer, running it through both the tail and the head of each shrimp. Place on the rack. Brush the shrimp with some of the basil oil and season lightly with salt and pepper. Broil (grill) the shrimp until firm and pink, about 4 minutes. Transfer to a platter, drizzle with a little more basil oil, and serve.

cook's tip This technique can be adapted for woodier herbs such as rosemary: In a small saucepan, bring 1 cup (8 fl oz/250 ml) olive oil and 2 rosemary sprigs to a boil. Remove from the heat and let stand for 15 minutes. Discard the rosemary.

Fresh basil, ½ cup (½ oz/15 g) leaves

Olive oil, ⅔ cup (5 fl oz/160 ml)

Large shrimp (prawns), 1½ lb (750 g), peeled and deveined

Salt and freshly ground pepper

MAKES ABOUT 28 SKEWERS

ham & spinach quiches

Savory Tart Dough (page 40), 1 disk

Flour, for rolling out dough

Unsalted butter, 1½ tablespoons

Shallots, 2, finely chopped

Baby spinach, 1 cup (2 oz/60 g) coarsely chopped

Egg, 1

Heavy (double) cream, ⅔ cup (5 fl oz/160 ml)

Dijon mustard, ½ teaspoon

Salt and freshly ground pepper

Red bell pepper (capsicum), 2 tablespoons finely chopped

Ham, 1 oz (30 g), chopped

Gruyère cheese, 2 oz (60 g), finely grated

MAKES 24 MINI QUICHES

1 Roll out the dough
On a lightly floured work surface, roll out the dough until ⅛ inch (3 mm) thick. Using a 2-inch (5-cm) biscuit cutter, cut out as many rounds from the dough as possible. Ease the rounds gently into the cups of 1 or 2 miniature muffin pans. The dough edges should be flush with the rim of the pan. Gather the scraps, roll out ⅛ inch thick, and cut out additional rounds. You should have 24 lined cups.

2 Make the filling
Preheat the oven to 400°F (200°C). In a frying pan over low heat, melt the butter. Add the shallots and cook, stirring, until softened, about 5 minutes. Raise the heat to medium-low, add the spinach, and cook, stirring, until the spinach is wilted, about 1 minute; set aside. In a bowl, whisk together the egg, cream, mustard, ½ teaspoon salt, and a pinch of pepper. Stir in the spinach mixture, bell pepper, ham, and cheese. Divide the filling among the lined cups.

3 Bake the quiches
Bake until the quiches are puffy and golden brown, about 20 minutes. Let cool in the pan on a rack for about 10 minutes. Run a knife around the sides of each cup, lift out the quiches, and serve warm.

spinach & goat cheese tartlets

1 Prepare the tartlet shells
Preheat the oven to 400°F (200°C). On a lightly floured work surface, roll out the dough until ⅛ inch (3 mm) thick. Using a 5-inch (13-cm) pastry cutter, cut out 6 rounds. Place each round into a 4-inch (10-cm) tartlet pan with a removable bottom, fitting it snugly into the corners and up the sides of the pans. Pierce all over with a fork. Place on a baking sheet and freeze for 15 minutes. Blind bake the tartlet shells (see page 409) until the edges are golden, about 15 minutes. Remove the foil and bake until the dough is golden brown, about 10 minutes. Let cool on the baking sheet on a wire rack.

2 Fill and bake tartlets
Preheat the broiler (grill). In a large saucepan over medium heat, warm the oil. Add the garlic and cook until lightly golden, about 1 minute. Add the spinach and cook until just wilted, about 2 minutes. Season with salt and pepper. Place equal amounts of the spinach mixture in each tartlet shell, top with the cheese, and sprinkle with the pine nuts. Broil (grill) until the cheese is golden, 2–3 minutes. Transfer the tartlets to a wire rack and let cool slightly. Remove the pan rims, slide the tarts onto plates, and serve warm.

Cream Cheese Dough (page 41), 1 disk

Flour, for rolling out dough

Olive oil, 1 tablespoon

Garlic, 1 clove, minced

Baby spinach, 1½ lb (750 g)

Salt and freshly ground pepper

Goat cheese, ¼ lb (125 g), crumbled

Pine nuts, 2 tablespoons, toasted

MAKES 6 TARTLETS

lamb meatballs

Olive oil, 2 tablespoons

Yellow onion, 1 small, minced

Ground (minced) lamb, 1 lb (500 g)

Eggs, 2, lightly beaten

Fresh flat-leaf (Italian) parsley leaves, ½ cup (¾ oz/20 g), minced

Fine dried bread crumbs, 2 tablespoons

Ground cumin, 1 teaspoon

Garlic, 4 large cloves, minced

Salt and freshly ground pepper

Plain yogurt, 1 cup (8 oz/250 g)

Fresh cilantro (fresh coriander), 2 tablespoons minced

MAKES ABOUT 42 MEATBALLS

1 Shape the meatballs
Preheat the broiler (grill). Lightly oil a rimmed baking sheet. In a frying pan over medium-low heat, warm the oil. Add the onion and sauté until soft, about 5 minutes. Transfer to a large bowl and add the lamb, eggs, parsley, bread crumbs, cumin, three-fourths of the garlic, 1 teaspoon salt, and ½ teaspoon pepper. Use your hands to mix evenly. Form the mixture into walnut-sized balls, rolling them lightly between your palms. Place in a single layer on the prepared baking sheet.

2 Cook the meatballs
Broil (grill) the meatballs, turning once, until brown and slightly crispy, 8–10 minutes total.

3 Make the sauce and serve
Meanwhile, in a small bowl, whisk together the yogurt, cilantro, remaining garlic, and ¼ teaspoon salt. Skewer each meatball with a toothpick, place on a platter, and serve alongside the sauce.

storage tip Uncooked meatballs can be refrigerated for up to 4 hours. Remove them 15 minutes before cooking. They can also be frozen for up to 1 month; thaw before cooking.

steak crostini with creamy horseradish

1 Prepare the steak and sauce
Preheat the oven to 350°F (180°C). Place a rack in a roasting pan. Brush both sides of the steak with 1 tablespoon of the oil. Season generously with salt and pepper. Place on the rack and let stand at room temperature. In a small bowl, whisk together the horseradish and sour cream.

2 Make the crostini
Arrange the baguette slices on a baking sheet and brush lightly with the remaining 2 tablespoons oil. Season with salt and pepper. Bake until golden, 10–15 minutes. Transfer to a platter. Preheat the broiler (grill).

3 Cook the steak
Broil (grill) the steak until firm but still quite pink in the center, about 6 minutes per side. Let rest for 5 minutes. Cut the steak with the grain into strips about 2 inches (5 cm) thick, then thinly cut the strips crosswise across the grain. Arrange 1 or 2 steak slices on each crostini, top with a dollop of the horseradish cream, and sprinkle with paprika. Transfer to a platter and serve. »

Flank steak, 1½ lb (750 g), trimmed of excess fat

Olive oil, 3 tablespoons

Salt and freshly ground pepper

Prepared horseradish, 2 tablespoons

Sour cream, 3 tablespoons

French or sourdough baguette, cut into slices about ½ inch (12 mm) thick

Paprika for garnish

MAKES ABOUT 28 CROSTINI

steak crostini variation

cook's tip

Instead of horseradish cream, serve these steak crostini topped with a spicy, garlicky aioli. To prepare a quick version, mix 1 teaspoon minced garlic and ½ teaspoon hot paprika into ½ cup (4 fl oz/125 ml) good-quality mayonnaise, and season to taste with salt.

grilled pork skewers

1 Marinate the pork
Place 22 short bamboo skewers in cold water to soak for 20 minutes. Prepare a gas or charcoal grill for direct grilling over medium heat, or preheat the broiler (grill). In a large bowl, stir together the pork, oil, and garlic. Season with salt and pepper and toss well. Let stand for 15 minutes.

2 Make the salsa
Meanwhile, in a glass or ceramic bowl, gently stir together the pineapple, onion, bell pepper, mint, cilantro, and ¼ teaspoon salt. Set aside.

3 Cook the pork
Thread 3 cubes of pork onto each skewer, pushing them snugly together. Place the skewers on the grill rack and cook, turning the skewers halfway through the cooking time, until firm and just lightly browned, about 6 minutes. (Or, arrange the skewers on a broiler pan and broil/grill, turning them halfway through the cooking time, for about 6 minutes.) Transfer the skewers to a platter and serve alongside the pineapple salsa.

> cook's tip The pineapple salsa can be made ahead and refrigerated for up to 4 hours before serving.

Boneless pork loin, 1 lb (500 g), cut into ¾-inch (2-cm) cubes

Olive oil, 2 tablespoons

Garlic, 2 cloves, minced

Salt and freshly ground pepper

Pineapple, 1½ cups (9 oz/280g) finely chopped

Red onion, ½, finely chopped

Large red bell pepper (capsicum), ½, finely chopped

Fresh mint, 6 leaves, minced

Fresh cilantro (fresh coriander), 2 teaspoons minced

MAKES 22 SKEWERS

smoked salmon pinwheels

Smoked salmon, 6 oz (185 g), thinly sliced

Cream cheese, ¼ lb (125 g), at room temperature

Fresh basil, 1 teaspoon roughly chopped

Fresh chives, 2 teaspoons roughly snipped

Freshly ground white pepper

Flour tortillas, 4, each about 8 inches (20 cm) in diameter

MAKES 24 PINWHEELS

1 **Mix the filling**
Set aside three-fourths of the largest smoked salmon slices. Place the remaining slices in a food processor with the cream cheese, basil, chives, and ¼ teaspoon pepper. Pulse to blend.

2 **Assemble the pinwheels**
Spread each tortilla with one-fourth of the cream cheese mixture. Divide the reserved salmon slices among the tortillas, placing them horizontally across the center. Starting from the bottom, roll up each tortilla firmly. Trim the ends and cut each roll into 6 pieces. Arrange the pinwheels on a platter and serve.

crostini with lemony chicken salad

1 Make the crostini
Preheat the oven to 350°F (180°C). Arrange the baguette slices on a baking sheet and brush lightly with the olive oil. Season with salt and pepper. Bake until golden, 10–15 minutes. Transfer to a platter and set aside.

2 Cook the chicken
Season both sides of the chicken breasts with salt and pepper. In a large frying pan over medium heat, warm the canola oil. Add the chicken and cook until golden brown and opaque in the center, 4–5 minutes per side. Transfer to a cutting board and let stand for 5 minutes.

3 Prepare the chicken salad
Into a mixing bowl, grate ½ teaspoon zest from the lemon. Halve the lemon and squeeze 1 teaspoon juice into the bowl. Add the fennel, green onion, ¾ teaspoon tarragon, mayonnaise, ¾ teaspoon salt, and pepper to taste. Mix until smooth. Chop the chicken finely. Add to the fennel mixture and toss until blended. Spoon the salad on the crostini, garnish with the remaining tarragon, and serve.

French or sourdough baguette, 28 slices, each about ½ inch (12 mm) thick

Olive oil, 2 tablespoons

Salt and freshly ground pepper

Skinless, boneless chicken breast halves, 2, about ¾ lb (375 g) total weight, pounded lightly to an even thickness and patted dry

Canola oil, 1 tablespoon

Lemon, 1

Fennel bulb, ½, trimmed, quartered lengthwise, and finely chopped

Green (spring) onion, 1, white and pale green parts, finely chopped

Fresh tarragon, ¾ teaspoon finely chopped, plus more for garnish

Mayonnaise, ⅓ cup (3 fl oz/80 ml)

MAKES 28 CROSTINI

mini potato pancakes with salmon

Small baking potatoes, 1¼ lb (625 g), peeled

Flour, ½ cup (2½ oz/75 g)

Yellow onion, ½ small, grated

Salt and freshly ground white pepper

Egg, 1, lightly beaten

Olive oil, 1 tablespoon

Unsalted butter, 1 tablespoon, melted

Crème fraîche or sour cream, 1 cup (8 oz/250 g)

Smoked salmon, 6 oz (185 g), cut into slivers

Fresh chives, 1 tablespoon finely snipped

MAKES ABOUT 24 PANCAKES

1 Form the pancakes
Bring a pan of lightly salted water to a boil. Add the potatoes and cook until almost tender, about 10 minutes. Drain and rinse under cold running water to stop the cooking. Drain well and pat dry with paper towels. Using the largest holes on a box grater-shredder, grate the potatoes into a large bowl. Add the flour, onion, ½ teaspoon salt, and ¼ teaspoon pepper and mix well with a fork. Stir in the egg. With lightly floured hands, form the mixture into walnut-sized balls, rolling them between your palms, then flatten the balls into patties.

2 Cook the pancakes
In a small bowl, combine the oil and butter. Place a large frying pan over medium heat and brush generously with the oil-butter mixture. Working in batches, cook the pancakes until golden and crisp, 4–5 minutes per side. Transfer to a paper towel–lined plate. Top each pancake with a dollop of the crème fraîche and a few slivers of salmon. Arrange on a platter, sprinkle with the chives, and serve.

cook's tip The pancakes can be kept warm in a 200°F (95°C) oven while the other batches are cooking.

goat cheese– stuffed tomatoes

1 Mix the filling
In a food processor, combine the goat cheese, cream cheese, and sour cream. Process until smooth, scraping down the sides if necessary.

2 Stuff the tomatoes
Using the small end of a melon baller, carefully scoop out the seeds and core from each tomato. Arrange the tomatoes cut side up on a cutting board. Using 2 small spoons, place about 1 teaspoon cheese filling in each tomato, mounding it slightly. Transfer to a platter, sprinkle with the chives, and serve.

cook's tip To make the stuffed tomatoes in advance, prepare the filling as directed in Step 1. Hollow out the tomatoes and arrange cut side down on a paper towel–lined baking sheet. Cover with plastic wrap and refrigerate along with the filling for up to 3 hours. Fill the tomatoes just before serving.

Fresh goat cheese,
¼ lb (125 g), at room temperature

Cream cheese, 3 oz (90 g), at room temperature

Sour cream,
2 tablespoons

Cherry tomatoes,
2½ cups (1 lb/500 g), about 40, stem ends trimmed

Fresh chives,
2 tablespoons finely snipped

MAKES ABOUT 40 TOMATOES

rosemary focaccia

Coarse cornmeal,
1 tablespoon

Yeast Dough (page 42),
1 ball, at room
temperature

Olive oil, 2 tablespoons

Fresh rosemary,
2 teaspoons minced

Coarse sea salt

MAKES ABOUT 16 PIECES

1 Shape the dough
Sprinkle the cornmeal evenly over
an 11-by-17-inch (28-by-43-cm) rimmed
baking sheet. Place the dough on the
prepared sheet. Press down on the center,
and, working from the center outward,
push and stretch the dough evenly to
the edges of the pan. (If the dough is
difficult to handle, set it aside, covered,
for 10 minutes and try again.) Cover the
flattened dough with a damp kitchen
towel and let rise for 15 minutes.

2 Bake the focaccia
Place a rack in the lower third of the
oven and preheat to 450°F (230°C). Make
dimples in the dough with your fingertips.
Drizzle with the oil and sprinkle with the
rosemary and a small amount of salt. Bake
until golden brown, 15–18 minutes. Cut
the focaccia into pieces and serve warm
or at room temperature.

cherry tomato & pesto pizza

1 Shape the dough

Sprinkle the cornmeal evenly over an 11-by-17-inch (28-by-43-cm) rimmed baking sheet. Place the dough on the prepared sheet. Press down on the center, and, working from the center outward, push and stretch the dough evenly to the edges of the pan. (If the dough is difficult to handle, set it aside, covered, for 10 minutes and try again.) Cover the flattened dough with a damp kitchen towel and let rise for at least 15 minutes.

2 Assemble and bake the pizza

Place a rack in the lower third of the oven and preheat to 450°F (230°C). Spread the pesto over the dough, leaving a ¼-inch (6-mm) border uncovered. Arrange the cheese and tomatoes over the pesto. Season with salt and pepper. Bake until the edges are golden brown and the cheese is bubbling, 15–18 minutes. Cut into pieces and serve warm. »

Coarse cornmeal, 1 tablespoon

Yeast Dough (page 42), 1 ball, at room temperature

Basil pesto, ½ cup (4 fl oz/125 ml), homemade (page 34) or purchased

Fresh mozzarella cheese, ½ lb (250 g), sliced

Cherry tomatoes, 1 cup (6 oz/185 g) quartered

Salt and freshly ground pepper

MAKES 1 PIZZA

cherry tomato & pesto pizza
continued

cook's tip

Vary the pizza topping by using cured meats
such as salami or pepperoni. Or, substitute
other quick-cooking, freshly cut vegetables,
like bell peppers (capsicums) or mushrooms.

olive & onion flatbread

1 Cook the onions
In a large frying pan over medium heat, warm the oil. Add the onions and season with salt and pepper. Cover and cook gently, stirring every 5 minutes or so, until tender and golden, about 20 minutes.

2 Shape the dough
Meanwhile, sprinkle the cornmeal evenly over an 11-by-17-inch (28-by-43-cm) rimmed baking sheet. Place the dough on the prepared sheet. Press down on the center, and, working from the center outward, push and stretch the dough evenly to the edges of the pan. (If the dough is difficult to handle, set it aside, covered, for 10 minutes and try again.) Cover the dough with a damp kitchen towel and let rise for at least 15 minutes.

3 Assemble and bake the flatbread
Place a rack in the lower third of the oven and preheat to 450°F (230°C). Spread the onion mixture over the dough, leaving a ¼-inch (6-mm) border uncovered. Scatter the anchovies and olives over the dough. Bake until the edges are golden brown, 15–18 minutes. Let stand for 3–5 minutes. Cut into pieces and serve warm.

Olive oil, ¼ cup (2 fl oz/ 60 ml)

Yellow onions, 1½ lb (750 g), thinly sliced

Salt and freshly ground pepper

Coarse cornmeal, 1 tablespoon

Yeast Dough (page 42), 1 ball, at room temperature

Canned anchovy fillets, 8, soaked in warm water for 5 minutes, drained, patted dry, and chopped

Niçoise or other brine-cured black olives, 8, pitted and roughly chopped

MAKES 1 LARGE FLATBREAD

feta & spinach filo roll

Olive oil, 1 tablespoon

Green (spring) onions,
8, white and pale green
parts, chopped

Baby spinach, 1 lb
(500 g), chopped

**Fresh flat-leaf (Italian)
parsley,** 3 tablespoons
finely chopped

Ground nutmeg,
½ teaspoon

**Salt and freshly ground
pepper**

Eggs, 3

Feta cheese, 6 oz (185 g),
crumbled

Filo dough, 6 sheets,
thawed

Unsalted butter, 3–4
tablespoons, melted and
slightly cooled

Sesame seeds,
2 tablespoons

MAKES 6 SERVINGS

1 Prepare the filling
Position a rack in the middle of the oven and preheat to 375°F (190°C). Line a baking sheet with parchment (baking) paper. In a large frying pan over medium heat, warm the oil. Add the onions and sauté for about 4 minutes. Add the spinach and sauté for about 1 minute. Remove from the heat and stir in the parsley and nutmeg, and season with salt and pepper. Let cool slightly. In a bowl, beat the eggs with a fork until blended and stir in the cheese. Add the spinach mixture and stir to combine.

2 Shape and bake the roll
Lay out 1 filo sheet on a work surface and lightly brush with butter. Cover with a second filo sheet and brush it with butter. Repeat with the remaining sheets, brushing each one with butter. Spoon the spinach mixture in a line on a long side of the filo stack, leaving a border of about 1½ inches (4 cm) uncovered on the ends and the sides. Fold the long border over the filling, fold in the ends, and then gently roll up the dough, encasing the filling. Place the roll, seam side down, on the prepared sheet. Brush the top with butter and sprinkle with the sesame seeds. Bake until golden brown, 30–35 minutes. Let cool slightly on the pan on a wire rack. Cut into slices and serve.

cheesy chive popovers

1 Make the batter
Preheat the oven to 450°F (230°C). Generously grease 2 nonstick mini muffin pans. In a large bowl, stir together the flour, ½ teaspoon salt, ¼ teaspoon pepper, and the chives. In another bowl, whisk together the milk, eggs, and butter. Pour the wet ingredients over the dry ingredients and whisk until just combined (don't worry if some lumps remain).

2 Bake the popovers
Fill the prepared muffin cups with batter to within about ¼ inch (6 mm) of the rims. Place a scant teaspoon grated cheese in the center of each filled cup. Bake, without opening the oven door, for 10 minutes. Reduce the oven temperature to 350°F (180°C) and bake until the popovers are brown and fully puffed, 8–10 minutes longer. Transfer to a platter and serve warm.

cook's tip If the popovers happen to get stuck, gently pry them out with a small icing spatula or offset spatula, as a paring knife may scratch the pan.

Flour, 1 cup (5 oz/155 g)

Salt and freshly ground pepper

Fresh chives, 1 tablespoon finely snipped

Milk, 1¼ cups (10 fl oz/310 ml), at room temperature

Eggs, 2, at room temperature

Unsalted butter, 1 tablespoon, melted

Gruyère cheese, 3 oz (90 g), coarsely grated

MAKES 24 POPOVERS

beef empanadas

Lean ground (minced) beef, 6 oz (185 g)

Pine nuts, 3 tablespoons, coarsely chopped

Yellow onion, ½, finely chopped

Tomato paste, 1 tablespoon

Red wine, ¼ cup (2 fl oz/60 ml)

Currants, 3 tablespoons

Ground cumin, ½ teaspoon

Dried oregano, ¼ teaspoon

Salt and freshly ground pepper

Savory Tart Dough (page 40), 1 disk

Egg, 1, whisked with 1 tablespoon water

MAKES ABOUT 24 EMPANADAS

1 Make the filling
In a frying pan over medium heat, cook the beef and the pine nuts until the beef is no longer pink, about 6 minutes. Transfer to a bowl. Add the onion to the pan and cook, stirring, until softened, about 5 minutes. Add the tomato paste and wine and cook, stirring, for about 3 minutes. Stir the onion mixture, currants, cumin, oregano, ¼ teaspoon salt, and ¼ teaspoon pepper into the beef.

2 Roll out the dough
Preheat the oven to 375°F (190°C). Line 2 baking sheets with parchment (baking) paper. On a floured work surface, roll out the dough until just less than ¼ inch (6 mm) thick. Using a 3-inch (7.5-cm) biscuit cutter, cut out as many rounds as possible from the dough. Transfer to the prepared baking sheets. Gather the scraps together, roll out again, and cut out additional rounds. Brush the rounds with the egg mixture.

3 Assemble the empanadas
Place a generous tablespoon of the filling in the center of each dough round. Fold the dough over the filling, lining up the edges. Firmly crimp the edges with a fork. Brush the tops of the empanadas with the egg mixture. Bake until golden brown, about 30 minutes, and serve warm.

pear compote with cheese

1 Toast the bread
Preheat the oven to 350°F (180°C). Arrange the baguette slices on a baking sheet and brush lightly with the oil. Bake until crisp and golden, 10–15 minutes. Transfer to a large platter.

2 Cook the pear compote
In a frying pan over medium-low heat, combine the pears, star anise, wine, and sugar. Bring to a gentle simmer and cook, stirring occasionally, until the pears are softened, about 12 minutes. Remove the star anise. Let cool to room temperature. (The compote may be refrigerated for up to 8 hours; bring it to room temperature before serving.)

3 Arrange the platter
Transfer the compote to a small bowl and place on the platter. Arrange the cheeses and crostini around the compote. Layer a slice of cheese and a dollop of compote on each crostini and serve.

cook's tip You will find many good-quality commercial compotes or chutneys at the market, especially those made with fruits such as mango or apple. Either would be a good substitution in this recipe.

French or sourdough baguette, 24 slices, each about ½ inch (12 mm) thick

Olive oil, 2 tablespoons

Pears such as Bartlett (Williams') or Bosc, 2, peeled, quartered, cored, and coarsely chopped

Star anise or cinnamon stick, 1

Fruity white wine such as Riesling, 2½ tablespoons

Sugar, 1 tablespoon, or to taste

Aged pecorino cheese, ¼ lb (125 g)

Maytag or other blue cheese, ¼ lb (125 g)

MAKES 24 PIECES

scallops with mango & avocado

Bay scallops or sea scallops, 1¼ lb (625 g), side muscles removed

Canola oil, 1–2 tablespoons

Lime juice, from 7–8 limes (1¼ cups/ 10 fl oz/310 ml)

Fresh cilantro (fresh coriander), 1½ tablespoons finely chopped

Salt and freshly ground pepper

Red pepper flakes, ¾ teaspoon

Hot pepper sauce such as Tabasco

Mango, 1, peeled, pitted, and cut into small cubes

Hass avocado, 1, halved, pitted, peeled, and cut into small cubes

Olive oil for drizzling

MAKES 6–8 SERVINGS

1 Cook the scallops
If using large sea scallops, cut the scallops in half hortizontally. In a large frying pan over medium-high heat, warm 1 tablespoon of the canola oil until hot but not smoking. Working in batches, sear the scallops for 1–2 minutes on each side, adding more oil to the pan if necessary. Transfer the seared scallops to a plate.

2 Flavor the scallops
In a glass or ceramic bowl, combine the lime juice, cilantro, 2 teaspoons salt, pepper flakes, and hot pepper sauce to taste. Add the seared scallops and toss. Gently stir in the mango and avocado. Spoon into martini glasses or small bowls. Drizzle with olive oil and serve.

cook's tip This Peruvian-inspired dish can also be made with fresh fish. Substitute 1¼ lb (750 g) halibut or cod fillet, cut into ½-inch (12-mm) cubes. Sear the cubes as you would the scallops for about 1 minute per side and proceed with the recipe.

appetizers made easy

With a well-stocked pantry and weekly menus, you'll have a solid foundation for small-plate meals for the family and even impromptu get-togethers for friends. In the following pages, you'll find tips on how to make the most of your time along with ideas for hosting parties with ease.

SIMPLE APPETIZERS

Charcuterie Arrange cured meats like salami, prosciutto, and *coppa* on a cutting board. Garnish the board with olives or cornichons, and place a ramekin of grainy mustard for spreading alongside. Serve with baguette slices.

Cheese platter Put together a platter of your favorite cheeses and accompaniments. Include a mixture of soft cheeses, such as goat cheese or Brie, and hard cheeses, such as Manchego or aged Cheddar. Serve with nuts, fresh fruit, and baguette slices or crackers.

Cheese puffs Wrap small squares or triangles of store-bought puff pastry around pieces of cheese and a pinch of fresh herbs, such as thyme, and bake in a 375°F (190°C) oven until golden, about 20 minutes.

Precut vegetables & fruit Supermarkets stock prewashed, precut fruits and vegetables, which can easily be assembled into crudité or dessert platters.

Shortcut ingredients If you like to entertain on the fly, consider stocking your kitchen with a number of essential ingredients that will boost the flavor of any selection you lay out and save you the time and effort of having to prepare them yourself.

- CAPONATA Available in jars in Italian specialty shops and some supermarkets, this chunky, sweet-and-sour Sicilian mixture of eggplant (aubergine), onion, celery, pine nuts, currants, capers, and vinegar makes a good summertime dip or a base for bruschetta. It can also be tossed with hot pasta for an easy sauce.

- HUMMUS Look in the refrigerator section of your supermarket for premade hummus. Make a quick sandwich or wrap filling by adding lemon juice, minced garlic, and a pinch of cumin. Or, top with a swirl of olive oil and serve with warmed pita slices or crudités such as broccoli florets, carrot sticks, or zucchini (courgette) spears.

- PESTO Look for freshly made versions of this vibrant summery sauce at Italian delicatessens, or stock up on flavorful jarred or frozen varieties. You can also make your own pesto very quickly if you have the right ingredients (see page 34). Spread on thin toasted baguette slices and top with sliced plum (Roma) tomatoes.

- SALSA There is a wide variety of fresh salsas to choose from at the supermarket, from tomato and tomatillo salsas to fruit salsas. Keep some on hand to serve with tortilla chips or quesadillas.

- SMOKED FISH Vacuum-packed smoked salmon and trout can be kept unopened in the refrigerator for several weeks. Serve with a dollop of sour cream or crème fraîche on toast points, homemade or packaged blini, or triangles of dense German-style rye bread or pumpernickel bread.

- TAPENADE This pungent spread, made from minced black olives and seasoned with garlic, is delicious lightly spread on toasted baguette slices or crackers.

Here are some ideas on how to create a satisfying supper by adding one or two side dishes to an appetizer recipe. "In Minutes" meals include appetizers and accompaniments that can be put together quickly. "Fit for Company" meals offer suggestions for stress-free get-togethers, complete with a wine suggestion.

IN MINUTES

Caprese Skewers (page 51)

sliced salami and prosciutto

warm focaccia with fresh thyme and olive oil

Guacamole & Sweet Potato Chips (page 55)

cheese quesadillas

black beans and rice

Shrimp & Basil Skewers (page 59)

orzo pasta with lemon

grilled asparagus

Smoked Salmon Pinwheels (page 66)

shaved zucchini (courgettes) with Parmesan

tomato slices with sea salt and olive oil

Crostini with Lemony Chicken Salad (page 67)

fresh fruit salad

FIT FOR COMPANY

Crab Salad Bites (page 48)

chilled cucumber soup

crusty bread

Champagne or Sauvignon Blanc

Antipasto Platter (page 54)

Olive & Onion Flatbread (page 73)

Chianti or Barbera

Ham & Spinach Quiches (page 60)

arugula (rocket) salad with Parmesan

Pinot Noir or Chardonnay

Lamb Meatballs (page 62)

spinach salad with feta cheese

Syrah or Zinfandel

Mini Potato Pancakes with Salmon (page 68)

sautéed green beans

dry Riesling

MEAL PLANNING TIPS

Appetizers aren't just for parties. Even if you're not in the mood for entertaining, you can easily incorporate the recipes in this chapter into your weekly family dinners.

Make small plates With the growing popularity of Spanish tapas, an assortment of small plates has become a festive way to enjoy any meal. Mix and match a few appetizers and pass them around the table on platters for a complete meal.

Round it out Many of the appetizers in this chapter can become the centerpiece of a dinner menu. Once you have decided which recipe to make for your main dish, you can choose from among a variety of quick and easy side dishes to complete the meal (see pages 16–17).

Adjust the yield Most of the recipe yields in this chapter are given in quantities rather than in number of servings. For instance, the recipe for Grilled Pork Skewers (page 65) makes about 22 skewers. You can easily halve or double the recipe depending on how many people you are serving and which accompaniments you choose.

salads

spinach, pear & walnut salad

1 Toast the walnuts
Preheat the oven to 350°F (180°C). Spread the walnuts in a single layer on a rimmed baking sheet and toast, stirring occasionally, until fragrant, 8–10 minutes; do not let them brown.

2 Make the dressing
Meanwhile, in a large bowl, whisk together the sour cream, mayonnaise, oil, vinegar, Worcestershire sauce, a dash of hot pepper sauce, and a pinch of pepper until well blended.

3 Assemble the salad
Add the spinach, pears, and toasted walnuts to the dressing and toss to coat evenly. Arrange on plates or in bowls, sprinkle with the cheese, and serve.

cook's tip Unlike many fruits, pears ripen off the tree, and they ripen from the inside out, so they may feel firm on the surface even when soft inside. To test for ripeness, press just to one side of the stem end; if it gives, the pear is ripe. To ripen pears quickly, put them in a paper bag with a banana. Check once a day to see how the ripening is progressing.

Walnut halves, ¾ cup (3 oz/90 g)

Sour cream, ¼ cup (2 oz/60 g)

Mayonnaise, 2 tablespoons

Walnut oil, 2 tablespoons

Red wine vinegar, 2 teaspoons

Worcestershire sauce, 1 teaspoon

Hot pepper sauce such as Tabasco

Freshly ground pepper

Baby spinach, 6 cups (6 oz/185 g)

Pears such as Bosc or Anjou, 4, peeled, halved, cored, and cut into thin wedges

Blue cheese, 2 oz (60 g), crumbled

MAKES 4 SERVINGS

greek salad

Lemon juice, from 1 lemon

Garlic, 1 clove, minced

Freshly ground pepper

Olive oil, ¼ cup (2 fl oz/60 ml), plus 1 tablespoon

Pita breads, 2 rounds

Dried oregano, ½ teaspoon

Hearts of romaine (cos) lettuce, 2, coarsely chopped

English (hothouse) cucumber, 1, halved crosswise and thickly sliced

Tomatoes, 2, cut into wedges

Assorted brine-cured olives, 1 cup (6 oz/185 g)

Feta cheese, ½ lb (250 g), crumbled

Green (spring) onions, 8, white and pale green parts, thinly sliced

MAKES 4 SERVINGS

1 **Make the vinaigrette**
In a large bowl, whisk together the lemon juice, garlic, and a generous amount of pepper. Gradually whisk in the ¼ cup oil until well blended.

2 **Warm the pita**
Preheat the oven to 300°F (150°C). Cut each pita into 4 wedges. Arrange on a baking sheet and brush both sides with the remaining 1 tablespoon oil. Sprinkle with the oregano and place in the oven to warm for about 10 minutes.

3 **Assemble the salad**
Add the lettuce, cucumber, and tomatoes to the vinaigrette and toss to coat evenly. Arrange on plates and top with the olives, cheese, and green onions. Place the warm pita wedges alongside the salads and serve.

cook's tip For picnic-style pita sandwiches, make the salad as directed, but pit and chop the olives. Slice leftover cooked chicken breasts and toss with the salad. Halve the pita rounds, stuff with the salad and chicken, and serve.

edamame, corn & tomato salad

1 Cook the corn and edamame
Have ready a bowl of ice water. Bring a saucepan of water to a boil, add the corn and edamame, and cook for 3 minutes. Using a slotted spoon, transfer the corn and edamame to the bowl of ice water. Drain, place in a large bowl, and add the tomatoes and avocado.

2 Assemble the salad
In a small bowl, whisk together the lime juice, 1 teaspoon salt, and ⅛ teaspoon pepper. Gradually whisk in the oil until well blended. Pour the dressing over the vegetables and gently toss to combine. Arrange the lettuce leaves on a serving platter and spoon the salad onto the leaves. Garnish with the cilantro and serve.

> **cook's tip** *Edamame* is the Japanese word for "soybean." It makes a delicious and healthy snack: lightly boil the pods in water and then salt them generously. Squeeze the beans from the pods and enjoy out of hand.

Fresh corn kernels, from 2 ears, or frozen corn kernels, ¾ cup (5 oz/155 g)

Frozen shelled edamame, 1½ cups (9 oz/280 g)

Cherry tomatoes, 12, halved

Hass avocado, 1 large, halved, pitted, peeled, and cubed

Fresh lime juice, 2 tablespoons

Salt and freshly ground pepper

Canola oil, 1 tablespoon

Romaine (cos) lettuce, 8 dark outer leaves

Fresh cilantro (fresh coriander), 2 tablespoons chopped

MAKES 4 SERVINGS

grilled asparagus & prosciutto salad

Asparagus, 1¼ lb (625 g), tough ends removed

Olive oil, 7 tablespoons (3½ fl oz/105 ml)

Salt and freshly ground pepper

Garlic, 1 clove, minced

Red wine vinegar, 2 tablespoons

Tarragon or Dijon mustard, 1 teaspoon

Fresh chives, 1 tablespoon finely snipped

Mixed baby greens, 6 cups (6 oz/185 g)

Prosciutto, 3 oz (90 g), thinly sliced and cut into strips

Parmesan cheese, 2 oz (60 g), shaved

MAKES 4 SERVINGS

1 **Grill the asparagus**
Prepare a gas or charcoal grill for direct-heat grilling over medium-high heat, or preheat a stovetop grill pan over medium-high heat. Brush the asparagus with 1 tablespoon of the oil and season with salt and pepper. Place the asparagus on the grill rack or in the grill pan and cook, turning occasionally, until slightly charred and tender, about 8 minutes.

2 **Make the vinaigrette**
In a large bowl, whisk together the garlic, vinegar, mustard, ¼ teaspoon salt, and a pinch of pepper. Gradually whisk in the remaining 6 tablespoons (3 fl oz/90 ml) oil until well blended. Stir in the chives.

3 **Assemble the salad**
Add the greens and prosciutto to the vinaigrette and toss gently to coat. Arrange the grilled asparagus on plates and top with the dressed greens and prosciutto. Top with the cheese and serve.

grapefruit, jicama & avocado salad

1 Prepare the grapefruits
Trim a slice from the top and bottom of each grapefruit, cutting through the peel and pith. Stand the grapefruit upright and, following the contour of the fruit, cut away the peel and pith, being careful not to remove too much of the flesh. Holding the grapefruit over a large bowl to catch the juice, cut between the membranes to release each segment. Cut the segments into pieces and set aside in another bowl.

2 Make the vinaigrette
Add the vinegar, mustard, ¼ teaspoon salt, and a pinch of pepper to the grapefruit juice and whisk to combine. Gradually whisk in the oil until blended. Stir in the basil.

3 Assemble the salad
Add the radicchio, jicama, and grapefruit pieces to the vinaigrette and toss to coat evenly. Arrange on plates, top with the avocados, and serve. »

Ruby grapefruits, 2

White wine vinegar, 1 tablespoon

Honey Dijon mustard, 1 teaspoon

Salt and freshly ground pepper

Olive oil, ⅓ cup (3 fl oz/80 ml)

Fresh basil, 1 tablespoon minced

Radicchio, 1 small head, cored and thinly sliced

Jicama, about ½ lb (250 g), peeled and cut into matchsticks

Hass avocados, 2, halved, pitted, peeled, and cut into cubes

MAKES 4 SERVINGS

grapefruit, jicama & avocado salad
continued

cook's tip

To make candied pecans as a garnish for the salad, line
a rimmed baking sheet with parchment (baking) paper.
In a saucepan over medium heat, bring ½ cup (4 oz/125 g)
sugar and ¼ cup (2 fl oz/60 ml) water to a boil and cook
until light amber. Add 1 cup (4 oz/125 g) pecan halves,
swirl the pan, then pour onto the prepared sheet and
spread in a single layer. Let cool.

grilled summer vegetable salad

1 Grill the vegetables
Prepare a gas or charcoal grill for direct-heat grilling over high heat, or preheat the broiler (grill). Place the eggplant and squash slices in a shallow dish and brush both sides with the 3 tablespoons oil. Season with salt and pepper and the oregano. Place the slices on the grill rack and cook, turning once, until tender and golden, 2–3 minutes. (Or, arrange the slices on a rimmed baking sheet and place under the broiler. Cook, turning once, for 2–3 minutes per side.)

2 Make the vinaigrette
In a large bowl, whisk together the vinegar, mustard, ¼ teaspoon salt, and a pinch of pepper. Gradually whisk in the remaining ¼ cup oil until well blended.

3 Assemble the salad
Cut the grilled vegetables into bite-sized pieces and add to the vinaigrette. Add the tomatoes and greens and toss to coat. Sprinkle with the cheese and serve.

Eggplant (aubergine), 1 large or 2 small, cut lengthwise into thick slices

Yellow summer squash or zucchini (courgettes), 3, cut lengthwise into thick slices

Olive oil, ¼ cup (2 fl oz/60 ml), plus 3 tablespoons

Salt and freshly ground pepper

Dried oregano, ½ teaspoon

Balsamic vinegar, 1 tablespoon

Dijon mustard, 1 teaspoon

Tomatoes, 4, cored and quartered

Mixed baby greens, 3 cups (3 oz/90 g)

Fresh goat cheese, ⅔ cup (3 oz/90 g) crumbled

MAKES 4 SERVINGS

couscous salad

Olive oil, ¼ cup
(2 fl oz/60 ml), plus
2 tablespoons

Yellow onion, 1, finely
chopped

Garlic, 2 cloves, minced

Chicken broth, 2¾ cups
(22 fl oz/680 ml), or
Chicken Stock (page 29)

**Salt and freshly ground
pepper**

Instant couscous,
1½ cups (9 oz/280 g)

Slivered almonds, ¾ cup
(3 oz/90 g)

**Chickpeas (garbanzo
beans),** 1 can (15 oz/
470 g), rinsed and
drained

**Red bell pepper
(capsicum),** 1, seeded
and chopped

Brine-cured black olives,
¾ cup (3½ oz/105 g),
pitted and chopped

Lemon juice, from
1 lemon

**Fresh flat-leaf (Italian)
parsley,** ¼ cup (⅓ oz/
10 g) finely chopped

MAKES 4 SERVINGS

1 Prepare the couscous
In a large saucepan over medium-low
heat, warm 1 tablespoon of the oil. Add
the onion and sauté until softened, about
4 minutes. Add the garlic and sauté for
1 minute. Add the broth, ½ teaspoon salt,
and several grinds of pepper and bring
to a boil. Place the couscous in a large
stainless-steel bowl and pour the hot liquid
over it. Blend well with a fork, cover, and
let stand for 5 minutes.

2 Toast the almonds
Meanwhile, in a large frying pan over
medium heat, warm 1 tablespoon of the
oil. Add the almonds and toast, stirring,
until crisp and golden, 5–7 minutes. Add
to the couscous.

3 Assemble the salad
Fluff the couscous with a fork, mixing
in the almonds. Add the chickpeas, bell
pepper, olives, lemon juice, parsley, and
remaining ¼ cup oil to the couscous. Toss
gently to combine. Season to taste with
salt and pepper and serve.

farro salad

1 Cook the farro
In a saucepan, combine the farro and 2 cups (16 fl oz/500 ml) water. Bring to a boil over high heat, then reduce the heat to low and simmer, covered, until the grains are plump and tender to the bite, about 30 minutes. Remove from the heat, uncover, and let cool slightly. (The farro can be prepared up to 1 day in advance and stored in the refrigerator.)

2 Make the vinaigrette
Meanwhile, in a large bowl, whisk together the lemon juice, ¼ teaspoon salt, and a pinch of pepper. Gradually whisk in the oil until well blended.

3 Assemble the salad
Add the radishes, cucumber, mint, and farro to the vinaigrette and toss to coat evenly. Gently toss in the spinach and cheese and serve.

Farro, 1 cup (5 oz/155 g)

Lemon juice, from 2 lemons

Salt and freshly ground pepper

Olive oil, ¼ cup (2 fl oz/60 ml)

Radishes, 8, thinly sliced

English (hothouse) cucumber, ½, peeled, halved lengthwise, and thinly sliced

Fresh mint, ⅓ cup (½ oz/15 g) loosely packed, finely chopped

Baby spinach, 6 cups (6 oz/185 g)

Feta cheese, 5 oz (155 g), crumbled

MAKES 4 SERVINGS

> cook's tip If you can't find farro, you can use bulgur instead. Place 1 cup (6 oz/185 g) bulgur in a large heatproof bowl and pour in 2 cups (16 fl oz/500 ml) boiling water. Let stand for 30 minutes, then fluff the grains with a fork.

mediterranean
potato salad

Salt and freshly ground pepper

Thin green beans, ¼ lb (125 g), trimmed

Red-skinned potatoes, 1¼ lb (625 g), quartered

Canned chickpeas (garbanzo beans) or kidney beans, 1 cup (7 oz/220 g) drained and rinsed

Red onion, 1 small, finely chopped

Fresh flat-leaf (Italian) parsley, ½ cup (¾ oz/20 g) roughly chopped

Fresh mint, ½ cup (¾ oz/20 g) roughly chopped

Sicilian or other green olives, 4, pitted and coarsely chopped

Capers, 1 tablespoon, rinsed and chopped

Whole-grain mustard, 1 tablespoon

Red wine vinegar, 1 tablespoon

Olive oil, 1 tablespoon

MAKES 4 SERVINGS

1 Cook the beans and potatoes

Have ready a bowl of ice water. Bring a large pot of water to a boil, add 1 tablespoon salt and the green beans, and cook until bright green and tender-crisp, about 3 minutes. Using a slotted spoon, transfer to the bowl of ice water and let stand for 1–2 minutes. Drain the beans and place in a large bowl. Add the potatoes to the boiling water and cook until just tender, about 10 minutes. Drain and add the potatoes to the beans.

2 Assemble the salad

Add the chickpeas, onion, parsley, mint, olives, and capers to the green beans and potatoes. In a small bowl, whisk together the mustard, vinegar, 1 teaspoon salt, and ⅛ teaspoon pepper. Gradually whisk in the oil until blended. Pour the mixture over the salad, toss to coat, and serve.

cook's tip For heartier fare, serve with 4–8 hard-cooked eggs. Follow the instructions on page 91 to boil the eggs. Drain the eggs, run under cold water, then peel and quarter and add to the salad plates.

chicken cobb salad

1 Cook the bacon

In a frying pan over medium heat, fry the bacon, stirring occasionally, until crisp and brown, about 5 minutes. Transfer to paper towels to drain.

2 Boil the eggs

In a small saucepan, combine the eggs with water to cover and bring to a boil over medium heat. As soon as the water boils, remove the pan from the heat and cover. Let stand for 10 minutes. Drain the water from the pan, then run cold water over the eggs until they are cool enough to handle. Peel and slice the eggs.

3 Assemble the salad

In a small bowl, whisk together the vinegar, mustard, garlic, ¼ teaspoon salt, and ¼ teaspoon pepper. Gradually whisk in the oil until blended. In a large bowl, toss the salad greens with the vinaigrette. Arrange the chicken, cheese, avocado slices, tomatoes, bacon, and eggs on top of the greens and serve.

cook's tip To save time, use a good-quality bottled vinaigrette. You can also try sliced roast beef, cubed ham, or sliced smoked turkey instead of the chicken and bacon.

Thick-cut bacon, 6 slices, chopped

Eggs, 2

Red wine vinegar, 2 tablespoons

Dijon mustard, 1 teaspoon

Garlic, 1 clove, minced

Salt and freshly ground pepper

Olive oil, ½ cup (4 fl oz/125 ml)

Mixed salad greens, 12 cups (¾ lb/375 g)

Classic Roast Chicken (page 267) or rotisserie chicken, 2½ cups (1 lb/500 g) coarsely chopped meat

Gorgonzola or other blue cheese, ¼ lb (125 g), crumbled

Hass avocados, 2, halved, pitted, peeled, and sliced

Tomatoes, 2, seeded and chopped

MAKES 4–6 SERVINGS

crab cake salad

Eggs, 2

Mayonnaise, ⅓ cup
(3 fl oz/80 ml), plus
1 tablespoon

Fresh lump crabmeat,
1 lb (500 g), picked over
for shell fragments and
squeezed to remove
excess water

**Fine fresh white bread
crumbs (page 214),**
½ cup (1 oz/30 g)

Green (spring) onions,
4, white and pale green
parts, finely chopped

**Salt and freshly ground
pepper**

Dijon mustard,
2 teaspoons

Lemon juice, from
1 lemon

Unsalted butter,
2 tablespoons

Butter (Boston) lettuce,
2 heads, torn into bite-
sized pieces

MAKES 4 SERVINGS

1 **Prepare the crab cakes**
In a bowl, whisk the eggs lightly. Add
the 1 tablespoon mayonnaise, crabmeat,
bread crumbs, green onions, 2 teaspoons
salt, and ½ teaspoon pepper. Stir with
a fork until well combined. Divide the
mixture into 8 equal portions and gently
form each portion into a small patty.

2 **Make the dressing**
In a small bowl, whisk together the
remaining ⅓ cup mayonnaise, mustard,
lemon juice, and ¼ teaspoon pepper
until well blended.

3 **Cook the crab cakes and serve**
In a large frying pan over medium-
low heat, melt the butter. Working in
batches if necessary, add the crab cakes
and cook without moving them until
golden brown on the first side, about
4 minutes. Turn and cook until golden
brown on the second side, 3–4 minutes
longer. Arrange the lettuce on plates
and place the crab cakes alongside.
Drizzle with the dressing and serve.

vietnamese shrimp & noodle salad

1 Prepare the noodles and dressing
In a large bowl, soak the noodles in hot water to cover for 15 minutes. Meanwhile, in another bowl, whisk together the lemongrass, ginger, lime juice, fish sauce, 2 teaspoons oil, and sugar until blended. Drain the noodles.

2 Cook the noodles
Bring a large pot of water to a boil. Plunge the reconstituted noodles into the boiling water for 5 seconds and drain immediately. Rinse well under cold running water and drain again. Add to the dressing and toss to coat evenly.

3 Cook the shrimp and serve
In a frying pan over medium-high heat, warm the remaining 1 tablespoon oil. Add the shrimp and cook, stirring frequently, until opaque throughout, 2–3 minutes. Add the shrimp, onions, and mint to the noodles and toss to combine. Arrange the lettuce on plates and top with the noodle-shrimp mixture. Sprinkle the peanuts on top and serve. »

Dried rice stick noodles, ½ lb (250 g)

Lemongrass, 2 stalks, pale inner core only, finely minced

Fresh ginger, 2 tablespoons finely grated

Lime juice, from 1 lime

Asian fish sauce, 3 tablespoons

Asian sesame oil, 2 teaspoons, plus 1 tablespoon

Sugar, 1 teaspoon

Small shrimp (prawns), 1 lb (500 g), peeled and deveined

Green (spring) onions, 12, white and pale green parts, thinly sliced

Fresh mint, ¼ cup (⅓ oz/10 g) coarsely chopped

Romaine (cos) lettuce, 1 head, pale inner leaves only, torn into bite-sized pieces

Roasted peanuts, ½ cup (2½ oz/75 g), chopped

MAKES 4 SERVINGS

vietnamese shrimp & noodle salad
continued

cook's tip

When using lemongrass, be sure to cut off the grassy top and trim the root end of the stalk, then peel away the tough outer layers from the bulblike base. If you are unable to find fresh lemongrass, substitute the finely grated zest and the juice of 1 lemon.

crab & mango salad

1 Make the vinaigrette
In a large bowl, whisk together the vinegar, ¼ teaspoon salt, and a pinch of pepper. Stir in the tarragon. Gradually whisk in the oil until well blended. Season to taste with salt and pepper.

2 Assemble the salad
Set aside one-third of the vinaigrette. Add the greens to the large bowl with the vinaigrette and toss to coat. Arrange on plates. In the same bowl, combine the crabmeat, mango, and reserved vinaigrette, and toss to moisten evenly. Mound the crabmeat mixture on the greens and serve.

White wine vinegar,
4 teaspoons

Salt and freshly ground white pepper

Fresh tarragon,
1 tablespoon minced

Olive oil, ¼ cup
(2 fl oz/60 ml)

Mixed salad greens,
8 cups (½ lb/250 g)

Fresh lump crabmeat,
¾ lb (375 g), picked over for shell fragments and squeezed to remove excess water

Mango, 1, peeled, pitted, and cubed

MAKES 4 SERVINGS

chicken & orzo salad

Basil Pesto (page 34) or purchased pesto, ⅔ cup (5 fl oz/160 ml)

White wine vinegar, 2 tablespoons

Salt and freshly ground pepper

Olive oil, 3 tablespoons

Orzo pasta, ¾ lb (375 g)

Classic Roast Chicken (page 267) or rotisserie chicken, 2½ cups (1 lb/ 500 g) shredded meat

Cherry tomatoes, ½ lb (250 g), halved

Baby spinach, 6 cups (6 oz/185 g)

MAKES 4 SERVINGS

1 Make the vinaigrette
In a large bowl, whisk together the pesto, vinegar, ¼ teaspoon salt, and a pinch of pepper. Gradually whisk in the oil until well blended.

2 Cook the orzo
Bring a large pot of water to a boil. Add 2 tablespoons salt and the orzo. Cook, stirring occasionally to prevent sticking, until the pasta is al dente, according to the package directions. Drain, rinse under cold running water, and drain again. Add the orzo to the vinaigrette and toss to coat evenly.

3 Assemble the salad
Add the chicken, tomatoes, and spinach to the orzo, toss gently to combine, and serve.

cook's tip In the past, if you wanted to serve pesto, you had to make it from scratch. Now it is available in plastic containers in the refrigerated section of many markets. Avoid the pesto sold in glass jars on store shelves, as it lacks the flavor that comes from the fresh herbs.

seared scallop & spinach salad

1 Prepare the bacon and spinach
In a frying pan over medium heat, cook the bacon, stirring occasionally, until crisp, about 5 minutes. Meanwhile, in a large bowl, stir together the vinegar, shallot, and a pinch of pepper. Add the spinach and toss to coat with the vinegar mixture. Using a slotted spoon, transfer the bacon to the bowl with the spinach, then drizzle 2 tablespoons of the bacon fat over the spinach and toss quickly to combine. Arrange the spinach-bacon mixture on plates. Reserve the remaining fat in the pan.

2 Sear the scallops and serve
Return the frying pan to medium-high heat and add the scallops. Cook, turning once, until golden brown on both sides but still slightly translucent in the center, about 2 minutes per side. Arrange on the spinach and serve.

Thick-cut bacon, 3 slices, chopped

White wine vinegar, 2 teaspoons

Shallot, 1, minced

Freshly ground pepper

Baby spinach, 12 cups (¾ lb/375 g)

Sea scallops, 1 lb (500 g), side muscles removed

MAKES 4 SERVINGS

chicken salad provençal

Red wine vinegar, 3 tablespoons

Dijon mustard, 1 tablespoon

Olive oil, ⅓ cup (3 fl oz/80 ml)

Salt and freshly ground pepper

Red-skinned potatoes, 1 lb (500 g) small

Thin green beans, ½ lb (250 g), trimmed

Butter (Boston) lettuce, 1 small head, leaves separated

Classic Roast Chicken (page 267) or rotisserie chicken, 2 cups (12 oz/ 375 g) shredded meat

Plum (Roma) tomatoes, 3, cut into wedges

Niçoise olives, ½ cup (2½ oz/75 g)

Red onion, 1 small, thinly sliced

Fresh basil, ¼ cup (⅓ oz/10 g) slivered

MAKES 4 SERVINGS

1 **Make the vinaigrette**
In a small bowl, whisk together the vinegar and mustard. Gradually whisk in the oil until smooth. Season with salt and pepper and set aside.

2 **Cook the vegetables**
In a large saucepan, combine the potatoes with water to cover and a generous pinch of salt. Bring to a boil over high heat, reduce the heat to medium, and cook for 8 minutes. Add the green beans and continue to cook until the potatoes are tender and the green beans are tender-crisp, 2–3 minutes longer. Drain the potatoes and green beans and let cool slightly. Slice the potatoes and place in a bowl. Add the beans and 3 tablespoons of the vinaigrette and toss to coat.

3 **Assemble the salad**
Line plates with the lettuce leaves. Top with the chicken, potatoes, green beans, tomatoes, and olives. Sprinkle with the onion and basil. Drizzle with the remaining vinaigrette and serve.

cook's tip The vegetables can be cooked and the vinaigrette prepared up to 1 day in advance. Store both in airtight containers in the refrigerator.

chicken & mango salad

1 Make the vinaigrette
In a food processor or blender, combine the peanut oil, vinegar, mustard, and chili oil, if using, and process until blended. Add the garlic and chutney and continue to process to a smooth purée.

2 Assemble the salad
In a bowl, combine the chicken, celery, onion, cashews, and mango. Add the vinaigrette and toss gently to coat. Divide the lettuce among plates, top with the chicken mixture, and serve. »

Peanut or canola oil,
⅔ cup (5 fl oz/160 ml)

White wine vinegar,
¼ cup (2 fl oz/60 ml)

Dijon mustard,
1 tablespoon

Asian chili oil,
2–3 teaspoons (optional)

Garlic, 2 cloves, minced

Mango chutney, ½ cup
(5 oz/155 g)

**Classic Roast Chicken
(page 267) or rotisserie
chicken,** 2 cups (12 oz/
375 g) shredded meat

Celery, 1 stalk, thinly
sliced

Red onion, 1 small,
halved and thinly sliced

**Roasted, salted
cashews,** ⅓ cup
(2½ oz/75 g), coarsely
chopped

Mango, 1, peeled, pitted,
and thinly sliced

Romaine (cos) lettuce,
4 cups (4 oz/125 g)
shredded

MAKES 4 SERVINGS

cook's tip

To prepare a mango, first peel it using a vegetable peeler or paring knife. Then, stand the mango on one of its narrow edges and use a sharp knife to cut down along one side of the stem end, just grazing the pit. Repeat on the other side. Cut each half into slices. Slice off any flesh left clinging to the pit.

fried chicken salad

1 Make the vinaigrette
In a large bowl, whisk together the mustard, vinegar, and 1 teaspoon salt. Whisk in the olive oil until blended.

2 Fry the chicken
Preheat the oven to 200°F (95°C). In a deep, heavy saucepan over high heat, pour in canola oil to a depth of ½ inch (12 mm) and heat to 360°F (182°C) on a deep-frying thermometer. Line a large rimmed baking sheet with a double layer of paper towels and place in the oven. In a large, resealable plastic bag, combine the flour and 1½ teaspoons each salt and pepper. Pour the buttermilk into a shallow bowl. Working in batches if necessary, dip the chicken pieces in the buttermilk. Remove, letting any excess drip back into the bowl, and place in the flour. Seal the bag and toss to coat evenly. Using tongs, add half of the chicken to the oil and fry, turning occasionally, until golden and opaque throughout, 2–4 minutes. Transfer to the prepared baking sheet and keep warm in the oven. Let the oil return to 360°F before frying the second batch.

3 Assemble the salad
Add the lettuce, tomato, onion, and pecans to the vinaigrette and toss to coat evenly. Arrange on plates, top with the fried chicken, and serve.

Honey Dijon mustard, 1 tablespoon

Red wine vinegar, 1 tablespoon

Salt and freshly ground pepper

Olive oil, ½ cup (4 fl oz/125 ml)

Canola oil, for frying

Flour, 1 cup (5 oz/155 g)

Buttermilk, 1 cup (8 fl oz/250 ml)

Skinless, boneless chicken breasts, 1 lb (500 g), cut into large bite-sized pieces

Romaine (cos) lettuce, 1 head, pale inner leaves only, torn into bite-sized pieces

Tomato, 1 large, cut into bite-sized chunks

Red onion, 1 small, halved and cut into thin slivers

Pecan halves, 1 cup (4 oz/125 g), coarsely chopped

MAKES 4 SERVINGS

asian chicken salad

Red onion, ½ small, thinly sliced, plus 2 tablespoons finely chopped

Fresh ginger, 1 teaspoon finely grated

White miso, 1½ tablespoons

Rice vinegar, 3 tablespoons

Honey, 1 tablespoon

Canola oil, 5 tablespoons (2½ fl oz/75 ml)

Asian sesame oil, 2 tablespoons

Red or yellow bell pepper (capsicum), 1, seeded and thinly sliced

Bean sprouts, ⅔ cup (2 oz/60 g)

Classic Roast Chicken (page 267) or rotisserie chicken, 4 cups (1½ lb/750 g) shredded meat

Fresh cilantro (fresh coriander), ¼ cup (⅓ oz/10 g) coarsely chopped

MAKES 4 SERVINGS

1 Make the dressing
In a blender or food processor, combine the chopped onion, ginger, miso, vinegar, honey, canola oil, and sesame oil. Pulse until smooth.

2 Assemble the salad
In a large bowl, combine the sliced onion, bell pepper, bean sprouts, chicken, and cilantro. Add the dressing and toss to coat evenly. Arrange on plates and serve.

chicken tostada salad

1 Prepare the salsa
In a bowl, whisk together the lime zest and juice, garlic, ½ teaspoon salt, and ⅛ teaspoon pepper. Gradually whisk in the oil until blended to make a vinaigrette. Transfer 3 tablespoons of the vinaigrette to a large bowl and add the beans, corn, tomatoes, and chiles, and mix gently. Reserve the remaining vinaigrette. Let the salsa stand for at least 10 minutes to blend the flavors.

2 Assemble the salad
Add the lettuce to the reserved vinaigrette and toss to coat. Arrange the tostada shells on plates and add the dressed lettuce. Spoon the salsa over the lettuce, top with the chicken, and serve.

cook's tip Deep-fried tostada shells are available in most well-stocked supermarkets. If you cannot find them, divide 4 cups (6 oz/185 g) good-quality corn tortilla chips among bowls, top with the chicken salad, and serve.

Lime zest and juice, from 2 limes

Garlic, 1 clove, minced

Salt and freshly ground pepper

Olive oil, ⅔ cup (5 fl oz/160 ml)

Black beans, 1 can (14½ oz/455 g), drained and rinsed

Fresh corn kernels, from 2 ears (about 2 cups/ 12 oz/375 g)

Plum (Roma) tomatoes, 2, seeded and diced

Canned green chiles, 4, diced

Romaine (cos) lettuce, 1 small head, cut into bite-sized pieces

Corn tostada shells, 4

Classic Roast Chicken (page 267) or rotisserie chicken, 2 cups (12 oz/ 375 g) shredded meat

MAKES 4 SERVINGS

chutney chicken & pistachio salad

Lemon, 1

Mayonnaise, ½ cup
(4 fl oz/125 ml)

Mango chutney, ¼ cup
(2½ oz/75 g)

Dijon mustard,
1 tablespoon

**Classic Roast Chicken
(page 267) or rotisserie
chicken,** 2 cups (12 oz/
375 g) diced meat

Seedless red grapes,
1 cup (6 oz/185 g), halved

Celery, 2–3 stalks,
roughly chopped

Red onion, 1 small, finely
chopped

Pistachios, ⅓ cup
(2 oz/60 g)

**Salt and freshly ground
pepper**

MAKES 4 SERVINGS

1 **Make the dressing**
Grate 1 teaspoon zest and squeeze
1 tablespoon juice from the lemon into a
large bowl. Add the mayonnaise, chutney,
and mustard, and stir to combine.

2 **Assemble the salad**
Add the chicken, grapes, celery,
onion, and pistachios to the dressing. Stir
gently to combine. Season to taste with
salt and pepper. Divide among salad
plates or bowls and serve.

cook's tip You can use ¾ lb
(12 oz/375 g) skinless, boneless
cooked turkey breast in place of
the chicken. For a light summertime
supper, serve the salad atop leaves
of green-leaf lettuce with a basket of
warm buttermilk biscuits.

vietnamese chicken salad

1 Make the vinaigrette
Grate 1 teaspoon zest and squeeze 2 tablespoons juice from the lime into a small bowl. Add the oil, fish sauce, and sugar and whisk until blended.

2 Assemble the salad
In a large bowl, combine the chicken, cabbage, green onions, and cilantro and toss to mix well. Drizzle with the lime vinaigrette and toss to coat. Season to taste with salt and pepper. Divide among plates, top with the peanuts, and serve.

cook's tip To turn this salad into a heartier main course, add 8 oz (250 g) cooked rice vermicelli noodles along with the chicken and cabbage and toss to coat with the vinaigrette.

Lime, 1 large

Peanut oil, 6 tablespoons (3 fl oz/90 ml)

Asian fish sauce, 2 tablespoons

Sugar, 1 tablespoon

Classic Roast Chicken (page 267) or rotisserie chicken, 2 cups (12 oz/ 375 g) shredded meat

Napa cabbage, 2 cups (6 oz/185 g) shredded or thinly sliced

Green (spring) onions, 4, white and pale green parts, thinly sliced

Fresh cilantro (fresh coriander), ¼ cup (⅓ oz/10 g) chopped

Salt and freshly ground pepper

Roasted peanuts, ¼ cup (1½ oz/45 g) coarsely chopped

MAKES 4 SERVINGS

curried chicken salad

Salt and freshly ground white pepper

Skinless, boneless chicken breasts, 1½ lb (750 g)

Mayonnaise, 1 cup (8 fl oz/250 ml)

Curry powder, 2 teaspoons

Honey, 1 tablespoon

White wine vinegar, 1 tablespoon

Celery, 4 stalks, chopped

Apples such as Fuji, Gala, or Granny Smith, 3, cored and cut into small cubes

Pecan halves, 1 cup (4 oz/125 g), toasted

Butter (Boston) lettuce, 1 head, pale inner leaves only

MAKES 4 SERVINGS

1 Poach the chicken
Bring a large saucepan of water to a boil over high heat. Add ½ teaspoon salt and the chicken, reduce the heat until the water is barely simmering, and cook until the chicken is opaque throughout, 8–10 minutes. Remove from the heat and let stand until cool enough to handle. Cut the chicken into bite-sized cubes.

2 Make the dressing
In a large bowl, whisk together the mayonnaise, curry powder, honey, vinegar, ½ teaspoon salt, and a pinch of pepper until well blended.

3 Assemble the salad
Add the chicken, celery, apples, and half of the pecans to the dressing and toss to coat. Arrange the lettuce on plates and top with the chicken mixture. Sprinkle with the remaining pecans and serve.

cook's tip You can save time by using a purchased rotisserie chicken in this recipe. Remove and discard the skin from the chicken, then pull off the meat from the bones. Cut the meat into bite-sized cubes. You will need about 4 cups (1½ lb/750 g).

grilled chicken caesar

1 Make the dressing
In a blender or food processor, combine the mayonnaise, lemon juice, garlic, anchovies to taste (if using), mustard, Worcestershire sauce, vinegar, 4 tablespoons (2 fl oz/60 ml) of the oil, ¼ teaspoon salt, and a generous amount of pepper. Process until smooth.

2 Grill the chicken
Prepare a gas or charcoal grill for direct-heat grilling over high heat, or preheat a stovetop grill pan over high heat. Brush both sides of the chicken breasts with the remaining 1 tablespoon oil and season with salt and pepper. Place the chicken on the grill rack or in the grill pan and cook, turning once, until opaque throughout, 4–5 minutes per side. Transfer the chicken to a cutting board and let stand for 5–7 minutes. Cut the chicken on the diagonal into slices.

3 Assemble the salad
In a large bowl, combine the lettuce and dressing and toss to coat. Arrange the dressed lettuce on plates, top with the chicken slices and cheese, and serve. »

Mayonnaise,
1 tablespoon

Lemon juice, from
1 lemon

Garlic, 2 cloves, minced

Anchovy fillets, 1–3,
finely chopped (optional)

Dijon mustard,
2 teaspoons

Worcestershire sauce,
1 teaspoon

Red wine vinegar,
1 teaspoon

Olive oil, 5 tablespoons
(2½ fl oz/75 ml)

**Salt and freshly ground
pepper**

**Skinless, boneless
chicken breasts,** 1¼ lb
(625 g), pounded lightly
to an even thickness

Romaine (cos) lettuce,
3 heads, pale inner
leaves only

Parmesan cheese, 3 oz
(90 g), shaved with a
vegetable peeler

MAKES 4 SERVINGS

cook's tip

Garlic crostini are a delicious accompaniment to this salad and take only minutes to prepare. To make them, preheat the oven to 400°F (200°C). Cut a baguette into ½-inch (12-mm) slices, brush with olive oil, and place on a baking sheet. Bake until golden, about 5 minutes. Peel a clove of garlic and rub it onto each warm slice of bread.

arugula, squash & salami salad

1 Make the *salsa verde*
In a blender or food processor, combine the garlic, parsley, mint, capers, mustard, ¼ cup oil, and 1 teaspoon of the vinegar. Process until smooth; set aside.

2 Roast the squash
Preheat the oven to 450°F (230°C). On a rimmed baking sheet, toss the squash cubes with 1 tablespoon of the oil, season generously with salt and pepper, and spread in an even layer. Roast, shaking the pan every 5 minutes, until the squash is tender, about 15 minutes. Let cool in the pan for 5 minutes. Add the *salsa verde* and toss gently to coat evenly.

3 Assemble the salad
In a large bowl, combine the arugula, salami, remaining 1 tablespoon oil, ¼ teaspoon salt, and a pinch of pepper. Toss to combine, add the remaining 2 teaspoons vinegar, and toss again. Arrange on plates, top with the squash, sprinkle with the pine nuts, and serve.

cook's tip The *salsa verde* for this salad can be made up to 4 hours ahead of time. Cover and refrigerate until just before serving.

Garlic, 1 clove, sliced

Fresh flat-leaf (Italian) parsley leaves, ¾ cup (¾ oz/20 g) firmly packed

Fresh mint leaves, ¼ cup (¼ oz/7 g) firmly packed

Capers, 2 teaspoons, rinsed and drained

Dijon mustard, 1 teaspoon

Olive oil, ¼ cup (2 fl oz/60 ml), plus 2 tablespoons

Red wine vinegar, 3 teaspoons

Butternut squash, 1 lb (500 g), halved, seeded, peeled, and cut into cubes

Salt and freshly ground pepper

Arugula (rocket), ½ lb (250 g)

Salami, ¼ lb (125 g), cut into thin strips

Pine nuts, 2 tablespoons, toasted

MAKES 4 SERVINGS

lentil, bacon & frisée salad

Garlic, 2 cloves, sliced

Shallots, 3, 1 sliced and
2 minced

Olive oil, ¾ cup
(6 fl oz/180 ml)

Sherry vinegar, ¼ cup
(2 fl oz/60 ml)

Dijon mustard,
1 tablespoon

**Salt and freshly ground
pepper**

Thick-cut bacon, 4 slices,
chopped

Celery, 1 stalk, finely
chopped

Carrot, 1, finely chopped

Green Lentils (page 37),
4 cups (28 oz/875 g)

Frisée, 1 bunch, tough
stems removed

MAKES 4 SERVINGS

1 Prepare the vinaigrette and bacon
In a blender or food processor, combine the garlic, sliced shallot, oil, vinegar, mustard, ¾ teaspoon salt, and ¼ teaspoon pepper. Process until smooth. (You will have more vinaigrette than you will need for the salad; store the remainder in an airtight container in the refrigerator for up to 1 week.) In a heavy saucepan over low heat, cook the bacon, stirring occasionally, until crisp, about 8 minutes. Using a slotted spoon, transfer to paper towels to drain.

2 Warm the lentils
Return the saucepan to low heat, add the minced shallots to the bacon fat and sauté until softened, about 4 minutes. Add the celery and carrot and cook, stirring occasionally, until wilted, 3–4 minutes. Add the lentils and cook, stirring gently, until warmed through, about 5 minutes.

3 Assemble the salad
Place half of the vinaigrette and the lentil mixture in a large bowl and toss to combine. Arrange the frisée on plates and top with the lentil mixture. Drizzle with a little more vinaigrette, sprinkle with the bacon, and serve.

warm escarole,
egg & bacon salad

1 Make the vinaigrette

Bring a small saucepan of water to a boil. Add the bacon and cook for 5 minutes. Drain, transfer to paper towels, and blot dry. Wipe clean the saucepan, place over medium-low heat, and add the oil, garlic, and bacon. Cook, stirring, until the garlic is golden and the bacon is crisp, about 3 minutes. Be careful not to let the garlic burn. Remove from the heat and discard the garlic. Stir in the mustard and 2 tablespoons vinegar; set aside.

2 Poach the eggs

Fill a large, wide pan with water, add the remaining 1 teaspoon vinegar, place over high heat, and bring to a rolling boil. Turn off the heat. Working quickly, crack each egg and release it just above the water, letting it ease into the water and spacing the eggs evenly. Cover the pan and let the eggs stand for 3–4 minutes.

3 Assemble the salads

Place the escarole in a large bowl. Bring the vinaigrette to a boil, then pour three-fourths of it over the escarole and toss to wilt the leaves slightly. Season to taste with salt and pepper. Toss again and arrange on plates. Using a slotted spoon, transfer a poached egg to the top of each salad, drizzle with the remaining vinaigrette, and serve.

Thick-cut bacon, 4 slices, finely chopped

Olive oil, ¼ cup (2 fl oz/60 ml)

Garlic, 1 clove, smashed

Whole-grain mustard, 1 tablespoon

Red wine vinegar, 2 tablespoons, plus 1 teaspoon

Eggs, 4

Escarole (Batavian endive), 2 heads, tough outer leaves removed, torn into bite-sized pieces

Salt and freshly ground pepper

MAKES 4 SERVINGS

chipotle beef & corn salad

Boneless sirloin or rib-eye steak, 1¼ lb (625 g) and 1½ inches (4 cm) thick

Olive oil, ¼ cup (2 fl oz/60 ml), plus 2 tablespoons

Salt and freshly ground pepper

Canned chipotle chiles in adobo, ¼ cup (1½ oz/45 g) with sauce

White wine vinegar, 1 tablespoon

Garlic, 1 large clove, sliced

Lime juice, from 2 limes

Corn kernels, from 2 ears (about 2 cups/12 oz/375 g)

Radishes, 6, chopped

Plum (Roma) tomatoes, 4, chopped

Fresh cilantro (fresh coriander), ¼ cup (⅓ oz/10 g) minced

Romaine (cos) lettuce, 2 heads, pale inner leaves only, torn into bite-sized pieces

MAKES 4 SERVINGS

1 Marinate the steak
Place the steak on a plate, brush both sides with the 2 tablespoons oil, and season both sides generously with salt and pepper. Let stand for 30 minutes.

2 Make the dressing and corn salsa
Meanwhile, in a blender or food processor, combine the chiles, remaining ¼ cup oil, vinegar, garlic, half of the lime juice, 1 tablespoon water, ¼ teaspoon salt, and a pinch of pepper. Process until smooth. In a bowl, toss together the corn, radishes, tomatoes, cilantro, remaining lime juice, and ¼ teaspoon salt.

3 Cook the steak and finish the salad
Prepare a gas or charcoal grill for direct-heat grilling over medium-high heat, or preheat a stovetop grill pan over medium-high heat. Place the steak on the grill rack or in the grill pan and cook, turning every 4 minutes, about 8 minutes total per side for medium-rare. Transfer the steak to a cutting board and let stand for 5–10 minutes. Cut the steak on the diagonal across the grain into thin slices. Arrange the lettuce on plates and top with the steak and corn salsa. Drizzle with the dressing and serve.

steak, arugula & pecorino salad

1 Make the vinaigrette
In a bowl, whisk together the vinegar, shallot, ½ teaspoon salt, and ¼ teaspoon pepper. Gradually whisk in the oil.

2 Make the salad
Thinly slice the steak across the grain. In a large bowl, combine the arugula, tomatoes, and steak slices. Add the vinaigrette and toss to coat evenly. Arrange the salad on plates, top with the cheese, and serve.

cook's tip You can make the vinaigrette up to 5 days in advance and store it in an airtight container in the refrigerator. Shake or whisk well before using. It is a good "house dressing," too, complementing almost any mixed green salad, so make a double batch to have extra on hand.

Red wine vinegar, 1½ tablespoons

Shallot, 1, minced

Salt and freshly ground pepper

Olive oil, ⅓ cup (3 fl oz/80 ml)

Grilled Flank Steak (page 305), ½ steak

Arugula (rocket), 10 oz (315 g), stems removed

Cherry or grape tomatoes, 1 lb (500 g), halved

Pecorino romano or Parmesan cheese, ¼ lb (125 g), shaved with a vegetable peeler

MAKES 4 SERVINGS

vietnamese beef salad

Garlic, 6 cloves, minced

Asian fish sauce,
2 teaspoons

Sugar, 1 teaspoon

**Salt and freshly ground
pepper**

Olive oil, 3 tablespoons

Sirloin steak, 1¼ lb
(625 g), trimmed of
excess fat and cut into
cubes

Red onion, 1 small,
halved and very thinly
sliced

Rice vinegar,
2 tablespoons

Canola oil, 2 teaspoons

Watercress, 6 oz (185 g),
tender leaves and stems
only

**Fresh cilantro (fresh
coriander),** 1 cup
(1 oz/30 g) loosely
packed leaves

MAKES 4 SERVINGS

1 **Marinate the beef**
In a large resealable plastic bag,
combine the garlic, fish sauce, sugar,
½ teaspoon salt, a pinch of pepper, and
2 tablespoons of the olive oil. Add the
steak, seal the bag, and squeeze to
distribute the ingredients. Let stand for
30 minutes at room temperature or
refrigerate for up to 1½ hours (return
to room temperature before cooking).

2 **Marinate the onion**
In a bowl, toss the onion with the
vinegar and season generously with
pepper. Let stand for 10–15 minutes. Add
the remaining 1 tablespoon olive oil and
toss to combine.

3 **Cook the beef and finish the salad**
Place a wok or deep, heavy frying
pan over high heat and add the canola
oil. Meanwhile, arrange the watercress
and cilantro on plates and top with the
marinated onion. When the oil is hot, add
the steak and its marinade and cook,
stirring, until the steak is browned on all
sides, 1½–2½ minutes. Do not overcook.
Arrange the steak on the salads and serve.

salads made easy

Salads can be easily adapted to suit any taste—and to make use of whatever you have in your refrigerator or pantry. Use the recipes in this book as a starting point, building on them with these simple ideas and tips to create your own quick and satisfying salads.

SIMPLE SALADS

Butter lettuce salad Combine Dijon mustard, white wine vinegar, and olive oil in a salad bowl. Add torn butter (Boston) lettuce leaves and snipped chives and toss well. Season to taste with salt and pepper.

Fennel-orange salad Trim and thinly slice 2 fennel bulbs. Peel 1–2 regular or blood oranges and slice crosswise. Gently toss with minced shallot and a Champagne vinaigrette.

Mediterranean salad Toss chunks of peeled cucumber, halved cherry tomatoes, sliced green (spring) or red onion, Kalamata olives, fresh oregano or mint, and crumbled feta cheese in a red wine vinaigrette.

Warm spinach salad Fry a few strips of bacon, then drain and chop. Make a dressing with cider vinegar, minced shallots, olive oil, and a bit of the bacon drippings. Warm the dressing and toss with the spinach. Top with chopped hard-boiled egg and the chopped bacon.

Wash greens well Fill a large bowl with cold water. Trim off the stem end of each head of lettuce and pull the leaves apart. Cut or tear into bite-sized pieces and toss into the water. Allow the greens to float to the top and let them stand for a few minutes. Dry in a salad spinner in small batches. (For cold storage tips, see page 9.)

Refresh greens To revive lettuce that is beginning to wilt, soak it in a bowl of ice water in the refrigerator for 30 minutes to 1 hour. When ready to use the lettuce, drain and dry as directed above.

Create contrasts Try to achieve a mix of colors, textures, and flavors when combining salad ingredients. For example, if you add a soft ingredient, such as avocado or blue cheese, balance it with something crunchy, like jicama or toasted walnuts. Add brightly colored ingredients, such as radishes, oranges, or beets to offset paler greens. Complement sweet and rich flavors with bright, acidic ingredients, like lemon juice or grapefruit segments.

Think beyond lettuce You can toss virtually any vegetable with dressing to make a salad. Add coarsely chopped fresh herbs such as dill, basil, chives, mint, and flat-leaf (Italian) parsley to salads for additional flavor and color.

Taste before you toss To taste a salad dressing, try it on a single leaf of lettuce, rather than tasting it with a spoon. You will get a better sense of how it will taste in the finished salad. Adjust the seasonings, adding more oil, acidic ingredients, herbs, or salt and pepper if needed, before dressing the salad.

Use dressing sparingly For lettuce salads, add the dressing just before serving to keep the greens from wilting. Err on the side of underdressing, drizzling in just enough dressing to moisten the greens and then tossing well to coat the greens. You can pass extra dressing at the table for those who want more.

shortcut ingredients

Smart cooks rely on high-quality packaged or prepared foods to help get dinner on the table in a hurry. These ingredients make the job of preparing a salad easier, either because they are already assembled and ready to use or because they add concentrated flavor without extra work. Here are some salad-making time savers.

Cherry tomatoes Purchase packaged cherry tomatoes, rinse them, drain and dry them well, and return them to their containers. Store at room temperature; toss whole or halved into salads.

Crumbled cheese Buy crumbled goat, feta, or blue cheese, and keep in the refrigerator to toss into salads.

Deli meats Sliced deli meats, such as prosciutto, ham, salami, and turkey, can be chopped and added to a salad for flavor and protein.

Frozen cleaned shrimp Keep a bag of peeled, deveined cooked shrimp (prawns) or bay shrimp (salad shrimp) in the freezer. They can be thawed and used to turn a salad into a more substantial meal.

Hard-boiled eggs Slices of hard-boiled egg add protein and flavor to a salad. Store them, cooled and unpeeled, in the refrigerator in an airtight container or resealable plastic bag. Peel and slice the eggs just before adding to a salad.

Mozzarella cheese Look for bite-sized fresh mozzarella balls (*bocconcini*), which can be tossed into salads without any prep.

Prewashed salad greens Buy cut-up mixed lettuces, spinach, romaine (cos), iceberg, slaw mix, and other salad greens in bags or plastic boxes. Refresh greens with cold water before serving.

Rotisserie chicken Purchase an extra rotisserie chicken, which can be stored in the refrigerator and quickly skinned, boned, and chopped for tossing into salads during the week.

Salad bar vegetables At the supermarket salad bar, fill a container with prepped and/or cooked vegetables, such as beets, broccoli, potatoes, snap peas, snow peas (mangetouts), cauliflower, carrots, and even lettuce greens to use in salads.

FROM THE PANTRY

These shortcut ingredients can be stored in the pantry for making salads in a pinch.

Bottled dressings Keep a variety of dressings on hand to use when you're pressed for time. Look for dressings and vinaigrettes that include natural ingredients.

Canned beans Kidney beans, chickpeas (garbanzo beans), and other legumes can be drained, rinsed under cold water, and added to salads.

Croutons Store-bought or homemade croutons contribute texture to all kinds of salads and will keep for a few weeks in an airtight container.

Dried fruit Dried cranberries, cherries, and other fruits add a hint of sweetness to salads.

Nuts Buy spiced or candied walnuts, pecans, almonds, pine nuts, or other nuts to sprinkle over salads for added crunch.

Olives Keep a variety of pitted green or black olives for adding to salads (either whole or coarsely chopped).

Tuna in oil Look for imported tuna packed in olive oil in jars or cans for a quick protein addition to a salad.

Asian sesame-miso dressing
In a blender or food processor, combine 1 clove chopped garlic, 2 tablespoons chopped red onion, 1 teaspoon grated fresh ginger, 5 tablespoons (2½ fl oz/75 ml) canola oil, 3 tablespoons rice vinegar, 2 tablespoons Asian sesame oil, 1½ tablespoons white miso, 1 tablespoon honey, and a pinch of cayenne pepper. Process until smooth. Season to taste with salt and pepper.

Blue cheese dressing In a small bowl, whisk together ¼ cup (2 fl oz/60 ml) each mayonnaise and olive oil, 2 tablespoons white wine vinegar, 2 teaspoons Dijon mustard, and 1 teaspoon Worcestershire sauce. Gently stir in ¼ cup (1 oz/30 g) crumbled blue cheese. Season to taste with salt and pepper.

Mustard vinaigrette In a small bowl, whisk together 2 cloves minced garlic, 1 minced shallot, 3 tablespoons red wine vinegar, and 1 tablespoon Dijon mustard. Gradually add ½ cup (4 fl oz/ 125 ml) olive oil, whisking constantly to form an emulsion. Season to taste with salt and pepper. Let the vinaigrette stand for at least 30 minutes to blend the flavors.

vinaigrette basics

The classic formula for a vinaigrette dressing is 1 part vinegar to 3 parts oil, plus salt and pepper to taste. Use these proportions as a guideline to create your own dressings.

- For the easiest vinaigrette, simply drizzle olive oil and good-quality vinegar over your salad, followed by plenty of coarse salt and freshly ground pepper, and then toss.

- To create smooth, emulsified vinaigrettes, combine all of the ingredients except the oil in a bowl. Add the oil in a slow, steady stream as you whisk constantly with a small whisk or fork. Or, mix the ingredients in a blender or mini food processor.

- Make extra vinaigrette and store it in a jar or airtight container in the refrigerator to use later in the week.

- Experiment with different kinds of vinegar, such as balsamic, cider, rice, or a flavor-infused vinegar. Or, substitute fresh citrus juice, such as lemon or lime, for half of the vinegar.

- Try different types of oil: a small amount of walnut or hazelnut (filbert) oil adds rich, nutty flavor to a vinaigrette.

- Make your own flavored oils by infusing olive oil with minced herbs, citrus zest, chile, or other flavorings. Use the same day, or store in a stoppered glass bottle in the refrigerator for a few weeks. Check for freshness before using.

- For extra flavor, add minced shallots or green (spring) onions to a vinaigrette, allowing them to sit in the dressing for 30 minutes or more before adding to a salad.

- Whisk mustard, yogurt, mayonnaise, or sour cream into vinaigrettes for a creamy flavor and consistency.

- Liven up the flavor of store-bought vinaigrettes by adding fresh ingredients, such as herbs, garlic, shallots, or yogurt. A squeeze of lemon or lime juice can also add a hint of freshness.

- Use vinaigrettes to marinate foods for grilling or to drizzle over warm vegetables just before serving.

- If storing a vinaigrette in the refrigerator, be sure to bring it to room temperature before using.

SAMPLE MEALS

"In Minutes" meals can be made when time is especially short. "Fit for Company" meals are easy ideas for stress-free get-togethers when you want to make an impression.

IN MINUTES

Spinach, Pear & Walnut Salad (page 81)

rotisserie chicken

Greek Salad (page 82)

warmed pita bread

hummus or baba ghanoush

Grilled Asparagus & Prosciutto Salad (page 84)

sliced heirloom tomatoes

crusty bread

Grapefruit, Jicama & Avocado Salad (page 85)

warm corn tortillas

Chicken & Orzo Salad (page 96)

garlic and herb crostini

assorted cheeses

Vietnamese Beef Salad (page 114)

steamed rice noodles with basil

FIT FOR COMPANY

Grilled Summer Vegetable Salad (page 87)

grilled halibut with pesto

Pinot Noir or dry Rosé

Couscous Salad (page 88)

pan-seared lamb chops with herbs

sliced tomatoes with feta cheese and oregano

Syrah or Zinfandel

Crab Cake Salad (page 92)

toasted focaccia with herbs and coarse sea salt

Sauvignon Blanc

Arugula, Squash & Salami Salad (page 109)

ravioli with butter and sage

Chianti or Sangiovese

Steak, Arugula & Pecorino Salad (page 113)

grilled corn with herb butter

Syrah or Merlot

MEAL PLANNING TIPS

Salads can be healthful and infinitely varied. Best of all, they don't require many steps or complicated cooking techniques. As a main dish or as a side dish, try to make salad a regular component of your weeknight meals.

A salad can be a complete meal With just a few accompaniments (see pages 16–17), most of the salads in this book can be served as complete meals. Adding main-dish salads to your weeknight menus is both healthful and time-saving, as they are generally rich in vegetables and require little cooking.

A salad can also be a first course When you have extra time or are entertaining guests, you can prepare any of the salads in this book as a starter simply by reducing the portion size by up to one-half, depending on how many people you are serving.

Mix and match components Once you find salad recipes you like, you can use their basic elements to create new combinations of your own. Vary the ingredients based on what is freshest and in season, and alter the dressings if necessary.

soups

tomato-basil soup

1 Roast the tomatoes
Preheat the oven to 400°F (200°C).
Arrange the tomato halves cut side up
in a large roasting pan. Sprinkle with the
garlic and 1 tablespoon of the basil and
drizzle with 4 tablespoons (2 fl oz/60 ml)
of the oil. Roast until the tomatoes are
soft when pierced with a fork, about
40 minutes. Remove and discard the skins.

2 Simmer the soup
In a saucepan over medium-high
heat, warm the remaining 1 tablespoon
oil. Add the shallots and sauté for about
2 minutes. Add the roasted tomatoes and
garlic, wine, and ½ cup (4 fl oz/125 ml)
water and bring to a boil. Reduce the heat
to medium-low and simmer, uncovered,
until the mixture has thickened, about
20 minutes. Season with salt and pepper.

3 Purée the soup
Using a food processor or blender,
purée the soup to the desired consistency.
Return to the pan and reheat to serving
temperature. Ladle the soup into bowls,
garnish with the remaining 3 tablespoons
basil, and serve.

Plum (Roma) tomatoes,
10, halved lengthwise

Garlic, 2 cloves, minced

Fresh basil,
4 tablespoons chopped

Olive oil, 5 tablespoons
(2½ fl oz/75 ml)

Shallots, 4, halved

Dry white wine, 1½ cups
(12 fl oz/375 ml)

**Salt and freshly ground
pepper**

MAKES 4 SERVINGS

chicken-tortilla soup

Olive oil, 1 tablespoon

White onion, ½, finely chopped

Chili powder, 2 teaspoons

Chicken broth or stock, 6 cups (48 fl oz/1.5 l), homemade (page 29) or purchased

Cooked chicken, 2 cups (12 oz/375 g) shredded meat (see Cook's Tip)

Lime juice, from 3–4 limes

Salt

Corn tortilla chips, 1½ cups (4 oz/125 g), broken into pieces

Queso fresco, ½ cup (2½ oz/75 g) crumbled, or Monterey jack cheese, ½ cup (2 oz/60 g) shredded

Hass avocado, 1, halved, pitted, peeled, and cubed

Fresh cilantro (fresh coriander), ¼ cup (⅓ oz/10 g) chopped

MAKES 4–6 SERVINGS

1 **Sauté the onion**
In a large saucepan over medium-high heat, warm the oil. When it is hot, add the onion and sauté until translucent, about 3 minutes. Add the chili powder and stir until fragrant, about 1 minute. Pour in the broth and bring to a boil.

2 **Finish the soup**
Add the shredded chicken, reduce the heat to medium, and simmer until the chicken is heated through, about 3 minutes. Add the lime juice and salt to taste. Ladle into bowls, garnish with the tortilla chips, *queso fresco*, avocado, and cilantro, and serve.

cook's tip This soup is best made with homemade chicken stock, and you will have cooked chicken meat leftover from making the stock. Alternatively, you can purchase chicken stock or low-sodium broth and buy a rotisserie chicken to use in this recipe.

french onion soup

1 **Caramelize the onions**
In a large frying pan over medium heat, melt the butter with 1 tablespoon of the oil. Add the onions and sauté until golden, 4–5 minutes. Reduce the heat to low, cover, and cook, stirring occasionally, for 15 minutes. Uncover, add the sugar and ½ teaspoon salt, and cook, stirring occasionally, until the onions are deeply browned, about 25 minutes. Add the flour and stir for 2–3 minutes.

2 **Simmer the soup**
In another saucepan, bring the broth and wine to a boil. Slowly stir in the onions. Add 1 teaspoon pepper. Reduce the heat to medium, cover partially, and simmer for about 45 minutes.

3 **Finish the soup**
Meanwhile, preheat the broiler (grill). Place the bread slices on a baking sheet, drizzle with the remaining 3 tablespoons oil, and toast, turning once, until golden, 3–4 minutes on each side. Rub the bread with the cut sides of the garlic. Reduce the oven temperature to 400°F (200°C). Place 6–8 ovenproof bowls on a baking sheet. Ladle the soup into the bowls. Top each with 2 slices of toast and sprinkle with the cheese. Bake until the cheese is golden brown, about 15 minutes. Remove from the oven and serve.

Unsalted butter, 4 tablespoons (2 oz/60 g)

Olive oil, 4 tablespoons (2 fl oz/60 ml)

Yellow onions, 2 lb (1 kg), thinly sliced

Sugar, ½ teaspoon

Salt and freshly ground pepper

Flour, 1½ tablespoons

Beef broth or stock, 2 qt (2 l), homemade (page 30) or purchased

Dry white wine, ½ cup (4 fl oz/125 ml)

Baguette, 12–16 slices, each about ½ inch (12 mm) thick

Garlic, 3 cloves, halved

Gruyère cheese, ½ lb (250 g), shredded

MAKES 6–8 SERVINGS

miso noodle soup

Udon noodles, 1 lb
(500 g)

**Vegetable broth or
stock,** 4 cups (32 fl oz/
1 l), homemade (page 27)
or purchased

Fresh ginger, 3 thin slices

Sake, 2 tablespoons

Red miso, 2 tablespoons

Silken tofu, ¼ lb (125 g),
cut into ½-inch (12-mm)
cubes

Button mushrooms,
2 large, thinly sliced

Carrot, 1 small, thinly
sliced

Green (spring) onion,
1 large, dark green part
only, thinly sliced
lengthwise

MAKES 4 SERVINGS

1 Cook the noodles

Fill a large pot half full with water
and bring to a boil over high heat. Add
the noodles, return the water to a boil,
and cook until the noodles are al dente,
2–3 minutes. Drain the noodles, rinse well
under cold running water, and drain again.
Divide among 4 soup bowls.

2 Make the soup

In a saucepan over medium-high
heat, warm the broth with the ginger and
sake until bubbles begin to form around
the edge of the pan. Reduce the heat to
medium-low and simmer for 5 minutes.
Remove and discard the ginger. Place
the miso in a small bowl and add ¼ cup
(2 fl oz/60 ml) of the hot broth. Stir until
the miso is dissolved and creamy, and
pour into the pot. Place the tofu in a sieve
and warm it under a slow stream of hot
running water. Divide the tofu among
the soup bowls. Ladle in the hot broth,
dividing it among the bowls. Garnish with
the sliced mushrooms, carrot, and green
onion, and serve.

> **cook's tip** Miso comes in many
> colors; if you cannot find red miso,
> you can substitute white miso, also
> known as *shiro miso*.

italian rice & pea soup

1 Sauté the vegetables
In a large saucepan over medium heat, melt the butter. Add the celery and shallot and sauté until the shallot is translucent, about 2 minutes. Add the rice and cook, stirring, until the grains are opaque, about 1 minute.

2 Cook the rice and peas
Raise the heat to medium-high, add the broth and 2 cups (16 fl oz/500 ml) water, and bring to a boil. Reduce the heat to low, cover, and simmer until the rice is tender, about 20 minutes. Add the peas and cook, stirring occasionally, for 5 minutes longer. Just before serving, stir in the cheese and parsley and season with salt and pepper. Ladle into bowls and serve. »

Unsalted butter, 2 tablespoons

Celery, 1 stalk, chopped

Shallot, 1, minced

Short-grain white rice such as Arborio, ½ cup (3½ oz/105 g)

Chicken broth or stock, 3 cups (24 fl oz/750 ml), homemade (page 29) or purchased

Frozen peas, 2 cups (12 oz/375 g)

Parmesan cheese, ½ cup (2 oz/60 g) freshly grated

Fresh flat-leaf (Italian) parsley, 1 tablespoon minced

Salt and freshly ground pepper

MAKES 4 SERVINGS

cook's tip

You can substitute 2 lb (1 kg) fresh English peas for the frozen peas, adding them with the broth and water. To shell the peas, hold each pod over a bowl, press your thumb against the seam to split it, and then sweep the peas into the bowl. This can be done up to 1 day in advance; store the peas in a resealable plastic bag in the refrigerator.

chicken noodle soup

1 Prepare the soup

In a large saucepan over medium heat, warm the oil. Add the celery, leek, and carrot and sauté until softened, about 5 minutes. Pour in the broth and add the bay leaf, thyme, and shredded chicken. Bring to a boil over medium-high heat. Stir in the noodles and cook just until the noodles are tender, about 10 minutes.

2 Season the soup

Remove and discard the bay leaf from the soup. Season to taste with salt and pepper. Ladle into bowls, garnish with the parsley, and serve.

> **cook's tip** To make chicken and rice soup, substitute 1 cup (5 oz/ 155 g) cooked rice for the noodles, adding it to the soup a few minutes before serving to heat through.

Olive oil, 2 tablespoons

Celery, 2 stalks, finely chopped

Leek, 1, white part only, halved, rinsed, and thinly sliced

Carrot, 1, finely chopped

Chicken broth or stock, 5 cups (40 fl oz/1.25 l), homemade (page 29) or purchased

Bay leaf, 1

Dried thyme, ¼ teaspoon

Cooked chicken, 2 cups (12 oz/375 g) shredded meat, reserved from Chicken Stock (page 29) or purchased rotisserie chicken

Dried egg noodles, ½ lb (250 g)

Salt and freshly ground pepper

Fresh flat-leaf (Italian) parsley, ¼ cup (⅓ oz/10 g) minced

MAKES 4 SERVINGS

creamy asparagus soup

Unsalted butter,
2 tablespoons

Shallot, 1, minced

**Vegetable broth or
stock,** 4 cups (32 fl oz/
1 l), homemade (page 27)
or purchased

Dry white wine, ½ cup
(4 fl oz/125 ml)

Asparagus, 1½ lb
(750 g), tough ends
removed, cut into
1-inch (2.5-cm) pieces

Heavy (double) cream,
¼ cup (2 fl oz/60 ml)

**Salt and freshly ground
pepper**

Fresh tarragon,
2 tablespoons chopped

MAKES 4 SERVINGS

1 **Simmer the asparagus**
In a large saucepan over medium
heat, melt the butter. Add the shallot and
sauté until translucent, about 1 minute.
Add the broth, wine, and asparagus, raise
the heat to medium-high, and bring to a
boil. Reduce the heat to low and simmer,
uncovered, until the asparagus is tender,
about 10 minutes.

2 **Purée the soup**
Using a food processor or blender,
process the soup to a smooth purée.
Return to the pan and place over low heat.
Stir in the cream and reheat to serving
temperature. Season to taste with salt
and pepper. Ladle the soup into bowls,
garnish with the tarragon, and serve.

minestrone with pesto

1 Cook the vegetables

In a large pot over medium-low heat, warm the oil. Add the onion and sauté until softened, about 5 minutes. Add the broth, cabbage, tomatoes, carrot, and potato. Season with 1 teaspoon salt and ½ teaspoon pepper. Raise the heat to high, cover, and bring to a boil. Reduce the heat to medium-low and cook, partially covered, until the vegetables are tender, about 30 minutes.

2 Finish the soup

Stir in the chickpeas and zucchini and simmer, partially covered, for 5 minutes. Raise the heat to medium and add the pasta. Cook, uncovered and stirring frequently, until the pasta is al dente, about 5 minutes. Taste and adjust the seasoning with salt and pepper. Ladle the soup into bowls and stir a spoonful of the pesto into each serving. Top with the cheese, if using, and serve.

> cook's tip A variety of vegetables can be used in minestrone. If you like, add 1 cup (4 oz/125 g) chopped celery or the same amount of chopped cauliflower instead of the potato and cabbage.

Olive oil, 5 tablespoons (2½ fl oz/75 ml)

Yellow onion, 1, finely chopped

Chicken broth or stock, 7 cups (56 fl oz/1.75 l), homemade (page 29) or purchased

Green cabbage, 1 head, shredded

Canned whole plum (Roma) tomatoes, 1 cup (8 fl oz/250 ml) chopped, with juice

Carrot, 1, finely chopped

Yellow potato, 1, diced

Salt and freshly ground pepper

Chickpeas (garbanzo beans), 1 can (15 oz/ 470 g), drained and rinsed

Zucchini (courgettes), 2 small, diced

Conchigliette, ditalini, or other small pasta, 1 cup (3½ oz/105 g)

Basil Pesto (page 34) or purchased pesto, 1 cup (8 fl oz/250 ml)

Parmesan cheese, ¼ cup (1 oz/30 g) freshly grated (optional)

MAKES 8 SERVINGS

spring vegetable soup

Vegetable broth or stock, 4 cups (32 fl oz/ 1 l), homemade (page 27) or purchased

Sugar snap peas, 1 lb (500 g), trimmed and coarsely chopped

Leek, 1, white part only, halved, rinsed, and thinly sliced

Green (spring) onions, 3, white part only, chopped

Salt and freshly ground pepper

Fresh flat-leaf (Italian) parsley, 2 tablespoons minced

Fresh chives, 2 tablespoons minced

Lemon, 1, quartered

MAKES 4 SERVINGS

1 **Simmer the vegetables**
In a saucepan over medium-high heat, bring the broth to a boil. Add the sugar snap peas, leek, and green onions. Reduce the heat to low and simmer, covered, until the peas are just tender, 10–15 minutes.

2 **Purée the soup**
Using a food processor or blender, process the soup to a coarse purée. Return to the pan and reheat to serving temperature. Season to taste with salt and pepper. Ladle the soup into bowls, garnish with the parsley and chives, and serve. Pass the lemon quarters at the table to squeeze over the soup.

cook's tip Instead of sugar snap peas, you can use 1 lb (500 g) freshly shelled English peas or 1 lb (500 g) sliced asparagus. They will take 15–25 minutes to cook, depending on their maturity.

chilled cucumber soup

1 Prepare the cucumbers
Cut each cucumber in half lengthwise. Using a teaspoon, scoop out and discard the seeds. Roughly chop 2½ of the cucumbers. Finely chop the remaining half and reserve for garnish.

2 Purée the soup
In a food processor or blender, combine the roughly chopped cucumbers, yogurt, garlic, onion, bread, broth, and 1 tablespoon of the mint. Process to a smooth purée. Season to taste with salt and white pepper.

3 Chill and serve the soup
Transfer the soup to an airtight container and refrigerate for 2–8 hours. Ladle the soup into chilled bowls. Garnish with the reserved cucumber and the remaining 1 tablespoon mint and serve.

cook's tip To chill soup quickly, fill a large bowl with ice water. Pour the soup into a smaller bowl and nest in the ice water. Stir the soup occasionally to hasten the cooling.

Cucumbers, 3, peeled

Plain yogurt, 1½ cups (12 oz/375 g)

Garlic, 1 clove, minced

Yellow onion, ½, coarsely chopped

White country bread, 1 large slice, crust removed, cubed

Chicken broth, ½ cup (4 fl oz/125 ml)

Fresh mint, 2 tablespoons chopped

Salt and freshly ground white pepper

MAKES 4 SERVINGS

greek chicken
& rice soup

Long-grain rice, 1 cup
(7 oz/220 g)

Chicken broth or stock,
3 cups (24 fl oz/750 ml),
homemade (page 29) or
purchased

**Skinless, boneless
chicken thighs or
breasts,** about 1½ lb
(750 g), cut into bite-sized
pieces

Cornstarch (cornflour),
1 teaspoon

Egg yolks, 3

Lemon juice, from
½ lemon

**Salt and freshly ground
pepper**

MAKES 4 SERVINGS

1 **Cook the rice and chicken**
Prepare the rice according to the
package directions and set aside.
Meanwhile, in a saucepan over medium-
high heat, bring the broth to a simmer.
Add the chicken, reduce the heat to low,
and simmer, uncovered, until the chicken
is opaque throughout, about 7 minutes.
Remove from the heat and set aside.

2 **Make the lemon-egg mixture**
In a small bowl, stir together the
cornstarch and 1 tablespoon water until
combined. In a small saucepan over low
heat, whisk together the egg yolks and
lemon juice. When the egg yolk mixture is
just warm, whisk in the cornstarch mixture
and then 1 cup (8 fl oz/250 ml) of the
warm broth. Raise the heat to medium
and continue to whisk until a thick sauce
has formed, about 5 minutes. Season to
taste with salt and pepper.

3 **Finish the soup**
Return the pan holding the broth and
chicken to medium heat and bring to a
simmer. Add the lemon-egg mixture while
whisking constantly; the soup will thicken
slightly. Stir in the rice and season to taste
with salt and pepper. Ladle the soup into
bowls and serve.

clam chowder

1 **Cook the bacon**
In a large saucepan over medium heat, cook the bacon, stirring often, until it starts to brown and has rendered some of its fat, about 3 minutes. Using a slotted spoon, transfer to paper towels to drain.

2 **Cook the vegetables**
Add the butter to the bacon drippings. When it melts, add the celery, onion, thyme, and bay leaf and sauté until the onion is translucent, about 2 minutes. Add the potatoes and stir well. Add the reserved clam liquor and 2 cups (16 fl oz/500 ml) water and bring to a boil. Reduce the heat to low, cover, and simmer until the potatoes are tender, about 15 minutes.

3 **Finish the soup**
Add the milk and cream and stir to combine. Add the clam meat, heat through, and season to taste with salt and pepper. Remove and discard the bay leaf. Ladle the chowder into bowls, garnish with the bacon, and serve. »

Thick-cut bacon, 3 slices, chopped

Unsalted butter,
1 tablespoon

Celery, 2 stalks, chopped

Yellow onion, ½, finely chopped

Dried thyme,
½ teaspoon

Bay leaf, 1

Red-skinned potatoes,
3, cubed

Clam meat, 2 cans (6½ oz/200 g each), drained, chopped, clam liquor reserved

Milk, 1½ cups (12 fl oz/375 ml)

Heavy (double) cream,
1 cup (8 fl oz/250 ml)

Salt and freshly ground pepper

MAKES 4 SERVINGS

cook's tip

If desired, you can use 2 lb (1 kg) fresh clams in their shells for this recipe. Discard any that fail to close to the touch, then steam them in a covered wide saucepan with 1 cup (8 fl oz/ 250 ml) water until they open. Discard any clams that do not open. Let cool, then remove the meat from the shells and chop the meat.

black bean soup with ham

1 Prepare the soup

In a large saucepan over medium heat, warm the oil. Add the onion, carrots, and celery. Cook, stirring occasionally, until the vegetables begin to soften, about 5 minutes. Add the garlic and cook until fragrant, about 1 minute longer. Add the beans, broth, and sherry. Cover and bring to a boil over high heat. Reduce the heat to medium-low and simmer, partially covered and stirring often, until the flavors are blended, about 15 minutes.

2 Finish the soup

In a blender or food processor, purée 2 cups (16 fl oz/500 ml) of the soup, then return to the pan. Add the diced ham and simmer over medium heat until the ham is heated through, about 5 minutes. Season with salt and pepper. Ladle into bowls, garnish with the sour cream, and serve.

> cook's tip This soup can easily be turned into a white bean soup by substituting canned cannellini or Great Northern beans for the black beans. If using white beans, omit the dry sherry and sour cream.

Olive oil, 2 tablespoons

Yellow onion, 1, finely chopped

Carrots, 2, finely chopped

Celery, 1 stalk, finely chopped

Garlic, 2 cloves, minced

Black beans, 2 cans (14½ oz/455 g each), drained and rinsed

Chicken broth or stock, 6 cups (48 fl oz/1.5 l), homemade (page 29) or purchased

Dry sherry, ½ cup (4 fl oz/125 ml)

Baked Ham (page 328) or purchased ham, 1 cup (6 oz/185 g) diced

Salt and freshly ground pepper

Sour cream, ¼ cup (2 oz/60 g), for garnish

MAKES 8 SERVINGS

italian white bean soup

Olive oil, 2 tablespoons

Pancetta or thick-cut bacon, 3 oz (90 g), chopped

Yellow onion, 1 small, finely chopped

Carrots, 2, finely chopped

Garlic, 2 cloves, minced

Dried oregano, ½ teaspoon

Tomato paste, 1 tablespoon

Chicken broth or stock, 4 cups (32 fl oz/1 l), homemade (page 29) or purchased

Cannellini beans, 2 cans (14½ oz/455 g each), drained and rinsed

Baby spinach, 2 cups (2 oz/60 g), chopped

Salt and freshly ground pepper

Fresh flat-leaf (Italian) parsley, 2 tablespoons minced

MAKES 4 SERVINGS

1 Sauté the vegetables

In a large saucepan over medium-low heat, warm the oil. Add the pancetta and sauté until it browns slightly, about 5 minutes. Raise the heat to medium, add the onion and carrots, and sauté until the vegetables are soft, about 5 minutes. Add the garlic and oregano and cook, stirring, until fragrant, about 2 minutes.

2 Finish the soup

Stir in the tomato paste, mixing well. Add the broth and the beans. Raise the heat to medium-high and bring to a boil, then reduce the heat to medium. Add the spinach and cook until it is wilted, about 10 minutes. Season to taste with salt and pepper. Ladle the soup into bowls, sprinkle with the parsley, and serve.

sweet potato soup

1 Sauté the vegetables
In a large saucepan over medium heat, melt the butter. Add the celery and leek and sauté until the leek is translucent, about 3 minutes. Add the sweet potatoes and broth, raise the heat to high, and bring to a boil. Reduce the heat to low, cover, and simmer until the sweet potatoes are tender, about 30 minutes.

2 Purée the soup
Using a food processor or blender, process the soup to a smooth purée. Return to the pan and reheat to serving temperature. Season to taste with salt and pepper. Ladle into bowls, garnish with the pecans, if using, and serve.

Unsalted butter, 1 tablespoon

Celery, 2 stalks, chopped

Leek, 1, white part only, halved, rinsed, and thinly sliced

Sweet potatoes, 2 large, peeled and cut into 2-inch (5-cm) pieces

Chicken or vegetable broth or stock, 4 cups (32 fl oz/1 l), homemade (page 29 or 27) or purchased

Salt and freshly ground pepper

Pecans, ¼ cup (1 oz/ 30 g), toasted and chopped (optional)

MAKES 4 SERVINGS

potato-cheddar soup

Thick-cut bacon, 4 slices, chopped

Leek, 1, white part only, halved, rinsed, and thinly sliced

Russet potatoes, 3 large, peeled and cubed

Chicken broth or stock, 2 cups (16 fl oz/500 ml), homemade (page 29) or purchased

Milk, 3 cups (24 fl oz/750 ml)

Salt and freshly ground pepper

Sharp Cheddar cheese, ½ cup (2 oz/60 g) shredded

MAKES 4 SERVINGS

1 Cook the bacon and vegetables
In a large saucepan over medium heat, cook the bacon until crisp, about 5 minutes. Using a slotted spoon, transfer the bacon to paper towels to drain. Pour off all but 2 tablespoons of the bacon drippings from the pan and return to medium heat. Add the leek and sauté until translucent, about 2 minutes. Add the potatoes and broth and stir. Bring to a boil, then reduce the heat to low. Cook, covered, until the potatoes are tender, about 15 minutes.

2 Purée the soup
Raise the heat to medium, add the milk and ½ teaspoon pepper, and bring just to a simmer. Using a food processor or blender, process the soup to a smooth purée. Return to the saucepan and reheat to serving temperature. Add the cheese and stir until melted. Season to taste with salt and pepper. Ladle the soup into bowls, sprinkle with the bacon, and serve.

> cook's tip Sautéed leeks are a flavorful base for many soups and stews. For a classic potato-leek soup, omit the bacon and the cheese in this recipe.

tortellini in broth

1 **Cook the tortellini**
In a large saucepan over medium-high heat, bring the broth to a boil. Add the tortellini and cook for about 5 minutes, or according to the package directions. Season to taste with salt and pepper.

2 **Garnish the soup**
Ladle the soup into bowls, garnish with the cheese and basil, and serve.

Beef broth or stock,
6 cups (48 fl oz/1.5 l), homemade (page 30) or purchased

Cheese tortellini, ¾ lb (375 g), purchased

Salt and freshly ground pepper

Parmesan cheese,
⅓ cup (1½ oz/45 g) freshly grated

Fresh basil, ¼ cup (⅓ oz/10 g) slivered

MAKES 4 SERVINGS

hot & sour soup

Soy sauce, 6 tablespoons
(3 fl oz/90 ml)

Worcestershire sauce,
3 tablespoons

Rice vinegar,
2 tablespoons

Asian sesame oil,
1 tablespoon

Chile paste, ½ teaspoon

Cornstarch (cornflour),
1 tablespoon

Canola or peanut oil,
2 tablespoons

Fresh ginger, 2
tablespoons grated

Green (spring) onions,
3, thinly sliced

**Pork tenderloin or
boneless loin,** ½ lb
(250 g), thinly sliced
across the grain and cut
into thin strips

**Shiitake mushrooms or
button mushrooms,** 6 oz
(185 g), stems discarded
and caps thinly sliced

Chicken broth or stock,
6 cups (48 fl oz/1.5 l),
homemade (page 29) or
purchased

MAKES 4 SERVINGS

1 Prepare the seasonings
In a small bowl, combine the soy
sauce, Worcestershire sauce, vinegar,
sesame oil, chile paste, and cornstarch.
Stir to dissolve the cornstarch; set aside.

2 Cook the soup
Heat a large, heavy saucepan over
high heat until hot and add the canola oil.
Add the ginger and all but 1 tablespoon
of the green onions and sauté for about
5 seconds until fragrant. Add the pork and
mushrooms and sauté until the pork is just
opaque, about 1 minute. Pour in the broth,
bring to a boil, and then reduce the heat
to low. Give the soup seasonings a quick
stir, add to the soup, stir well, and simmer,
stirring occasionally, until the soup begins
to thicken slightly, about 5 minutes. Ladle
into bowls, garnish with the reserved
green onions, and serve.

cook's tip This soup can be
prepared a day in advance. Let cool,
transfer to an airtight container, and
store in the refrigerator; reheat just
before serving. You can also freeze
the soup for up to 3 months. Thaw
in the refrigerator.

mexican pork & rice soup

1 Brown the pork
In a large saucepan over medium-high heat, warm 1 tablespoon of the oil. Working in batches if necessary to avoid crowding, add the pork and cook, turning as needed, until golden brown on all sides, about 6 minutes. Using a slotted spoon, transfer to a plate.

2 Simmer the soup
Reduce the heat to medium and add the remaining 1 tablespoon oil. Add the onion, garlic, chiles, and rice and stir to coat with the oil. Pour in the broth and bring to a boil. Reduce the heat to low, cover, and simmer until the rice is tender, about 20 minutes.

3 Finish the soup
Return the pork to the pan, stir in the cilantro and lime juice, and cook until the pork is opaque throughout, about 5 minutes. Season to taste with salt and pepper. Ladle into bowls and serve. »

Olive oil, 2 tablespoons

Boneless pork loin, 1 lb (500 g), cut into cubes

Yellow onion, 1 small, chopped

Garlic, 2 cloves, minced

Serrano chiles, 3, seeded and chopped

Long-grain rice, ¼ cup (2 oz/60 g)

Chicken broth or stock, 5 cups (40 fl oz/1.25 l), homemade (page 29) or purchased

Fresh cilantro (fresh coriander), ¼ cup (⅓ oz/10 g) minced

Lime juice, from 1 lime

Salt and freshly ground pepper

MAKES 4 SERVINGS

cook's tip

You can dress up this soup with a colorful garnish of chopped avocado and tomato. Serve with warm corn tortillas.

spicy gazpacho

1 Make the soup

In a food processor or blender, combine half each of the tomatoes, cucumber, bell pepper, and onion with all of the chiles and garlic. Process to a coarse paste. Add half of the cilantro and all of the olive oil, tomato juice, and red wine vinegar and process to a smooth purée. Season to taste with salt and pepper.

2 Garnish the soup

Transfer to an airtight container and refigerate for 2–8 hours or up to 2 days. Ladle the soup into bowls. Garnish with the remaining tomatoes, cucumber, bell pepper, onion, and cilantro, top with the croutons, and serve.

Plum (Roma) tomatoes, 8, chopped

Cucumber, 1, peeled, halved, seeded, and chopped

Red bell pepper (capsicum), 1 small, seeded and chopped

Red onion, 1 small, chopped

Serrano chiles, 2, seeded

Garlic, 2 cloves

Fresh cilantro (fresh coriander), ½ cup (¾ oz/20 g) chopped

Olive oil, 1 tablespoon

Tomato juice, 1½ cups (12 fl oz/375 ml), chilled

Red wine vinegar, 2 tablespoons

Salt and freshly ground pepper

Croutons, 1½ cups (2½ oz/75 g), homemade (page 155) or purchased

MAKES 4 SERVINGS

creamy mushroom bisque

Unsalted butter,
4 tablespoons (2 oz/60 g)

Shallot, 1 large, chopped

Cremini mushrooms,
10 oz (315 g), chopped

Flour, 3 tablespoons

**Mushroom broth or
stock,** 3 cups (24 fl oz/
750 ml), homemade
(page 28) or purchased

Brandy, ¼ cup
(2 fl oz/60 ml)

Heavy (double) cream,
½ cup (4 fl oz/125 ml),
plus more for garnish

**Salt and freshly ground
pepper**

MAKES 4 SERVINGS

1 Cook the soup
In a large, heavy saucepan over medium heat, melt the butter. Add the shallot and sauté until translucent, about 2 minutes. Add the mushrooms, cover, and cook until their juices are released, about 3 minutes. Stir in the flour and cook, stirring, until thoroughly blended, about 1 minute. Pour in the broth and brandy. Bring to a boil, cover, reduce the heat to medium, and simmer for 15–20 minutes.

2 Finish the soup
Transfer the soup to a blender and process to a smooth purée. Add the ½ cup cream and pulse twice just to blend. Return to the pan and place over low heat. Reheat to serving temperature. Season to taste with salt and pepper. Ladle into bowls, drizzle with cream, and serve.

split pea soup

1 Cook the soup
In a frying pan over medium heat, warm the oil. Add the onion and garlic and sauté until softened, 4–5 minutes. Place the ham hock in the center of a Dutch oven or slow cooker and add the sautéed onion and garlic, the split peas, carrots, celery, broth, thyme, 1 teaspoon salt, and ½ teaspoon pepper and stir. If using a Dutch oven, bring to a simmer over medium-high heat, then reduce the heat to medium-low, cover, and cook until the peas are tender, 50–60 minutes. (If using a slow cooker, cover and cook on the high-heat setting for 4–5 hours or the low-heat setting for 8–10 hours.)

2 Finish the soup
Transfer the ham hock to a platter or cutting board and let cool for about 15 minutes. Remove the ham meat from the bone, shredding or cutting it into bite-sized pieces. Stir the ham into the soup along with the parsley. Ladle the soup into bowls and serve.

Olive oil, 2 tablespoons

Yellow onion, 1, finely chopped

Garlic, 2 cloves, minced

Smoked ham hock, 1, about 1½ lb (750 g)

Green split peas, 1 lb (500 g), picked over and rinsed

Carrots, 3, chopped

Celery, 2 stalks, chopped

Chicken broth or stock, 6 cups (48 fl oz/1.5 l), homemade (page 29) or purchased

Dried thyme, 1 teaspoon

Salt and freshly ground pepper

Fresh flat-leaf (Italian) parsley, ½ cup (¾ oz/20 g) minced

MAKES 6–8 SERVINGS

vietnamese beef noodle soup

Beef eye of round roast,
½ lb (250 g), cut across
the grain into slices
⅛ inch (3 mm) thick

Canola oil, 2 tablespoons

Asian fish sauce,
3½ teaspoons

Salt

Beef broth or stock,
6 cups (48 fl oz/1.5 l),
homemade (page 30)
or purchased

Fresh ginger, 3-inch
(7.5-cm) piece, thinly
sliced

Coriander seeds,
1 teaspoon

Cinnamon stick, ½-inch
(12-mm) piece

Rice vermicelli, 8–10 oz
(250–315 g)

Bean sprouts, ¼ lb
(125 g)

**Fresh basil, preferably
Thai,** ½ cup (¾ oz/20 g)
coarsely chopped

Limes, 2, quartered

MAKES 4 SERVINGS

1 Marinate the beef
In a large resealable plastic bag, combine the beef, 1 tablespoon of the oil, 1½ teaspoons of the fish sauce, and ¼ teaspoon salt. Seal the bag and turn to distribute the marinade. Set aside at room temperature for 15 minutes or in the refrigerator for up to overnight.

2 Cook the broth and noodles
In a large saucepan over medium-high heat, combine the broth, ginger, coriander seeds, cinnamon stick, and remaining 2 teaspoons fish sauce. Bring to a boil. Reduce the heat to low, cover, and simmer for 30 minutes. Bring a large pot of water to a boil, add the vermicelli, and cook until tender, according to the package directions. Drain, rinse under cold water, and divide evenly among bowls.

3 Finish the soup
In a frying pan over high heat, warm the remaining 1 tablespoon oil. Add the beef and its marinade and cook, stirring, until the beef is seared on both sides, about 4 minutes total. Remove from the pan and set aside. Strain the broth, return to the saucepan, and bring to a boil over medium-high heat. Add the bean sprouts, basil, and beef and cook for about 3 minutes. Ladle over the vermicelli and serve. Pass the lime quarters at the table.

thai chicken-coconut soup

1 **Make the soup base**
Grate 1 tablespoon zest and squeeze ½ cup (4 fl oz/125 ml) juice from the orange. In a large saucepan over medium-high heat, combine the orange zest and juice, coconut milk, broth, and fish sauce. Stir well and bring to a boil.

2 **Cook the chicken and mushrooms**
Reduce the heat to low, add the chicken, and simmer, uncovered, for 5 minutes. Add the mushrooms and continue to cook until the chicken is opaque throughout and the mushrooms are tender, about 5 minutes longer. Add the lime juice and season to taste with salt and pepper. Ladle into bowls, garnish with the basil, and serve. »

Orange, 1

Unsweetened coconut milk, 3 cups (24 fl oz/ 750 ml)

Chicken broth or stock, 1½ cups (12 fl oz/375 ml), homemade (page 29) or purchased

Asian fish sauce, 2 teaspoons

Skinless, boneless, chicken breast halves, 2, cut into bite-sized pieces

Button mushrooms, 6 oz (185 g), quartered

Lime juice, from 1 lime

Salt and freshly ground pepper

Fresh basil, preferably Thai, ¼ cup (⅓ oz/10 g) chopped

MAKES 4 SERVINGS

cook's tip

For a spicier soup, add 2 seeded and minced Thai
or serrano chiles. Use kitchen gloves to protect
your hands while mincing and seeding chiles, as
they have volatile oils that will irritate your skin.

chicken & corn chowder

1 Cook the bacon
In a saucepan over medium heat, fry the bacon until crisp, about 5 minutes. Using a slotted spoon, transfer to paper towels to drain. Pour off all but about 3 tablespoons of the bacon drippings from the pan.

2 Cook the vegetables and chicken
Add the bell pepper, corn, and potatoes to the drippings over medium heat. Cook, stirring frequently, until the pepper is just softened, 4–5 minutes. Add the broth and wine, bring to a boil, cover, and cook until the potatoes are almost tender, about 5 minutes. Add the chicken and cook, covered, until opaque throughout, 5–7 minutes.

3 Finish the chowder
Stir in the onions, thyme, and half-and-half. Bring to a simmer over medium heat, reduce the heat to medium-low, and cook, uncovered, until heated through, about 3 minutes. Season to taste with salt and pepper. Ladle the chowder into bowls, sprinkle with the bacon, and serve.

Thick-cut bacon, 4 slices, chopped

Red bell pepper (capsicum), 1 large, seeded and chopped

Fresh or frozen corn kernels, 4 cups (1½ lb/750 g)

Yukon gold potatoes, ¾ lb (375 g), cut into ½-inch (12-mm) chunks

Chicken broth or stock, 3 cups (24 fl oz/750 ml), homemade (page 29) or purchased

Dry white wine, ½ cup (4 fl oz/125 ml)

Skinless, boneless chicken thighs, ¾ lb (375 g) total weight, cut into ½-inch (12-mm) chunks

Green (spring) onions, 6, white and pale green parts, thinly sliced

Fresh thyme, 3 tablespoons minced

Half-and-half (half cream), 2½ cups (20 fl oz/625 ml)

Salt and freshly ground pepper

MAKES 4 SERVINGS

roasted root vegetable soup

Celery root (celeriac),
1 large or 2 small, peeled
and cut into slices 1 inch
(2.5 cm) thick

Parsnips, 2, peeled and
quartered lengthwise

Leeks, 2 large, white part
only, halved and rinsed

Garlic, 1 head, top
one-third cut off

Olive oil, ¼ cup
(2 fl oz/60 ml)

Herbes de Provence,
1 teaspoon

**Salt and freshly ground
pepper**

Vermouth or brandy,
1 teaspoon

**Half-and-half (half
cream),** 2½ cups
(20 fl oz/625 ml)

Chicken broth or stock,
3 cups (24 fl oz/750 ml),
homemade (page 29) or
purchased

MAKES 4 SERVINGS

1 **Roast the vegetables**
Preheat the oven to 325°F (165°C).
Arrange the celery root, parsnips, leeks
(cut side down), and garlic (cut side up) in
a single layer on a rimmed baking sheet.
Sprinkle with the olive oil, herbes de
Provence, and a little salt and pepper.
Roast for 30 minutes. Turn the vegetables,
cover the pan loosely with aluminum foil,
and continue to roast until the vegetables
are very tender, about 30 minutes longer.

2 **Purée the soup**
Squeeze the pulp from the garlic into
a food processor or blender, discarding
the skins. In batches, add the rest of the
roasted vegetables and purée. Transfer
to a large saucepan over medium-high
heat. Add the vermouth, half-and-half,
and broth, stir well, and bring to a boil.
Reduce the heat to low, cover, and simmer
for 10–15 minutes to blend the flavors.
Season to taste with salt and pepper.
Ladle the soup into bowls and serve.

> **cook's tip** If you can't find celery
> root, use ¾ lb (375 g) russet potatoes,
> peeled and sliced, and 1–2 celery
> stalks, cut into 2-inch (5-cm) pieces.
> Roast on the baking sheet with the
> other vegetables as directed.

beef & barley soup

1 Cook the barley
In a saucepan over medium-high heat, bring 3 cups (24 fl oz/750 ml) water to a boil. Add 1 teaspoon salt and the barley and return to a boil. Reduce the heat to low, cover, and cook just until tender, about 1½ hours. Drain and set aside.

2 Prepare the soup base
Meanwhile, in a large saucepan over medium heat, melt the butter. Add the onion and mushrooms and cook, stirring frequently, until the onion is translucent and the mushrooms have released their juices, about 5 minutes. Add the broth and beef, reduce the heat to low, and simmer, uncovered, for about 10 minutes.

3 Finish the soup
When the barley is ready, add it to the soup base and simmer over medium heat for 5 minutes to blend the flavors. Season to taste with salt and pepper. Ladle into bowls and serve.

cook's tip For an earthier soup, replace the button mushrooms with a variety of mushrooms, such as cremini, chanterelles, stemmed shiitakes, or porcini (ceps).

Salt and freshly ground pepper

Pearl barley, ¼ cup (2 oz/60 g)

Unsalted butter, 2 tablespoons

Yellow onion, 1 small, chopped

Button mushrooms, ½ lb (250 g), finely chopped

Beef broth or stock, 4 cups (32 fl oz/1 l), homemade (page 30) or purchased

Boneless beef sirloin, ½ lb (250 g), cut into thin slices and then finely chopped

MAKES 4 SERVINGS

lentil & spinach soup

Thick-cut bacon, 3 slices, chopped

Carrot, ½, finely chopped

Yellow onion, ½ small, finely chopped

Garlic, 2 cloves, minced

Fresh thyme, 1 teaspoon minced

Salt and freshly ground pepper

Dried lentils, 1 cup (7 oz/220 g), picked over and rinsed

Chicken broth or stock, 4 cups (32 fl oz/1 l), homemade (page 29) or purchased

Tomato paste, 2 tablespoons

Baby spinach, 3 cups (3 oz/90 g), chopped

MAKES 4 SERVINGS

1 **Cook the bacon and vegetables**
In a large saucepan over medium heat, sauté the bacon until the fat is rendered, about 5 minutes. Add the carrot and onion and sauté until the onion is translucent, about 2 minutes. Add the garlic, thyme, and 1 teaspoon salt and sauté until the garlic is soft, about 1 minute. Stir in the lentils.

2 **Finish the soup**
Add the broth, tomato paste, and 1 cup (8 fl oz/250 ml) water, raise the heat to high, and bring to a boil. Reduce the heat to low, cover partially, and simmer until the lentils are tender, 25–30 minutes. Add the spinach and simmer until wilted, about 2 minutes longer. Season the soup to taste with salt and pepper. Ladle into bowls and serve.

cook's tip For an almost instant soup, use canned lentils instead of dried. Add them to the soup in Step 2 and cook for 5 minutes before stirring in the spinach.

hungarian beef stew

1 Cook the onions and beef
In a Dutch oven over high heat, warm the oil. Add the beef and onions, season with salt and pepper, and cook, stirring frequently, until the beef is browned and the onions begin to caramelize, about 10 minutes. Stir in the garlic, paprika, and tomato paste. Add the broth, bring to a boil, reduce the heat to low, cover, and braise until the meat is nearly fork-tender, about 1 hour.

2 Finish the stew
Add the potatoes, bell pepper, and carrots, and continue to braise, covered, until the vegetables are tender, about 30 minutes longer. Ladle the stew into shallow bowls and serve.

cook's tip There are many different varieties of paprika, so be sure to use a good-quality brand. Hungarian and Spanish paprika are the most popular and they come in sweet and hot varieties. For this recipe, use sweet paprika or a combination of sweet and hot.

Olive oil, 2 tablespoons

Boneless beef chuck, 2 lb (1 kg), trimmed of excess fat and cut into 1½-inch (4-cm) pieces

Yellow onions, 2 large, chopped

Salt and freshly ground pepper

Garlic, 3 large cloves, minced

Sweet smoked paprika, 1½ tablespoons

Tomato paste, 2 tablespoons

Chicken broth or stock, 4 cups (32 fl oz/1 l), homemade (page 29) or purchased

Boiling potatoes, 1 lb (500 g), quartered

Red bell pepper (capsicum), 1, seeded and cut into ½-inch (12-mm) strips

Carrots, 2, peeled and cut into 1-inch (2.5-cm) chunks

MAKES 4–6 SERVINGS

hearty beef &
vegetable soup

Olive oil, 2 tablespoons

Boneless beef chuck,
1 lb (500 g), cut into
chunks

Yellow onion, 1 large,
chopped

Carrots, 2, chopped

Celery, 2 stalks, chopped

Red-skinned potatoes,
2, cut into chunks

**Crushed plum (Roma)
tomatoes,** 1 can
(28 oz/875 g), with juice

Green beans, ½ lb
(250 g), trimmed

**Fresh flat-leaf (Italian)
parsley,** 2 tablespoons
chopped

**Salt and freshly ground
pepper**

MAKES 6–8 SERVINGS

1 Cook the beef and vegetables
In a large saucepan over medium-high heat, warm 1 tablespoon of the oil. Working in batches, sauté the beef in the oil until browned, about 4 minutes. Transfer to a plate. Add the remaining 1 tablespoon oil to the pan and reduce the heat to medium. Add the onion, carrots, and celery, cover, and cook, stirring occasionally, until the onion is softened, about 5 minutes. Return the beef and any juices from the plate to the pan.

2 Simmer the soup
Add 6 cups (48 fl oz/1.5 l) water to the pan and bring to a boil over high heat. Reduce the heat to medium-low and simmer, partially covered, for 1 hour. Add the potatoes, tomatoes, and green beans, and stir well. Simmer until the beef and potatoes are tender, about 20 minutes. Stir in the parsley and season to taste with salt and pepper. Ladle into bowls and serve.

cook's tip To freeze, transfer the cooled soup to 1-qt (1-l) airtight containers, leaving ½ inch (12 mm) at the top to allow for expansion. Freeze for up to 2 months. Thaw overnight in the refrigerator.

soups made easy

Even the heartiest soups don't have to involve a lot of work. Most of the recipes in this book require less than 30 minutes of hands-on time to prepare. If you plan ahead and stock your kitchen, you'll be able to put delicious homemade soups on the table in record time.

BROTHS & STOCKS

The recipes in this book give you a choice between using purchased broths or homemade stocks. If you are short on time, good-quality broths can be found in cans and aseptic boxes on market shelves. Read the labels carefully to avoid unwholesome ingredients. If you have time to make your own, homemade stocks will deliver much better flavor. Several stocks are included in the Basic Recipes chapter (see page 14). Be sure to make a big batch so you can freeze some for later use.

STORING & THAWING

Remember that many soups and stews can be made a day or two ahead and refrigerated (or frozen for a longer period). Dishes like these even improve in flavor a day after they are made. (See page 12 for tips on storage and thawing.)

Shortcut ingredients Whatever you are cooking, certain ingredients can make the job easier and save prep time, either because they are precooked or because they add concentrated, intense flavor. Here are some time-saving soup ingredients.

- CANNED BEANS Save soaking and simmering time by using canned beans. Always drain the liquid and rinse the beans well before using.

- CANNED TOMATOES Use canned tomatoes rather than mealy, out-of-season fresh tomatoes for better flavor. Because they are already peeled, you'll save kitchen time, too.

- COOKED SAUSAGES Slice fully cooked sausages, such as andouille, smoked chorizo, chicken with apple, or kielbasa, and add directly to soups, or brown first for extra flavor.

- DRIED MUSHROOMS The concentrated flavor of dried porcini, shiitake, or other mushrooms complements many soups. To reconstitute, place the mushrooms in a heatproof bowl, cover with boiling water, cover the bowl, and soak until soft and flexible, at least 10 minutes. Strain the flavorful soaking liquid and add to soups.

- FROZEN VEGETABLES Keep a supply of frozen peas, mixed Italian-style vegetables, and corn on hand to spruce up a variety of soups.

- ROTISSERIE CHICKEN Buy enough chicken for dinner one night plus leftovers, and cut up the leftover chicken meat to add to soup the next night. Save the carcass and refrigerate or freeze, and then use it to enrich purchased chicken broth.

- TOMATO PASTE Buy tomato paste in a tube and refrigerate after opening. Add a small amount to soups to intensify flavor.

cooking tips for soup

One of the best things about soup is its versatility: You can make it with nearly any vegetable—from peas and chard to turnips and cauliflower—and it's a great way to use extra ingredients in the refrigerator. Use the recipes in this book as a starting point, building on them with these basic techniques to create your own soups.

BASIC TECHNIQUES

Prep Use a food processor to make quick work of chopping vegetables. Prep vegetables for two nights: when you are chopping vegetables for dinner, chop extra vegetables for recipes on your menu and store them in an airtight container in the refrigerator for the next night. Keep a selection of cut-up frozen vegetables to use when you don't have time to buy or prep fresh ones.

Sauté Many of the recipes in this book begin with sautéing aromatic seasonings and vegetables (onions, garlic, carrots, celery) in butter or oil to create a flavorful base for the soup. If you have a heavy soup pot or Dutch oven, you can use it for this step, then continue making the soup in the same pot.

Roast Roasting vegetables or other ingredients (beets, tomatoes, meats, poultry) before using them in soups intensifies their flavor. Because the oven does most of the work, it's a method that requires little hands-on time and delivers a big payoff.

For easy cleanup, line a roasting pan with aluminum foil and brush the foil with a little olive oil to help prevent sticking. Most ingredients can be roasted a day or two ahead of time and stored in an airtight container in the refrigerator. Make extra roasted vegetables to serve on another night.

Simmer Most soups are simmered gently over low heat, requiring little attention other than occasional stirring and skimming. When making thicker soups, use a heavy-bottomed pot to avoid scorching and a wooden spoon or spatula to stir, drawing it across the bottom each time.

Purée The tall, narrow shape of a blender effectively purées mixtures with a high proportion of liquid and some chunky ingredients, making it the best tool for puréeing soups, though a food processor or immersion blender can also be used. Puréeing some, but not all, of a soup is an easy way to give it a more substantial, chunky texture.

When puréeing hot soups, fill the blender no more than two-thirds full. Cover with the lid, making sure it is secure, and then drape a kitchen towel over the lid in case there is splattering. Hold the lid down with one hand, start the motor on the slowest speed, and then increase the speed as necessary.

Season & enrich Season soups during cooking as directed, then taste the finished soup before serving to adjust the seasoning with salt and pepper as needed. Adding a small amount of fresh lemon juice or vinegar just before serving can brighten the flavor of many soups. Use only a few drops at a time, tasting as you go. Some soups are enriched with heavy (double) cream, sour cream, yogurt, butter, or olive oil just before serving. Stir these ingredients in gradually, and don't allow the soup to boil if you are adding sour cream or yogurt, which can curdle at high temperatures. Add garnishes after dividing the soup in serving bowls.

easy garnishes

A garnish is an easy way to elevate the flavor and the presentation of a bowl of soup. Many garnishes, such as croutons and crumbled bacon, also add texture to creamy soups.

- BREAD CRUMBS Drizzle fresh bread crumbs with olive oil, sprinkle with salt and pepper, then toast in a toaster oven or in a 350°F (180°C) oven until golden.

- CROUTONS To make your own croutons, drizzle thin slices or cubes of baguette or other crusty bread with olive oil, sprinkle with salt, and then toast in a toaster oven or on a baking sheet in a 350°F (180°C) oven until lightly browned.

- CRUMBLED BACON Brown some extra bacon when cooking it for a soup base, then chop and sprinkle over each serving.

- CRUMBLED TORTILLA CHIPS Sprinkle over Latin-inspired soups to add texture and color; pass additional crumbled chips at the table.

- EXTRA-VIRGIN OLIVE OIL Drizzle a little fruity, bright green olive oil over each serving, making a spiral or zigzag pattern. It will add flavor and style to many Italian and other Mediterranean soups and is particularly appealing on the surface of thick vegetable purées.

- FETA OR BLUE CHEESE Crumble fresh feta cheese or a mild blue cheese over each serving to add another layer of flavor.

- FRESH CHIVES Snip with kitchen scissors, allowing the bits to fall directly onto a bowl of soup.

- FRESH LEAFY HERBS Strip leaves from stems and then roughly chop any large leaves if necessary.

- PARMESAN OR AGED PECORINO CHEESE Grate or shave directly onto a bowl of soup for the best flavor.

- QUESO FRESCO Crumble this soft, white cheese over each serving; it is ideal for Latin-inspired soups.

- SALSA Top Latin-inspired soups with a dollop of purchased salsa. If desired, add a small spoonful of sour cream and top it with a fresh cilantro (fresh coriander) leaf.

- SOUR CREAM, PLAIN YOGURT, OR CRÈME FRAÎCHE Thin with milk or cream and, using a teaspoon, drizzle over a bowl of soup.

"In Minutes" meals include soups and accompaniments that can be put together quickly. "Fit for Company" meals include ideas for stress-free get-togethers, complete with a wine suggestion.

IN MINUTES

Spring Vegetable Soup (page 128)

rotisserie chicken

———

Greek Chicken & Rice Soup (page 130)

broiled (grilled) sausages and zucchini (courgettes)

———

Clam Chowder (page 131)

mixed salad greens with balsamic vinaigrette

———

Sweet Potato Soup (page 135)

spinach salad with bacon and honey-mustard vinaigrette

———

Mexican Pork & Rice Soup (page 139)

roasted poblano chiles stuffed with jack cheese

———

Spicy Gazpacho (page 141)

mixed salad greens with sautéed shrimp (prawns)

chips and guacamole

FIT FOR COMPANY

French Onion Soup (page 121)

mixed salad greens with red wine vinaigrette

Beaujolais or Pinot Noir

———

Chilled Cucumber Soup (page 129)

seared salmon

Pinot Gris or Merlot

———

Italian White Bean Soup (page 134)

braised sausages and greens

Chianti

———

Tortellini in Broth (page 137)

garlic crostini

arugula (rocket) and Parmesan salad with balsamic vinaigrette

Cabernet Sauvignon

———

Thai Chicken-Coconut Soup (page 145)

sliced cucumber and red onion salad with rice vinegar dressing

Dry Riesling

MEAL PLANNING TIPS

Getting into the habit of making a weekly meal plan can save you hours of shopping and kitchen time. Once you have mapped out your meals, you can take stock of what you already have in your refrigerator and pantry and draw up a list of ingredients you need to make the recipes.

Soup is the perfect anchor for a meal Soup is flavorful, filling, and easy to cook, serve, store, and reheat. And whether light and meatless or hearty and substantial, soup can be a healthful mainstay as well as an inexpensive dinnertime solution. Use this book to build a repertoire of reliable soups that you and your family can enjoy throughout the year.

Soup can be a first course or a main course Serve a lighter soup, such as Spring Vegetable Soup (page 128) or Chilled Cucumber Soup (page 129), as a first course before a meat or fish main course. Or, offer a heartier soup, such as Beef & Barley Soup (page 149) or Lentil & Spinach Soup (page 150), as the centerpiece of the meal, accompanying it with a simple side dish to round out the meal (see pages 16–17).

pasta & grains

spaghetti carbonara

1 Make the sauce

Bring a large pot of water to a boil. In a large frying pan over medium heat, warm 1 tablespoon of the oil. Add the pancetta and 3 tablespoons water and cook until the water has evaporated. Add the garlic and the remaining 2 tablespoons oil and cook, stirring occasionally, until the pancetta is slightly browned, about 4 minutes. Stir in the wine and cook until the wine evaporates slightly, about 1 minute; set aside. In a large serving bowl, beat the eggs with the cheese and ¾ teaspoon salt; set aside.

2 Cook the pasta

Meanwhile, add 2 tablespoons salt and the pasta to the boiling water. Cook, stirring occasionally to prevent sticking, until al dente, according to the package directions. Drain, reserving about ½ cup (4 fl oz/125 ml) of the cooking water. Working quickly, add the hot pasta to the egg mixture and toss to combine. Add as much of the cooking water as needed to achieve a nice coating consistency for the sauce. Add the pancetta, a generous amount of pepper, and the parsley. Toss again and serve.

Olive oil, 3 tablespoons

Pancetta or thick-cut bacon, ¼ lb (125 g), chopped

Garlic, 2 large cloves, minced

Dry white wine, ⅓ cup (3 fl oz/80 ml)

Eggs, 3, at room temperature, beaten

Parmesan cheese, ⅓ cup (1½ oz/45 g) freshly grated

Salt and freshly ground pepper

Spaghetti, 1 lb (500 g)

Fresh flat-leaf (Italian) parsley, ¼ cup (⅓ oz/ 10 g) minced

MAKES 4 SERVINGS

pasta with hearty beef ragù

Olive oil, 6 tablespoons
(3 fl oz/90 ml)

Yellow onion, 1 small,
finely chopped

Garlic, 3 large cloves,
minced

Carrot, 1, finely chopped

Celery, 1 stalk, finely
chopped

Fresh rosemary,
1 teaspoon minced

Ground (minced) beef,
¾ lb (375 g)

Dry red wine, ½ cup
(4 fl oz/125 ml)

Tomato paste,
3 tablespoons

**Canned whole plum
(Roma) tomatoes,**
2½ cups (20 fl oz/625 ml),
chopped, with juice

**Salt and freshly ground
pepper**

Penne or rigatoni, 1 lb
(500 g)

MAKES 4 SERVINGS

1 Make the ragù
In a large, deep frying pan or Dutch oven over medium-low heat, warm the oil. Add the onion, garlic, carrot, celery, and rosemary and cook, stirring frequently, until the vegetables are softened, about 8 minutes. Add 1–2 tablespoons water if necessary to keep the vegetables from browning. Add the beef and cook, breaking it up with a wooden spoon, until it is browned, about 10 minutes. Add the wine and tomato paste. Cook, stirring occasionally, until the wine evaporates slightly, 3–4 minutes. Add the tomatoes, 1 teaspoon salt, and ½ teaspoon pepper. Reduce the heat to low, cover partially, and cook, stirring occasionally, until the ragù is thick and aromatic, about 1 hour.

2 Cook the pasta
Just before the sauce is done, bring a large pot of water to a boil. Add 2 tablespoons salt and the pasta to the boiling water. Cook, stirring occasionally to prevent sticking, until al dente, according to the package directions. Drain and add to the sauce, stirring to combine. Warm briefly over low heat to blend the flavors. Season to taste with salt and pepper and serve.

chicken & arugula pesto pasta

1 **Make the arugula pesto**
Bring a large pot of water to a boil. In a food processor, combine the garlic, pine nuts, arugula, and ¼ cup (1 oz/30 g) of the Parmesan cheese. Pulse to chop. With the machine running, gradually add the oil. Season with ¼ teaspoon salt and several grindings of pepper.

2 **Cook the pasta**
Add 2 tablespoons salt and the pasta to the boiling water. Cook, stirring occasionally to prevent sticking, until al dente, according to the package directions. Drain, reserving about ½ cup (4 fl oz/125 ml) of the cooking water. Return the pasta to the pot.

3 **Finish the pasta**
While the pasta is cooking, in a large frying pan over medium-high heat, melt the butter. Add the chicken and cook, stirring occasionally, until heated through, 3–4 minutes. Add the chicken to the drained pasta along with the pesto, tomatoes, *ricotta salata*, and remaining ¼ cup Parmesan cheese. Toss, adding as much of the cooking water as needed to achieve a nice sauce consistency. Season with salt and pepper and serve.

Garlic, 1 small clove

Pine nuts, 2 tablespoons

Baby arugula (rocket), 1¼ cups (1¼ oz/40 g)

Parmesan cheese, ½ cup (2 oz/60 g) freshly grated

Olive oil, ¼ cup (2 fl oz/60 ml)

Salt and freshly ground pepper

Ziti, 1 lb (500 g)

Unsalted butter, 2 tablespoons

Classic Roast Chicken (page 267) or rotisserie chicken, 2 cups (12 oz/ 375 g) shredded meat

Cherry tomatoes, ½ lb (250 g), halved

Ricotta salata, 1 cup (4 oz/125 g) crumbled

MAKES 4–6 SERVINGS

pasta with brown butter & asparagus

Salt and freshly ground pepper

Asparagus, 1 lb (500 g), tough ends removed, cut into 1-inch (2.5-cm) pieces

Unsalted butter, ½ cup (4 oz/125 g)

Hazelnuts (filberts), 1 cup (5 oz/155 g), toasted, skinned, and coarsely chopped

Gemelli or other short pasta such as penne, 1 lb (500 g)

Parmesan cheese, ½ cup (4 oz/125 g) freshly grated

MAKES 4 SERVINGS

1 Blanch the asparagus
Bring a large pot of water to a boil. Add 2 tablespoons salt and the asparagus to the boiling water and cook just until tender, about 4 minutes. Using a skimmer or slotted spoon, transfer the asparagus to a colander and drain; set aside. Return the water to a boil.

2 Make the butter sauce
In a large frying pan over low heat, melt the butter. Cook until the butter is lightly browned, about 2 minutes; be careful that it doesn't burn. Add the hazelnuts and season to taste with salt. Add the reserved asparagus and toss. Remove from the heat.

3 Cook the pasta
Meanwhile, add the pasta to the boiling water. Cook, stirring occasionally to prevent sticking, until al dente, according to the package directions. Drain, reserving about ½ cup (4 fl oz/125 ml) of the cooking water. Add the drained pasta to the sauce and toss to combine. Warm briefly over low heat to blend the flavors. Add as much of the cooking water as needed to achieve a nice coating consistency for the sauce. Season to taste with salt and pepper, top with the cheese, and serve.

capellini with lemon, garlic & parsley

1 **Make the sauce**
Bring a large pot of water to a boil. In a large frying pan over low heat, warm the oil. Add the garlic and sauté until fragrant but not golden, 1–2 minutes. Remove from the heat and stir in the lemon zest, lemon juice, and 1 teaspoon salt. Season to taste with pepper. Transfer to a large serving bowl.

2 **Cook the pasta**
Meanwhile, add 2 tablespoons salt and the pasta to the boiling water. Cook, stirring occasionally to prevent sticking, until al dente, according to the package directions. Drain, reserving about ½ cup (4 fl oz/125 ml) of the cooking water. Add the drained pasta and the parsley to the sauce and toss to coat. Add as much of the cooking water as needed to achieve a nice coating consistency for the sauce. Season to taste with salt and pepper and serve. »

Olive oil, ½ cup (4 fl oz/125 ml)

Garlic, 4 large cloves, minced

Lemon zest, from 1 lemon

Lemon juice, from ½ lemon

Salt and freshly ground pepper

Capellini or spaghettini, 1 lb (500 g)

Fresh flat-leaf (Italian) parsley, ½ cup (¾ oz/ 20 g) minced

MAKES 4 SERVINGS

cook's tip

For colorful and flavorful variations, add ½ cup (3 oz/90 g) halved cherry tomatoes; ½ cup (2½ oz/75 g) chopped, pitted black or green olives; or 1 tablespoon each minced fresh thyme, rosemary, and sage to the pasta when you add the parsley.

farfalle with salsa cruda

1 Prepare the sauce
In a large bowl, combine the tomatoes, garlic, basil, oil, vinegar, and red pepper flakes. Stir well and let stand at room temperature for about 15 minutes to blend the flavors. Stir in the cheese and let stand for about 10 minutes longer.

2 Toast the pine nuts
Meanwhile, in a small frying pan over medium-high heat, toast the pine nuts, stirring often, until fragrant, 1–2 minutes. Transfer to a plate and set aside.

3 Cook the pasta
Bring a large pot of water to a boil. Add 2 tablespoons salt and the pasta and cook, stirring occasionally to prevent sticking, until al dente, according to the package directions. Drain and add to the sauce, along with the prosciutto and toasted pine nuts. Toss to combine and slightly soften the cheese. Season to taste with salt and black pepper and serve.

cook's tip Make this dish in the summer when ripe, juicy tomatoes of many varieties, including heirlooms, are abundant. At other times of the year, use plum (Roma) tomatoes.

Tomatoes, 1½ lb (750 g), cored and coarsely chopped

Garlic, 2 cloves, minced

Fresh basil, ½ cup (¾ oz/20 g) slivered

Olive oil, ½ cup (4 fl oz/125 ml)

Balsamic vinegar, 3 tablespoons

Red pepper flakes, ½ teaspoon

Smoked or fresh mozzarella cheese, ½ lb (250 g), cubed

Pine nuts, ¼ cup (1¼ oz/40 g)

Salt and freshly ground black pepper

Farfalle or other medium pasta, 1 lb (500 g)

Prosciutto, 2 oz (60 g) thinly sliced, chopped

MAKES 4 SERVINGS

penne with vodka sauce

Unsalted butter,
4 tablespoons (2 oz/60 g)

Heavy (double) cream,
1 cup (8 fl oz/250 ml)

Tomato paste, ¼ cup
(2 oz/60 g)

Vodka, ⅓ cup (3 fl oz/
80 ml) plus 2 tablespoons

Fresh basil,
2 tablespoons slivered

Red pepper flakes,
pinch

Salt

**Penne or other tubular
pasta,** 1 lb (500 g)

Parmesan cheese, ½ cup
(2 oz/60 g) freshly grated

MAKES 4 SERVINGS

1 Make the sauce
Bring a large pot of water to a boil. In a large frying pan over medium-low heat, melt the butter with the cream. In a small bowl, stir the tomato paste with the vodka until smooth. Stir into the cream mixture. Add the basil, red pepper flakes, and 1 teaspoon salt. Cook until the alcohol evaporates slightly and the sauce is thick enough to coat the back of a spoon, about 5 minutes.

2 Cook the pasta
Meanwhile, add 2 tablespoons salt and the pasta to the boiling water. Cook, stirring occasionally to prevent sticking, until al dente, according to the package directions. Drain, reserving about ½ cup (4 fl oz/125 ml) of the cooking water. Add the drained pasta to the sauce and warm over low heat to blend the flavors. Add the cheese and toss to combine. Add as much of the cooking water as needed to achieve a nice sauce consistency and serve.

cook's tip For a new version of classic vodka sauce, add a splash of brandy or Cognac to the ⅓ cup vodka, and substitute 2 tablespoons brandy or Cognac for the remaining 2 tablespoons vodka.

tagliatelle with crab

1 Make the sauce
Bring a large pot of water to a boil. In a large frying pan over medium heat, melt the butter with the oil. Add the leek and shallot and sauté until softened, about 7 minutes. Add the crabmeat and cook, stirring occasionally, until just warmed through, about 4 minutes. Add the wine and cook until the wine evaporates slightly, about 1 minute. Reduce the heat to medium-low and add the cream, half of the tarragon, and 1 teaspoon salt. Cook, stirring occasionally, until the sauce is warmed through, about 3 minutes. Do not let it boil. Remove from the heat.

2 Cook the pasta
Meanwhile, add 2 tablespoons salt and the pasta to the boiling water. Cook, stirring occasionally to prevent sticking, until al dente, according to the package directions. Drain, reserving about ½ cup (4 fl oz/125 ml) of the cooking water. Add the drained pasta to the sauce and toss to combine. Add as much of the cooking water as needed to achieve a nice coating consistency for the sauce. Sprinkle with the remaining tarragon, season to taste with pepper, and serve.

Unsalted butter, 4 tablespoons (2 oz/60 g)

Olive oil, 2 tablespoons

Leek, 1, white and pale green parts, halved, rinsed, and thinly sliced

Shallot, 1 large, minced

Fresh lump crabmeat, ¾ lb (375 g), picked over for shell fragments

Dry white wine, ½ cup (4 fl oz/125 ml)

Heavy (double) cream, 1 cup (8 fl oz/250 ml)

Fresh tarragon, 3 tablespoons minced

Salt and freshly ground white pepper

Tagliatelle or linguine, 1 lb (500 g)

MAKES 4 SERVINGS

pasta with roasted squash & bacon

Butternut or other winter squash, 2 lb (1 kg), peeled, seeded, and cut into small cubes

Yellow onion, 1 large, halved and thinly sliced

Thick-cut bacon, 4 strips, cut into ½-inch (12-mm) pieces

Olive oil, 2 tablespoons

Fresh sage, 1 tablespoon minced

Salt and freshly ground pepper

Rigatoni or other large pasta, 1 lb (500 g)

Parmesan cheese, ½ cup (2 oz/60 g) freshly grated, plus more for serving

MAKES 4 SERVINGS

1 Roast the squash and onions
Preheat the oven to 425°F (220°C). On a large rimmed baking sheet, toss the squash, onion, and bacon with the oil. Sprinkle with the sage and season with salt and pepper. Spread on the sheet in a single layer. Roast until the squash is deep golden brown and tender and the bacon is crisp, 15–20 minutes. Remove from the oven and set aside.

2 Cook the pasta
Meanwhile, bring a large pot of water to a boil. Add 2 tablespoons salt and the pasta to the boiling water. Cook, stirring occasionally to prevent sticking, until al dente, according to the package directions. Drain, reserving about ½ cup (4 fl oz/ 125 ml) of the cooking water. Return the pasta to the pot. Add the squash mixture and toss for 1 minute over high heat, adding as much of the cooking water as needed to achieve a nice coating consistency for the sauce. Add the ½ cup cheese, toss to combine, and serve. Pass additional cheese at the table.

pappardelle with shredded beef ragù

1 Cook the vegetables
In a large frying pan over medium heat, sauté the pancetta until browned, about 5 minutes. Using a slotted spoon, transfer the pancetta to a plate. Add the leeks and fennel to the pan and sauté until softened, about 5 minutes. Add the garlic and sauté until softened, about 1 minute.

2 Make the ragù
Add the brisket with sauce and the tomatoes to the pan with the vegetables. Raise the heat to high and bring to a gentle boil. Reduce the heat to medium and simmer, stirring occasionally, until the flavors are blended and the sauce is slightly reduced, about 10 minutes. Stir in the basil and cook for 1 minute longer. Stir in the reserved pancetta.

3 Cook the pasta
While the ragù is simmering, bring a large pot of water to a boil. Add 2 tablespoons salt and the pasta to the boiling water and cook, stirring occasionally to prevent sticking, until al dente, according to the package directions. Drain the pasta, add to the ragù, and toss to combine. Divide among shallow bowls and serve. Pass the cheese at the table.

Pancetta or thick-cut bacon, 2 oz (60 g), diced

Leeks, 2 large, white and pale green parts, halved, rinsed, and thinly sliced

Fennel bulb, 1 small, trimmed and chopped

Garlic, 2 cloves, minced

Braised Brisket (page 320), 2 cups (12 oz/375 g) shredded meat, plus 1 cup (8 fl oz/250 ml) sauce from brisket

Diced tomatoes, 1 can (14½ oz/455 g), with juice

Fresh basil, ¼ cup (⅓ oz/10 g) minced

Salt

Pappardelle or other wide egg noodles, ¾ lb (375 g)

Parmesan cheese, ½ cup (2 oz/60 g) freshly grated

MAKES 4 SERVINGS

spaghetti amatriciana

Olive oil, 2 tablespoons

Pancetta or thick-cut bacon, 3 oz (90 g), chopped

Yellow onion, 1 small, finely chopped

Red pepper flakes, 1 teaspoon

Dry white wine, ½ cup (4 fl oz/125 ml)

Tomato paste, 2 tablespoons

Canned whole plum (Roma) tomatoes, 2½ cups (20 fl oz/625 ml), chopped, with juice

Salt

Spaghetti, 1 lb (500 g)

Pecorino romano or Parmesan cheese, ½ cup (2 oz/60 g) freshly grated

MAKES 4 SERVINGS

1 Make the sauce
Bring a large pot of water to a boil. In a large frying pan over medium-low heat, warm the oil. Add the pancetta, onion, and red pepper flakes and sauté until the onion is softened and the pancetta is lightly browned, about 6 minutes. Stir in the wine and tomato paste. Reduce the heat to low and cook until the wine evaporates slightly, about 1 minute. Add the tomatoes and ½ teaspoon salt. Raise the heat to medium-low and simmer, stirring occasionally, until the sauce is thickened, about 20 minutes.

2 Cook the pasta
Meanwhile, add 2 tablespoons salt and the pasta to the boiling water. Cook, stirring occasionally to prevent sticking, until al dente, according to the package directions. Drain, reserving about ½ cup (4 fl oz/125 ml) of the cooking water. Add the drained pasta to the sauce and toss to combine. Sprinkle with one-third of the cheese and toss again. Add as much of the cooking water as needed to achieve a nice sauce consistency. Serve, passing the remaining cheese at the table.

three-cheese macaroni

1 Make the cheese sauce

Bring a large pot of water to a boil. In a small saucepan over medium heat, warm the milk until small bubbles begin to form around the edge of the pan. Remove from the heat. In a large saucepan over low heat, melt the butter. Add the flour, whisking to incorporate. Raise the heat to medium-low and cook the mixture, whisking constantly, until very lightly golden, 3–4 minutes. Gradually whisk in the hot milk. Cook, stirring frequently, until the mixture is thick and creamy, about 15 minutes. Add the Gruyère and Fontina cheeses, and the cayenne, if using. Season to taste with salt. Cook, stirring frequently, until the cheeses are melted, 2–3 minutes. Stir in the Parmesan cheese. Remove the sauce from the heat and set aside.

2 Cook the pasta

Meanwhile, add 2 tablespoons salt and the pasta to the boiling water. Cook, stirring occasionally to prevent sticking, until al dente, according to the package directions. Drain, reserving about ½ cup (4 fl oz/125 ml) of the cooking water. Add the drained pasta to the sauce and stir to combine. Add as much of the cooking water as needed to achieve a nice sauce consistency and serve. »

Milk, 3 cups (24 fl oz/ 750 ml)

Unsalted butter, 5 tablespoons (2½ oz/ 75 g)

Flour, 3 tablespoons

Gruyère cheese, ¾ cup (3 oz/90 g) shredded

Fontina cheese, ¾ cup (3 oz/90 g) shredded

Cayenne pepper, ¼ teaspoon (optional)

Salt

Parmesan cheese, ½ cup (2 oz/60 g) freshly grated

Macaroni, shells, or penne, 1 lb (500 g)

MAKES 4 SERVINGS

three-cheese macaroni variation

cook's tip

For a classic baked macaroni and cheese, preheat the oven
to 400°F (200°C). Increase the milk by ¼ cup (2 fl oz/60 ml).
Undercook the pasta by 2 minutes, drain, and add to the
sauce. Pour into a buttered baking dish. Sprinkle with
½ cup (1 oz/30 g) fresh bread crumbs (see tip, page 214),
and bake until golden brown, 10–12 minutes.

linguine with clams

1 Cook the clams
Bring a large pot of water to a boil. In a large frying pan over medium-low heat, warm the oil, garlic, and red pepper flakes until the garlic is fragrant, about 3 minutes. Discard any clams that fail to close to the touch. Add the clams to the pan along with the wine and 1 teaspoon salt and cover with a tight-fitting lid. Raise the heat to medium and cook, shaking the pan vigorously and often, until the clams open, about 10 minutes. Discard any empty shells and any unopened clams. Add the parsley. Remove from the heat.

2 Cook the pasta
Meanwhile, add 2 tablespoons salt and the pasta to the boiling water. Cook, stirring occasionally to prevent sticking, until al dente, according to the package directions. Drain, add the pasta to the clam mixture, and toss to combine. Warm briefly over low heat and serve.

cook's tip Medium-sized shrimp (prawns) can be substituted for the clams. Peel and devein 1½ lb (750 g) shrimp, leaving the tails intact. Cook the shrimp with the garlic until they turn opaque, about 3 minutes, then finish the recipe as directed.

Olive oil, ½ cup (4 fl oz/125 ml)

Garlic, 5 large cloves, minced

Red pepper flakes, ¼ teaspoon

Small clams such as littleneck or Manila, 3½ lb (1.75 kg), scrubbed

Dry white wine, ½ cup (4 fl oz/125 ml)

Salt

Fresh flat-leaf (Italian) parsley, ⅓ cup (½ oz/ 15 g) finely chopped

Linguine or spaghetti, 1 lb (500 g)

MAKES 4 SERVINGS

spaghetti & meatballs

Day-old coarse country bread, crusts removed, ¾ cup (¾ oz/20 g) cubed

Milk, ⅓ cup (3 fl oz/80 ml)

Ground (minced) beef, 1 lb (500 g)

Yellow onion, 1 small, shredded

Fresh flat-leaf (Italian) parsley, 2 tablespoons minced

Fresh thyme, 1 teaspoon minced

Egg, 1, beaten

Parmesan cheese, 1 cup (3 oz/90 g) freshly grated

Salt and freshly ground pepper

Olive oil for frying

Tomato-Basil Sauce (page 31) or purchased pasta sauce, 2½ cups (20 fl oz/625 ml)

Spaghetti, 1 lb (500 g)

MAKES 6 SERVINGS

1 Prepare the meatballs
In a small bowl, combine the bread and milk. Let stand for about 3 minutes, then squeeze the bread dry, discarding the milk. In a large bowl, combine the soaked bread, beef, onion, parsley, thyme, egg, ¼ cup (1 oz/30 g) of the cheese, 1 teaspoon salt, and ½ teaspoon pepper. Mix gently with your hands. Form the beef mixture into balls about 1 inch (2.5 cm) in diameter.

2 Cook the meatballs
In a large frying pan over medium heat, pour oil to a depth of ½ inch (12 mm). Add the meatballs and cook, turning occasionally, until browned on all sides, 10–12 minutes. Transfer to a plate lined with paper towels to drain. Discard the oil and place the pan over medium-low heat. Pour the tomato sauce into the pan, stirring and scraping up any browned bits from the pan bottom. Add the meatballs and cook, covered, for about 15 minutes.

3 Cook the pasta
Meanwhile, bring a large pot of water to a boil. Add 2 tablespoons salt and the pasta. Cook, stirring occasionally, until al dente, according to the package directions. Drain, add to the sauce, and toss to combine. Serve, passing the remaining cheese at the table.

vegetable rigatoni with goat cheese

1 Prepare the vegetables
Bring a large pot of water to a boil. In a large frying pan over medium heat, warm the oil. Add the garlic and sauté until fragrant, about 1 minute. Add the tomatoes and cook, stirring often, until they give off their juices, about 3 minutes. Add the chopped vegetables and cook, stirring frequently, until heated through, about 5 minutes. Season to taste with salt and pepper. Reduce the heat to low to keep warm.

2 Cook the pasta
Add 2 tablespoons salt and the pasta to the boiling water. Cook, stirring occasionally to prevent sticking, until al dente, according to the package directions. Drain, reserving about ½ cup (4 fl oz/125 ml) of the cooking water. Return the pasta to the pot. Add the vegetables, goat cheese, and basil and toss to combine. Add as much of the cooking water as needed to achieve a nice coating consistency for the sauce. Cook briefly over low heat to blend the flavors. Serve, passing the Parmesan cheese at the table.

cook's tip Any tube-shaped pasta, such as ziti or penne, can be served with this chunky, rustic sauce.

Olive oil, 3 tablespoons

Garlic, 2 cloves, minced

Cherry tomatoes, 1 lb (500 g), halved

Summer Vegetable Kebabs (page 205), 4 kebabs, vegetables removed and coarsely chopped

Salt and freshly ground pepper

Rigatoni, 1 lb (500 g)

Fresh goat cheese, 1 cup (4 oz/125 g) crumbled

Fresh basil, ¼ cup (⅓ oz/10 g) minced

Parmesan cheese, 1 cup (4 oz/125 g) freshly grated

MAKES 4–6 SERVINGS

pasta shells
with cauliflower

Salt

Cauliflower, 1 medium head, cut into florets then coarsely chopped

Olive oil, 8 tablespoons (4 fl oz/125 ml)

Garlic, 4 large cloves, minced

Green (spring) onions, 6–8, white and tender green parts, thinly sliced

Fresh marjoram, 2 teaspoons minced

Red pepper flakes, ½ teaspoon

Fresh flat-leaf (Italian) parsley, 3 tablespoons minced

Chicken or vegetable broth or stock, 2 cups (16 fl oz/ 500 ml), homemade (page 29 or 27) or purchased

Conchiglie or other small pasta shells, ¾ lb (375 g)

Fresh bread crumbs, ¼ cup (½ oz/15 g) (see tip, page 214)

MAKES 4 SERVINGS

1 Cook the cauliflower
Bring a large pot of water to a boil. Add 2 tablespoons salt and the cauliflower to the boiling water and cook until tender, about 7 minutes. Transfer the cauliflower to a colander to drain; set aside. Return the water to a boil.

2 Make the sauce
In a large frying pan over medium-low heat, warm 4 tablespoons of the oil. Add the garlic, green onions, marjoram, and red pepper flakes and sauté for about 4 minutes. Stir in the cooked cauliflower, parsley, and broth. Raise the heat to medium and cook, stirring, until the liquid is slightly reduced, about 12 minutes.

3 Cook the pasta
In a small frying pan over medium heat, warm the remaining 4 tablespoons oil. Add the bread crumbs and cook, stirring frequently, until golden, about 2 minutes. Meanwhile, add the pasta to the boiling water and cook, stirring occasionally, until al dente, according to the package directions. Drain, reserving about ½ cup (4 fl oz/125 ml) of the cooking water. Add the drained pasta to the sauce and toss. Add as much of the cooking water as needed to achieve a nice coating consistency for the sauce. Sprinkle the bread crumbs over the pasta and serve.

ziti with pesto & potatoes

1 Cook the potatoes

Add the potatoes to a saucepan with water to cover. Bring to a boil over high heat, reduce the heat to medium, and cook until tender, about 20 minutes. Drain and let cool. Peel the potatoes and cut into small cubes.

2 Cook the pasta and green beans

Meanwhile, bring a large pot of water to a boil. Add 2 tablespoons salt and the pasta. Cook, stirring occasionally to prevent sticking, until al dente, according to the package directions. Add the beans about 5 minutes before the pasta is ready.

3 Finish the dish

Drain the pasta and beans, reserving about ½ cup (4 fl oz/125 ml) of the cooking water. In a large serving bowl, mix a few tablespoons of the cooking water with the pesto. Add the potato cubes, drained pasta, and beans and toss to combine. Add as much of the remaining cooking water as needed to achieve a nice coating consistency for the sauce. Serve, passing the cheese at the table.

White boiling potatoes, 3, about 5 oz (155 g) total weight

Salt

Ziti, penne, or other tubular pasta ¾ lb (375 g)

Green beans, about ⅓ lb (5 oz/155 g), trimmed and cut crosswise into thirds

Basil Pesto (page 34) or purchased pesto, 1 cup (8 fl oz/250 ml)

Parmesan cheese, ½ cup (2 oz/60 g) freshly grated

MAKES 4 SERVINGS

stuffed cannelloni

Salt and freshly ground pepper

Cannelloni pasta, ½ lb (250 g)

Baby spinach, 1½ lb (750 g), coarsely chopped

Fresh ricotta cheese, 3 cups (1½ lb/750 g)

Egg yolks, 2, lightly beaten

Ground nutmeg, ¼ teaspoon

Parmesan cheese, 1 cup (4 oz/125 g) freshly grated

Bolognese Sauce (page 32) or purchased pasta sauce, 4 cups (32 fl oz/1 l)

MAKES 4–6 SERVINGS

1 Cook the pasta
Bring a large pot of water to a boil. Add 2 tablespoons salt and the pasta. Cook, stirring occasionally, until not quite al dente, about 2 minutes less than the package directions. Drain and rinse under cool running water.

2 Prepare the filling
Add the spinach and ½ cup (4 fl oz/ 125 ml) water to a large frying pan over medium heat. Cook, stirring frequently, until wilted, about 2 minutes. Drain, pressing on the spinach with the back of a large spoon to remove as much water as possible. In a large bowl, mix together the drained spinach, ricotta, egg yolks, nutmeg, ½ teaspoon salt, ¼ teaspoon pepper, and half of the Parmesan cheese.

3 Stuff and bake the cannelloni
Preheat the oven to 375°F (190°C). Coat the bottom of a 10-by-12-inch (25-by-30-cm) baking dish with a large spoonful of the sauce. Using a teaspoon, stuff the cannelloni with the spinach filling. Place the stuffed pasta in the dish and spoon the remaining sauce over the top. Sprinkle with the remaining Parmesan cheese and cover with aluminum foil. Bake for 15 minutes. Remove the foil and bake until bubbly, about 10 minutes longer. Let cool for 10–15 minutes before serving.

pasta with chickpeas

1 **Simmer the chickpeas**
In a large pot over medium-high heat, combine the chickpeas and broth. Bring to a boil, reduce the heat to low, and cook, partially covered, until the chickpeas are very tender, about 15 minutes. Remove 1 cup (7 oz/220 g) of the chickpeas and pass them through a potato ricer or purée in a food processor or blender. Return to the pot and stir to blend.

2 **Cook the pasta and serve**
In a frying pan over medium-low heat, warm the 3 tablespoons oil. Add the pancetta and sauté until lightly browned, about 3 minutes. Stir in the onion, garlic, and sage and sauté until the vegetables are softened, about 2 minutes. Add the tomato paste and ½ cup (4 fl oz/125 ml) of the chickpea broth and stir to combine. Add the mixture in the frying pan to the pot with the chickpeas. Bring to a gentle boil over medium heat and cook for about 10 minutes. Add the pasta and cook, stirring frequently, until al dente, according to the package directions. Season to taste with salt and pepper. Ladle into bowls, drizzle with olive oil, sprinkle with the parsley, and serve. »

Canned chickpeas (garbanzo beans), 4 cups (28 oz/875 g), drained and rinsed

Chicken broth or stock, 8 cups (64 fl oz/2 l), homemade (page 29) or purchased

Olive oil, 3 tablespoons, plus more for drizzling

Pancetta or thick-cut bacon, 3 oz (90 g), chopped

Yellow onion, 1, chopped

Garlic, 3 large cloves, minced

Fresh sage or rosemary, 1 tablespoon minced

Tomato paste, 2 tablespoons

Ditali or other small soup pasta, ¼ lb (125 g)

Salt and freshly ground pepper

Fresh flat-leaf (Italian) parsley, 3 tablespoons chopped

MAKES 4 SERVINGS

cook's tip

In a simple, rustic dish such as this one,
it is important to use the best ingredients.
Look for premium extra-virgin olive oil
with a greenish tint and peppery kick for
drizzling on the soup.

creamy mushroom stroganoff

1 Make the sauce
Bring a large pot of water to a boil. In a large frying pan over medium-high heat, melt the butter. Add the shallot and sauté until lightly golden, 2–3 minutes. Add the mushrooms and cook, stirring, until they have softened and released most of their liquid, about 5 minutes. Add the flour and stir to incorporate. Stir in the wine and the broth and cook until the wine evaporates slightly, about 2 minutes. Remove from the heat and stir in the sour cream and the 2 tablespoons parsley. Season with salt and pepper.

2 Cook the pasta
Add 2 tablespoons salt and the noodles to the boiling water. Cook, stirring occasionally to prevent sticking, until al dente, according to the package directions. Drain, reserving about ½ cup (4 fl oz/125 ml) of the cooking water. Add the pasta to the mushroom sauce and toss to combine. Warm briefly over low heat to blend the flavors. Add as much of the cooking water as needed to achieve a nice sauce consistency. Garnish with parsley and serve.

Unsalted butter,
6 tablespoons (3 oz/90 g)

Shallot, 1 large, thinly sliced

Mixed mushrooms, such as stemmed shiitake, oyster, and cremini, 2 lb (1 kg), thinly sliced

Flour, 2 tablespoons

Dry white wine, 1 cup (8 fl oz/250 ml)

Chicken or vegetable broth or stock, 1 cup (8 fl oz/250 ml), homemade (page 29 or 27) or purchased

Sour cream, ½ cup (4 oz/125 g)

Fresh flat-leaf (Italian) parsley, 2 tablespoons minced, plus more for garnish

Salt and freshly ground pepper

Wide egg noodles or pappardelle, 1 lb (500 g)

MAKES 4 SERVINGS

sausage lasagna

Olive oil, 1 tablespoon

Sweet Italian sausage, 1½ lb (750 g), casings removed and meat crumbled

Fresh ricotta cheese, 2 cups (1 lb/500 g)

Milk, ¼ cup (2 fl oz/ 60 ml)

Nutmeg, ⅛ teaspoon freshly grated

Tomato-Basil Sauce (page 31) or purchased pasta sauce, 2½ cups (20 fl oz/625 ml)

No-cook lasagna noodles, 1 lb (500 g)

Mozzarella cheese, ½ lb (250 g), shredded

Parmesan cheese, ½ cup (2 oz/60 g) freshly grated

MAKES 6 SERVINGS

1 Cook the sausage
Preheat the oven to 400°F (200°C). In a frying pan over medium heat, warm the oil. Add the sausage and sauté until browned, about 10 minutes.

2 Assemble the lasagna
In a bowl, stir together the ricotta, milk, and nutmeg. Spread about ¼ cup (2 fl oz/60 ml) of the tomato sauce on the bottom of a 10-by-12-by-2-inch (25-by-30-by-5-cm) baking dish. Cover with a single layer of noodles without overlapping them. Spread with one-third of the remaining sauce, half of the ricotta mixture, and one-third of the sausage. Add another layer of noodles, half of the sauce, the remaining ricotta mixture, and half of the sausage. Top with another layer of noodles and the remaining sauce and sausage. Top evenly with the mozzarella and Parmesan cheeses.

3 Bake the lasagna
Cover the dish with aluminum foil and bake for 45 minutes. Uncover and bake until the cheese is golden and bubbly, about 10 minutes. Let stand for 10 minutes. Cut into squares and serve.

baked rigatoni with ricotta & sausage

1 Prepare the sauce
Preheat the oven to 350°F (180°C) and lightly oil a deep 2½-quart (2.5-l) baking dish. Bring a large pot of water to a boil. In a large frying pan over medium-high heat, warm the oil. Add the sausage and sauté, breaking up the sausage with a spoon, until browned, about 6 minutes. Drain any excess fat from the pan. Stir in the tomato sauce and olives, season to taste with salt and pepper, and set aside.

2 Cook the pasta
Add 2 tablespoons salt and the pasta to the boiling water. Cook, stirring occasionally to prevent sticking, until the pasta is not quite al dente, about 2 minutes less than the package directions. Drain, rinse under cold running water, and drain again.

3 Bake the pasta
Return the pasta to the cooking pot and gently stir in the tomato-sausage mixture and ricotta cheese. Spread the pasta and sauce in the prepared dish and sprinkle with the Parmesan cheese. Bake until golden and bubbly, about 25 minutes. Let cool for 5 minutes and serve.

Olive oil, 2 tablespoons

Italian sausage, 1 lb (500 g), casings removed

Roasted Tomato Sauce (page 33) or purchased pasta sauce, 3 cups (24 fl oz/750 ml)

Pitted black Mediterranean olives, 1 cup (5 oz/155 g) coarsely chopped

Salt and freshly ground pepper

Rigatoni, 1 lb (500 g)

Fresh ricotta cheese, 1¾ cups (15 oz/470 g)

Parmesan cheese, ¼ cup (1 oz/30 g) freshly grated

MAKES 4–6 SERVINGS

shanghai noodles with pork

Fresh Chinese egg noodles, 1 lb (500 g)

Canola or peanut oil, 5 tablespoons (2½ fl oz/75 ml)

Soy sauce, ¼ cup (2 fl oz/60 ml)

Worcestershire sauce, 3 tablespoons

Rice vinegar, 2 tablespoons

Sugar, 1 teaspoon

Freshly ground white pepper

Boneless pork loin, ½ lb (250 g), cut across the grain into thin strips

Yellow onion, 1, thinly sliced

Red bell peppers (capsicums), 2, seeded and thinly sliced crosswise

Garlic, 2 cloves, minced

Napa cabbage, ½ head, finely shredded

MAKES 4 SERVINGS

1 Parboil the noodles
Bring a large pot of water to a boil. Separate the noodles, drop into the boiling water, and boil for 2 minutes. Drain and rinse with cold running water. Place in a bowl, add 1 tablespoon of the oil, and toss to coat evenly.

2 Make the sauce
In a small bowl, stir together ⅓ cup (3 fl oz/80 ml) warm water and the soy sauce, Worcestershire sauce, vinegar, sugar, and a pinch of pepper.

3 Stir-fry the pork and noodles
Heat a wok or large nonstick frying pan over high heat until very hot and add 2 tablespoons of the oil. Add the pork and stir-fry just until browned, 2–3 minutes. Using a slotted spoon, transfer the pork to a bowl. Return the pan to high heat and add the remaining 2 tablespoons oil. Add the onion and bell peppers and stir-fry just until tender, about 5 minutes. Add the garlic and cabbage and stir-fry until the cabbage begins to wilt, about 3 minutes. Add the sauce and bring to a boil. Stir in the noodles and pork and mix well. Cover, reduce the heat to low, and cook, stirring once or twice, until the noodles have absorbed the sauce, about 10 minutes. Transfer to bowls and serve.

shrimp pad thai

1 Cook the noodles and sprouts
Bring a large saucepan of water to a boil. Add the noodles, turn off the heat, and let stand, stirring occasionally, until soft, about 10 minutes. Stir in the bean sprouts. Drain the noodles and sprouts.

2 Stir-fry the shrimp
Meanwhile, in a small bowl, combine the ketchup, black bean sauce, chile sauce, and fish sauce. In a wok or deep frying pan over medium heat, warm the oil. Add the minced onions and ginger and stir-fry until fragrant, about 30 seconds. Add the shrimp and stir-fry until opaque throughout, 1–2 minutes.

3 Finish the dish
Add the ketchup mixture to the wok. Pour the egg into the middle of the sauce and stir just until cooked. Immediately add the noodles and sprouts, toss to coat evenly with the sauce, and cook until heated through, about 2 minutes. Taste and adjust the seasoning with ketchup or chile sauce. Transfer to a platter. Garnish with the sliced onions and the peanuts and serve. Pass the lime wedges at the table, if using.

Medium rice noodles, 10 oz (315 g)

Bean sprouts, 2 cups (8 oz/250 g)

Ketchup, ⅓ cup (3 fl oz/ 80 ml), plus more for seasoning

Black bean sauce, scant 1 tablespoon

Chile sauce such as Sriracha, 1 teaspoon, plus more for seasoning

Asian fish sauce, 3 tablespoons

Peanut or canola oil, 1 tablespoon

Green (spring) onions, 3, white parts minced and green tops thinly sliced

Fresh ginger, 1 tablespoon minced

Shrimp (prawns), ⅓ lb (155 g), peeled, deveined, and halved lengthwise

Egg, 1, lightly beaten

Dry-roasted peanuts, 2 tablespoons chopped

Lime, 1, cut into wedges (optional)

MAKES 4 SERVINGS

creamy polenta with asparagus

Mascarpone cheese,
⅔ cup (6 oz/185 g), at
room temperature

Lemon zest, from
1 lemon, finely grated

Asparagus, 1½ lb (750 g),
tough ends removed

Olive oil, 1 tablespoon

**Salt and freshly ground
pepper**

Milk, 2 cups
(16 fl oz/500 ml)

Instant polenta, 1 cup
(7 oz/220 g)

Parmesan cheese, ½ cup
(2 oz/60 g) freshly shaved
shards

MAKES 4 SERVINGS

1 **Cook the asparagus**
Preheat the broiler (grill). In a small
bowl, mix together the mascarpone and
lemon zest; set aside. Place the asparagus
on a rimmed baking sheet, lightly toss with
the oil, and season with salt and pepper.
Broil (grill) until tender-crisp and slightly
charred, about 6 minutes. Transfer the
asparagus to a platter and cover with
aluminum foil to keep warm.

2 **Cook the polenta**
In a saucepan over high heat,
bring 1½ cups (12 fl oz/375 ml) of the
milk and 1½ cups water to a boil and add
1 teaspoon salt. Whisk in the polenta.
Reduce the heat to low and cook, whisking
occasionally, until the polenta is thick and
smooth, 3–5 minutes. Whisk the remaining
½ cup (4 fl oz/125 ml) milk into the polenta.
Spoon into shallow bowls and top with
the asparagus. Top with a dollop of the
mascarpone, sprinkle with the Parmesan
cheese, and serve.

grilled polenta with sausage

1 Cook the polenta
In a saucepan over high heat, bring the milk and 1½ cups (12 fl oz/375 ml) water to a boil and add 1 teaspoon salt. Whisk in the polenta. Reduce the heat to low and cook, whisking, until the polenta is thick and smooth, 3–5 minutes. Spread the polenta into an oiled 9-inch (23-cm) round baking pan. Set aside to cool.

2 Cook the broccoli and sausage
In a large saucepan over medium-high heat, warm 1 tablespoon of the oil. Add the sausages and sauté until browned, about 5 minutes. Add the garlic and cook for about 1 minute. Add the broccoli rabe and broth and bring to a boil. Reduce the heat to medium-low, cover, and simmer, stirring occasionally, until the broccoli rabe is tender-crisp, about 10 minutes. Add the red pepper flakes and season with salt.

3 Grill the polenta
Prepare a grill for direct grilling over medium-high heat and lightly oil the grill rack. Or, preheat a grill pan over medium-high heat. Turn the polenta out onto a cutting board, cut into 8 wedges, and brush with the remaining 1 tablespoon oil. Place on the grill rack or grill pan and cook, turning once, until heated through, about 5 minutes. Arrange on plates with the sausage and broccoli rabe and serve. **»**

Milk, 2 cups
(16 fl oz/500 ml)

Salt

Instant polenta, 1 cup
(7 oz/220 g)

Olive oil, 2 tablespoons

Italian sausages, 1 lb
(500 g), casings removed
and meat crumbled

Garlic, 2 cloves, minced

Broccoli rabe, 2 lb (1 kg),
coarsely chopped

Chicken broth, ½ cup
(4 fl oz/125 ml)

Red pepper flakes,
¼ teaspoon

MAKES 4 SERVINGS

cook's tip

If you cannot find broccoli rabe, you can use chopped kale, Swiss chard, or other hearty greens instead. Wash thoroughly to remove any grit, remove the stems, and coarsely chop.

farro with tomatoes & mozzarella

1 Soak the farro
Place the farro in a bowl with 3 cups (24 fl oz/750 ml) water and let stand at room temperature for 2 hours.

2 Simmer the farro
Drain the farro and place in a saucepan. Add the broth and bring to a boil over medium-high heat, then reduce the heat to medium-low, cover, and simmer until the farro is tender, about 30 minutes. Let stand, covered, for 10 minutes. Transfer to a bowl and let cool to room temperature.

3 Assemble the salad
Add the tomatoes and cheese to the farro. In a small bowl, whisk together the vinegars, 1 teaspoon salt, and ⅛ teaspoon pepper. Whisk in the oil until smooth. Pour over the salad, add the basil, and toss with a fork. Spoon into bowls and serve.

Farro, ¾ cup (4 oz/125 g)

Vegetable broth or stock, 2½ cups (20 fl oz/625 ml), homemade (page 27) or purchased

Plum (Roma) tomatoes, 2 large, halved lengthwise, seeded, and coarsely chopped

Fresh mozzarella cheese balls (*bocconcini*), ¼ lb (125 g), halved

Balsamic vinegar, 2 teaspoons

Red wine vinegar, 2 teaspoons

Salt and freshly ground pepper

Olive oil, 1 tablespoon

Fresh basil, 8 large leaves, cut into thin strips

MAKES 4 SERVINGS

cook's tip Farro is an Italian variety of the grain known as spelt. Look for it in specialty-food stores or Italian markets. You can also use barley in place of farro. Cook it according to the package directions.

greek bulgur salad

Bulgur, 1 cup (6 oz/185 g)

Fresh lemon juice,
2 tablespoons

Olive oil, 1 tablespoon

Garlic, 1 small clove,
minced

**Salt and freshly ground
pepper**

Fresh mint, ¾ cup
(1 oz/30 g) minced

Cherry tomatoes, 2 cups
(12 oz/375 g) halved

Cucumber, 1 small,
peeled, seeded, and
cubed

Romaine (cos) lettuce,
4 large leaves

MAKES 4 SERVINGS

1 Prepare the bulgur
Bring 3 cups (24 fl oz/750 ml) water
to a boil. Place the bulgur in a heatproof
bowl, pour in the boiling water, and set
aside until the bulgur is soft, about
20 minutes. Drain through a fine-mesh
sieve and return to the bowl. Add the
lemon juice, oil, garlic, ½ teaspoon salt,
and ⅛ teaspoon pepper, and stir well.
Stir in the mint, tomatoes, and cucumber.

2 Assemble the salad
Line a platter with the lettuce leaves.
Mound the bulgur salad on top and serve.

cook's tip For a heartier salad,
mix 1 cup (5 oz/155 g) crumbled feta
cheese into the bulgur and serve
with toasted pita bread.

chicken couscous

1 **Cook the vegetables**
Grate 1½ teaspoons zest from the lemons and squeeze ⅓ cup (2 fl oz/60 ml) juice. In a large saucepan over medium heat, warm 3 tablespoons of the oil. Add the onion and sauté until softened, about 4 minutes. Add the garlic and sauté for 1–2 minutes. Stir in the cumin and cinnamon, and then mix in the chicken, lemon zest and juice, dried fruits, and broth. Bring to a boil, reduce the heat to medium-low, cover, and simmer for 5 minutes to blend the flavors.

2 **Cook the couscous and serve**
Stir in the couscous, re-cover the pan, and remove from the heat. Let stand until the liquid is absorbed and the couscous is softened, about 5 minutes. Add the cilantro and toss with a fork. Garnish with the almonds and serve.

> **cook's tip** This one-dish meal is perfect for a picnic or potluck: it is easily transported and it tastes great at room temperature. If making the dish ahead, try to keep it refrigerated until about 1 hour before serving.

Lemons, 2

Olive oil, 4 tablespoons (2 fl oz/60 ml)

Yellow onion, 1 small, chopped

Garlic, 3 cloves, minced

Ground cumin, 1½ teaspoons

Ground cinnamon, ¾ teaspoon

Classic Roast Chicken (page 267) or rotisserie chicken, 2 cups (12 oz/ 375 g) shredded meat

Mixed dried fruits such as pitted dates and apricots, 1 cup (6 oz/ 185 g) chopped

Chicken broth or stock, 3 cups (24 fl oz/750 ml), homemade (page 29) or purchased

Instant couscous, 2 cups (6 oz/185 g)

Fresh cilantro (fresh coriander), ¼ cup (⅓ oz/10 g) minced

Sliced (flaked) almonds, ½ cup (2 oz/60 g), toasted

MAKES 4 SERVINGS

mushroom risotto

Dried porcini mushrooms, about 2 tablespoons, rinsed

Vegetable broth or stock, 5½ cups (44 fl oz/ 1.35 l), homemade (page 27) or purchased

Dry white wine, 1 cup (8 fl oz/250 ml)

Unsalted butter, 1 tablespoon

Olive oil, 1 tablespoon

Yellow onion, 1 small, finely chopped

Arborio rice, 2 cups (14 oz/440 g)

Frozen peas, 1 cup (5 oz/155 g)

Parmesan cheese, ½ cup (2 oz/60 g) freshly grated, plus shavings for garnish

Salt and freshly ground pepper

MAKES 4 SERVINGS

1 Prepare the mushrooms
Place the mushrooms in a small heatproof bowl. Add ⅓ cup (3 fl oz/ 80 ml) hot water and let stand until the mushrooms are soft, about 20 minutes. Drain and finely chop.

2 Cook the rice
Meanwhile, in a saucepan over medium heat, bring the broth and wine to a gentle simmer and maintain over low heat. In a heavy-bottomed saucepan over medium heat, melt the butter with the oil. Add the onion and sauté until softened, about 4 minutes. Add the rice and cook, stirring, until the grains are well coated, about 1 minute. Add 2 cups (16 fl oz/ 500 ml) of the simmering broth and cook, stirring, until the liquid is absorbed, 3–4 minutes. Reduce the heat to medium-low and continue to add the broth 1 cup (8 fl oz/250 ml) at a time, stirring occasionally, and adding more only after the previous addition has been absorbed.

3 Finish the risotto
When the rice is tender and creamy but still al dente, after about 20 minutes, stir in the mushrooms and peas and cook for 2 minutes. Stir in the ½ cup cheese. Season to taste with salt and pepper, garnish with the shaved cheese, and serve.

crab & lemon risotto

1 **Heat the broth**
In a saucepan over medium-low heat, bring the broth, onion tops, and 2 cups (16 fl oz/500 ml) water to a gentle simmer and maintain over low heat.

2 **Cook the rice**
In a large frying pan over medium-low heat, warm the oil and minced onions. Add the rice and cook, stirring, until the grains are well coated, about 1 minute. Strain the broth mixture over the rice, discarding the onion tops. Season the rice with ¼ teaspoon salt and cook at an active simmer, stirring every few minutes, until the liquid is nearly absorbed, about 20 minutes. Meanwhile, return the saucepan to low heat, add 1 cup (8 fl oz/250 ml) water, and bring to a gentle simmer. The rice should be tender and creamy but still firm to the bite. If it is still underdone, add ½ cup (4 fl oz/125 ml) of the simmering water and cook for 3–4 minutes longer.

3 **Finish the risotto**
Gently stir in the crabmeat, lemon zest and juice, and ½ cup of the simmering water. Cook until the liquid is nearly absorbed. Stir in the butter, season to taste with salt, and serve.

Chicken broth or stock, 2 cups (16 fl oz/500 ml), homemade (page 29) or purchased

Green (spring) onions, 2, white and pale green parts minced and dark green tops reserved

Olive oil, 2 tablespoons

Arborio rice, 2 cups (14 oz/440 g)

Salt

Fresh lump crabmeat, ½ lb (250 g), picked over for shell fragments

Finely grated lemon zest and juice, from 2 lemons

Unsalted butter, 1 tablespoon

MAKES 4 SERVINGS

wild rice salad

Wild rice, ¾ cup (4½ oz/ 140 g)

Salt and freshly ground pepper

Celery, 1 large stalk, chopped

Dried cranberries, ⅓ cup (2 oz/60 g)

Walnuts, ⅓ cup (2½ oz/75 g) lightly toasted and chopped

Oranges, 1–2, preferably navel, peeled, sectioned, and chopped (see cook's tip)

Fresh orange juice, ¼ cup (2 fl oz/60 ml)

Walnut or canola oil, 1 tablespoon

Pomegranate seeds, ¼ cup (1 oz/30 g) (optional)

MAKES 4 SERVINGS

1 Cook the rice
In a large saucepan, combine the rice, 3 cups (24 fl oz/750 ml) water, and ½ teaspoon salt. Bring to a boil over medium-high heat. Reduce the heat to medium-low, cover, and simmer until the rice is just tender, about 40 minutes. Drain and place in a bowl.

2 Assemble the salad
Add the celery, cranberries, walnuts, chopped oranges, and orange juice to the rice. Add the oil and stir with a fork to combine. Season to taste with salt and pepper. Spoon the salad into a serving bowl. Sprinkle with the pomegranate seeds, if using, and serve.

cook's tip To peel and section an orange, cut a thin slice off the top and bottom. Set the orange on one end on a cutting board. Working from top to bottom, slice off the peel in vertical strips, also cutting away the white pith. Holding the orange over a bowl to collect the juice, slide the knife down the membrane on either side of each section, and let the section drop into the bowl.

pasta & grains made easy

Having a collection of easy pasta and grain recipes on hand is a good starting point for getting dinner on the table quickly, especially during the week when time is limited. With a well-stocked kitchen, you'll be able to whip up a wonderful pasta meal in record time any night of the week.

PASTA SHAPES

Bucatini long, hollow strands

Capellini thin, long strands

Conchiglie shells

Ditali little thimbles

Ditalini tiny thimbles

Farfalle bow ties or butterflies

Fettuccine long ribbons

Fusilli twists

Gemelli twisted spiral tubes

Lasagna wide, flat noodles

Linguine long, flat strands

Macaroni elbows

Orecchiette little ears

Orzo barley-shaped pasta

Pappardelle long, wide ribbons

Penne tubes

Rigatoni large, grooved tubes

Spaghetti long, round strands

Spaghettini long, thin strands

Tagliatelle long, thin ribbons

Ziti long tubes

Stock your pantry Pasta and grain dishes are especially useful for the busy cook because many can be made with pantry ingredients like garlic, olive oil, and canned tomatoes or tomato paste.

- STOCK A SELECTION OF PASTA SHAPES Add variety to your menus by stocking pasta types that work with different types of sauces and soups, such as short, stubby shapes; ribbon and strand varieties; and soup pasta. The flavor and texture of imported Italian dried pasta are superior. The pasta has an elasticity that allows it to stand up to cooking without becoming mushy. Good-quality pasta is a sunny color with tiny specks of wheat visible. Couscous is another versatile meal element that looks and acts like a grain but is actually a form of pasta. Instant couscous, which cooks in about 5 minutes, makes an easy meal or hearty side dish.

- STOCK A SELECTION OF RICES A mix of rices can add welcome variety to your meals: choose brown and white rice, which are available in short-grain and long-grain versions. Wild rice, actually the seed of an aquatic grass, is another good option. For risotto, you'll want medium-grain Arborio rice. Some long-grain rice varieties have distinct fragrances and flavors, such as jasmine rice and basmati, favored for Thai and Indian food, respectively.

- GO WHOLE GRAIN Check the aisles and bulk food bins at your local supermarket for whole-grain alternatives to your usual starchy side dishes. Polenta, the Italian form of boiled cornmeal, is available in instant or precooked forms that shave time off your meal preparation. Instant polenta can be boiled and topped with vegetables or meat, and precooked polenta can be sliced and grilled. Barley is nutty and chewy; it is a nice change from rice and a good addition to soups. Bulgur wheat can be added to many salads beyond tabbouleh, and farro, another form of wheat, lets you bring a taste of Tuscany to your dinner table in the form of hearty salads and side dishes.

dos and don'ts of perfect pasta

Cooking and serving perfect pasta every time is fast and easy if you follow these ten simple rules of preparation.

DO use the finest-quality Italian dried pasta Find a good source, then purchase a few different shapes.

DO boil pasta in plenty of water To cook 1 lb (500 g) of pasta, fill a large pot no more than three-fourths full with about 5 qt (5 l) water. Cook pasta just before serving, never in advance.

DON'T add oil to the water Contrary to popular belief, adding oil to the cooking water does not keep the pasta from sticking. Instead, it coats the pasta, preventing the sauce from clinging to it.

DO add plenty of salt to the water Once the water is boiling, add about 2 tablespoons kosher salt along with the pasta.

DO stir from the outset Start stirring the pasta with a long spoon as soon as you drop it into the water and continue to stir occasionally to prevent it from sticking together.

DON'T overcook the pasta Use the package directions as a guide to cooking time, but check the pasta once or twice before the time has elapsed. It should be tender yet still slightly firm at the center (this is known as al dente).

DO save some cooking water Many recipes call for reserving about ½ cup (4 fl oz/125 ml) of the cooking water. Some sauces require more cooking water to thin them and keep the pasta moist.

DO drain the pasta immediately to prevent overcooking Never rinse the drained pasta with water, or you'll remove some of the starch that helps the sauce adhere.

DO sauce the pasta just after draining If the sauce is hot, add the drained pasta directly to the sauce and toss or stir over low heat for a few seconds, just until the pasta is coated.

DON'T let the pasta cool off To keep pasta from cooling once it is served, warm the individual plates or shallow bowls for a few minutes in a 200°F (95°C) oven.

MATCHING SAUCES & PASTAS

While most pasta shapes can be used with most sauces, here is a general pairing guide.

Butter sauces conchiglie, farfalle, tagliatelle

Cheese sauces bucatini, conchiglie, farfalle, fusilli, gemelli, macaroni

Cream sauces gemelli, pappardelle, penne, tagliatelle

Oil-based sauces capellini, farfalle, spaghetti, spaghettini

Pesto bucatini, linguine, penne

Ragù & meat sauces bucatini, conchiglie, fettuccine, fusilli, gemelli, linguine, orecchiette, pappardelle, penne, rigatoni, spaghetti, ziti

Seafood sauces linguine, spaghetti, spaghettini

Tomato sauces conchiglie, farfalle, linguine, penne, spaghetti, spaghettini, tagliatelle

Vegetable sauces cavatelli, gemelli, orecchiette, penne, rigatoni, ziti

Baked pastas cannelloni, lasagna, penne, rigatoni, ziti

Broths & soups small pasta shapes such as ditali, ditalini, orzo, tubetti

cooking rice & risotto

Grains are essential to many cuisines around the world. Both a variety of rices and risotto make excellent side dishes as well as substantial main dishes. Using the proportions here, you can cook rice dishes as accompaniments and also pair them with a vegetable or salad to make a complete meal.

Rice A staple in Asian cooking, long-grain rice such as jasmine and basmati cooks up to a dry, light texture, while medium- and short-grain rices are softer and moister. If you eat a lot of rice, consider investing in a rice cooker (see page 10), which cooks steamed rice conveniently and consistently.

The exact ratio of water to rice varies with different types of rice, but here are general directions for cooking rice on the stove top: For 3 cups (15 oz/470 g) cooked rice, place 1 cup (7 oz/220 g) rice in a fine-mesh sieve and rinse until the water runs clear. Transfer the rice to a heavy saucepan and add 1½ cups (12 fl oz/375 ml) water. Bring to a boil, give the rice a quick stir, reduce the heat to low, cover, and cook, undisturbed, for 20 minutes. Let rest, covered, off the heat for 10 minutes, then fluff before serving. Cook twice as much rice as you need and refrigerate the extra for up to 2 days. Leftover rice can be used in a variety of dishes from soups to fried-rice to rice pudding.

NOTE: Brown and wild rice cook the same way as regular rice, but with a water-to-rice ratio of about 3-to-1 for wild rice and a longer simmering time (about 40 minutes) for both brown and wild rice.

Risotto Good risotto requires a particular kind of starchy rice. The Arborio variety is most widely available because it was the first Italian rice exported on a large scale. Risotto is prepared by adding hot liquid (usually broth) a little at a time and stirring often as the rice slowly simmers. This breaks down the outer layer of the rice and slowly releases its starch, thickening the cooking liquid and giving the dish its characteristic creaminess. The liquid-to-rice ratio depends on the desired consistency, but is usually about 3-to-1. Do not rinse the rice before cooking risotto as this causes the starch to begin releasing too soon. Most of the flavoring ingredients for risotto are added toward the end of cooking, so rice for risotto may be cooked ahead of time and finished over the stove just before serving.

"In Minutes" meals include easy recipes and accompaniments that can be put together quickly. "Fit for Company" meals include ideas for stress-free get-togethers, complete with a wine suggestion.

IN MINUTES

Spaghetti Carbonara (page 157)

roasted asparagus

garlic crostini

——

Three-Cheese Macaroni (page 169)

grilled chicken sausages and zucchini (courgettes)

——

Linguine with Clams (page 171)

mixed salad greens with citrus vinaigrette

crusty bread

——

Ziti with Pesto & Potatoes (page 175)

pan-seared salmon fillets with lemon wedges

——

Baked Rigatoni with Ricotta & Sausage (page 181)

mixed salad greens with balsamic vinaigrette

——

Grilled Polenta with Sausage (page 185)

sliced tomatoes with sea salt

FIT FOR COMPANY

Pasta with Hearty Beef Ragù (page 158)

braised greens with balsamic vinegar

Syrah or Zinfandel

——

Pasta with Brown Butter & Asparagus (page 160)

grilled flank steak

Zinfandel

——

Tagliatelle with Crab (page 165)

butter lettuce and grapefruit salad

Sauvignon Blanc

——

Shrimp Pad Thai (page 183)

sautéed green beans with red pepper flakes and Thai basil

steamed rice

Riesling or Pinot Gris

——

Mushroom Risotto (page 190)

arugula (rocket) and Parmesan salad with red wine vinaigrette

Pinot Noir

With a little planning and a well-organized kitchen, you can become a smarter cook who regularly turns out delicious pasta and grain-based dishes with ease and speed.

Pasta and grains are versatile Think of pasta and grains as healthy and delicious foundations for many flavor combinations, from sautéed vegetables and simmered seafood to spicy tomato sauces and hearty meat ragùs. For variety, alternate serving meat- or vegetable-based pasta sauces with creamy pastas, and don't forget that both pasta and grains are great additions to soups.

Pasta can be a first course or a main course Serve a pasta dish as a first course before meat or fish in the traditional Italian way, or offer it as a main course accompanied by a salad or vegetables for a lighter meal (see pages 16–17).

Plan seasonally Choose recipes that call for the fresh produce and other ingredients of the season. Plan dishes that match the weather: robust meat sauces and baked pasta dishes in the cool months, pesto or light vegetable and herb sauces using fresh tomatoes in summer.

vegetables

spring vegetable stir-fry

1 Parboil the vegetables
Bring a large pot of water to a boil. Add the asparagus and sugar snap peas and cook for 2 minutes. Add the frozen peas and cook for 10 seconds. Drain and rinse under cold running water.

2 Make the sauce
In a small bowl, combine ¼ cup (2 fl oz/60 ml) water and the hoisin sauce, soy sauce, vinegar, sesame oil, and cornstarch. Stir to dissolve the cornstarch.

3 Stir-fry the vegetables
Heat a wok or large frying pan over high heat until hot and add 1 tablespoon of the canola oil. Add the leek and ginger and stir-fry until the leek is tender, about 2 minutes. Add the remaining 1 tablespoon canola oil, stir in the asparagus, sugar snap peas, and peas, and stir-fry until heated through, about 2 minutes. Give the sauce a quick stir, add to the pan, and stir until thickened, about 1 minute. Serve with the rice.

cook's tip To remove the tough ends of asparagus, hold each spear near both ends and bend it until it snaps. Discard the woody base.

Asparagus, ½ lb (250 g), tough ends removed and cut into bite-sized pieces

Sugar snap peas, ½ lb (250 g), trimmed

Frozen petite peas, 1 cup (5 oz/155 g)

Hoisin sauce, 1 tablespoon

Soy sauce, 1 tablespoon

Rice vinegar, 1 tablespoon

Asian sesame oil, 1 teaspoon

Cornstarch (cornflour), ½ teaspoon

Canola or peanut oil, 2 tablespoons

Leek, 1, white part only, halved, rinsed, and thinly sliced

Fresh ginger, 1 tablespoon minced

Steamed rice, for serving

MAKES 4 SERVINGS

artichokes
with lemon aioli

Lemon, 1

Baby artichokes, 14

Salt and freshly ground pepper

Olive oil, ¼ cup
(2 fl oz/60 ml)

Mayonnaise, ⅔ cup
(5 fl oz/160 ml)

Garlic, 1 clove, minced

MAKES 6–8 SERVINGS

1 Trim the artichokes
Grate 1 teaspoon zest from the lemon. Halve the lemon and squeeze 2 teaspoons juice from one half. Reserve both lemon halves. Snap off the tough outer leaves from each artichoke and trim the spiny tops and the stem. Remove any fibrous portions around the base. Halve the artichokes. As you work, rub all the cut areas with the lemon halves.

2 Cook the artichokes
Bring a large pot of lightly salted water to a boil. Add the 2 lemon halves and the artichokes, reduce the heat to medium, and simmer until the artichoke bases are tender, about 6 minutes. Drain and rinse under cold running water. Discard the lemon halves. Preheat a grill pan over medium heat. In a bowl, toss the artichokes with the olive oil until evenly coated. Season with salt and pepper and toss again. Cook the artichokes, turning occasionally, until grill marks appear, about 10 minutes.

3 Make the aioli
Meanwhile, in a bowl, whisk together the mayonnaise, garlic, and lemon zest and juice. Transfer the artichokes to a platter and serve with the aioli.

eggplant with spicy chile sauce

1 Prepare the grill
Prepare a grill for direct-heat grilling over high heat. If using a gas grill, turn one burner on high and the other burner(s) on low. If using a charcoal grill, arrange the coals into a slope.

2 Make the chile sauce
In a small frying pan over medium-high heat, warm the 1 tablespoon oil. Add the shallot, garlic, and chile and sauté until the shallot softens without browning, about 1 minute. Remove from the heat, add the fish sauce, lime juice, and brown sugar, and stir to dissolve the sugar.

3 Grill the eggplants
Brush the eggplants with oil. Lightly oil the grill rack. Place the eggplants over the cooler area of the grill, and cover. Cook, turning occasionally, until tender, about 6 minutes. Chop the eggplants into 1-inch (2.5-cm) chunks and add to the sauce. Stir gently to combine. Spoon the rice into bowls, top with the eggplant and sauce, sprinkle with the basil, and serve.

cook's tip Thai basil, which has purple stems, is sold at Asian grocery stores and many supermarkets. If it's unavailable, substitute Italian basil.

Canola oil, 1 tablespoon, plus more for brushing

Shallot, 1, minced

Garlic, 2 cloves, minced

Red chile, preferably Thai, 1, seeded and minced

Asian fish sauce, ⅓ cup (3 fl oz/80 ml)

Lime juice, from 1 lime

Brown sugar, 1 tablespoon firmly packed

Asian eggplants (slender aubergines), 6, halved lengthwise

Steamed rice, for serving

Fresh basil, preferably Thai, 3 tablespoons slivered

MAKES 4 SERVINGS

potato-cauliflower gratin

Heavy (double) cream, 2 cups (16 fl oz/500 ml)

Garlic, 3 cloves, crushed

Fresh thyme, 2 sprigs

Salt and freshly ground pepper

Cauliflower, 1 small head, separated into florets

Yukon gold potatoes, 2 lb (1 kg), peeled and thinly sliced

Gruyère cheese, 2 cups (8 oz/250 g) shredded

Parmesan cheese, 1 cup (4 oz/125 g) freshly grated

Fresh bread crumbs, ¼ cup (½ oz/15 g) (see tip, page 214)

MAKES 4–6 SERVINGS

1 Cook the cauliflower
Preheat the oven to 400°F (200°C). Butter a 2-qt (2-l) baking dish. In a saucepan over high heat, combine the cream, garlic, thyme, 1 teaspoon salt, and ¼ teaspoon pepper. Bring to a boil, add the cauliflower, reduce the heat to low, and simmer until the cauliflower is just tender and the sauce has thickened, 8–10 minutes. Remove the garlic and thyme and discard.

2 Assemble and bake the gratin
Layer the potatoes in the prepared dish and sprinkle evenly with ½ cup (2 oz/60 g) each of the Gruyère and Parmesan cheeses. Using a slotted spoon, remove the cauliflower from the sauce and arrange in the dish. Top with the remaining cheeses. Pour the sauce evenly over the vegetables and sprinkle with the bread crumbs. Bake until the potatoes are just tender and the top is golden brown, about 30 minutes. Let cool for about 5 minutes before serving.

cook's tip To slice potatoes thinly, use the slicer attachment on a food processor. Or, use a mandoline for a similar result.

roasted squash with spiced couscous

1 **Roast the squash**
Preheat the oven to 400°F (200°C). Brush the squash halves with the oil and season with salt and pepper. Place the halves, cut side down, on a rimmed baking sheet. Roast until a thin knife easily pierces the squash, about 20 minutes.

2 **Make the spiced couscous**
Meanwhile, in a saucepan, bring the broth to a boil. Stir in the couscous, cinnamon, ginger, ½ teaspoon salt, and pepper to taste. Cover and set aside for 5 minutes. Using a fork, fluff the couscous. Stir the almonds, currants, onions, and apple into the couscous. Spoon the couscous mixture into the roasted squash halves and serve. »

Acorn squash, 2, each 1¼ lb (750 g), halved and seeds removed

Olive oil, 2 teaspoons

Salt and freshly ground pepper

Vegetable broth or stock, 1 cup (8 fl oz/ 250 ml), homemade (page 27) or purchased

Instant couscous, ¾ cup (4½ oz/140 g)

Ground cinnamon, ½ teaspoon

Ground ginger, ¼ teaspoon

Sliced (flaked) almonds, 3 tablespoons, toasted

Dried currants, 2 tablespoons

Green (spring) onions, 2, white and green parts, finely chopped

Golden Delicious apple, ½, cored and chopped

MAKES 4 SERVINGS

roasted squash with spiced couscous

cook's tip

Other small winter squash, such as butternut
squash, will work well in this dish, as the orange
flesh is sweet and will be complemented by the
spiced couscous. Cut the squash into cubes, roast,
and stir into the cooked couscous. Decrease the
roasting time by about 10 minutes.

spicy corn cakes
with black beans

1 Prepare the beans
In a saucepan over medium heat, stir together the beans, oregano, and 1 teaspoon of the chili powder. Cook, stirring occasionally, until the beans are heated through. Remove from the heat, cover, and set aside.

2 Make the batter
In a bowl, whisk together the cornmeal, flour, baking soda, remaining 1 teaspoon chili powder, ½ teaspoon salt, and ⅛ teaspoon pepper. In another bowl, whisk together the butter, buttermilk, and egg. Mix the wet ingredients quickly into the dry ingredients until just blended, leaving small lumps. Fold in the corn.

3 Make the cakes
Heat a large cast-iron frying pan over medium-high heat. Brush it with 1 teaspoon of the oil. Working in batches, add the batter ¼ cup (2 fl oz/60 ml) at a time. Cook the cakes, turning once, until browned and puffy, about 4 minutes total. Transfer to a plate and cover with aluminum foil. Stir the batter and brush the pan with oil between batches. Arrange the cakes on plates, top with the beans, sour cream, and salsa, and serve.

Black beans, 1 can (14½ oz/ 455 g), rinsed and drained

Fresh oregano, 1 teaspoon chopped

Chili powder, 2 teaspoons

Stone ground yellow cornmeal, ⅔ cup (3 oz/90 g)

Flour, 2 tablespoons

Baking soda (bicarbonate of soda), ¼ teaspoon

Salt and freshly ground pepper

Unsalted butter, 3 tablespoons, melted

Buttermilk, 1 cup (8 fl oz/ 250 ml)

Egg, 1

Frozen corn kernels, ½ cup (3 oz/90 g), thawed

Canola oil, 2 teaspoons

Sour cream, for serving

Fresh tomato salsa, for serving, homemade (page 206) or purchased

MAKES 4 SERVINGS

dry-fried green beans with pork

Green beans, 1 lb (500 g), cut into bite-sized pieces

Beef broth, ½ cup (4 fl oz/125 ml)

Soy sauce, 3 tablespoons

Rice vinegar, 1 tablespoon

Cornstarch (cornflour), 1 teaspoon

Sugar, ½ teaspoon

Canola or peanut oil, 2 tablespoons

Ground (minced) pork, ¼ lb (125 g)

Fresh ginger, 1 tablespoon minced

Garlic, 2 cloves, minced

Green (spring) onion, 1, white and green parts, chopped

Red or green jalapeño chile, 1 small, seeded and minced

Steamed rice, for serving (optional)

MAKES 4 SERVINGS

1 Parboil the green beans
Bring a large pot of lightly salted water to a boil. Add the beans and cook for 2 minutes. Drain. Place under cold running cold water to halt the cooking. Pat the beans dry.

2 Make the sauce
In a small bowl, combine the broth, soy sauce, vinegar, cornstarch, and sugar and stir to dissolve the cornstarch.

3 Stir-fry the beans
Heat a wok or large frying pan over high heat until hot and add the oil. Add the pork and stir-fry until no longer pink, about 2 minutes. Add the ginger, garlic, green onion, and chile and stir-fry for about 10 seconds until fragrant. Stir in the green beans. Give the sauce a quick stir, then add to the pan and stir-fry until the beans are heated through and the sauce thickens, about 1 minute. Serve with the steamed rice, if using.

summer vegetable kebabs

1 Prepare the grill
Prepare a grill for direct-heat grilling over high heat. Soak 8 long bamboo skewers in water to cover for 20 minutes.

2 Prepare the vegetables
In a large bowl, whisk together the wine, ½ teaspoon salt, and ½ teaspoon pepper. Whisk in the oil. Add the eggplant, zucchini, yellow squashes, onion, bell pepper, and mushrooms and toss gently to coat. Let stand for 5 minutes. Thread the vegetables onto the skewers. Pour any remaining marinade into a bowl.

3 Grill the kebabs
Lightly oil the grill rack. Place the skewers on the grill and cover. Grill, turning and basting occasionally with the reserved marinade, until the vegetables are tender, 8–10 minutes. Drizzle the kebabs with the pesto and serve.

storage tip You can serve 4 of the kebabs and store the rest for another meal (see pages 173 and 206). Remove the vegetables from the skewers and let cool to room temperature. Refrigerate in an airtight container for up to 3 days.

Dry white wine, ½ cup (4 fl oz/125 ml)

Salt and freshly ground pepper

Olive oil, ¼ cup (2 fl oz/ 60 ml)

Eggplant (aubergine), 1 small, cut into chunks

Zucchini (courgettes), 2, cut into chunks

Yellow squashes, 2, cut into chunks

Red onion, 1, quartered lengthwise and separated into double-thick wedges

Red bell pepper (capsicum), 1, seeded and cut into large pieces

Cremini mushrooms, 16 large

Basil Pesto (page 34) or purchased pesto, 2 tablespoons

MAKES 8 KEBABS

vegetable quesadillas

Flour tortillas, 8, each 8 inches (20 cm) in diameter

Pepper jack or Monterey jack cheese, 2 cups (8 oz/250 g) shredded

Summer Vegetable Kebabs (page 205), 4 kebabs, vegetables removed and coarsely chopped

Canola oil, about 1 tablespoon

Fresh cilantro (fresh coriander), 3 tablespoons coarsely chopped

Fresh tomato salsa, 1 cup (8 fl oz/250 ml), homemade (see Cook's Tip) or purchased

MAKES 4 SERVINGS

1 Prepare the quesadillas
Spread out the tortillas on a work surface. Sprinkle the bottom half of each tortilla with some of the cheese and then some of the chopped vegetables. Fold in half to enclose the filling and press firmly. Stack the quesadillas on a plate and set aside. Preheat the oven to 200°F (95°C).

2 Cook the quesadillas
Preheat a large frying pan over medium heat until hot. Brush the pan lightly with oil. Place 2 quesadillas in the pan and cook, turning once, until lightly toasted, about 2 minutes on each side. Transfer to a baking sheet and keep warm in the oven. Repeat with the remaining quesadillas, brushing the pan with oil between batches. Cut the quesadillas into wedges. Sprinkle with the cilantro and serve, passing the salsa at the table.

cook's tip To make a quick tomato salsa, combine 1 tomato, seeded and chopped; ½ onion, chopped; 2 tablespoons chopped fresh cilantro (fresh coriander); ½ jalapeño chile, seeded and diced (if desired), and fresh lime juice, salt, and pepper to taste.

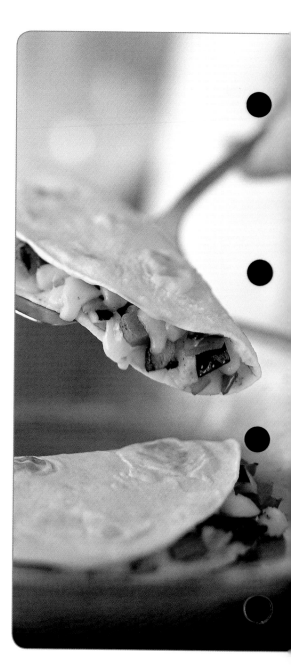

roasted vegetables with romesco

1 Roast the potatoes
Preheat the oven to 450°F (230°C). In a small saucepan over medium-low heat, warm the oil. Add the garlic and cook until golden, about 5 minutes. Remove from the heat and discard the garlic. Place the potatoes on a large, rimmed baking sheet. Drizzle with 1 tablespoon of the garlic oil and toss to coat. Roast for 10 minutes.

2 Add the vegetables
In a large bowl, toss the zucchini, eggplant, bell pepper, and onion with the remaining garlic oil. Add to the baking sheet with the potatoes. Roast, turning occasionally, until the vegetables are tender, 20–30 minutes. Season to taste with salt and pepper. Transfer to a platter, top with the romesco sauce, and serve.

Olive oil, ¼ cup (2 fl oz/ 60 ml)

Garlic, 2 cloves, smashed

Red-skinned potatoes, 1 lb (500 g) small, halved

Zucchini (courgettes), 2 large, halved lengthwise and cut into chunks

Asian eggplants (slender aubergines), 2, cut into chunks

Red bell pepper (capsicum), 1 large, seeded and cut into chunks

Red onion, 1, thickly sliced

Salt and freshly ground pepper

Romesco Sauce (page 35), 1 cup (8 fl oz/250 ml)

MAKES 4–6 SERVINGS

vegetable &
tofu stir-fry

Firm tofu, 1 lb (500 g), drained and cut into bite-sized cubes

Cornstarch (cornflour), 1 tablespoon

Vegetable broth or stock, ¼ cup (2 fl oz/ 60 ml), homemade (page 27) or purchased

Black bean sauce, 1 tablespoon

Sugar, 1 teaspoon

Peanut oil, ⅓ cup (3 fl oz/80 ml)

Red pepper flakes, ⅛ teaspoon

Bok choy, 1 small head, trimmed and cut into bite-sized pieces

Zucchini (courgette), 1 small, cut into bite-sized pieces

Red bell pepper (capsicum), 1, seeded and sliced

Sugar snap peas, ¼ lb (125 g), trimmed

MAKES 4 SERVINGS

1 **Prepare the tofu and sauce**
Line a baking sheet with a double thickness of paper towels. Arrange the tofu in a single layer on the towels. Top with another layer of towels and pat the tofu dry. In a small bowl, stir together the cornstarch and broth until the cornstarch dissolves. Stir in the bean sauce and sugar.

2 **Stir-fry the tofu and vegetables**
Heat a wok or large frying pan over high heat and add the oil. Carefully add the tofu and cook for 3 minutes. Turn and cook until golden, 3–4 minutes. Using a slotted spoon, transfer to paper towels to drain. Pour off all but 1 tablespoon oil and return the wok to high heat. Add the red pepper flakes, bok choy, zucchini, bell pepper, and snap peas and stir-fry until the vegetables are tender-crisp, about 3 minutes. Return the tofu to the wok. Give the sauce a quick stir, add to the pan, and cook, stirring, until the sauce thickens, about 1 minute. Serve in shallow bowls.

cook's tip Also called bean curd, tofu is sold in blocks with textures ranging from silken to extra-firm. Firm tofu holds its shape when stir-fried. Soft, silken tofu is best gently cooked in recipes such as soups.

indian vegetable curry

1 Sauté the aromatics and spices
In a frying pan over medium-high heat, warm the oil. Add the onions and garlic and sauté until softened, about 5 minutes. Add the ginger, coriander, turmeric, and cumin seeds and sauté until fragrant, about 1 minute. Add 1 cup (8 fl oz/250 ml) hot water and deglaze the pan, stirring to scrape up the browned bits on the pan bottom. When the water comes to a boil, remove from the heat.

2 Cook the curry
Put the potatoes, cauliflower, and green beans in a Dutch oven or slow cooker and add the contents of the frying pan. Sprinkle with 1½ teaspoons salt and stir to combine. If using a Dutch oven, partially cover and cook over low heat until the vegetables are tender and the sauce is thick, about 30 minutes. (If using a slow cooker, cover and cook on the high-heat setting for 4 hours or the low-heat setting for 8 hours.) Stir in the cilantro, season to taste with salt, and serve. »

Canola oil, ¼ cup
(2 fl oz/60 ml)

Yellow onions, 2, chopped

Garlic, 4 cloves, minced

Fresh ginger,
3 tablespoons minced

Ground coriander,
1½ teaspoons

Ground turmeric,
1 teaspoon

Cumin seeds, 1 teaspoon

Boiling potatoes, 1 lb
(500 g), peeled and cut into chunks

Cauliflower, 1 large head, separated into florets

Green beans, ¾ lb
(375 g), coarsely chopped

Salt

Fresh cilantro (fresh coriander), ¼ cup
(⅓ oz/10 g) chopped

MAKES 4 SERVINGS

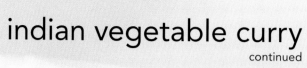

cook's tip

For a complete meal, serve the curry over steamed long-grain white rice such as basmati. Accompany with a colorful tomato and cucumber salad drizzled with plain yogurt and sprinkled with chopped fresh cilantro (fresh coriander).

lentil, potato & spinach curry

1 Sauté the aromatics and spices
In a heavy-bottomed saucepan or Dutch oven over medium-high heat, warm the oil. Add the onion and sauté until browned, about 8 minutes. Stir in the garlic, garam masala, cumin, and coriander and sauté until the spices are fragrant, about 1 minute.

2 Cook the vegetables
Add the potatoes, lentils, and 1 cup (8 fl oz/250 ml) water to the saucepan and bring to a boil. Reduce the heat to medium-low and simmer, uncovered, until the potatoes are tender, about 10 minutes. Stir in the spinach and cook just until it wilts, about 2 minutes. Season to taste with salt and pepper. Spoon the rice into bowls and top with the vegetable mixture. Garnish with the yogurt and serve.

> **cook's tip** Round out the meal with steamed rice or warmed naan. Chopped mustard greens or kale can be used in place of the spinach.

Canola oil, 2 tablespoons

Yellow onion, 1 large, chopped

Garlic, 2 cloves, minced

Garam masala, 1½ teaspoons

Ground cumin, 1 teaspoon

Ground coriander, ½ teaspoon

Red-skinned potatoes, 2 large, cut into bite-sized pieces

Green Lentils (page 37), 2 cups (14 oz/440 g)

Baby spinach, 2 cups packed (3 oz/90 g)

Salt and freshly ground pepper

Steamed white or brown basmati rice, for serving

Plain yogurt, ¼ cup (2 oz/60 g), for garnish

MAKES 4 SERVINGS

roasted vegetables
with sage butter

Golden or red beets,
2, peeled and cut into
wedges

Turnip, 1, peeled, if
desired, and cut into
wedges

**Delicata or butternut
squash,** 1, 6 oz (185 g),
peeled, seeded, and cut
into chunks

Fennel bulb, 1 small,
trimmed and sliced

Parsnip, 1, peeled and
cut into chunks

Baby carrots, 8

Garlic, 4 cloves, halved
lengthwise

Unsalted butter,
4 tablespoons (2 oz/60 g),
melted

Fresh sage,
3 tablespoons minced

**Salt and freshly ground
pepper**

White balsamic vinegar,
1 tablespoon

MAKES 4 SERVINGS

1 **Roast the vegetables**
Preheat the oven to 400°F (200°C).
Place the beets, turnip, squash, fennel,
parsnip, carrots, and garlic on a rimmed
baking sheet. Pour the butter over the
vegetables. Sprinkle with the sage,
1 teaspoon salt, and ¼ teaspoon pepper.
Toss to coat, then spread in an even layer.
Roast, stirring occasionally, for about
30 minutes. Continue to roast, without
stirring, until the vegetables are tender,
20–30 minutes longer. Using a large
spatula, transfer the vegetables to a
serving bowl. Reserve the pan juices.

2 **Finish the vegetables**
Pour the pan juices into a small bowl
and whisk in the vinegar. Drizzle over the
vegetables, toss, and serve.

sweet potato hash
with poached eggs

1 Cook the potatoes

Place both potatoes in a saucepan and add water to cover. Bring to a boil, reduce the heat to medium-high, and cook until the potatoes are almost tender, about 10 minutes. Drain.

2 Assemble the hash

Meanwhile, in a large frying pan over medium-high heat, warm the oil. Add the pepper and red onion and sauté until the red onion is translucent, about 2 minutes. Add the potatoes, spreading them in one layer. Reduce the heat to medium and cook, stirring occasionally, until the potatoes start to brown, about 6 minutes. Stir in the green onion. Season to taste with salt and pepper and cook, stirring, until the potatoes start to break down, about 1 minute. Transfer to plates.

3 Poach the eggs

Meanwhile, in a deep frying pan, bring 8 cups (64 fl oz/2 l) water to a gentle simmer over medium heat. Mix in the vinegar and 1 teaspoon salt. One at a time, crack the eggs into a small bowl then slide them into the water. After 1 minute, slip a spatula under the eggs to prevent them from sticking to the bottom of the pan. Cook the eggs for 3–4 minutes. Using a slotted spoon, carefully transfer the eggs to the plates with the hash and serve.

Red-skinned potato, 1 large, peeled and cut into bite-sized cubes

Sweet potato, 1 large, peeled and cut into bite-sized cubes

Canola oil, 2 tablespoons

Red bell pepper (capsicum), 1 small, seeded and chopped

Red onion, 1 small, finely chopped

Green (spring) onion, 1, white and dark green parts, chopped

Salt and freshly ground pepper

Distilled white vinegar, 1 tablespoon

Eggs, 4

MAKES 4 SERVINGS

asparagus milanese

Asparagus, 1 lb (500 g), tough ends removed

Unsalted butter, 2 tablespoons

Eggs, 4

Salt and freshly ground pepper

Shallot, 1 tablespoon minced

Fresh bread crumbs, 2 tablespoons (see tip)

MAKES 4 SERVINGS

1 Steam the asparagus

Fill a frying pan with 1 inch (2.5 cm) of water and bring to a boil. Add the asparagus, cover, and cook until bright green and tender-crisp, 3–4 minutes. Drain and arrange on plates. Wipe out the pan with a paper towel.

2 Cook the eggs

In the same pan over medium heat, melt the butter. Carefully break each egg into the pan. Season to taste with salt and pepper. Cook until the whites and yolks are set, about 4 minutes. Using a wide spatula, transfer the eggs to the plates with the asparagus. Add the shallot and bread crumbs to the pan and sauté until the crumbs are golden, about 2 minutes. Sprinkle over the eggs and serve.

cook's tip Whenever you have leftover day-old bread, preferably a baguette or rustic white loaf, cut it into slices and trim off the crusts, then place on a baking sheet and cook in a 300°F (150°C) oven for about 10 minutes. Process the toasted bread in a food processor to make fresh bread crumbs. Store the crumbs in an airtight container in the freezer for up to 4 months.

potato & gruyère tartlets

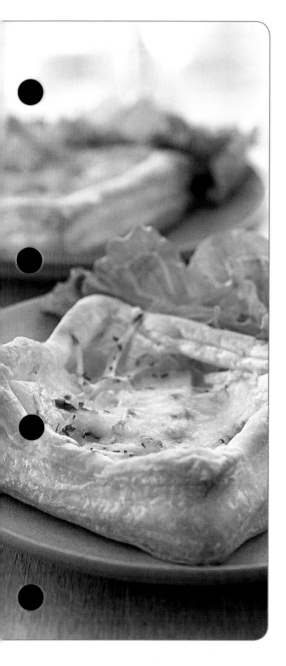

1 Make the filling

Preheat the oven to 400°F (200°C). In a bowl, stir together the oil, rosemary, ½ teaspoon salt, and ⅛ teaspoon pepper. Add the potato and onion and toss well.

2 Prepare the pastry

Lay the pastry squares on a baking sheet. With a sharp paring knife, make a cut ½ inch (12 mm) from the edge all the way around each square, being careful not to cut more than halfway through the pastry. Inside the border, prick the pastry all over with a fork.

3 Fill and bake the tartlets

Sprinkle 2 tablespoons of the cheese inside the border of each pastry square. Divide the potato and onion mixture among the squares and sprinkle with the remaining cheese. Bake until the borders of the tartlets are puffed and brown and the potatoes are tender, about 20 minutes. Serve warm or at room temperature.

> **cook's tip** As a quick side dish, accompany the tartlets with thin green beans. Bring a saucepan of lightly salted water to a boil, add the beans, and cook until tender, about 4 minutes. Run under cold water.

Olive oil, 2 tablespoons

Fresh rosemary, 1 tablespoon minced

Salt and freshly ground pepper

Russet or baking potato, 1, peeled, halved lengthwise, and thinly sliced

Yellow onion, 1 small, halved and thinly sliced

Frozen puff pastry, 1 sheet, thawed and cut into four 5-inch (13-cm) squares

Gruyère cheese, 1 cup (4 oz/125 g) shredded

MAKES 4 SERVINGS

herbed
sweet potatoes with feta

Sweet potatoes, 4 large, peeled and thickly sliced

Olive oil, 3 tablespoons

Salt and freshly ground pepper

Feta cheese, ¼ lb (125 g), crumbled

Pine nuts, ⅓ cup (2 oz/ 60 g)

Fresh thyme, 1 tablespoon minced

Lemon juice, from 1 lemon

MAKES 4–6 SERVINGS

1 **Season the sweet potatoes**
Preheat the oven to 400°F (200°C). Place the potatoes in a 2-qt (2-l) gratin or baking dish. Drizzle with the oil, season with salt and pepper, and toss to coat. Spread the potatoes in a single layer.

2 **Bake the sweet potatoes**
Cover the dish with aluminum foil and bake for about 20 minutes. Uncover, sprinkle with the cheese, pine nuts, and thyme, and continue to bake, uncovered, until the cheese is golden and the sweet potatoes are tender, 8–10 minutes longer. Remove from the oven, drizzle with the lemon juice, and serve.

spring vegetable tart

1 Prepare the pastry

Preheat the oven to 400°F (200°C). Line a rimmed baking sheet with parchment (baking) paper. Lay the puff pastry on the baking sheet. Fold over the edges to make a 1-inch (2.5-cm) border, overlapping the pastry at the corners and pressing it lightly. Inside the border, prick the pastry all over with a fork.

2 Fill and bake the tart

Sprinkle half of the cheese evenly over the pastry inside the border. Lay the asparagus in a row from one side of the pastry to the other. Sprinkle with the leeks. Bake for 15 minutes. Meanwhile, in a bowl, beat the eggs, milk, ½ teaspoon salt, and pepper to taste until well combined. Pour the egg mixture over the asparagus and leeks and sprinkle with the remaining cheese. Bake until the pastry is puffed and golden, about 10 minutes. Let stand for 10 minutes. Cut into pieces and serve. »

Frozen puff pastry, 1 sheet, thawed

Fontina cheese, 1 cup (4 oz/125 g) shredded

Asparagus, 15–20 thin spears, tough ends removed

Leek, 1 small, white part only, halved, rinsed, and thinly sliced

Eggs, 2

Milk, ¼ cup (2 fl oz/60 ml)

Salt and freshly ground pepper

MAKES 4 SERVINGS

cook's tip

To clean a leek quickly, trim off the dark green tops. Cut the stalk in half lengthwise, leaving the root end intact. Rinse the leek under cold running water, separating the layers to remove any embedded dirt. Prepare as directed, removing the root end.

curried chickpea
& potato stew

1 Prepare the aromatics
In a blender, combine 1 tablespoon water with the onion, ginger, garlic, and chile and process until a paste forms. In a small bowl, stir together the curry powder and ½ teaspoon salt.

2 Sauté the vegetables
Heat a large frying pan over high heat until hot and add 2 tablespoons of the oil. Add the potatoes and sauté until lightly browned, about 5 minutes. Season with ¼ teaspoon salt. Using a slotted spoon, transfer to a bowl. Return the pan to high heat and add 1 tablespoon of the oil. Add the okra, if using, and sauté until slightly crisp, about 5 minutes. Transfer to the bowl with the potatoes.

3 Cook the stew
Return the pan to medium-high heat and add the remaining 1 tablespoon oil. Add the onion-garlic paste and fry until fragrant, about 2 minutes. Stir in the curry mixture and broth, mix well, and bring to a boil. Return the vegetables to the pan and add the chickpeas. Reduce the heat to low and cook, uncovered, until the potatoes are tender, 15–20 minutes. Season to taste with salt. Serve over rice.

Yellow onion, 1, coarsely chopped

Fresh ginger, 2 tablespoons chopped

Garlic, 4 cloves, chopped

Red or green jalapeño chile, 1 small, seeded and chopped

Curry powder, 1½ tablespoons

Salt

Canola or peanut oil, 4 tablespoons (2 fl oz/ 60 ml)

Boiling potatoes, 2 large, peeled and cut into small cubes

Okra, ½ lb (250 g) fresh or frozen, thickly sliced (optional)

Chicken or vegetable broth or stock, 1½ cups (12 fl oz/375 ml), homemade (page 29 or 27) or purchased

Chickpeas (garbanzo beans), 1 can (15 oz/ 470 g), drained and rinsed

Steamed rice, for serving

MAKES 4 SERVINGS

mushroom tart

Cream Cheese Dough (page 41), 1 disk

Unsalted butter, 2 tablespoons

Mixed fresh mushrooms, such as cremini and stemmed shiitake, 1½ lb (750 g), halved or quartered

Shallot, 1 large, chopped

Crème fraîche or heavy (double) cream, ½ cup (4 fl oz/125 ml)

Fresh oregano, 1 teaspoon chopped

Salt and freshly ground pepper

MAKES 6 SERVINGS

1 Bake the tart shell
Preheat the oven to 400°F (200°C). On a lightly floured work surface, roll out the dough into a 12-inch (30-cm) round. Fit into a 9-inch (23-cm) round tart pan and trim the dough to allow a ½-inch (12-mm) overhang. Fold the overhang over itself and pinch to create a sturdy edge. Prick the dough all over with a fork. Freeze for 15 minutes. Blind bake the tart shell (see page 409) until lightly golden, about 15 minutes. Let cool on a wire rack.

2 Make the filling and finish the tart
In a large frying pan over medium heat, melt the butter. Add the mushrooms and shallot and sauté until lightly browned, 8–10 minutes. Add the crème fraîche and oregano, season to taste with salt and pepper, and stir to combine. Spread the mushroom mixture in the tart shell. Bake until the crust is golden brown, about 15 minutes. Let cool briefly on a wire rack. Remove the pan rim, cut the tart into wedges, and serve.

mushroom & broccoli rice pilaf

1 Cook the rice

Preheat the oven to 350°F (180°C). In a saucepan over medium heat, combine the stock and sherry and heat until steaming, 8–10 minutes. In a heavy-bottomed ovenproof saucepan or Dutch oven over medium-high heat, melt the butter. Add the onion and sauté until translucent, 4–5 minutes. Add the rice and stir until well coated with the butter, about 1 minute. Pour in the hot broth. Add the thyme, ½ teaspoon salt, and pepper to taste. Bring to a boil, cover, and bake in the oven for 35 minutes.

2 Finish the pilaf

Remove the rice from the oven and stir in the broccoli and chickpeas. Cover and bake until the broccoli is tender, 10–15 minutes. Let stand, covered, for 5 minutes. Fluff with a fork, sprinkle with the nuts and red pepper flakes, and serve.

cook's tip Regular long-grain or short-grain brown rice can be used in place of the basmati. Check the package as the cooking time may vary. Thawed frozen corn kernels or chopped red bell pepper (capsicum) can be substituted for the broccoli and chickpeas.

Mushroom broth or stock, 2½ cups (20 fl oz/ 625 ml), homemade (page 28) or purchased

Dry sherry, 2 tablespoons

Unsalted butter, 2 tablespoons

Yellow onion, 1, finely chopped

Brown basmati rice, 1 cup (7 oz/220 g)

Fresh thyme leaves, 1 tablespoon

Salt and freshly ground pepper

Broccoli, 1 small head, separated into florets

Canned chickpeas (garbanzo beans), 1 cup (7 oz/220 g), rinsed and drained

Salted roasted cashews, ½ cup (2 oz/60 g) coarsely chopped

Red pepper flakes, pinch

MAKES 4 SERVINGS

spicy tofu with peas

Oyster sauce, ¼ cup
(2 fl oz/60 ml)

Soy sauce, ¼ cup
(2 fl oz/60 ml)

Rice vinegar, ¼ cup
(2 fl oz/60 ml)

**Chile sauce such as
Sriracha, or tomato
paste,** 2 teaspoons

Asian sesame oil,
2 tablespoons

Sugar, 2 teaspoons

Cornstarch (cornflour),
1 teaspoon

Canola or peanut oil,
¼ cup (2 fl oz/60 ml)

Fresh ginger,
2 tablespoons minced

Garlic, 4 cloves, minced

Firm tofu, 2 lb (1 kg),
drained and cut into bite-
sized cubes

Frozen petite peas,
1 cup (5 oz/155 g)

Steamed rice, for serving
(optional)

MAKES 4 SERVINGS

1 **Make the sauce**
In a small bowl, combine ¼ cup
(2 fl oz/60 ml) water and the oyster sauce,
soy sauce, vinegar, chile sauce, sesame oil,
sugar, and cornstarch and stir to dissolve
the sugar and cornstarch.

2 **Stir-fry the tofu**
Heat a wok or large frying pan over
medium-high heat until hot and add the
canola oil. Add the ginger and garlic and
stir-fry for about 5 seconds until fragrant.
Reduce the heat to medium, give the sauce
a quick stir, and add to the pan along with
the tofu. Stir-fry gently until the sauce
thickens slightly, about 1 minute. Add the
peas and cook until heated through, about
1 minute longer. Serve over the rice, if using.

vegetable chow mein

1 Prepare the noodles and sauce
Bring a large pot of water to a boil. Add the noodles and cook for 2 minutes. Drain and rinse well with cold running water. Place in a bowl, add 1 tablespoon of the canola oil, and toss to coat evenly. In a small bowl, stir together 3 tablespoons water and the oyster sauce, soy sauce, vinegar, and sesame oil.

2 Stir-fry the vegetables
Heat a wok or large frying pan over high heat until very hot and add 2 tablespoons of the canola oil. Add the onion and bell pepper and stir-fry just until tender, about 2 minutes. Add the mushrooms and zucchini and stir-fry until golden brown, about 2 minutes. Transfer the vegetables to a bowl.

3 Stir-fry the noodles
Return the pan to high heat and add the remaining 2 tablespoons canola oil. Stir in the ginger and garlic and stir-fry for about 5 seconds until fragrant. Add the noodles and stir-fry until heated through, about 5 minutes. Return the vegetables to the pan, add the sauce, and continue to stir and toss until all the ingredients are well combined and heated through, about 1 minute. Transfer to a platter and serve.

Fresh Chinese egg noodles, ½ lb (250 g)

Canola or peanut oil, 5 tablespoons (2½ fl oz/ 75 ml)

Oyster sauce, 2 tablespoons

Soy sauce, 2 tablespoons

Rice vinegar, 2 tablespoons

Asian sesame oil, 1 tablespoon

Yellow onion, ½, thinly sliced

Red bell pepper (capsicum), 1, seeded and thinly sliced

Shiitake mushrooms, ¼ lb (125 g), stems discarded and caps thinly sliced

Zucchini (courgette), 1, cut into matchsticks

Fresh ginger, 1 tablespoon grated

Garlic, 2 cloves, minced

MAKES 4 SERVINGS

endive & radicchio gratin

Belgian endive (chicory/witloof), 4 large heads, halved lengthwise and cut into wide ribbons

Radicchio, 2 small heads, halved lengthwise and cut into wide ribbons

Milk, 1½ cups (12 fl oz/375 ml)

Unsalted butter, 3 tablespoons

Flour, 2 tablespoons

Gruyère or Comté cheese, 1 cup (4 oz/125 g) shredded

Salt and freshly ground pepper

Parmesan cheese, ¼ cup (1 oz/30 g) freshly grated

MAKES 4 SERVINGS

1 **Prepare the vegetables**
Preheat the oven to 400°F (200°C). Butter a shallow 2-qt (2-l) gratin or baking dish. Add the endive and radicchio to the prepared dish and toss to combine.

2 **Make the sauce**
In a small saucepan over medium heat, warm the milk until small bubbles begin to appear around the edge of the saucepan. Remove from the heat. In another saucepan over low heat, melt 2 tablespoons of the butter. Add the flour and whisk to incorporate. Raise the heat to medium-low and cook, stirring often, for 2 minutes. Gradually whisk in the hot milk. Cook, stirring frequently, until the sauce is thick enough to coat the back of a spoon, 3–4 minutes. Add ¾ cup (3 oz/90 g) of the Gruyère cheese and stir until it melts. Season to taste with salt and pepper.

3 **Finish the gratin**
Spoon the sauce over the vegetables and dot with the remaining 1 tablespoon butter. Sprinkle with the Parmesan cheese and remaining ¼ cup (1 oz/30 g) Gruyère cheese. Bake until the vegetables are tender and the top of the gratin is golden, about 30 minutes. Serve hot.

roasted
eggplant lasagna

1 **Roast the eggplant**
Preheat the oven to 450°F (230°C). Brush the eggplant slices with oil, season with salt and pepper, and place on 2 rimmed baking sheets. Roast, turning once, until the slices are nicely browned, about 20 minutes total.

2 **Layer the eggplant**
Meanwhile, in a saucepan over medium heat, warm the Bolognese sauce. Reduce the oven temperature to 375°F (190°C). Spread a large spoonful of the sauce onto the bottom of a 10-by-12-inch (25-by-30-cm) baking dish. Lay one-third of the eggplant slices on the bottom of the dish, overlapping them slightly. Top with 1 cup (8 fl oz/250 ml) of the sauce and one-third of the mozzarella cheese slices. Repeat to make 2 more layers, ending with the mozzarella. Sprinkle the Parmesan cheese on top.

3 **Bake the lasagna**
Bake until the eggplant is warmed through and the cheese is melted, about 20 minutes. Let stand for 10 minutes. Serve garnished with the basil. »

Eggplants (aubergines), 2, about 1½ lb (750 g) total weight, cut crosswise into thick slices

Olive oil, for brushing

Salt and freshly ground pepper

Bolognese Sauce (page 32), 3 cups (24 fl oz/750 ml)

Fresh mozzarella cheese, 1 lb (500 g), sliced

Parmesan cheese, ½ cup (2 oz/60 g) freshly grated

Fresh basil, ¼ cup (1 oz/30 g) slivered

MAKES 4–6 SERVINGS

cook's tip

If you have the time, use salt to draw out
moisture from the eggplant, making it easier
to cook. Sprinkle the eggplant slices with coarse
salt on both sides and place in a colander set
over a plate. Let drain for about 30 minutes.
Wipe with paper towels to remove excess salt.

red pepper &
goat cheese frittata

1 **Cook the vegetables**
In a heavy 10-inch (25-cm) ovenproof frying pan over medium heat, warm the oil. Add the onion and sauté until golden, 5–6 minutes. Add the red pepper and sauté until warmed through, 1–2 minutes.

2 **Prepare the frittata**
In a bowl, whisk together the eggs, oregano, ½ teaspoon salt, and ¼ teaspoon pepper. Spread the sautéed vegetables evenly in the pan, and then pour in the egg mixture. Reduce the heat to medium-low and cook, without stirring, until the edges begin to look set, about 3 minutes. Using a spatula, carefully lift up the edges of the frittata and let the uncooked egg run underneath. Continue to cook, without stirring, until the eggs are almost set on top, 5–8 minutes longer.

3 **Finish the frittata**
While the frittata is cooking, preheat the broiler (grill). Sprinkle the frittata with the cheese and place under the broiler. Broil (grill) until the top is set and the cheese is melted, about 2 minutes. Cut into large wedges and serve.

Olive oil, 3 tablespoons

Yellow onion, 1, thinly sliced

Roasted red pepper (capsicum), ⅔ cup (4 oz/125 g) chopped

Eggs, 8

Fresh oregano, 2 tablespoons chopped

Salt and freshly ground pepper

Fresh goat cheese, 3 oz (90 g), crumbled

MAKES 4 SERVINGS

vegetable enchiladas

Corn tortillas, 15, halved

Canola oil, 2 tablespoons

Salt

Monterey jack cheese,
1 cup (4 oz/125 g)
shredded

White Cheddar cheese,
1 cup (4 oz/125 g)
shredded

Corn kernels, 2 cups
(12 oz/370 g) fresh or
frozen

Zucchini (courgettes),
2, halved lengthwise and
thinly sliced

Yellow onion, 1 large,
halved and thinly sliced

Tomatillo salsa, 2 jars
(12½ oz/390 g each)

**Sour cream or Mexican
crema,** ¼ cup (2 oz/60 g)

Queso fresco **or feta
cheese,** ½ cup (2½ oz/
75 g) crumbled

MAKES 4–6 SERVINGS

1 Toast the tortillas
Preheat the oven to 400°F (200°C).
Brush the tortilla halves with the oil,
sprinkle with salt, and arrange on a baking
sheet. Bake until they begin to crisp, about
3 minutes. Remove from the oven and
reduce the oven temperature to 300°F
(150°C). In a small bowl, stir together the
Monterey jack and Cheddar cheeses, corn,
zucchini, and onion.

2 Assemble the enchiladas
Reserve one-fourth of the salsa for
serving. Cover the bottom of a 9-inch
(23-cm) round baking dish with a thin layer
of salsa. Lay 10 tortilla halves over the
salsa, overlapping them if necessary. Top
with one-fourth of the remaining salsa and
one-third of the shredded cheese mixture.
Repeat the layers two more times. Top the
final layer of shredded cheese mixture with
the remaining salsa. Spoon the sour cream
evenly over the top, then sprinkle with
the *queso fresco*.

3 Bake the enchiladas
Cover the dish with aluminum foil
and bake until the vegetables are tender,
about 20 minutes. Uncover and continue
to bake until the cheese is golden,
10–15 minutes longer. Let stand briefly
before serving. Pass the remaining salsa
at the table.

vegetables made easy

Many people feel they should eat more fresh vegetables than they do. With the recipes in this chapter and the helpful tips, tools, and techniques in the following pages, you'll be using vegetables as the stars of well-balanced and delicious meals in no time.

TIME-SAVING TOOLS

Grill pan This ridged cast iron or anodized aluminum pan is used on the stove top and produces grill marks and nearly the same taste as cooking on an outdoor grill. To ensure that vegetables are well seared, always let the pan preheat over high heat for about 5 minutes.

Steamer insert or basket Steaming vegetables is usually preferred over boiling because it is faster and the vegetables' nutrients are not lost in the cooking water. A steamer insert or collapsible basket is necessary when steaming vegetables. Look for a steamer insert that will fit in one of your saucepans that has a lid.

Wok With its generous size, sloping sides, and rounded bottom, a wok is the ideal implement for cooking Asian stir-fries. The shape and depth of the pan guarantee that all the ingredients will be exposed to the hot surface and that they can be tossed and stirred without spilling over the rim.

cooking methods for vegetables

Boiling & steaming These moist-heat cooking methods are the simplest and most common ways to cook vegetables. Steaming calls for cooking over a small amount of boiling water, while boiling calls for immersing in a generous amount of boiling water. Whichever method you choose, it won't take long to cook the vegetables, so keep an eye on them. Vegetables should be tender-crisp and brightly colored. Good candidates for boiling and steaming include beets, broccoli, cauliflower, corn, green beans, and potatoes.

Grilling Almost all types of sturdy vegetables are good for grilling. Larger vegetables should be cut into thick slices, while smaller vegetables can be left whole. Let vegetables sit in a marinade or toss them with olive oil, salt, and ground pepper before grilling. Good candidates for grilling include corn, eggplants (aubergines), fennel, onions, bell peppers (capsicums), and zucchini (courgettes).

Roasting This dry-heat method concentrates the natural sugars in vegetables and heightens their flavor. Cut medium or large vegetables into halves or chunks, toss with olive oil, and sprinkle with salt, pepper, and other complementary seasonings before roasting. Remember to keep an eye on the vegetables to prevent burning or scorching. Good candidates for roasting include broccoli, Brussels sprouts, cauliflower, eggplants (aubergines), parsnips, potatoes, squashes, sweet potatoes, and tomatoes.

Sautéing & stir-frying Both sautéing and stir-frying call for cooking vegetables quickly over high heat. The combination of high temperature and hot oil sears vegetables, imparting an appealing flavor. Try to cut the vegetables into uniform pieces to ensure even cooking. For safety reasons, be sure to pat the vegetables dry before adding them to the hot oil. Good candidates for sautéing and stir-frying include asparagus, carrots, green beans, peas, and zucchini (courgettes).

SAMPLE MEALS

These menus are designed to help you plan your weekly meals. Consider your schedule, and then mix and match the main dishes and accompaniments to create the plan that works best for you. "In Minutes" meals include vegetable dishes and accompaniments that can be put together quickly. "Fit for Company" meals offer ideas for stress-free get-togethers, complete with a wine suggestion.

IN MINUTES	FIT FOR COMPANY
Vegetable & Tofu Stir-Fry (page 208)	**Artichokes with Lemon Aioli** (page 198)
steamed jasmine rice	**Potato & Gruyère Tartlets** (page 215)
———	Chardonnay
Vegetable Chow Mein (page 223)	———
steamed broccoli	**Asparagus Milanese (page 214)**
fried rice with egg	sautéed sliced red potatoes with butter and herbs
———	arugula (rocket) and Parmesan salad with red wine vinaigrette
Roasted Eggplant Lasagna (page 225)	Pinot Gris or Pinot Noir
mixed greens with balsamic vinaigrette	———
warm focaccia with olive oil	**Herbed Sweet Potatoes with Feta** (page 216)
———	rotisserie chicken
Vegetable Enchiladas (page 228)	Merlot or Pinot Noir
black beans and rice	———
———	**Spring Vegetable Tart** (page 217)
Red Pepper & Goat Cheese Frittata (page 227)	butter lettuce and avocado salad with citrus vinaigrette
roasted asparagus	Sauvignon Blanc
herbed biscuits	

VEGETARIAN MEALS

Sticking to a vegetarian diet can be challenging, especially on those days when you don't have much time to cook. Here are several ideas for easy-to-fix vegetarian dishes.

Burritos Keep flour tortillas in the refrigerator for preparing burritos or soft tacos using cheese, salsa, rice, and canned refried pinto or black beans. Warm the tortilla, fill with the ingredients, and roll up to eat.

Eggs It's a good idea to keep a supply of eggs on hand. Make a quick frittata (page 227) or prepare a simple omelet using chopped leftover vegetables and cheese and serve it with sautéed potatoes. Hard-boiled eggs are easy to make and can be used in numerous dishes.

Hummus Prepared hummus is widely available in many supermarkets. Spread it on toasted pita stuffed with shredded carrot, tomato slices, and store-bought tahini. Or, serve hummus alongside olives, feta cheese, stuffed grape leaves, and cherry tomatoes.

Marinated tofu Pressed, marinated, and baked, these ready-to-eat tofu squares make a great base for a sandwich, salad, or vegetable stir-fry.

seafood

trout amandine

1 Toast the almonds
Place the fillets on a plate and season on both sides with salt and pepper. Heat a large frying pan over medium-low heat. Add the almonds and toast, stirring frequently, until they turn golden brown, 3–5 minutes. Transfer to a plate.

2 Cook the trout
Return the pan to medium-low heat. Spread the flour on a large plate. Roll the fillets in the flour, coating both sides well and shaking off any excess. Add the oil to the pan and raise the heat to medium. Add the fillets, skin side up, and cook until browned, about 4 minutes. Turn and cook until the fillets flake easily near the tail ends, about 2 minutes longer. Transfer the fillets, skin side down, to plates.

3 Make the sauce
Wipe any oil from the pan with a paper towel. Return the pan to medium heat and add the butter. When the butter has melted, add the lemon juice and parsley. Stir in the almonds and season to taste with salt and pepper. Spoon the sauce over the fillets and serve.

Trout fillets, 4, 1½ lb (750 g) total weight

Salt and freshly ground pepper

Slivered almonds, ¼ cup (1 oz/30 g)

Flour, ⅓ cup (2 oz/60 g)

Olive oil, 2 tablespoons

Unsalted butter, 4 tablespoons (2 oz/60 g)

Lemon juice, from 1 lemon

Fresh flat-leaf (Italian) parsley, ¼ cup (⅓ oz/ 10 g) minced

MAKES 4 SERVINGS

fish tacos

Tilapia, cod, or other mild white fish fillets, 1 lb (500 g), pin bones removed

Ground cumin, ¼ teaspoon

Dried oregano, ¼ teaspoon

Salt

Olive oil, 1 tablespoon

Lime juice, from 1 lime

Corn tortillas, 12

Green cabbage, 2 cups (6 oz/185 g) finely shredded

Fresh tomatillo salsa, 1 cup (8 fl oz/250 ml)

Sour cream, ⅓ cup (3 oz/90 g)

Fresh cilantro (fresh coriander), 2 tablespoons coarsely chopped

MAKES 4 SERVINGS

1 Season the fish
If using tilapia, split the fillets lengthwise along the seam. Place the fish on a plate. In a small bowl, combine the cumin, oregano, and ½ teaspoon salt. Sprinkle over both sides of the fish. Drizzle with the oil and lime juice.

2 Heat the tortillas
Preheat a cast-iron or other heavy frying pan over medium-low heat, and a stovetop grill pan over medium-low heat on another burner. One at a time, warm the tortillas in the frying pan until flexible, turning once, 30–60 seconds each. Stack them on a plate and cover with a kitchen towel to keep warm.

3 Cook the fish and make the tacos
Raise the heat under the grill pan to medium-high. When the pan is hot, add the fish and cook until golden, about 3 minutes. Turn and cook until golden around the edges, 1–2 minutes longer, depending on fish type and thickness. Transfer the fish to a plate and cut into bite-sized pieces. Place an equal amount of the fish on each warm tortilla and top with some of the shredded cabbage, a spoonful of salsa, and a dollop of sour cream. Sprinkle with cilantro and serve.

sea bass with ginger

1 Make the sauce
Preheat the oven to 425°F (220°C). In a small bowl, combine 3 tablespoons water and the soy sauce, oyster sauce, sesame oil, canola oil, sugar, cornstarch, and a pinch of white pepper. Stir well to dissolve the sugar and cornstarch.

2 Cook the sea bass
Place the fillets in a baking dish just large enough to hold them in a single layer. Scatter the green onions and ginger over the fillets and then drizzle evenly with the sauce. Cover the dish tightly with aluminum foil. Bake until the fillets are opaque throughout, 12–15 minutes. Carefully remove the foil. Spoon the pan juices over the fillets, garnish with the cilantro, and serve with the rice.

cook's tip Any firm white-fleshed fish, such as cod or halibut, can be substituted for the sea bass. Before cooking, quickly check for errant bones by running your fingers lightly along the seams of each fillet. If you detect any bones, remove them with needle-nosed pliers or a paring knife.

Soy sauce, 2 tablespoons

Oyster sauce,
1 tablespoon

Asian sesame oil,
1 tablespoon

Canola or peanut oil,
1 teaspoon

Sugar, ½ teaspoon

Cornstarch (cornflour),
¼ teaspoon

Freshly ground white pepper

Sea bass fillets, 4,
1½ lb (750 g) total weight, pin bones removed

Green (spring) onions,
3, thinly sliced

Fresh ginger,
2 tablespoons thinly sliced strips

Fresh cilantro (fresh coriander), 3 tablespoons chopped

Steamed rice, for serving

MAKES 4 SERVINGS

roast halibut
with herb butter

Unsalted butter,
4 tablespoons (2 oz/60 g),
at room temperature

**Fresh flat-leaf (Italian)
parsley,** 2 teaspoons
minced

Fresh thyme, 1 teaspoon
minced, plus 3 or 4 sprigs

Fresh chives, 1 teaspoon
minced

Lemon zest, from
1 lemon, finely grated

Lemon juice, from
2 lemons

**Salt and freshly ground
pepper**

Yellow onion, 1 large,
thickly sliced

Halibut fillet, 2 lb (1 kg),
pin bones removed

Olive oil, 1½ teaspoons

MAKES 4 SERVINGS

1 Make the herb butter
In a bowl, using a fork, beat the butter until soft and light. Add the minced herbs, lemon zest and juice, and a pinch each of salt and pepper and beat until thoroughly blended. Taste and adjust the seasonings with salt and pepper. (The herb butter may be prepared up to 2 days in advance and stored, tightly covered, in the refrigerator.)

2 Season the halibut
Preheat the oven to 400°F (200°C). Oil a baking dish just large enough to hold the halibut. Spread the onion slices in a single layer in the prepared dish. Scatter the thyme sprigs on top. Rub the halibut with the oil and season lightly with salt and pepper. Place on the onions.

3 Roast the halibut
Roast until an instant-read thermometer inserted into the thickest part of the halibut reads 120°F (49°C). The total cooking time will be about 10 minutes per inch (2.5 cm) of thickness, but start checking 5 minutes before the halibut is scheduled to be done to avoid overcooking. Divide the fillet into individual portions and transfer to plates. Top with the herb butter, place the onion slices alongside, and serve.

creole striped bass

1 Season the fish
In a small bowl, combine the chile powder, paprika, thyme, garlic powder, ½ teaspoon salt, ¼ teaspoon black pepper, and ¼ teaspoon white pepper. Place the fillets on a plate and season on both sides with the spice mixture.

2 Cook the fish
In a large frying pan over medium heat, warm the oil. Add the fish and cook until well browned on the first side, about 4 minutes. Turn and cook until opaque throughout, 2–4 minutes more, depending on thickness. Transfer the fillets to plates.

3 Make the sauce
Wipe any oil from the pan with a paper towel. Return the pan to medium heat and add the lemon juice and 1–2 tablespoons water. Stir, scraping up any browned bits from the pan bottom. Stir in the butter and season to taste with salt and pepper. Spoon the sauce over the fish and serve. »

Ancho chile powder, ½ teaspoon

Paprika, ½ teaspoon

Dried thyme, ¼ teaspoon

Garlic powder, ⅛ teaspoon

Salt and freshly ground black pepper

Freshly ground white pepper

Striped bass or other firm white fish fillets, 4, 1½ lb (750 g) total weight, pin bones removed

Olive oil, 2 tablespoons

Lemon juice, from 1 lemon

Unsalted butter, 2 tablespoons

MAKES 4 SERVINGS

cook's tip

The mixture of salt, chiles, and other spices used to flavor this dish is typical of Louisiana cooking. It is a homemade version of the various packaged Creole or Cajun blends sold in stores. To save time, use 2 ½ teaspoons of one of these premixed seasonings in place of the chile powder, paprika, thyme, garlic powder, salt, and black and white peppers.

ginger salmon cakes

1 Combine the seasonings and fish
In a food processor, combine the ginger and green onions and process until finely chopped, stopping once or twice to scrape down the sides of the work bowl. Sprinkle the salmon with the cornstarch and add to the processor with the egg white, a pinch of salt, and the fish sauce. Using quick pulses, process until the mixture resembles coarsely ground meat. Do not overprocess the mixture or the cakes will be heavy.

2 Form and chill the cakes
Divide the salmon mixture into 8 equal portions. With moistened hands, gently shape each portion into a patty about ½ inch (12 mm) thick. Transfer to a plate, cover with plastic wrap, and refrigerate for 5–10 minutes.

3 Cook the cakes
In a large frying pan over medium heat, warm the 1 tablespoon oil. Add the salmon cakes and cook until golden brown on the first side, about 3 minutes. Turn, adding more oil if needed, and cook until the cakes are slightly springy to the touch and have lost their raw color in the center, 2–3 minutes longer. Transfer to plates and sprinkle with the sesame seeds. Serve, passing the soy sauce, chile sauce, and lemon wedges at the table.

Fresh ginger, 2 tablespoons coarsely chopped

Green (spring) onions, 2, white and pale green parts, coarsely chopped

Salmon fillet, 1 lb (500 g), skin and pin bones removed, cut into small pieces

Cornstarch (cornflour), 1 teaspoon

Egg white, 1

Salt

Asian fish sauce, 1 teaspoon

Canola oil, 1 tablespoon, or as needed

Sesame seeds, 1 tablespoon, toasted

Soy sauce, for serving

Chile sauce such as Sriracha, for serving

Lemon or lime, 1, cut into wedges

MAKES 4 SERVINGS

baked sole with lemon-butter sauce

Asparagus, 1 lb (500 g) medium-sized stalks, tough ends removed

Salt and freshly ground pepper

Sole or flounder fillets, 4 large or 8 small, 1½ lb (750 g) total weight

Unsalted butter, 1 tablespoon

Finely grated lemon zest and juice, from 1 lemon

Flour, 1 tablespoon

Chicken broth or stock, 1 cup (8 fl oz/250 ml), homemade (page 29) or purchased

MAKES 4 SERVINGS

1 Bake the fish and asparagus
Preheat the oven to 400°F (200°C) and butter a 9-by-13-inch (23-by-33-cm) baking dish. Arrange the asparagus in a single layer in the prepared dish and season with salt. Season the fillets on both sides with salt and pepper and place on top of the asparagus. Bake until the fillets are beginning to flake at the tail ends and the asparagus is tender-crisp, about 7 minutes, depending on the thickness of the fillets.

2 Make the sauce
Meanwhile, in a saucepan over low heat, melt the butter with the lemon zest. Whisk in the flour and cook, stirring, until the mixture just begins to color, about 3 minutes. Add the broth and the lemon juice and whisk vigorously to break up any lumps. Cook, whisking occasionally, until thick, about 5 minutes. Season to taste with salt and pepper. Arrange the fillets and asparagus on plates, top with the sauce, and serve.

baked halibut
with salsa verde

1 Cook the halibut
Preheat the oven to 300°F (150°C). Oil a shallow baking dish just large enough to hold the fillets in a single layer. Season the fillets lightly on both sides with salt and pepper and place, skin side down, in the prepared dish. Bake until opaque throughout, about 8 minutes; start checking the fish after about 5 minutes to avoid overcooking.

2 Prepare the sauce
In a food processor, combine the garlic, parsley, tarragon, oil, anchovy paste, if using, and 1 tablespoon vinegar. Process until smooth, stopping once or twice to scrape down the sides of the work bowl. Season to taste with salt, pepper, and more vinegar, if desired. Transfer the fillets to plates, top with the sauce, and serve.

cook's tip If you prefer a mellow-tasting sauce, you can first blanch the garlic and herbs. Bring a small saucepan of water to a boil, add the garlic, and cook for 1 minute. Add the parsley and tarragon and cook just until wilted. Drain into a fine-mesh sieve and let cool briefly before puréeing in Step 2.

Halibut or salmon fillets, 4, 1½ lb (750 g) total weight, pin bones removed

Salt and freshly ground pepper

Garlic, 2 cloves

Fresh flat-leaf (Italian) parsley, 1 cup (1 oz/30 g) loosely packed leaves

Fresh tarragon, 1 tablespoon leaves

Olive oil, 5 tablespoons (2½ fl oz/75 ml)

Anchovy paste, 1 teaspoon (optional)

Sherry vinegar, 1 tablespoon, or to taste

MAKES 4 SERVINGS

fried catfish & greens

Catfish fillets, 4, 1½ lb
(750 g) total weight

**Salt and freshly ground
black pepper**

Buttermilk, ½ cup
(4 fl oz/125 ml)

Fine yellow cornmeal,
1 cup (5 oz/155 g)

Cayenne pepper,
¼ teaspoon

Peanut or canola oil,
3 tablespoons

Yellow onion, 1, halved
and thinly sliced

Garlic, 1 clove, sliced

**Collard, mustard, or
turnip greens,**
2 bunches, 1 lb (500 g)
total weight, shredded

Lemons, 2, cut into
wedges

MAKES 4 SERVINGS

1 Season the catfish
Put the fillets in a shallow bowl or baking dish and season lightly with salt and black pepper. Add the buttermilk and let stand for 5–10 minutes. On a plate, stir together the cornmeal and cayenne.

2 Cook the greens
In a deep frying pan over low heat, warm 1 tablespoon of the oil. Add the onion and cook, stirring occasionally, until it begins to soften, about 10 minutes. Raise the heat to medium, add the garlic and greens, cover, and cook, stirring occasionally, until the greens are tender, about 15 minutes. Season to taste with salt and black pepper and keep warm.

3 Fry the catfish
Meanwhile, in a large frying pan over medium heat, warm the remaining 2 tablespoons oil. Lift each fillet from the buttermilk, letting any excess drip into the bowl. Roll the fillets in the cornmeal mixture, coating both sides well and shaking off any excess. Place in the pan and cook until golden brown, about 4 minutes. Turn and cook until opaque throughout, 2–3 minutes longer. Transfer to paper towels to drain. Arrange the fillets on plates, place the greens and lemon wedges alongside, and serve.

miso-marinated salmon

1 Marinate the fish
In a shallow glass or ceramic dish just large enough to hold the fillets in a single layer, stir together the miso, mirin, sake, brown sugar, and soy sauce. Add the fillets and turn to coat. Let stand at room temperature for 10 minutes, turning the fillets occasionally, or cover and refrigerate for up to overnight.

2 Cook the fish
Preheat the broiler (grill). Remove the fillets from the marinade, reserving the marinade. Line a rimmed baking sheet with aluminum foil. Arrange the fillets on the prepared sheet. Add the bok choy to the reserved marinade and turn to coat. Remove the bok choy, reserving the marinade, and arrange around the salmon. Broil (grill) until the fillets and bok choy are deep golden brown and lightly charred on the edges, 3–4 minutes. Turn the fillets and bok choy, and brush with the reserved marinade. Broil until the salmon is slightly charred on the outside and just opaque throughout and the bok choy is tender-crisp, 3–4 minutes longer. Transfer to plates and serve.

White or yellow miso,
½ cup (5 oz/155 g)

Mirin or dry sherry,
⅓ cup (3 fl oz/80 ml)

Sake or dry white wine,
¼ cup (2 fl oz/60 ml)

Light brown sugar,
3 tablespoons firmly packed

Soy sauce, 2 tablespoons

Salmon fillets, 4, about 1½ lb (750 g) total weight, skin and pin bones removed

Baby bok choy, 2 or 3 heads, cut in half lengthwise

MAKES 4 SERVINGS

spicy snapper with tomatoes & olives

Yellow onion, 1, sliced

Snapper, rockfish, or other firm white fish fillets, 4, 1½ lb (750 g) total weight, pin bones removed

Salt

Limes, 2, halved

Canned crushed tomatoes, 1 cup (8 fl oz/ 250 ml) with juice

Green olives, 6, pitted and chopped

Capers, 1 teaspoon

Pickled jalapeño chiles, 1 tablespoon chopped

Fresh cilantro (fresh coriander), 1 tablespoon coarsely chopped (optional)

MAKES 4 SERVINGS

1 Prepare the onion and fish
Preheat the oven to 400°F (200°C). Oil a baking dish just large enough to hold the fish in a single layer. Spread the onion slices in an even layer in the prepared dish and place in the oven as it preheats. Place the fish fillets on a plate and season lightly on both sides with salt. Squeeze the lime halves over the fish.

2 Cook the fish
Remove the baking dish from the oven and arrange the fillets, skin side down, on top of the onion. Top with the tomatoes, then scatter with the olives, capers, and chiles. Cover the dish tightly with aluminum foil and cook until the fillets are opaque throughout, about 10 minutes for thin fillets or 12–15 minutes for fillets about 1 inch (2.5 cm) thick. Sprinkle with the cilantro, if using, and serve.

> **cook's tip** Pickled jalapeños give this Mexican dish a piquant chile flavor. If you prefer the flavor of fresh jalapeños, cut them in half lengthwise, remove the seeds and membranes, and put them in the baking dish along with the onion in Step 1.

seared salmon with mashed potatoes

1 Prepare the potatoes
Place the potatoes in a saucepan with water to cover. Add ½ teaspoon salt, cover, and bring to a boil. Reduce the heat to low and cook until the potatoes are tender, about 15 minutes. Drain, reserving about ½ cup (4 fl oz/125 ml) of the cooking water. Return the potatoes to the pan over low heat and add the milk and butter. Using a potato masher, mash the potatoes until creamy, adding some of the reserved cooking water if the potatoes are too thick. Season with salt and pepper and cover the pan to keep warm.

2 Cook the parsley and salmon
While the potatoes are cooking, in a large frying pan over medium-high heat, warm the oil. Add the parsley and cook until crisp, 10–15 seconds. Using tongs, transfer to a paper towel to drain. Add the salmon and cook until browned on the first side, about 4 minutes. Turn and cook until opaque throughout, 2–4 minutes longer. Add the lemon slices to the pan and let warm as the salmon finishes cooking. Arrange the potatoes, salmon, lemon slices, and parsley on plates and serve. »

Russet potatoes, 1½ lb (750 g), peeled and quartered

Salt and freshly ground pepper

Milk, ¼ cup (2 fl oz/ 60 ml), warmed

Unsalted butter, 2 tablespoons

Olive oil, 3 tablespoons

Fresh flat-leaf (Italian) parsley, 4 large sprigs

Salmon fillets, 4, 1½ lb (750 g) total weight, pin bones removed

Lemons, 2, sliced

MAKES 4 SERVINGS

seared salmon with mashed potatoes

continued

cook's tip

For variety, replace the parsley with basil, tarragon, or another fairly sturdy fresh herb. Tiny or especially delicate herbs such as thyme, dill, and chervil are more difficult to fry successfully but are also possible substitutions.

seared tuna
with white beans

1 Warm the beans
In a saucepan over medium heat, warm the beans, stirring frequently, until heated through, about 2 minutes.

2 Sear the tuna
Season the tuna steaks on both sides with salt and pepper. In a frying pan over medium-high heat, warm the oil. Add the tuna and sear until crisp and browned, about 2 minutes on each side for rare. Add the parsley to the beans and toss. Arrange the beans and tuna steaks on plates and serve.

White Beans (page 36), 2 cups (14 oz/440 g)

Tuna steaks, 4, each about ¾ inch (2 cm) thick

Salt and freshly ground pepper

Olive oil, 3 tablespoons

Fresh flat-leaf (Italian) parsley, 2 tablespoons minced

MAKES 4 SERVINGS

stovetop smoked salmon

Sugar, 1 teaspoon

Salt and freshly ground white pepper

Salmon fillet, 1½ lb (750 g), skin intact and pin bones removed

MAKES 4 SERVINGS

1 Season the salmon
In a bowl, combine the sugar, 1½ teaspoons salt, and a scant ¼ teaspoon white pepper. Rinse the fillet and pat dry. Spread the seasonings over the bone side of the fillet, applying them more heavily on the thickest parts.

2 Set up the smoking pan
Choose a deep frying pan (avoid nonstick) large enough to hold the fillet on a footed wire rack inside the pan. Line the pan with a piece of heavy-duty aluminum foil 18 inches (45 cm) wide and 3 times as long as the width of the rack, pressing it against the surface. Sprinkle a large handful of fine hardwood smoking chips in the middle of the pan and set the rack on top. Place the fillet, skin side down, on the rack. Bring the edges of the foil up and crimp together to form a tent over the fillet, leaving a small vent.

3 Smoke the salmon
Turn on the kitchen exhaust fan, if you have one. Heat the pan over medium-high heat until smoke begins to emerge from the vent. Reduce the heat to medium-low, crimp the vent closed, and cook the salmon until opaque throughout, about 10 minutes. If necessary, reseal and continue to cook until done. Carve the fillet and serve.

indian fish curry

1 Make the curry base
In a deep frying pan or wok over medium-low heat, warm the oil. Add the onion, garlic, and ginger and cook until the onion is softened, about 5 minutes. Stir in the curry powder and cook for 1 minute. Add the coconut milk, chiles, and 1 teaspoon salt. Cook until fragrant and slightly thickened, about 15 minutes.

2 Season the fish
Meanwhile, place the fillets in a shallow bowl. Sprinkle with the turmeric and ½ teaspoon salt and toss to coat.

3 Finish the curry
Add the tomatoes, lemon juice, and ½ cup (4 fl oz/125 ml) hot water to the curry base and bring to a simmer over medium heat. Taste and adjust the seasoning with salt. Add the fish and cook until the fish begins to flake apart, about 5 minutes. Transfer to bowls and serve.

> **cook's tip** For a heartier meal, add ½ cup (2½ oz/75 g) frozen petite peas to the pan when you add the fish. Or, add 1 zucchini (courgette), cut into small pieces, along with the coconut milk. Serve the curry over steamed rice.

Canola oil or clarified butter, 1 tablespoon

Yellow onion, 1, halved and thinly sliced

Garlic, 2 cloves, minced

Fresh ginger, 1 tablespoon minced

Curry powder, 1 tablespoon

Unsweetened coconut milk, 1 can (14 fl oz/430 ml)

Jalapeño or serrano chiles, 2 small, halved and seeded

Salt

Rockfish, snapper, cod, or other firm white fish fillets, 1 lb (500 g), pin bones removed, cut into bite-sized pieces

Ground turmeric, ¼ teaspoon

Plum (Roma) tomatoes, 2, seeded and chopped

Lemon juice, from 1 lemon

MAKES 4 SERVINGS

tilapia with sweet peppers

Olive oil, 3 tablespoons

Red, orange, or yellow bell peppers (capsicums), 3, seeded and sliced

Garlic, 1 large clove, sliced

Dried oregano, ¼ teaspoon

Chicken or vegetable broth, ¼ cup (2 fl oz/ 60 ml)

Salt and freshly ground pepper

Tilapia fillets, 4, 1½ lb (750 g) total weight, pin bones removed

Paprika, ¼ teaspoon

Flour, ¼ cup (1½ oz/45 g)

Sherry vinegar, ½ teaspoon

MAKES 4 SERVINGS

1 Sauté the peppers
In a deep frying pan over medium heat, warm 2 tablespoons of the oil. Add the peppers and sauté for about 2 minutes. Add the garlic, oregano, broth, ¼ teaspoon salt, and a pinch of pepper. Cover and cook until the peppers are tender, about 20 minutes.

2 Cook the fish
Meanwhile, place the fillets on a plate. Season on both sides with the paprika and then sprinkle with salt. Preheat a large, heavy frying pan over low heat. When the peppers are nearly done, raise the heat under the pan to medium-high. Add the remaining 1 tablespoon oil. Sprinkle the fillets on both sides with the flour, shaking off any excess. Add to the pan and cook until golden brown, about 3 minutes. Turn and cook until just opaque throughout, about 3 minutes. Stir the vinegar into the peppers and season to taste with salt and pepper. Transfer the fillets and peppers to plates and serve.

cook's tip The pepper mixture, a simple version of a Basque *pipérade*, is equally good with just about any type of mild white fish or tuna.

halibut with tomatoes & leeks

1 Roast the leeks

Preheat the oven to 450°F (230°C). In a large roasting pan, toss the leeks with 2 tablespoons of the oil and season with salt and pepper. Spread the leeks out in a single layer. Roast until just tender, about 10 minutes. Remove the pan from the oven and add the tomatoes to the pan. Preheat the broiler (grill).

2 Cook the halibut

Season the halibut with salt and pepper and lay the fillets over the leeks and tomatoes. Drizzle with the remaining 1 tablespoon oil. Broil (grill) until the fillets are just opaque throughout, about 8 minutes. Transfer the fillets to plates, top with the leeks and tomatoes, and serve.

Leeks, 3 lb (1.5 kg), white and pale green parts, halved, rinsed, and thinly sliced

Olive oil, 3 tablespoons

Salt and freshly ground pepper

Cherry tomatoes, 2 cups (12 oz/375 g)

Halibut fillets, 4, about 6 oz (185 g) each

MAKES 4 SERVINGS

> cook's tip When fresh basil is in season, use strips of it to garnish the halibut. To cut the basil leaves into strips, stack the leaves on top of one another and roll them tightly lengthwise. Using a chef's knife or kitchen shears, cut the leaves crosswise into thin strips.

cajun shrimp boil

Seafood boil seasoning such as Old Bay, 6 tablespoons

Yellow onions, 2 large, quartered

Garlic, 1 head, unpeeled and halved crosswise

Lemons, 2, halved

Red-skinned potatoes, 2 lb (1 kg) small

Corn, 4 ears, each cut into thirds

Smoked pork or chicken sausages, 1½ lb (750 g), cut into slices 1 inch (2.5 cm) thick

Large shrimp (prawns), 3 lb (1.5 kg), unpeeled and tails intact

MAKES 6 SERVINGS

1 Simmer the potatoes
Fill a large pot with water and place over high heat. Add the seafood seasoning, onions, garlic, and lemon halves and bring to a boil. Add the potatoes, reduce the heat to low, and simmer until the potatoes are tender, 15–20 minutes.

2 Cook the shrimp
Add the corn and sausages to the pot and cook for 5 minutes. Remove from the heat, add the shrimp, cover, and let stand until the shrimp are opaque, about 4 minutes. Pour the contents of the pot into a colander to drain. Return the shrimp, sausage, and vegetables to the pot, or place in a large serving bowl, and serve.

thai green curry mussels

1 Make the curry base

Add ¼ cup (2 fl oz/60 ml) of the coconut milk and the curry paste to a wok or large saucepan and set over medium-low heat. Cut the bottom one-third of the lemongrass stalk into 1-inch (2.5-cm) pieces. Crush the pieces with the flat side of a chef's knife. Add to the wok along with the lime leaf, if using. Bring the curry mixture to a simmer over medium heat and cook, stirring occasionally, until fragrant, about 5 minutes.

2 Cook the mussels

Add the remaining coconut milk, ½ cup (4 fl oz/125 ml) water, and the fish sauce to the curry base and stir to blend. Discard any mussels that do not close to the touch, then raise the heat to high and add the mussels to the wok. When a few start to open, cover the pan and cook for 2 minutes. Uncover and, using a slotted spoon, transfer the opened mussels to bowls. Cover again and continue to cook until the remaining mussels open, about 2 minutes longer. Transfer the mussels to the bowls, discarding any that have failed to open. Remove and discard the lemongrass stalk and lime leaf, if using. Ladle the broth over the mussels, garnish with the basil, and serve.

Unsweetened coconut milk, 1 can (14 fl oz/430 ml)

Thai green curry paste, 1 tablespoon

Lemongrass, 1 stalk

Kaffir lime leaf, 1 (optional)

Asian fish sauce, 1 tablespoon

Mussels, 1½ lb (750 g), scrubbed and debearded if necessary

Fresh basil or mint, 3 tablespoons slivered

MAKES 4 SERVINGS

lime shrimp
with coconut rice

Unsalted butter,
5 tablespoons (2½ oz/
75 g)

Long-grain white rice,
1 cup (7 oz/220 g)

**Unsweetened coconut
milk,** 1 cup (8 fl oz/
250 ml)

Lime, 1

Garlic, 6 cloves, minced

Large shrimp (prawns),
1 lb (500 g) total weight,
peeled and deveined

Green (spring) onions,
8, white and pale green
parts, thinly sliced

**Fresh cilantro (fresh
coriander),** ¼ cup
(⅓ oz/10 g) minced

MAKES 4 SERVINGS

1 Cook the rice
In a saucepan over medium heat,
melt 1 tablespoon of the butter. Add the
rice and cook, stirring constantly, until
the grains are well coated, about 1 minute.
Stir in 1 cup (8 fl oz/250 ml) water and the
coconut milk and bring to a boil. Reduce
the heat to low, cover, and cook until the
liquid is absorbed and the rice is tender,
about 20 minutes.

2 Cook the shrimp
Meanwhile, grate 1 teaspoon zest
and squeeze 2 tablespoons juice from the
lime. About 5 minutes before the rice is
ready, in a large frying pan over medium
heat, melt the remaining 4 tablespoons
(2 oz/60 g) butter. Add the garlic and lime
zest and juice and stir until the mixture is
bubbly. Add the shrimp and onions and
sauté until the shrimp are just opaque
throughout, about 3 minutes. Stir in half
of the cilantro.

3 Finish the rice
Fluff the rice with a fork and gently
stir in the remaining cilantro. Arrange the
rice and shrimp on plates and serve.

salt & pepper shrimp

1 **Make the spice mixture**
In a small bowl, stir together the sugar, five-spice powder, and ¼ teaspoon each salt and pepper.

2 **Sear the shrimp**
Heat a wok or large frying pan over high heat until very hot and add 2 tablespoons of the oil. Spread the cornstarch on a plate. Dip each shrimp into the cornstarch, coating both sides and shaking off the excess. Add the shrimp to the pan in a single layer and sear, turning once, just until opaque throughout, about 1 minute on each side. Using a slotted spoon, transfer the shrimp to a bowl.

3 **Finish the dish**
Return the pan to high heat and add the remaining 2 tablespoons oil. Add the ginger, garlic, and chile and stir-fry until fragrant, about 5 seconds. Add the spice mixture and mirin, return the shrimp to the pan, and stir-fry until the shrimp are coated with the spice mixture and are heated through, 15–20 seconds. »

Sugar, ¼ teaspoon

Chinese five-spice powder, ¼ teaspoon

Salt and freshly ground pepper

Canola or peanut oil, 4 tablespoons (2 fl oz/ 60 ml)

Cornstarch (cornflour), ¼ cup (1 oz/30 g)

Large shrimp (prawns), 1½ lb (750 g), peeled and deveined

Fresh ginger, 2 tablespoons minced

Garlic, 3 cloves, minced

Red or green jalapeño chile, 1, seeded and minced

Mirin, 2 tablespoons

MAKES 4 SERVINGS

cook's tip

For extra flavor, you can serve the shrimp with a citrus-soy
dipping sauce: stir together 3 tablespoons fresh lemon juice,
2 tablespoons soy sauce, 1 tablespoon water, ½ teaspoon
minced fresh cilantro (fresh coriander), ¼ teaspoon sugar,
and 1 clove garlic, minced. The sauce can be made a day
in advance, covered, and refrigerated; bring to room
temperature before serving.

five-spice scallops with noodles

1 Prepare the oranges and noodles
Grate 1 teaspoon zest and squeeze ½ cup (4 fl oz/125 ml) juice from the oranges; set aside. Bring a large pot of water to a boil. Add the noodles and cook, stirring, until tender, according to the package directions. Drain.

2 Cook the scallops
Meanwhile, sprinkle the scallops on both sides with the five-spice powder and season lightly with salt and pepper. In a large frying pan over high heat, warm 3 tablespoons of the oil. Working in batches if necessary, add the scallops to the pan in a single layer and cook until well browned, about 1 minute. Turn and cook until well browned and just opaque in the center, 1–2 minutes. Transfer to a plate.

3 Cook the vegetables
Add the remaining 1 tablespoon oil to the same pan over high heat. Add the ginger and garlic and stir-fry just until fragrant, about 30 seconds. Add the sugar snap peas and stir-fry just until tender-crisp, about 1 minute. Stir in the orange zest and juice, wine, and soy sauce and cook until slightly reduced, 1–2 minutes. Add the cooked noodles and green onions and toss gently. Arrange in shallow bowls, top with the scallops, and serve.

Oranges, 2

Fresh Chinese egg noodles, ½ lb (250 g)

Large sea scallops, 1¼ lb (625 g) total weight, side muscles removed

Chinese five-spice powder, 2 teaspoons

Salt and freshly ground pepper

Peanut or canola oil, 4 tablespoons (2 fl oz/ 60 ml)

Fresh ginger, 1 tablespoon finely chopped

Garlic, 3 cloves, minced

Sugar snap peas, 1¼ lb (625 g)

Dry white wine, ½ cup (4 fl oz/125 ml)

Soy sauce, 2 tablespoons

Green (spring) onions, 4, white and pale green parts, chopped

MAKES 4 SERVINGS

chile-garlic prawns

Soy sauce, 6 tablespoons (3 fl oz/90 ml)

Rice vinegar, ¼ cup (2 fl oz/60 ml)

Asian sesame oil, 4 teaspoons

Ketchup, ¼ cup (2 oz/60 g)

Sugar, 2 teaspoons

Cornstarch (cornflour), 2 teaspoons

Canola or peanut oil, 3 tablespoons

Tiger prawns, 2 lb (1 kg), peeled and deveined

Fresh ginger, 2 tablespoons minced

Garlic, 4 cloves, minced

Red or green jalapeño chile, 1, seeded and minced

Green (spring) onions, 6, white and pale green parts, thinly sliced

Steamed rice, for serving (optional)

MAKES 4 SERVINGS

1 **Make the sauce**
In a small bowl, combine the soy sauce, vinegar, sesame oil, ketchup, sugar, cornstarch, and 6 tablespoons (3 fl oz/ 90 ml) water and and stir to dissolve the cornstarch and sugar.

2 **Stir-fry the prawns**
Heat a wok or large frying pan over high heat until hot and add 2 tablespoons of the canola oil. Add the prawns and sear, turning once, until browned on both sides, about 2 minutes total. Using a slotted spoon, transfer the prawns to a bowl. Return the pan to high heat and add the remaining 1 tablespoon canola oil. Add the ginger, garlic, chile, and two-thirds of the green onions and stir-fry until fragrant, about 10 seconds. Give the sauce a quick stir, add to the pan, and stir until it begins to bubble. Add the prawns and stir-fry until the prawns are opaque throughout and the sauce has thickened slightly, about 1 minute. Garnish with the remaining green onions and serve over the rice, if using.

lobster rolls

1 Extract the lobster meat

Twist off the claws from the body. Using a lobster cracker or mallet, break the shell on each claw and remove the meat. Using a large, sharp knife, cut the lobster in half lengthwise from head to tail. Discard the black vein that runs the length of the body and the small sand sac at the base of the head. Remove the meat from the body and tail. Twist off the small legs where they join the body to check for other chunks of meat.

2 Make the lobster salad

Chop the lobster meat and place in a bowl. Add the celery, bell pepper, mayonnaise, and mustard. Stir to blend and season to taste with salt.

3 Toast the rolls

Heat a frying pan over medium heat. Butter the cut sides of the rolls. Place the rolls, buttered side down, in the pan and toast until golden brown, about 3 minutes. Transfer the rolls to plates, fill with the lobster salad, and serve.

> cook's tip These rolls can also be made with ½ lb (250 g) cooked crabmeat or ½ lb cooked and roughly chopped shrimp (prawns).

Cooked lobster, 1, 1½ lb (750 g)

Celery, 1 large stalk, finely chopped

Red bell pepper (capsicum), ½, seeded and finely chopped

Mayonnaise, 3 tablespoons

Dijon mustard, ½ teaspoon

Salt

Unsalted butter, 1 tablespoon, at room temperature

Soft rolls, 4, split

MAKES 4 SERVINGS

fritto misto

Peanut oil for frying

Cake (soft-wheat) flour,
2 cups (8 oz/250 g)

Salt and freshly ground pepper

Squid bodies and tentacles, ¾ lb (375 g), bodies cut crosswise into rings

Medium shrimp (prawns), ¾ lb (375 g), peeled and deveined, tails intact

Lemon, 1, very thinly sliced

MAKES 4 SERVINGS

1 Heat the oil
Preheat the oven to 250°F (120°C). Line a rimmed baking sheet with paper towels, set a rack on top of the towels, and place in the oven. Fill a large, heavy saucepan with oil to a depth of about 2 inches (5 cm). Heat the pan over high heat until the oil reaches 400°F (200°C) on a deep-frying thermometer.

2 Cook the seafood
In a large, shallow bowl, whisk together the flour, 1 teaspoon salt, and 1 teaspoon pepper. Working in small batches, toss the squid and shrimp in the flour mixture, coating them evenly and shaking off any excess. Using a wire skimmer, lower the seafood into the hot oil. Fry, turning once, until golden, 3–4 minutes. Remove from the oil and place on the prepared baking sheet in the oven. Let the oil return to 400°F between batches. Transfer to a platter, garnish with the lemon slices, and serve.

cook's tip To make a dipping sauce, combine ½ cup (4 fl oz/ 125 ml) mayonnaise, 1 tablespoon lemon juice, and ½ teaspoon cayenne pepper. Season to taste with salt and pepper.

shrimp scampi

1 Cook the shrimp
In a frying pan over medium heat, warm the oil. Add the shrimp and cook, stirring, just until opaque throughout, about 4 minutes. Transfer to a plate.

2 Make the sauce
Return the pan to medium heat. Add the garlic, parsley, thyme, and basil and sauté until fragrant, about 30 seconds. Add the wine and stir, scraping up any browned bits on the bottom of the pan. Cook until the wine evaporates slightly, then remove the pan from the heat and add the butter and a pinch of pepper. Stir until the butter melts, then return the shrimp to the pan and toss to coat with the sauce. Taste and adjust the seasoning with salt and pepper and serve. »

Olive or canola oil, 1 tablespoon

Shrimp (prawns), 1½ lb (750 g), peeled and deveined, tails intact

Garlic, 2 cloves, minced

Fresh flat-leaf (Italian) parsley, 1 tablespoon minced

Fresh thyme, 1 teaspoon minced

Fresh basil, 1 teaspoon minced

Dry white wine, 3 tablespoons

Unsalted butter, 2 tablespoons

Salt and freshly ground pepper

MAKES 4 SERVINGS

cook's tip

For an easy pasta dish, boil 1 lb (500 g) fresh or dried fettuccine, linguine, or spaghetti in lightly salted water until al dente, then drain, reserving some of the cooking water. Toss the drained pasta in the pan with the cooked shrimp and sauce, adding a little of the reserved cooking water to achieve a nice sauce consistency.

ale-steamed clams

1 **Steam the clams**
In a large saucepan, Dutch oven, or stockpot, combine the ale and shallot. Add the clams, discarding any that do not close to the touch. Cover, bring to a boil over high heat, and cook, shaking the pan occasionally, for 3–4 minutes. Uncover and, using a slotted spoon, transfer any fully opened clams to serving bowls. Re-cover the pan and continue to cook until the remaining clams open. The total cooking time will be 5–10 minutes, depending on the size of the clams. Transfer the opened clams to the bowls, discarding any that have failed to open.

2 **Finish the broth**
Add the butter to the hot broth and stir until melted. Ladle some broth into each bowl. Serve with bread for dipping into the broth.

cook's tip Look for an ale that has a sweet malt flavor and is not too bitter. The best choice is a wheat-based Bavarian-style *hefeweizen* or a white ale in the Belgian tradition. A highly hopped ale may yield a broth that is overly bitter.

Wheat, white, or brown ale, 1 cup (8 fl oz/250 ml), at room temperature

Shallot, 1, minced

Littleneck, Manila, or other small clams, 4 dozen, scrubbed

Unsalted butter, 2 tablespoons

Baguette or other crusty white bread, for serving

MAKES 4 SERVINGS

classic crab cakes

Eggs, 2

Mayonnaise, ½ cup
(4 fl oz/125 ml)

Dijon mustard,
2 tablespoons

Worcestershire sauce,
2 tablespoons

**Hot pepper sauce such
as Tabasco,** ½ teaspoon

Fresh lump crabmeat,
2 lb (1 kg), picked over
for shell fragments and
squeezed to remove
excess water

Dried bread crumbs,
½ cup (1 oz/30 g)

Fresh chives,
4 tablespoons minced

Canola oil, ⅔ cup
(5 fl oz/160 ml)

Mixed salad greens,
4 cups (4 oz/125 g)

Lemon wedges, for
serving

MAKES 6 SERVINGS

1 Prepare the crab cakes
In a large bowl, beat the eggs lightly. Add the mayonnaise, mustard, Worcestershire sauce, hot pepper sauce, crabmeat, bread crumbs, and chives. Stir with a fork until well mixed. Gently form the mixture into small patties about 1½ inches (4 cm) in diameter. You should have 18–20 patties. Transfer the patties to a baking sheet and refrigerate for 15–30 minutes or place in the freezer (see tip, below).

2 Cook the crab cakes
In a large frying pan over medium heat, warm the oil. Working in batches if necessary, add the crab cakes and cook, without moving them, until golden brown, about 4 minutes. Turn and cook until golden brown on the second sides, 3–4 minutes longer. Arrange the greens on plates, top with the crab cakes, and serve with the lemon wedges.

cook's tip Freeze the uncooked crab cakes on a baking sheet until firm, about 2 hours. Wrap the cakes in plastic wrap and place in a plastic freezer bag. Freeze for up to 1 month. Thaw the cakes overnight in the refrigerator before cooking.

seafood made easy

Incorporating seafood dishes into your weekly menus is a good way to put nutritious meals on the table with minimum time or effort. Because seafood cooks quickly, planning ahead will pay off: when it's time to make dinner, you'll be able to prepare a memorable dish in just minutes.

FISH FACTS

Healthful benefits All types of fish are high in protein, and most are low in fat. Those that are not, such as salmon, are high in omega-3 fatty acids, which can lower cholesterol. For these reasons, many nutritionists advise eating fish at least twice a week.

Cautions The relatively high mercury content of some fish, including swordfish, shark, and king mackerel, has caused alarm. Doctors have warned pregnant women about eating these fish. Nursing mothers, young children, and anyone who may become pregnant may want to avoid them as well. Salmon is not included in this category, but farmed salmon can be high in toxins.

Fish at risk A number of the most popular types of fish are now considered endangered due to overfishing or pollution. Ask your fishmonger for substitutes and ensure that the source is a trusted and sustainable one.

Choosing seafood Fish and shellfish are sold in a variety of forms—fresh, frozen, or thawed—and in supermarkets, warehouse stores, and ethnic and specialty markets. In some areas, you may be able to buy fish directly from the fishmonger or from a local source at a farmers' market. Wherever you shop, here are some tips that will help you choose the best seafood to prepare.

- ASK QUESTIONS Fresh fish is always ideal, but some types are frozen so that they can be shipped long distances. Ask if the seafood you are buying is fresh or frozen, or wild or farmed.

- TRUST YOUR INSTINCTS Although a fish market will never have the aroma of a bakery, it should smell like the sea, and the fish and shellfish should be chilled, preferably on a bed of ice.

- CHECK APPEARANCES Fresh fish fillets should be shiny. Dull colors and dry surfaces are warning signs that something is not right. Purchase whole fish only with clear—not cloudy—eyes. Bivalves such as clams and mussels should have tightly closed shells, or shells that close when touched. Live crabs or lobsters should still be active in the tank.

- BE FLEXIBLE Many seafood recipes have more than one option for the type of fish or shellfish that can be used. If the exact type you are looking for is not available, ask for a substitute. Or, purchase the freshest catch of the day and build your menu around it.

Cooking seafood Seafood can be cooked in a number of different ways, but one rule applies to every method, from grilling to roasting to frying: don't overcook it. Shrimp (prawns) are cooked when they turn pink. Most fin fish is done when it is opaque throughout and the texture is firm and flaky but still moist. The two exceptions are tuna and salmon, which are often quickly seared and eaten rare to medium-rare. When cooking any type of seafood, check it for doneness often to prevent overcooking.

seafood preparation

Peeling shrimp Working with one shrimp (prawn) at a time, pull off the small legs on the underside. Starting with the section of shell closest to the head, gently pull it up and lift it away. Leave the tail intact or remove it, depending on your preference or as the recipe directs. To remove it, hold firmly as you pull so the meat remains.

Deveining shrimp Use a small, sharp paring knife to make a shallow cut down the center of the outer curve of the shrimp. With the tip of the knife, gently lift out the long vein and pull it out, scraping it away or rinsing it out if necessary.

Cleaning clams and mussels Using a stiff-bristled brush, scrub clams and mussels well under cold running water to rid them of grit. Discard any mollusks that do not close to the touch.

Removing pin bones from fish The small pin bones found in salmon, halibut, and other types of fish fillets should be removed before cooking. Lay the fillet skin side down and run a fingertip along the seams to locate the bones. Using fish tweezers or needle-nosed pliers, pull the bones out one by one, gripping the tip of each bone and pulling up diagonally.

Skinning a fish fillet Position the tail end of the fillet near the edge of the cutting board. Using a fillet knife or other slim, long-bladed knife, hold the edge of the skin at the tail end securely, and position the blade at a slight upward angle between the skin and the flesh. Gently slide the blade forward along the skin, moving up along the fillet, until the meat is loosened. Discard the skin.

Cooking a fish fillet Be sure your pan or grill is hot before adding fish fillets. Because they cook quickly, a cool pan will extend the cooking time and compromise the texture of the final dish.

Testing for doneness An instant-read thermometer is useful for checking thick fish steaks or other large cuts (follow the recipe's temperature guidelines). For fillets, insert a knife or skewer into the center; it should enter easily. Clams and mussels should be cooked until they open; discard any that fail to open. Crab and lobster are done when their shells turn bright red.

FROZEN SEAFOOD

Frozen seafood is a convenient item to have on hand. Look for packages that are free of ice crystals and are kept in the coldest area of the freezer. Put them in your shopping cart just before checking out, and transfer them to your own freezer as soon as possible.

Fish fillets At the market, buy individually frozen fish fillets. They will thaw more quickly than those frozen together in a solid block. Fillets can often be baked or steamed while still frozen; add 3–5 minutes to the cooking time, depending on the thickness of the fillet.

Scallops While freshly caught scallops are ideal, quick-frozen scallops are frozen as soon as they are shucked and often have a better flavor than those that have been sitting for several days before being delivered to the market.

Shrimp Most shrimp is frozen before it reaches the store, so frozen shrimp is often of a better quality than fresh and can be used for anything from salads to curries to stir-fries. The best way to thaw frozen shrimp is in the refrigerator. If you are short on time, thaw under running cold water.

Below are some general tips on storing seafood. See the storage chart on page 420 for seafood storage times.

Keeping it cold Be sure to refrigerate seafood as soon as possible after you purchase it. The best way to store just-purchased seafood is in its original wrapping in the coldest part of the refrigerator, usually in the back.

Storing fish Most fish should be used the same day you purchase it to maintain its flavor and texture. If you need to refrigerate the fish overnight, put the package in a resealable plastic bag and store it on top of ice cubes placed in a baking dish. Or, simply set the package on top of frozen ice packs.

Storing shellfish Store live shellfish such as clams or mussels in a bowl and cover with a damp towel. Because they need air to survive, never wrap live shellfish tightly or submerge them in water. Shrimp (prawns) should be stored in a resealable plastic bag on a bed of ice. As with fish, try to use shellfish within a day of purchasing for the best flavor and texture.

types of fish & shellfish

There are hundreds of varieties of fish and shellfish. Learning the best way to cook each type will make your seafood meals more satisfying, and knowing which variety can be substituted for another in a recipe will make it easy to use what's fresh and available at the market. Most fin fish are defined by texture, flavor, and fat content; shellfish are divided into two main groups, mollusks and crustaceans.

- **FISH: LEAN & MILD** The majority of fish you prepare in your kitchen will be of this variety. Some of the most common examples include sea bass, catfish, rockfish (snapper), sole, tilapia, and trout. Because of the delicate texture of these fish, they are best when cooked with liquid or some fat to keep them moist. Suitable cooking methods include poaching, steaming, and sautéing.

- **FISH: RICH & FULL FLAVORED** These fish are typically those with a high oil content and a deep color and flavor. Both salmon and tuna fall into this category, as do sardines and mackerel. They take well to bold flavors and marinades and can withstand harsh, drier cooking methods, such as roasting, broiling, and grilling.

- **FISH: THICK & MEATY** This category consists of fish that are too large to be cooked whole. Its members can be from the rich and full flavored category, such as tuna, or the lean and mild category, like halibut and swordfish. These fish are often sliced crosswise into thick steaks, which makes them ideal candidates for pan-searing, grilling, broiling, and roasting.

- **SHELLFISH: CRUSTACEANS** These animated shellfish have legs or fins, and their delicate bodies are protected by a tough external skeleton. Crabs, lobsters, and shrimp (prawns) are the most popular and common shellfish in this category. Crabs and lobsters are often steamed or boiled, while shrimp can be cooked by many methods, such as boiling, sautéing, and stir-frying.

- **SHELLFISH: MOLLUSKS** There are two main categories of mollusk: bivalves and cephalopods. Bivalves are shellfish that live within two hinged shell halves and include clams, mussels, and scallops. Cephalopods have pinlike shells that are contained within their bodies. The most common cephalopod is squid. Clams and mussels are frequently steamed in wine or ale. Scallops are delicious when seared. Squid is either cooked briefly or slow cooked.

SAMPLE MEALS

"In Minutes" meals include recipes and accompaniments that can be put together quickly. "Fit for Company" meals include ideas for stress-free get-togethers, complete with a wine suggestion.

IN MINUTES

Fish Tacos (page 232)

black beans with crumbled *queso fresco*

———

Ginger Salmon Cakes (page 237)

mixed salad greens with cucumber and sesame dressing

———

Fried Catfish & Greens (page 240)

creamy polenta or grits

———

Indian Fish Curry (page 247)

sautéed petite peas

steamed basmati rice

———

Shrimp Scampi (page 259)

fresh fettuccine

butter lettuce salad

———

Ale-Steamed Clams (page 261)

mixed salad greens with citrus vinaigrette

crusty bread

FIT FOR COMPANY

Creole Striped Bass (page 235)

grilled corn on the cob

rice pilaf

Albariño or Viognier

———

Spicy Snapper with Tomatoes & Olives (page 242)

roasted new potatoes

braised chard with garlic

Chardonnay or Pinot Noir

———

Seared Salmon with Mashed Potatoes (page 243)

roasted broccoli

Merlot or Rosé

———

Fritto Misto (page 258)

spinach sautéed with garlic, pine nuts, and raisins

Prosecco or Pinot Grigio

———

Classic Crab Cakes (page 262)

butter lettuce salad with Champagne vinaigrette

Sauvignon Blanc

QUICK FISH SEASONINGS

When you have fresh fish fillets, but are short on time, here are some quick and easy seasoning ideas from the pantry. Drizzle or sprinkle your fillets to taste with one of the following seasonings, then grill, broil, or pan-fry, and dinner is served.

INFUSED OILS
- Chile-infused oil
- Garlic-infused oil
- Herb-infused oil

SPICE MIXTURES
- Chili powder (serve with lime)
- Creole seasoning
- Curry powder
- Garam masala

VINEGARS & VINAIGRETTES
- Balsamic vinegar
- Flavored vinegars
- Purchased vinaigrette

OTHER FLAVORINGS
- Citrus zest and juice from lemons, limes, or oranges
- Crushed fennel seeds
- Dried ground wild mushrooms such as porcini, chanterelles, or shiitakes
- Herbes de Provence
- Sesame seeds
- Soy sauce

poultry

classic roast chicken

1 Roast the chicken
Preheat the oven to 450°F (230°C).
Place the chicken, breast side up, on a
rack in a large roasting pan. Rub with the
rosemary and a generous amount of salt
and pepper. Roast for 20 minutes. Reduce
the oven temperature to 400°F (200°C)
and continue to roast until an instant-read
thermometer inserted into the thickest
part of a thigh away from the bone reads
170°F (77°C), about 40 minutes longer.
Transfer to a carving board and let rest
for 10 minutes.

2 Make the pan sauce
Pour off all but about 1½ teaspoons
fat from the roasting pan. Place over
medium-high heat and add the broth
and wine. Bring to a boil and stir, scraping
up the browned bits on the pan bottom.
Cook until slightly reduced, about 1 minute.
Season to taste with salt and pepper. Carve
the chicken, top with the sauce, and serve.

> **storage tip** Roast 2 chickens so
> you have leftovers for another meal
> (see page 13 for a list of recipes).
> Let the chicken cool, then remove
> the meat and store in an airtight
> container or resealable plastic bag
> in the refrigerator for up to 3 days.

Whole chicken, 1, 4 lb
(2 kg)

**Fresh rosemary or
tarragon,** 2 tablespoons
minced

**Salt and freshly ground
pepper**

Chicken broth, ¾ cup
(6 fl oz/180 ml)

**Dry white wine or
chicken broth,** ¼ cup
(2 fl oz/60 ml)

MAKES 4 SERVINGS

chicken &
spinach quesadillas

Canola oil, 3 tablespoons

Button mushrooms,
6 oz (185 g), sliced

Baby spinach, 2 cups
(4 oz/125 g) packed

**Classic Roast Chicken
(page 267) or rotisserie
chicken,** 2 cups (12 oz/
375 g) shredded meat

Flour tortillas, 8, each
10 inches (25 cm) in
diameter

Monterey jack cheese,
2 cups (8 oz/250 g)
shredded

Sour cream, ½ cup
(4 oz/125 g)

Fresh salsa, ½ cup
(4 fl oz/125 ml),
homemade (page 206)
or purchased

MAKES 4 SERVINGS

1 Prepare the filling
In a large, heavy frying pan over
medium heat, warm 1 tablespoon of the
oil. Add the mushrooms and sauté until
tender, about 3 minutes. Add the spinach
and chicken and sauté just until the
spinach is wilted, about 30 seconds.
Transfer to a bowl.

2 Assemble the quesadillas
Spread out the tortillas on a work
surface. Sprinkle the bottom half of each
tortilla with some of the cheese and then
some of the filling. Fold in half to enclose
the filling and press firmly. Stack the
quesadillas on a plate and set aside.

3 Cook the quesadillas
Wipe out the frying pan with a paper
towel and return to medium heat. Brush
lightly with some of the remaining oil.
Working in batches, add the quesadillas
and cook until golden brown, 1–2 minutes.
Carefully turn and cook until golden on
the second side and the cheese is melted,
2–3 minutes longer. Serve, passing the
sour cream and salsa at the table.

pan-seared chicken with mustard sauce

1 **Cook the chicken**
Place each chicken breast half between 2 sheets of plastic wrap and lightly pound with a meat mallet or the bottom of a heavy pan to an even thickness of about ½ inch (12 mm). Season with salt and pepper. In a large frying pan over medium-high heat, melt the butter. Add the chicken and cook, turning once, until opaque throughout, 8–10 minutes total. Transfer to a plate.

2 **Make the sauce**
Stir the mustard seeds into the pan drippings and cook over medium-high heat, stirring, for about 15 seconds. Add the wine and broth and bring to a simmer. Reduce the heat to medium and cook, stirring, until slightly reduced, 1–2 minutes. Stir in the cream and mustard and cook for 1 minute to blend the flavors. Return the chicken and any juices from the plate to the pan and simmer over medium heat, about 1 minute. Season to taste with salt and pepper. Slice the chicken and serve drizzled with the sauce.

Skinless, boneless chicken breast halves, 4, 2 lb (1 kg) total weight

Salt and freshly ground pepper

Unsalted butter, 3 tablespoons

Mustard seeds, 1 teaspoon

Dry white wine, ⅓ cup (3 fl oz/80 ml)

Chicken broth, ⅓ cup (3 fl oz/80 ml)

Heavy (double) cream, ¼ cup (2 fl oz/60 ml)

Dijon mustard, 2 tablespoons

MAKES 4 SERVINGS

cuban chicken stew

Whole chicken, 4 lb (2 kg), cut into 8 serving pieces

Salt and freshly ground pepper

Olive oil, 3 tablespoons

Garlic, 8 cloves, coarsely chopped

Orange juice, ¾ cup (6 fl oz/180 ml)

Lime juice, ¾ cup (6 fl oz/ 180 ml), from 6–8 limes

Bay leaf, 1

Yellow onion, 1, thinly sliced

Fresh flat-leaf (Italian) parsley, ½ cup (¾ oz/ 20 g) minced

Limes, 2, cut into wedges

MAKES 6 SERVINGS

1 Brown the chicken

Season the chicken pieces with salt and pepper. In a large frying pan over medium-high heat, warm the oil. Add the chicken, in batches if necessary, and cook, turning frequently, until browned, about 10 minutes total. Transfer to a Dutch oven or slow cooker. Pour off all but about 1 tablespoon fat from the frying pan and return to medium-high heat. Add the garlic and sauté until fragrant, about 1 minute. Add the orange and lime juices. Raise the heat to high, bring to a boil, and stir, scraping up the browned bits on the pan bottom. Pour the contents of the pan over the chicken in the Dutch oven. Add the bay leaf, onion, and 1 teaspoon salt and stir to combine.

2 Cook the stew

If using a Dutch oven, cover and cook over medium-low heat until the chicken is opaque throughout and very tender, about 1 hour. (If using a slow cooker, cover and cook on the high-heat setting for 2½ hours or the low-heat setting for 5 hours.) Remove and discard the bay leaf. Transfer the chicken to a serving dish. Season the sauce to taste with salt and pepper. Spoon the onions and sauce over the chicken, garnish with the parsley, and serve with the lime wedges.

chicken & dumplings

1 **Cook the chicken and vegetables**
Season the chicken with salt and pepper. In a Dutch oven over medium-high heat, melt the 2 tablespoons butter. Add the chicken and cook, stirring often, until golden, about 4 minutes. Add the carrots, onion, and celery, season with salt and pepper, and cook until the vegetables begin to soften and the chicken is opaque throughout, 4–5 minutes. Sprinkle with the 2 tablespoons flour and cook, stirring, for about 2 minutes. Pour in the chicken broth, add the peas, and bring to a boil.

2 **Make the dumpling dough**
Meanwhile, in a bowl, combine the 2 cups flour, the baking powder, and 1 teaspoon salt. Using a pastry blender or 2 knives, cut in the ½ cup butter until the mixture forms coarse crumbs the size of peas. Add the milk and stir, then knead a few times until a soft dough forms.

3 **Finish the stew**
Drop heaping tablespoons of the dough over the top of the boiling stew. Reduce the heat to low, cover the pot, and cook until the dumplings have nearly doubled in size, 7–10 minutes. Sprinkle with the parsley and serve. »

Skinless, boneless chicken thighs, 1½ lb (750 g), cut into bite-sized pieces

Salt and freshly ground pepper

Unsalted butter, ½ cup (4 oz/125 g), cold, cut into small pieces, plus 2 tablespoons

Carrots, 3, thinly sliced

Yellow onion, 1, chopped

Celery, 2 stalks, thinly sliced

Flour, 2 cups (10 oz/315 g), plus 2 tablespoons

Chicken broth or stock, 4 cups (32 fl oz/1 l), homemade (page 29) or purchased

Frozen petite peas, ½ cup (2½ oz/75 g)

Baking powder, 2 teaspoons

Milk, ½ cup (4 fl oz/ 125 ml)

Fresh flat-leaf (Italian) parsley, 2 tablespoons minced

MAKES 4 SERVINGS

cook's tip

To add extra flavor to the stew, you can make cheese or herb dumplings. Stir 1 cup (4 oz/125 g) grated Cheddar or asiago cheese or 1 tablespoon minced fresh chives, basil, or flat-leaf (Italian) parsley into the dry ingredients in Step 2 and proceed with the recipe.

chicken & leek pie

1 Prepare the filling
Preheat the oven to 375°F (190°C). In a large ovenproof frying pan over medium-high heat, melt 4 tablespoons (2 oz/60 g) of the butter. Add the leeks, season with salt and pepper, and sauté until softened, about 5 minutes. Sprinkle with the ⅓ cup flour and cook, stirring, for 2 minutes. Stir in the wine and broth and bring to a boil. Reduce the heat to low and simmer, stirring occasionally, until the liquid thickens slightly, about 5 minutes. Stir in the chicken and peas and season with salt and pepper.

2 Make the topping and bake the pie
In a bowl, combine the 2 cups flour, the baking powder, and ½ teaspoon salt. Using a pastry blender or 2 butter knives, cut in the remaining 5 tablespoons butter until the mixture forms coarse crumbs. Add the milk and stir until moistened. Place heaping spoonfuls of the batter evenly over the chicken filling. Bake until the topping is golden brown and the filling is bubbling, about 25 minutes, then serve.

Unsalted butter, 9 tablespoons (4½ oz/140 g)

Leeks, 2 large, white and pale green parts, halved, rinsed, and thinly sliced

Salt and freshly ground pepper

Flour, ⅓ cup (2 oz/60 g), plus 2 cups (10 oz/315 g)

Dry white wine, ¼ cup (2 fl oz/60 ml)

Chicken broth or stock, 4 cups (32 fl oz/1 l), homemade (page 29) or purchased

Classic Roast Chicken (page 267) or rotisserie chicken, about 4 cups (1½ lb/750 g) shredded meat

Frozen petite peas, 1 cup (5 oz/155 g)

Baking powder, 4 teaspoons

Milk, 1½ cups (12 fl oz/375 ml)

MAKES 4–6 SERVINGS

baked
chicken parmesan

Skinless, boneless chicken breast halves, 4, 2 lb (1 kg) total weight

Salt and freshly ground pepper

Olive oil, 2 tablespoons

Kale, 1 bunch, stems removed and leaves torn into large pieces

Tomato-Basil Sauce (page 31) or purchased marinara sauce, 2 cups (16 fl oz/500 ml), warmed

Fresh mozzarella cheese, 8 slices, ¼ inch (6 mm) thick

Parmesan cheese, ½ cup (2 oz/60 g) freshly grated

MAKES 4 SERVINGS

1 **Brown the chicken**
Preheat the oven to 400°F (200°C). Season the chicken with salt and pepper. In a large ovenproof frying pan over medium-high heat, warm the oil. Add the chicken and cook, turning once, until golden brown, about 7 minutes total. Transfer to a plate.

2 **Bake the chicken**
Add the kale to the pan and sauté over medium-high heat until wilted, about 1 minute. Return the chicken to the pan and pour the tomato sauce over the chicken and kale. Place 2 mozzarella cheese slices on each chicken breast. Sprinkle evenly with the Parmesan cheese. Bake until the cheese is golden and the chicken is opaque throughout, about 20 minutes, then serve.

cook's tip For an easy side dish, cook egg noodles or another type of pasta until al dente, according to the package directions. Toss the pasta with a little butter or olive oil and some chopped fresh flat-leaf (Italian) parsley.

apricot-glazed chicken

1 Brown the chicken
Preheat the oven to 425°F (220°C). Season the chicken with salt and pepper. In a large ovenproof frying pan over high heat, warm the oil. Add the chicken and cook, turning once or twice, until golden brown, 8–10 minutes total.

2 Bake the chicken
Meanwhile, in a large bowl, stir together the jam, vinegar, mustard, garlic, and ½ teaspoon salt. Brush the glaze over the chicken breasts, leaving about 1 tablespoon glaze in the bowl. Add the fennel to the bowl and toss with the remaining glaze. Spoon the fennel over the chicken. Bake until the chicken is opaque throughout, about 10 minutes. Arrange the chicken on plates, top with the fennel, and serve.

Skin-on, bone-in chicken breast halves, 4, 4 lb (2 kg) total weight

Salt and freshly ground pepper

Canola oil, 2 tablespoons

Apricot jam, ½ cup (5 oz/155 g)

Red wine vinegar, 2 tablespoons

Whole-grain or Dijon mustard, 2 tablespoons

Garlic, 2 cloves, minced

Fennel bulb, 1 large, trimmed, quartered lengthwise, and thinly sliced

MAKES 4 SERVINGS

oven-fried chicken

Lemon, 1

Buttermilk, ¾ cup
(6 fl oz/180 ml)

Fresh marjoram,
3 tablespoons chopped

**Salt and freshly ground
pepper**

Whole chicken, 1,
4 lb (2 kg), cut into
10 serving pieces

Cornmeal, ⅔ cup
(3½ oz/105 g)

**Fine dried bread
crumbs,** ⅓ cup
(1½ oz/45 g)

Parmesan cheese, ¼ cup
(1 oz/30 g) freshly grated

Unsalted butter,
4 tablespoons (2 oz/60 g),
melted

MAKES 4–6 SERVINGS

1 **Soak the chicken**
Preheat the oven to 425°F (220°C).
Grate 1 teaspoon zest and squeeze
2 tablespoons juice from the lemon. In a
shallow glass or ceramic dish, stir together
the buttermilk, lemon juice, 1 tablespoon
of the marjoram, and ¼ teaspoon each salt
and pepper. Add the chicken pieces, turn
to coat, and let stand for 10 minutes.

2 **Coat the chicken**
In a shallow bowl, stir together the
cornmeal, bread crumbs, cheese, lemon
zest, remaining 2 tablespoons marjoram,
and ½ teaspoon each salt and pepper.
One piece at a time, remove the chicken
from the buttermilk, letting the excess drip
into the dish, and dip into the cornmeal
mixture, turning to coat evenly. Arrange
the pieces, skin side up and in a single
layer, in a shallow roasting pan. Drizzle
with the butter.

3 **Cook the chicken**
Bake until the chicken is crisp and
browned on the outside and opaque
throughout, 35–45 minutes. Transfer
to a platter and serve.

spiced chicken & rice

1 Brown the chicken
In a large Dutch oven over medium-high heat, warm the oil. Add the chicken, season with salt and pepper, and cook, stirring, until browned on all sides, about 4 minutes. Transfer to a plate.

2 Make the rice
Add the ginger and curry powder to the pot and cook, stirring, until fragrant, about 30 seconds. Stir in the broth, scraping up any browned bits from the pan bottom. Bring to a boil, then add the rice, raisins, lemon zest and juice, and 1 teaspoon salt. Return the chicken and any juices from the plate to the pot. Bring to a boil, reduce the heat to medium, cover, and cook until the rice is tender and the chicken is opaque throughout, about 20 minutes. Add the peas, cover, and let stand for about 10 minutes. Sprinkle the cilantro and cashews over the rice, stir to combine, and serve.

> **cook's tip** Top this dish with ½ cup (2 oz/ 60 g) sweetened, shredded, dried coconut that has been toasted to enhance its nutty flavor (see page 366).

Canola oil, 3 tablespoons

Skinless, boneless chicken breasts, 1½ lb (750 g), cut into 1-inch (2.5-cm) pieces

Salt and freshly ground pepper

Fresh ginger, 2 tablespoons minced

Curry powder, 1½ teaspoons

Chicken broth or stock, 2½ cups (20 fl oz/625 ml), homemade (page 29) or purchased

Long-grain rice such as basmati, 1 cup (7 oz/220 g)

Golden raisins (sultanas), ¼ cup (1½ oz/45 g)

Finely grated zest and juice, from 1 lemon

Frozen petite peas, 1 cup (5 oz/155 g), thawed

Fresh cilantro (fresh coriander), ½ cup (¾ oz/20 g) minced

Roasted cashews, ½ cup (3 oz/90 g), coarsely chopped

MAKES 4 SERVINGS

chicken-pesto panini with mozzarella

Basil Pesto (page 34) or purchased pesto, 6 tablespoons (3 fl oz/ 90 ml)

Crusty white sandwich bread, 8 slices

Fresh mozzarella cheese, 10 oz (315 g), cut into 16 thin slices

Marinated roasted red peppers (capsicums), 2 small, halved

Classic Roast Chicken (page 267) or rotisserie chicken, thinly sliced breast meat

Arugula (rocket), 6 cups (¾ lb/375 g), stems removed

Unsalted butter, 6 tablespoons (3 oz/ 90 g), at room temperature

MAKES 4 SERVINGS

1 **Prepare the sandwiches**
Spread the pesto on the bread slices. For each sandwich, layer 2 cheese slices, a roasted red pepper half, one-fourth of the chicken, one-fourth of the arugula, and 2 more cheese slices.

2 **Refrigerate the sandwiches**
Spread both sides of each sandwich with one-fourth of the butter. Put the sandwiches on a sheet of waxed paper and refrigerate until the butter is firm, about 20 minutes.

3 **Cook the sandwiches**
Preheat a ridged grill pan or frying pan over medium heat until hot. Place 2 sandwiches in the pan and weight with a second frying pan. Cook until the undersides are golden, about 2½ minutes. Turn and weight the sandwiches again. Cook until the second sides are golden, about 2½ minutes more. Repeat with the remaining 2 sandwiches. Cut the sandwiches in half and serve.

orange-chipotle chicken with corn

1 Marinate the chicken

Prepare a gas or charcoal grill for direct-heat grilling over high heat. Place each chicken breast half between 2 sheets of plastic wrap and lightly pound with a meat mallet or the bottom of a heavy pan to an even thickness. In a shallow glass or ceramic dish, combine the orange zest and juice, vinegar, oil, garlic, oregano, chile powder, and ¾ teaspoon salt. Add the chicken and turn to coat evenly. Cover and let stand while the grill heats. (The chicken can be refrigerated for up to 4 hours; turn occasionally in the marinade.)

2 Grill the corn and chicken

Lightly oil the grill rack. Place the corn on the grill, cover, and cook for 10 minutes. Add the chicken breasts with any clinging marinade, cover, and cook, turning the corn and chicken occasionally, until the corn husks are charred and the chicken is nicely browned on the outside and feels firm when pressed, about 10 minutes longer. Transfer the chicken and corn to a platter and serve. »

Skinless, boneless, chicken breast halves, 4, 2 lb (1 kg) total weight

Grated orange zest and juice, from 1 large orange

Balsamic vinegar, 2 tablespoons

Olive oil, 2 tablespoons

Garlic, 1 clove, minced

Dried oregano, 1 teaspoon

Chipotle chile powder or other chile powder, ¼ teaspoon

Salt

Corn, 4 ears, unhusked

MAKES 4 SERVINGS

cook's tip

Lime butter is a fine way to embellish corn on the cob. Finely grate the zest from 1 lime into a bowl and add ½ cup (4 oz/125 g) room-temperature unsalted butter. Mix well, season with salt and freshly ground pepper, and let stand at room temperature for about 30 minutes to blend the flavors.

sesame chicken stir-fry

1 Prepare the chicken
Season the chicken with salt and pepper. Sprinkle with the sesame seeds, coating evenly and patting firmly so they adhere to the chicken.

2 Cook the chicken and vegetables
In a wok or large frying pan over high heat, warm the peanut oil. Add the chicken and cook, stirring often, until golden and nearly opaque throughout, 3–4 minutes. Transfer the chicken to a plate. Add the bell pepper, sugar snap peas, and garlic and stir-fry until the vegetables are barely tender-crisp, 1–2 minutes.

3 Finish the dish
Return the chicken to the pan with the vegetables and add the broth, soy sauce, vinegar, and sesame oil. Reduce the heat to medium and simmer until the chicken is opaque throughout and the sauce is slightly reduced, about 2 minutes. Transfer to plates or shallow bowls, sprinkle with the cilantro, and serve.

Skinless, boneless chicken breast halves, 1½ lb (750 g) total weight, cut into thin strips

Salt and freshly ground pepper

Sesame seeds, 3 tablespoons

Peanut oil, 3 tablespoons

Red bell pepper (capsicum), 1, seeded and thinly sliced

Sugar snap peas, ½ lb (250 g)

Garlic, 3 cloves, minced

Chicken broth, ⅔ cup (5 fl oz/150 ml)

Soy sauce, 3 tablespoons

Rice vinegar, 2 tablespoons

Asian sesame oil, 1 tablespoon

Fresh cilantro (fresh coriander), ¼ cup (⅓ oz/10 g) chopped

MAKES 4 SERVINGS

braised chicken
with mushrooms

Skin-on, bone-in, chicken breast halves, 4, 4 lb (2 kg) total weight

Salt and freshly ground pepper

Unsalted butter, 3 tablespoons

Yellow onion, 1 small, chopped

Wild and/or cultivated mushrooms, 1 lb (500 g), sliced

Madeira or dry sherry, ¼ cup (2 fl oz/60 ml)

Worcestershire sauce, 1 tablespoon

Fresh tarragon, 1 tablespoon chopped

MAKES 4 SERVINGS

1 Brown the chicken
Season the chicken with salt and pepper. In a large frying pan over medium-high heat, melt 2 tablespoons of the butter. Add the chicken and cook, turning once or twice, until golden brown on both sides, about 8 minutes total. Transfer the chicken to a plate.

2 Cook the vegetables
Melt the remaining 1 tablespoon butter in the pan over medium heat. Add the onion and sauté until barely softened, about 3 minutes. Add the mushrooms and sauté until their juices are released, about 5 minutes. Stir in the Madeira and Worcestershire sauce.

3 Braise the chicken
Return the chicken and any juices from the plate to the pan, and spoon the mushrooms over the chicken. Cover, reduce the heat to medium-low, and cook until the chicken is opaque throughout, 20–25 minutes. Stir in the tarragon and season to taste with salt and pepper. Transfer the chicken to plates, top with the mushrooms, and serve.

chicken saltimbocca

1 Prepare the chicken
Preheat the broiler (grill). Cut each chicken breast half in half lengthwise to make 8 pieces total. Place each piece of chicken between 2 sheets of plastic wrap and lightly pound with a meat mallet or the bottom of a heavy pan to an even thickness of about ¼ inch (6 mm). Season the chicken with salt and pepper, then sprinkle with the sage.

2 Cook the chicken
In a large frying pan over medium-high heat, melt 3 tablespoons of the butter. Add the chicken and cook until golden, 2–3 minutes. Turn and cook until just opaque throughout, about 3 minutes. Top each piece with 1 cheese slice and 1 prosciutto slice. Transfer to a baking sheet and cook under the broiler to melt the cheese, about 1 minute.

3 Make the sauce and serve
Add the remaining 1 tablespoon butter to the pan. Add the shallots and sauté until softened, about 1 minute. Add the Marsala and cook, stirring to scrape up the browned bits on the pan bottom, until the sauce is slightly reduced, 1–2 minutes. Squeeze in 1 teaspoon lemon juice and stir to blend. Transfer the chicken to plates, top with the shallot sauce, and serve.

Skinless, boneless chicken breast halves, 4, 2 lb (1 kg) total weight

Salt and freshly ground pepper

Fresh sage, 2 tablespoons minced

Unsalted butter, 4 tablespoons (2 oz/60 g)

Fontina cheese, 8 thin slices, about 3 oz (90 g) total weight

Prosciutto or boiled ham, 4 large thin slices, 2 oz (60 g) total weight, halved

Shallots, 2, minced

Marsala or chicken broth, ½ cup (4 fl oz/ 125 ml)

Lemon, ½

MAKES 4–6 SERVINGS

bourbon-molasses chicken

Canola oil, 1 tablespoon

Yellow onion, 1 small, finely chopped

Garlic, 2 cloves, minced

Ketchup, 1 cup (8 fl oz/250 ml)

Molasses, ¼ cup (3 oz/90 g)

Balsamic vinegar, ¼ cup (2 fl oz/60 ml)

Bourbon, ¼ cup (2 fl oz/60 ml)

Whole chicken, 1, 4 lb (2 kg), cut into 8 serving pieces

Salt and freshly ground pepper

MAKES 4 SERVINGS

1 Prepare the sauce

Prepare a gas or charcoal grill for indirect-heat grilling over high heat. If using a charcoal grill, arrange the hot coals on either side of the grill and place a drip pan in the center. If using a gas grill, preheat the grill using all of the burners, then turn off the burner directly below where the chicken will sit. In a heavy saucepan over medium heat, warm the oil. Add the onion and sauté until golden, about 5 minutes. Stir in the garlic and cook until fragrant, about 1 minute. Stir in the ketchup, molasses, vinegar, and bourbon and bring to a boil. Reduce the heat to medium-low and simmer until the sauce is slightly thickened, about 10 minutes. Remove from the heat.

2 Grill the chicken

Season the chicken pieces with salt and pepper. Lightly oil the grill rack. Place the chicken pieces, skin side down, on the coolest part of the grill, positioning the legs, thighs, and wings closest to the heat. Cover and grill, turning the pieces occasionally, until an instant-read thermometer inserted into the thickest part of a thigh or breast away from the bone reads 170°F (77°C), about 50 minutes. During the last 10 minutes of grilling, brush the pieces with the sauce. Remove from the grill and serve.

indian chicken curry

1 Brown the chicken
Season the chicken with salt and pepper. In a large, deep frying pan over medium-high heat, warm the oil. Add the chicken and cook, turning once or twice, until golden brown, 5–7 minutes total. Using a slotted spoon, transfer the chicken to a plate.

2 Cook the vegetables
Add the onion to the drippings in the pan and sauté until softened, 4–5 minutes. Stir in the garlic and ginger and sauté until softened, about 1 minute. Stir in the tomato sauce and broth.

3 Finish the dish
Return the chicken and any juices from the plate to the pan, spooning the liquid over the chicken. Bring to a simmer, cover, reduce the heat to medium-low, and simmer, stirring once or twice, until the chicken is opaque throughout, 20–25 minutes. Remove from the heat and stir in the yogurt, garam masala, and 2 tablespoons of the cilantro. Spoon the mixture over bowls of rice, if using, or directly into shallow bowls. Sprinkle with the cashews and remaining 1 tablespoon cilantro and serve.

Boneless, skinless chicken thighs, 1½ lb (750 g), cut into 1-inch (2.5-cm) chunks

Salt and freshly ground pepper

Canola oil, 3 tablespoons

Yellow onion, 1, sliced

Garlic, 2 large cloves, minced

Fresh ginger, 2 tablespoons finely chopped

Tomato sauce, ½ cup (4 fl oz/125 ml)

Chicken broth, ⅔ cup (5 fl oz/150 ml)

Plain yogurt, ⅔ cup (5 oz/155 g)

Garam masala, 2 teaspoons

Fresh cilantro (fresh coriander), 3 tablespoons chopped

Steamed basmati rice, for serving (optional)

Roasted cashews, ½ cup (2½ oz/75 g), coarsely chopped

MAKES 4 SERVINGS

thai pumpkin & chicken curry

Sugar pie pumpkin or butternut squash, 1 small, 1½ lb (750 g), halved, seeded, peeled, and cut into bite-sized cubes

Shallots, 2, chopped

Garlic, 3 cloves, coarsely chopped

Thai red curry paste, 1 tablespoon

Unsweetened coconut milk, 1 can (14 fl oz/ 430 ml)

Asian fish sauce, 2 tablespoons

Lime juice, from 1 lime

Light brown sugar, 2 teaspoons firmly packed

Canola or peanut oil, 3 tablespoons

Skinless, boneless chicken thighs, 1 lb (500 g), cut into bite-sized cubes

Fresh basil, preferably Thai, 2 tablespoons slivered

Steamed rice, for serving

MAKES 4 SERVINGS

1 Cook the pumpkin
Bring a large pot of water to a boil. Add the pumpkin and boil just until barely tender, about 7 minutes. Drain well.

2 Prepare the curry base
In a blender, combine the shallots, garlic, and curry paste with 2 tablespoons water and process until smooth. In a small bowl, combine the coconut milk, fish sauce, lime juice, and sugar and stir to dissolve the sugar.

3 Cook the curry
Season the chicken with salt and pepper. In a wok or large frying pan over medium heat, warm 2 tablespoons of the oil. Add the chicken and sauté until light brown on all sides, 5–7 minutes. Using a slotted spoon, transfer the chicken to a bowl. Return the pan to medium heat and add the remaining 1 tablespoon oil. Add the curry paste mixture and cook, stirring, for about 10 seconds until fragrant. Stir in the coconut milk mixture and bring to a boil. Add the chicken and pumpkin, reduce the heat to low, and simmer until the pumpkin is tender and the chicken is opaque throughout, about 5 minutes longer. Transfer to a bowl, garnish with the basil, and serve with rice.

arroz con pollo

1 Brown the chicken and vegetables
Preheat the oven to 350°F (180°C). Season the chicken with salt and pepper. In a large ovenproof frying pan with a tight fitting lid over medium-high heat, warm the oil. Add the chicken and cook, turning once or twice, until golden brown, about 6 minutes total. Transfer the chicken to a plate. Add the onion, peppers, and garlic to the drippings in the pan, reduce the heat to medium and sauté until the vegetables are softened, 4–5 minutes.

2 Cook the chicken and rice
Gently stir the saffron into the vegetables. Add the rice, stirring to coat. Stir in the broth and oregano and bring to a simmer. Return the chicken and any juices from the plate to the pan. Remove from the heat, cover, and bake in the oven for 45 minutes. Uncover and stir in the tomatoes. Cover and continue to cook until the rice is tender and most of the liquid is absorbed, about 15 minutes longer. Season to taste with salt and pepper and serve. »

Skin-on, bone-in chicken thighs, breast halves, and/or drumsticks, 3 lb (1.5 kg)

Salt and freshly ground pepper

Olive oil, 3 tablespoons

Yellow onion, 1, chopped

Roasted red bell peppers (capsicums), 3, thickly sliced

Garlic, 4 large cloves, minced

Saffron threads, ¼ teaspoon, crushed

Long grain white rice, 2 cups (14 oz/440 g)

Chicken broth or stock, 3 cups (24 fl oz/750 ml), homemade (page 29) or purchased

Fresh oregano, 2 tablespoons minced

Diced tomatoes, 1 can (14½ oz/455 g), with juice

MAKES 4–6 SERVINGS

cook's tip

For a quick paella, use 3 tablespoons minced fresh marjoram in place of the oregano, substitute ½ cup (4 fl oz/125 ml) dry white wine for an equal amount of the broth, and stir in 1 cup (5 oz/155 g) frozen petite peas with the tomatoes. You can also add Manila clams, shrimp (prawns), or sliced Spanish chorizo during the last 10 minutes of cooking.

chicken & sausage gumbo

1 Brown the chicken and sausage
Season the chicken with salt and pepper. In a large saucepan over medium-high heat, melt 2 tablespoons of the butter. Add the chicken and sauté until lightly browned, 2–3 minutes. Add the sausage and sauté until browned, about 2 minutes. Transfer the chicken and sausage to a plate.

2 Cook the vegetables
Add the celery, onion, bell pepper, and garlic to the pan and cook until the vegetables begin to soften, 3–5 minutes. Add the remaining 2 tablespoons butter and the flour and cook, stirring, for about 2 minutes. Gradually stir in the broth and bring to a boil.

3 Finish the gumbo
Return the chicken and sausage and any juices to the pan. Add the okra, reduce the heat to medium, and simmer until the chicken is opaque throughout and the gumbo has thickened, about 10 minutes. Season with salt and pepper, ladle into bowls, and serve.

cook's tip For more flavor, add ½ lb (250 g) cooked, peeled, and deveined shrimp (prawns) along with the browned chicken and sausage.

Skinless, boneless chicken thighs, 3, about 1 lb (500 g) total weight, cut into bite-sized pieces

Salt and freshly ground pepper

Unsalted butter, 4 tablespoons (2 oz/60 g)

Andouille or other spicy smoked sausage, 1 lb (500 g), thinly sliced

Celery, 4 stalks, chopped

Yellow onion, 1 large, chopped

Green bell pepper (capsicum), 1, seeded and chopped

Garlic, 3 cloves, minced

Flour, 2 tablespoons

Chicken broth or stock, 6 cups (48 fl oz/1.5 l), homemade (page 29) or purchased

Okra, 12 pods, cut into ½-inch (12-mm) pieces, or 2 cups (12 oz/375 g) frozen okra pieces

MAKES 4–6 SERVINGS

chicken posole

Olive oil, 2 tablespoons

Yellow onions, 2 large, finely chopped

Celery, 2 stalks, chopped

Serrano or jalapeño chiles, 2, cored, seeded, and minced

Garlic, 2 cloves, minced

Whole chicken, 1, 4 lb (2 kg), cut into 10 serving pieces

Hominy, 2 cans (15 oz/ 470 g each), drained and rinsed

Chili powder, 2 tablespoons

Dried oregano, 1 teaspoon crumbled

Salt and freshly ground pepper

Green cabbage, ¼ head, cored and thinly sliced

MAKES 6 SERVINGS

1 Cook the chicken

In a large pot over medium-high heat, warm the oil. Set aside ¼ cup (1 oz/30 g) of the chopped onions for serving. Add the remaining onions and the celery to the pot and sauté until softened, 4–5 minutes. Add the chiles and garlic and cook until fragrant, about 30 seconds. Add the chicken and 4 cups (32 fl oz/1 l) water and bring to a boil. Reduce the heat to medium-low and simmer until the chicken is opaque throughout, about 1 hour.

2 Finish the soup

Add the hominy, chili powder, and oregano and simmer until the hominy is heated through and the flavors have blended, 5–10 minutes. Season with salt and pepper to taste. Ladle the posole into bowls, top with the cabbage and reserved onion, and serve.

green chicken enchiladas

1 Make the tomatillo sauce
Preheat the oven to 400°F (200°C). In a large frying pan over medium heat, warm 1 tablespoon of the oil. Add the onion and sauté until softened, about 5 minutes. Add the garlic and chile and sauté for 1 minute. Transfer to a food processor, add the tomatillos and cilantro, and process until puréed. Return the pan to medium heat, add 1 tablespoon of the oil, and then add the tomatillo mixture. Bring to a boil and cook briskly until the sauce reduces slightly, about 5 minutes. Set aside.

2 Assemble and bake the enchiladas
In a frying pan over medium heat, warm the remaining 1 tablespoon oil. Add the chicken and sauté just until warm, about 3 minutes. Meanwhile, lightly oil a 9-by-13-inch (23-by-33-cm) baking dish. Spoon ½ cup (4 fl oz/125 ml) of the tomatillo sauce into the dish. Line the dish with 5 of the tortillas. Sprinkle with half of the chicken and ¾ cup (3 oz/90 g) of the cheese, then top with one-third of the remaining sauce. Repeat with 5 more tortillas, the remaining chicken, ¾ cup cheese, and half of the remaining sauce. Finish with the remaining tortillas, sauce, and finally, cheese. Pour the cream evenly on top. Bake until the sauce is bubbling around the edges, about 20 minutes. Let stand for 5 minutes, then serve.

Canola oil, 3 tablespoons

Yellow onion, 1 large, chopped

Garlic, 2 cloves, minced

Jalapeño chile, 1, seeded and minced

Tomatillos, 2 cans (28 oz/875 g each), drained

Fresh cilantro (fresh coriander), ¼ cup (⅓ oz/10 g) chopped

Classic Roast Chicken (page 267) or rotisserie chicken, 2½ cups (1 lb/500 g) coarsely chopped meat

Corn tortillas, 15, day old

Monterey jack cheese, 2 cups (8 oz/250 g) shredded

Heavy (double) cream, ½ cup (4 fl oz/125 ml)

MAKES 6 SERVINGS

lemongrass
chicken & asparagus

Skinless, boneless chicken breast halves, 4, 2 lb (1 kg) total weight, cut into thin strips

Salt and freshly ground pepper

Peanut or canola oil, 2 tablespoons

Green (spring) onions, ¾ cup (2½ oz/75 g) thinly sliced

Fresh ginger, 2 tablespoons minced

Lemongrass, 1 stalk, pale inner core only, finely chopped

Garlic, 3 cloves, minced

Slender asparagus, ½ lb (250 g), tough ends removed and sliced on the diagonal

Chicken broth, ¾ cup (6 fl oz/180 ml)

Asian fish sauce, 2 tablespoons

Peanuts, ¼ cup (1½ oz/45 g) chopped

Steamed white rice, for serving

MAKES 4 SERVINGS

1 Stir-fry the chicken

Season the chicken with salt and pepper. In a wok or large frying pan over high heat, warm the oil. Add the chicken and stir-fry until golden on the outside and opaque throughout, 2–3 minutes. Transfer to a plate. Add the green onions and stir-fry until fragrant, 1–2 minutes. Add the ginger, lemongrass, and garlic and stir-fry for 30 seconds. Add the asparagus and stir-fry just until tender-crisp, 2–3 minutes.

2 Finish the dish

Add the broth and fish sauce to the pan and bring to a simmer. Return the chicken and any juices from the plate to the pan, reduce the heat to medium-low, and simmer for 1 minute to heat through. Sprinkle with the peanuts. Spoon the rice onto plates, top with the chicken and asparagus mixture, and serve.

chicken in orange-riesling sauce

1 Prepare the orange and chicken
Finely grate 2 teaspoons zest and squeeze ¼ cup (2 fl oz/60 ml) juice from the orange; set aside. Place each chicken breast half between 2 sheets of plastic wrap and lightly pound with a meat mallet or the bottom of a heavy pan to an even thickness of about ½ inch (12 mm). Season with salt and pepper.

2 Cook the chicken
In a large frying pan over medium-high heat, melt 2 tablespoons of the butter. Working in batches if necessary, add the chicken and cook, turning once, until golden on both sides and opaque throughout, 6–8 minutes total. Transfer to a plate.

3 Make the sauce
Melt the remaining 1 tablespoon butter in the pan over medium heat. Add the shallot and sauté until lightly browned, about 1 minute. Add the wine, marjoram, and orange zest and juice. Cook, stirring to scrape up the browned bits on the pan bottom, until the sauce is bubbly and slightly reduced, about 3 minutes. Return the chicken and any juices from the plate to the pan and heat through, about 1 minute. Season to taste with salt and pepper. Transfer the chicken to a platter, top with the sauce, and serve.

Orange, 1 large

Skinless, boneless chicken breast halves, 4, 2 lb (1 kg) total weight

Salt and freshly ground pepper

Unsalted butter, 3 tablespoons

Shallot, 1, minced

Riesling or other fruity white wine, ½ cup (4 fl oz/125 ml)

Fresh marjoram, 1 tablespoon finely chopped

MAKES 4 SERVINGS

grilled chicken with tuscan herbs

Dried oregano,
2 teaspoons

Dried rosemary,
2 teaspoons

Dried sage, 2 teaspoons

Fennel seeds,
½ teaspoon, crushed

Salt and freshly ground pepper

Olive oil, 2 tablespoons

Garlic, 2 cloves, minced

Whole chicken legs, 4,
3 lb (1.5 kg) total weight

Lemon, 1 large, cut into wedges

MAKES 4 SERVINGS

1 Season the chicken
Prepare a gas or charcoal grill for indirect-heat grilling over high heat. If using a charcoal grill, arrange the hot coals on either side of the grill and place a drip pan in the center. If using a gas grill, preheat the grill using all of the burners, then turn off the burner directly below where the chicken will sit. In a small bowl, stir together the oregano, rosemary, sage, fennel, ½ teaspoon salt, and ½ teaspoon pepper. In a shallow glass or ceramic dish, stir together the oil and garlic. Add the chicken and turn to coat evenly. Sprinkle the herb mixture evenly over the chicken. Cover and let stand while the grill heats. (The chicken can be covered and refrigerated for up to overnight; bring to room temperature before grilling.)

2 Grill the chicken
Lightly oil the grill rack. Place the chicken, skin side down, on the coolest area of the grill. Cover and cook for 25 minutes. Turn the chicken and cook until an instant-read thermometer inserted in the thickest part of a thigh away from the bone reads 170°F (77°C), about 20 minutes longer. Serve with the lemon wedges.

cashew chicken

1 Marinate the chicken

In a large bowl, stir together 2 tablespoons of the soy sauce, the wine, and the ginger. Add the chicken and turn to coat evenly. Set aside for 15 minutes.

2 Make the sauce

In a small bowl, combine 2 tablespoons water, the remaining 1 tablespoon soy sauce, Worcestershire sauce, sesame oil, sugar, and cornstarch and stir to dissolve the sugar and cornstarch.

3 Stir-fry the chicken

Heat a wok or large frying pan over high heat until hot and add 2 tablespoons of the canola oil. Remove the chicken from the marinade, draining it well, and discard the marinade. Add the chicken to the pan and stir-fry until opaque, about 3 minutes. Using a slotted spoon, transfer the chicken to a bowl. Return the pan to medium heat and add the remaining 1 tablespoon canola oil. Add the onions and stir-fry for about 10 seconds until fragrant. Return the chicken to the pan and add the cashews. Give the sauce a quick stir, add to the pan, and stir until the sauce thickens slightly, 1–2 minutes. Serve with the rice. »

Soy sauce, 3 tablespoons

Rice wine or dry sherry, 1 tablespoon

Fresh ginger, 2 teaspoons grated

Skinless, boneless chicken thighs, 1 lb (500 g), cut into bite-sized pieces

Worcestershire sauce, 1 teaspoon

Asian sesame oil, 1 teaspoon

Sugar, ½ teaspoon

Cornstarch (cornflour), ¼ teaspoon

Canola or peanut oil, 3 tablespoons

Green (spring) onions, 2, white and pale green parts, chopped

Salted roasted cashews, 1 cup (5½ oz/170 g)

Steamed rice, for serving

MAKES 4 SERVINGS

cook's tip

For a quick and easy side dish, separate 1 lb (500 g) broccoli into small florets. Bring a pot of salted water to a boil, add the broccoli, and cook just until bright green and tender-crisp, about 3 minutes. Drain well, place in a dish, drizzle lightly with soy sauce and chile or sesame oil, toss, and serve.

balsamic
chicken & peppers

1 Cook the chicken
Season the chicken with salt and pepper. In a large frying pan over medium-high heat, warm 2 tablespoons of the oil. Add the chicken and cook, turning once, until golden brown on both sides, about 7 minutes total. Transfer to a plate.

2 Cook the vegetables
Add the remaining 2 tablespoons oil to the pan over medium-high heat. Add the bell peppers and onion and sauté until softened, about 6 minutes. Add the garlic and sauté for 1 minute.

3 Finish the chicken
Add the vinegar and half each of the basil and thyme and stir, scraping up the browned bits on the pan bottom. Return the chicken and any juices from the plate to the pan, spooning the peppers over the chicken. Reduce the heat to medium and simmer until the chicken is opaque throughout, 2–3 minutes. Stir in the remaining basil and thyme and season to taste with salt and pepper, then serve.

Skinless, boneless chicken breast halves or thighs, 4, 2 lb (1 kg) total weight

Salt and freshly ground pepper

Olive oil, 4 tablespoons (2 fl oz/60 ml)

Red bell pepper (capsicum), 1, seeded and sliced

Yellow bell pepper (capsicum), 1, seeded and sliced

Yellow onion, 1 large, thinly sliced

Garlic, 3 cloves, minced

Balsamic vinegar, 3 tablespoons

Fresh basil, ¼ cup (⅓ oz/10 g) minced

Fresh thyme, 1 tablespoon minced

MAKES 4 SERVINGS

turkey-poblano chili

Olive oil, 2 tablespoons

Poblano chiles, 2,
seeded and chopped

Yellow onion, 1 large,
chopped

Ground (minced) turkey,
2 lb (1 kg)

Garlic, 4 cloves, minced

Chili powder,
4 tablespoons (1 oz/30 g)

**Salt and freshly ground
pepper**

**Crushed plum (Roma)
tomatoes,** 1 can
(14½ oz/455 g) with juice

Kidney or pinto beans,
2 cans (14½ oz/455 g),
drained and rinsed

Chicken broth, 1 cup
(8 fl oz/250 ml)

Sour cream, ½ cup
(4 oz/125 g)

MAKES 4–6 SERVINGS

1 **Brown the vegetables and turkey**
In a Dutch oven over medium-high heat, warm the oil. Add the chiles and onion and sauté until softened, about 4 minutes. Add the turkey and cook, stirring to break up any clumps, until the meat begins to brown, 7–8 minutes.

2 **Finish the chili**
Add the garlic and chili powder, season with salt and pepper, and cook, stirring frequently, for 1 minute. Add the tomatoes, beans, and broth. Bring to a simmer, reduce the heat to medium-low, and cook, uncovered, until thickened, about 10 minutes. Season to taste with salt and pepper. Ladle the chili into bowls, garnish with the sour cream, and serve.

cook's tip Chili powder, a commercial blend of dried chiles and spices, is often confused with chile powder, the lightly toasted ground powder of an individual variety of chile, such as pasilla or New Mexican. Experiment with different chili and chile powders to find one that you prefer.

turkey breast in mole

1 Make the mole

In a frying pan over high heat, warm the oil. Add the onion and almonds and sauté until just golden, 8–10 minutes. Stir in the chile powder, cumin, and cinnamon and sauté until fragrant, about 30 seconds longer. Add the tomatoes, chocolate, oregano, 1 teaspoon salt, ½ teaspoon pepper, and ½ cup (4 fl oz/125 ml) of the broth. Stir until the chocolate has melted, about 1 minute. Transfer the sauce to a food processor or blender and process to a smooth purée. Return the purée to the frying pan over medium-high heat. Stir in the remaining ½ cup broth and bring to a simmer.

2 Cook the turkey

Place the turkey in a Dutch oven or slow cooker and add the hot mole sauce. If using a Dutch oven, cover and cook over low heat until an instant-read thermometer inserted into the thickest part of the breast registers 160°F (71°C), 1–1½ hours. (If using a slow cooker, cover and cook on the high-heat setting for 4 hours or the low-heat setting for 8 hours.) Transfer the turkey to a cutting board and let stand until cool enough to handle. Slice the turkey and arrange on a platter. Top with the mole sauce, garnish with the sesame seeds, if using, and serve.

Olive oil, 1½ tablespoons

Yellow onion, 1, chopped

Slivered almonds, ¼ cup (1½ oz/45 g)

Chile powder, 1½ teaspoons

Ground cumin, ½ teaspoon

Ground cinnamon, ¼ teaspoon

Diced tomatoes, ½ can (7 oz/220 g), drained

Bittersweet chocolate, 2 tablespoons chopped

Dried oregano, ½ teaspoon

Salt and freshly ground pepper

Chicken broth, 1 cup (8 fl oz/250 ml)

Bone-in turkey breast half, 1, 3 lb (1.5 kg), skin removed

Sesame seeds, for garnish (optional)

MAKES 4 SERVINGS

turkey cutlets with herbed pan gravy

Turkey cutlets, 4, each about 6 oz (185 g) and ½ inch (12 mm) thick

Salt and freshly ground pepper

Fresh sage, 1 tablespoon minced

Fresh thyme, 1 tablespoon minced

Fresh marjoram, 1 tablespoon minced

Unsalted butter, 5 tablespoons (2½ oz/ 75 g)

Celery, 2 stalks, finely chopped

Yellow onion, 1 small, finely chopped

Flour, 3 tablespoons

Chicken broth or stock, 2½ cups (20 fl oz/625 ml), homemade (page 29) or purchased

Madeira or sherry, 2 tablespoons

MAKES 4 SERVINGS

1 **Cook the turkey cutlets**
Season the turkey cutlets on both sides with salt and pepper. In a small bowl, combine the sage, thyme, and marjoram. Sprinkle half of the herb mixture on the cutlets, then pat it firmly into the meat. Set the remaining herb mixture aside. In a large frying pan over medium-high heat, melt 2 tablespoons of the butter. Add the cutlets in a single layer and cook, turning once, until golden on the outside and opaque throughout, 6–8 minutes total. Transfer to a plate.

2 **Make the gravy**
Melt the remaining 3 tablespoons butter in the pan over medium heat. Add the celery and onion and sauté until softened, about 5 minutes. Stir in the flour and cook, stirring, until the mixture is thickened and begins to turn pale gold, 1–2 minutes. Slowly stir in the broth, Madeira, and remaining herb mixture. Cook, stirring, until the gravy is smooth, thickened, and bubbly, 3–4 minutes. Return the cutlets and any juices to the pan and simmer until heated through, about 1 minute. Serve with the gravy.

poultry made easy

Poultry's versatility makes it a mainstay of dinner tables around the world. Whether roasted, baked, boiled, braised, stir-fried, or grilled, it is the perfect canvas for almost any flavoring. It is also one of the most useful leftovers—sliced or shredded, it can be used in countless meals.

cooking poultry

Safety Poultry is highly perishable. It should not be allowed to sit at room temperature for more than 2 hours at most. To err on the side of caution, especially in hot weather, don't let it sit out for more than 30 minutes. Before and after you handle raw poultry, wash your hands thoroughly with warm water and lots of soap. Be sure to thoroughly wash any cutting surfaces, dishware, and kitchen tools that come in contact with the raw poultry.

Checking for doneness Poultry should be cooked to the minimum temperature specified in recipes to kill food-borne bacteria such as salmonella. However, take care not to overcook it, which will affect flavor and texture. To test for doneness, use a thermometer for absolute certainty, but use your senses of touch and sight as well.

- To test whole birds for doneness, insert an instant-read thermometer into the thickest part of the thigh, not touching any bones. It should register 170–175°F (77–80°C).

- To test boneless cuts for doneness, press in the center of the cut with a fingertip. It should feel firm and spring back right away.

- To test bone-in cuts for doneness, make an incision near the bone. The meat should look opaque throughout with no sign of pink.

Carryover cooking When food is removed from the cooking source, it retains heat, so its internal temperature will rise a few more degrees. The phenomenon, called carryover cooking, should be taken into account when determining the doneness temperatures of poultry. The amount of increase depends on the size and shape of the bird as well as on the cooking temperature. A big turkey, for instance, may go up 5° to 10°F (3° to 6°C) after being removed from the heat source, while the temperature of a smaller chicken will usually rise less. Allow poultry to stand as directed in recipes to ensure optimum doneness.

Here are some ideas for creating meals centered on poultry. "In Minutes" meals include recipes and accompaniments that can be put together quickly. "Fit for Company" meals offer ideas for stress-free get-togethers, complete with a wine or beer suggestion.

IN MINUTES

Orange-Chipotle Chicken with Corn (page 279)

spinach salad with citrus vinaigrette

fresh sliced watermelon

Sesame Chicken Stir-Fry (page 281)

steamed basmati rice

Chicken Saltimbocca (page 283)

mashed yams

sautéed spinach with pine nuts, raisins, and red pepper flakes

---

Lemongrass Chicken & Asparagus (page 292)

steamed frozen pot stickers

steamed short-grain rice

Turkey-Poblano Chili (page 298)

warm corn tortillas

mixed greens salad with cilantro-lime vinaigrette

FIT FOR COMPANY

Braised Chicken with Mushrooms (page 282)

creamy polenta

redleaf lettuce salad with balsamic vinaigrette

Pinot Noir or Sangiovese

Chicken in Orange-Riesling Sauce (page 293)

scalloped potatoes

spinach salad with blue cheese and walnuts

off-dry Riesling

Grilled Chicken with Tuscan Herbs (page 294)

mashed potatoes

broiled (grilled) asparagus

Barbera

Turkey Breast in Mole (page 299)

steamed long-grain white rice

tropical fruit salad

Mexican lager or ale

STORING POULTRY

Below are tips for storing and thawing poultry. See the storage chart on page 420 for a full list of storage times.

In the refrigerator Refrigerate fresh poultry in the coolest part of the refrigerator for up to 48 hours after purchase. If the poultry has an unpleasant odor when the package is opened, don't panic, as it may be a result of oxygen depletion. Rinse the bird under cold water and pat dry with paper towels. If the odor is still unpleasant after the bird has been exposed to air for 5 minutes, discard the bird (or return it to the market if very recently purchased).

In the freezer To freeze poultry, remove it from its original packaging and rinse it well under cold water. Pat the meat dry with a paper towel and wrap in freezer-weight plastic wrap or put in a resealable plastic freezer bag.

Thawing poultry Thaw poultry in the refrigerator, never at room temperature. Allow a full 24 hours for every 5 pounds (2.5 kg) (a large chicken can take a full day and night to thaw). Do not thaw and refreeze poultry.

meat

steaks with herb butter

1 Prepare the herb butter
In a small dish, stir together the butter, chives, rosemary, and a pinch each of salt and pepper.

2 Cook the steaks
Meanwhile, prepare a gas or charcoal grill for direct-heat grilling over high heat and oil the grill rack. Or, preheat a broiler (grill). Season the steaks generously with salt and pepper, patting them firmly into the meat. Place the steaks on the grill rack, or put them on a rimmed baking sheet and place under the broiler. Cook, turning once, for 6–8 minutes total for medium-rare, or until done to your liking. Arrange on plates, top with the butter, and serve.

Unsalted butter,
3 tablespoons, at room temperature

Fresh chives,
2 tablespoons snipped

Fresh rosemary,
1 tablespoon minced

Salt and freshly ground pepper

Rib-eye steaks, 4, each 1 inch (2.5 cm) thick

MAKES 4 SERVINGS

chimichurri steak

Olive oil, ⅓ cup
(3 fl oz/80 ml)

Sherry vinegar, ⅓ cup
(3 fl oz/80 ml)

Fresh oregano,
3 tablespoons leaves

**Fresh flat-leaf (Italian)
parsley,** ½ cup (½ oz/
15 g) coarsely chopped

Garlic, 7 cloves, coarsely
chopped

Red pepper flakes,
½–¾ teaspoon

T-bone steaks, 4, each
1 inch (2.5 cm) thick

Salt

MAKES 4 SERVINGS

1 Marinate the steaks
In a food processor, combine the oil, vinegar, oregano, parsley, and garlic and process until finely chopped. Pour into a shallow glass or ceramic dish large enough to hold the steaks in a single layer, then stir in the red pepper flakes to taste. Season the steaks with salt, then add them to the marinade and turn to coat. Let stand at room temperature for 10 minutes.

2 Cook the steaks
Meanwhile, prepare a gas or charcoal grill for direct-heat grilling over high heat and oil the grill rack. Or, preheat a broiler (grill). Remove the steaks from the marinade, reserving the marinade. Place the steaks on the grill rack, or put them on a rimmed baking sheet to cook under the broiler. Brush the steaks with the remaining marinade and cook, turning once, for about 8 minutes total for medium-rare, or until done to your liking. Arrange on plates and serve.

> **cook's tip** Rosemary potato wedges are an excellent side dish. Toss Yukon gold potato wedges with a little olive oil, minced rosemary, and salt. Roast in a 375°F (190°C) oven until tender, about 30 minutes.

grilled flank steak

1 Marinate the steak
In a shallow glass or ceramic dish, whisk together the wine, soy sauce, oil, garlic, and ¼ teaspoon pepper. Add the flank steak and turn to coat evenly. Cover and let stand for 1 hour, or refrigerate, turning occasionally, for up to overnight.

2 Grill the steak
Prepare a gas or charcoal grill for direct-heat grilling over high heat. Oil the grill rack. Remove the steak from the marinade, discarding the marinade. Place the steak on the grill rack and cover. Cook, turning once, for 8–10 minutes total for medium-rare, or until done to your liking. Transfer the steak to a platter and let stand for 3–5 minutes. Thinly slice across the grain and serve.

> **storage tip** You can double this recipe so you have leftovers for another recipe (see pages 306 and 307). To store the second unused steak, let cool to room temperature, wrap tightly in aluminum foil or plastic wrap, and refrigerate for up to 2 days. Do not slice the chilled steak until ready to serve.

Full-bodied red wine, ½ cup (4 fl oz/125 ml)

Soy sauce, 3 tablespoons

Canola oil, 2 tablespoons

Garlic, 2 cloves, coarsely chopped

Freshly ground pepper

Flank steak, 1, 1½ lb (750 g)

MAKES 4–6 SERVINGS

steak & tomato sandwiches

Mayonnaise, ½ cup
(4 fl oz/125 ml)

Prepared horseradish,
2 tablespoons

Country-style bread,
8 slices

**Grilled Flank Steak
(page 305),** ½ steak

Tomatoes, 2, thickly
sliced

Red-leaf lettuce, 4 large
leaves

MAKES 4 SERVINGS

1 Flavor the mayonnaise
In a small bowl, stir together the
mayonnaise and horseradish. Spread
the mayonnaise mixture generously on
each slice of bread.

2 Assemble the sandwiches
Thinly slice the steak across the grain.
Divide the steak, tomatoes, and lettuce
among 4 of the bread slices, top with the
remaining slices, and serve.

steak tacos with guacamole

1 Warm the tortillas and steak
Preheat the oven to 350°F (180°C). Stack the tortillas, wrap in aluminum foil, and heat in the oven until hot, about 10 minutes. Thinly slice the steak across the grain, wrap in aluminum foil, and warm in the oven with the tortillas.

2 Make the guacamole
Meanwhile, in a bowl, using a fork, mash the avocados. Add the salsa and lime juice and stir to combine. Season to taste with salt and pepper. Transfer to a serving bowl.

3 Serve the tacos
Unwrap the tortillas and place in a napkin-lined basket. Unwrap the steak and arrange on a plate. Place the lettuce in a bowl. To serve, put the steak, tortillas, guacamole, and lettuce on the table and let guests make their own tacos.

Corn tortillas, 12

Grilled Flank Steak (page 305), ½ steak

Hass avocados, 2, halved, pitted, and peeled

Fresh tomato salsa, 1 cup (8 fl oz/250 ml), homemade (page 206) or purchased

Fresh lime juice, from 1 lime

Salt and freshly ground pepper

Romaine (cos) lettuce, ½ small head, thinly shredded

MAKES 4 SERVINGS

cook's tip When you don't have the time to make guacamole or salsa from scratch, you can find good-quality prepared guacamole and fresh salsa in the refrigerated section of the supermarket.

hearty beef stew

Thick-cut bacon, 4 oz (125 g), chopped

Flour, 3 tablespoons

Salt and freshly ground pepper

Boneless beef chuck, 3 lb (1.5 kg), trimmed of excess fat and cut into chunks

Baby carrots, ½ lb (250 g)

Cremini mushrooms, ¾ lb (375 g), halved if large

Frozen pearl onions, ½ lb (250 g)

Garlic, 3 cloves, minced

Dry red wine, 1 cup (8 fl oz/250 ml)

Beef broth, 1 cup (8 fl oz/250 ml)

Tomato paste, 2 tablespoons

Fresh rosemary, 1 tablespoon minced

MAKES 6 SERVINGS

1 Cook the bacon and brown the beef
In a large frying pan over medium heat, sauté the bacon until crisp, 5–7 minutes. Transfer to paper towels to drain. Pour off all but about 2 tablespoons of the drippings from the pan. In a large resealable plastic bag, combine the flour, 1 teaspoon salt, and ½ teaspoon pepper. Add the beef and shake to coat evenly. Return the frying pan to medium-high heat. Working in batches if necessary, add the beef and cook, turning, until well browned, about 10 minutes total. Transfer to a Dutch oven or slow cooker. Scatter the carrots, mushrooms, onions, and garlic on top of the beef.

2 Cook the stew
Return the frying pan to medium-high heat and add the wine, broth, and tomato paste. Bring to a boil, stirring to scrape up the browned bits on the pan bottom. Pour over the vegetables and beef. If using a Dutch oven, cover and cook over low heat until the beef is tender, about 2 hours. (If using a slow cooker, cover and cook on the high-heat setting for 4–5 hours or the low-heat setting for 8–9 hours.) Stir in the reserved bacon and the rosemary and cook, uncovered, over medium heat (or the high-heat setting of the slow cooker), for 10 minutes to thicken the sauce slightly. Season with salt and pepper and serve.

bbq beef sandwiches

1 Cook the beef
In a large frying pan over medium-high heat, warm the oil. Add the onion and garlic and sauté until softened, about 5 minutes. Add the beef, season with salt and pepper, and cook, stirring to break up any clumps, until browned, about 8 minutes. Add the barbecue sauce, reduce the heat to low, and cook until the meat is well coated and the sauce is heated through, about 5 minutes longer.

2 Assemble the sandwiches
Lightly toast the rolls. Place the open rolls on plates. Spoon the beef on the bottom halves, set the top halves in place, and serve. »

Olive oil, 2 tablespoons

Yellow onion, 1 large, chopped

Garlic, 3 large cloves, minced

Ground (minced) beef, 1½ lb (750 g)

Salt and freshly ground pepper

Barbecue sauce, 1½ cups (12 fl oz/375 ml)

Crusty sandwich rolls, 4, split

MAKES 4 SERVINGS

cook's tip

For a delicious, homemade coleslaw to accompany the sandwiches, mix together ⅓ cup (3 fl oz/80 ml) mayonnaise, 2 tablespoons apple cider vinegar, 1 tablespoon Dijon mustard, and ½ head green cabbage, shredded. Toss well to combine and let stand for up to 20 minutes until the flavors have come together and the cabbage has wilted slightly.

thai red curry beef

1 Make the sauce
In a small bowl, stir together the coconut milk, fish sauce, brown sugar, and lime juice.

2 Stir-fry the vegetables
Heat a wok or large frying pan over medium-high heat until hot and add 2 tablespoons of the oil. Add the onion and bell pepper and stir-fry just until tender, about 3 minutes. Using a slotted spoon, transfer to a bowl.

3 Cook the beef
Return the pan to medium-high heat and add the remaining 2 tablespoons oil. Add the red curry paste and stir-fry until fragrant, about 1 minute. Stir in the sauce, bring to a gentle boil, adjust the heat to maintain a gentle boil, and cook until the sauce begins to thicken, 5–7 minutes. Return the vegetables to the pan, stir in the beef, and simmer just until the beef is cooked through, about 2 minutes. Transfer to a serving bowl, garnish with the peanuts and basil, and serve with the rice.

Unsweetened coconut milk, 1 cup (8 fl oz/ 250 ml)

Asian fish sauce, ¼ cup (2 fl oz/60 ml)

Light brown sugar, 2 teaspoons firmly packed

Fresh lime juice, from ½ lime

Canola or peanut oil, 4 tablespoons (2 fl oz/ 60 ml)

Yellow onion, 1, thinly sliced

Red or green bell pepper (capsicum), 1, seeded and thinly sliced

Thai red curry paste, 1 tablespoon

Beef sirloin or tenderloin, 1 lb (500 g), cut across the grain into thin, bite-sized strips

Peanuts, 2 tablespoons toasted and chopped

Fresh basil, preferably Thai, ¼ cup (⅓ oz/10 g) slivered

Steamed rice, for serving

MAKES 4 SERVINGS

cuban beef picadillo

Olive oil, 1 tablespoon

Yellow onion, 1, chopped

Ground (minced) beef chuck, 1½ lb (750 g) total weight

Garlic, 2 cloves, minced

Chili powder, 2 tablespoons

Ground cinnamon, ¾ teaspoon

Ground allspice, ½ teaspoon (optional)

Diced tomatoes, 1 can (28 oz/875 g), with juice

Beef broth, 1¾ cups (14 fl oz/430 ml), or Beef Stock (page 30)

Raisins or currants, ⅔ cup (4 oz/125 g)

Tomato paste, 2 tablespoons

Red wine vinegar, ¼ cup (2 fl oz/60 ml)

Salt and freshly ground pepper

Steamed rice, for serving (optional)

MAKES 4 SERVINGS

1 Cook the onion and meat
In a large, deep frying pan over medium-high heat, warm the oil. Add the onion and sauté until translucent, 3–4 minutes. Add the beef and cook, stirring to break up any clumps, until the meat begins to brown, 7–8 minutes. Spoon off and discard the excess fat.

2 Cook the tomatoes and seasonings
Add the garlic, chili powder, cinnamon, and allspice, if using, and cook, stirring frequently, for 1 minute. Stir in the tomatoes, broth, raisins, tomato paste, and vinegar. Bring to a simmer, reduce the heat to medium, and cook, uncovered, until thickened toa stewlike consistency, 10–15 minutes. Season with salt and pepper. Serve the picadillo over the rice, if using.

> **cook's tip** This Cuban-inspired dish is also delicious wrapped in corn tortillas as a filling for soft tacos or in flour tortillas for burritos. Or, serve it over spaghetti and top with shredded Cheddar for a quick version of Cincinnati-style chili.

meatball sandwiches

1 **Prepare the meatballs**
In a large bowl, combine the bread crumbs and milk. Let stand for 5 minutes. In a frying pan over medium-high heat, warm the 1 tablespoon oil. Add the onion and garlic and sauté for about 5 minutes. Let cool slightly and add to the bread crumb mixture. Add the egg, parsley, 1 teaspoon salt, ¼ teaspoon pepper, and the beef and mix gently with your hands. Form into 12 equal-sized meatballs.

2 **Cook the meatballs**
In a large frying pan over medium heat, pour oil to a depth of ½ inch (12 mm). When the oil is hot, add the meatballs. Cook, turning, until browned on all sides, about 8 minutes. Transfer to paper towels to drain. Discard the oil and place the pan over medium-low heat. Add the tomato sauce and stir, scraping up any browned bits on the pan bottom. Add the meatballs and cook, covered, until heated through, about 10 minutes. Meanwhile, preheat the oven to 450°F (230°C). Place the rolls, cut sides up, on a rimmed baking sheet. Spread some of the sauce on the bottom half of each roll. Arrange 3 meatballs on each roll and top with the cheese. Bake until the cheese melts, about 5 minutes. Transfer to plates, top with the remaining sauce and roll tops, and serve.

Fresh bread crumbs,
½ cup (1 oz/30 g)
(see tip, page 214)

Milk, 2 tablespoons

Olive oil, 1 tablespoon,
plus more for frying

Yellow onion, 1 small,
finely chopped

Garlic, 1 clove, minced

Egg, 1, beaten

**Fresh flat-leaf (Italian)
parsley,** 3 tablespoons
minced

**Salt and freshly ground
pepper**

Ground (minced) beef,
1½ lb (750 g)

**Roasted Tomato Sauce
(page 33) or purchased
marinara sauce,** 2 cups
(16 fl oz/500 ml)

Crusty rolls, 4, each
6 inches (15 cm) long,
split

**Fresh mozzarella
cheese,** 6 oz (180 g),
thinly sliced

MAKES 4 SERVINGS

italian meatloaf

Ground (minced) beef chuck, ¾ lb (375 g)

Ground (minced) pork, ¾ lb (375 g)

Basil Pesto (page 34) or purchased pesto, ½ cup (4 fl oz/125 ml),

Fine fresh bread crumbs, 1 cup (2 oz/60 g) (see tip, page 214)

Oil-packed sun-dried tomatoes, ⅔ cup (4 oz/125 g) chopped

Egg, 1

Salt

MAKES 4–6 SERVINGS

1 Mix the meatloaf
Preheat the oven to 350°F (180°C). Have ready an 11-by-7-inch (28-by-18-cm) shallow baking dish. In a large bowl, combine the beef, pork, pesto, bread crumbs, sun-dried tomatoes, egg, and ½ teaspoon salt. Mix gently with your hands. Form the mixture into a rough 9-by-5-inch (23-by-13-cm) loaf in the center of the baking dish, then smooth the top.

2 Bake the meatloaf
Bake until the loaf is firm, the top is richly browned, and an instant-read thermometer inserted into the center registers 160°F (71°C). Let the loaf stand in the pan for 5–10 minutes before slicing. Serve warm.

> cook's tip Leftover meatloaf makes great sandwiches. Spread slices of French or Italian bread with pesto-flavored mayonnaise, layer each sandwich with slices of meatloaf and ripe tomatoes, and top with mixed greens.

italian burgers with peppers & onions

1 Ready the ingredients for grilling
Prepare a gas or charcoal grill for direct-heat grilling over high heat. In a bowl, toss the onion and bell pepper with the oil to coat, then season with salt and pepper. Place the vegetables in the center of a sheet of heavy-duty aluminum foil 12 inches (30 cm) long. Fold the sheet and pleat at the top and sides to enclose the vegetables. In a bowl, combine the beef, 2 tablespoons of the pesto, the garlic, 1 teaspoon salt, and ½ teaspoon pepper and mix well. Form into 4 equal patties. In a small bowl, combine the mayonnaise and the remaining 2 tablespoons pesto.

2 Grill the vegetables and patties
Lightly oil the grill rack. Place the vegetable packet on the grill and cover. Cook, turning occasionally, for 14 minutes. Add the patties to the grill, cover, and cook, turning once, until nicely browned on both sides, about 3 minutes on each side for medium-rare, or until done to your liking. At this point, the vegetables should be tender when pierced with a small knife (open the packet to check). During the last minute, add the rolls, cut sides down, to the grill to toast lightly. Serve the patties on the rolls with the onion, pepper, and pesto mayonnaise.

Yellow onion, 1 large, cut into half-moons ¼ inch (6 mm) thick

Red bell pepper (capsicum), 1, seeded and cut lengthwise into strips ¼ inch (6 mm) wide

Olive oil, 2 tablespoons

Salt and freshly ground pepper

Ground (minced) beef, 1½ lb (750 g)

Basil Pesto (page 34) or purchased pesto, 4 tablespoons (2 fl oz/60 ml)

Garlic, 2 cloves, minced

Mayonnaise, ½ cup (4 fl oz/125 ml)

Round Italian rolls, 4, split

MAKES 4 SERVINGS

chipotle beef chili

Flour, ¼ cup (1½ oz/45 g)

Salt and freshly ground pepper

Boneless beef chuck, 3 lb (1.5 kg), trimmed of excess fat and cut into chunks

Olive oil, 4–6 tablespoons (2–3 fl oz/60–90 ml)

Dried oregano, 1½ teaspoons

Garlic, 4 cloves, minced

Red onions, 2, finely chopped

Beef broth or dark Mexican beer, 2 cups (16 fl oz/500 ml)

Chipotle chiles in adobo sauce, 1 can (7 oz/220 g)

MAKES 6–8 SERVINGS

1 Brown the beef
In a resealable plastic bag, combine the flour, 1 teaspoon salt, and ½ teaspoon pepper. Add the beef and shake to coat evenly; reserve the excess flour mixture. In a large frying pan over medium-high heat, warm 4 tablespoons (2 fl oz/60 ml) of the oil. Add half of the coated beef and cook, turning, until evenly browned, 10–12 minutes. Transfer to paper towels to drain briefly, and then transfer to a Dutch oven or slow cooker. Repeat with the remaining beef, adding extra oil if needed. Sprinkle the browned beef with the oregano.

2 Finish the chili
Return the frying pan to medium-high heat. Add the garlic and all but about ½ cup (2½ oz/75 g) of the onions and sauté for 1 minute. Sprinkle with the reserved flour mixture and sauté for 1 minute longer. Pour in the broth and chiles. Raise the heat to high, bring to a boil, and stir to scrape up the browned bits on the pan bottom. Pour over the beef. If using a Dutch oven, place over medium-high heat and bring to a simmer. Reduce the heat to medium and cook, stirring frequently, until the beef is tender, 1–1½ hours. (If using a slow cooker, cook on the high-heat setting for 3–4 hours or the low-heat setting for 6–8 hours.) Serve, sprinkled with the remaining ½ cup onion.

grilled
thai beef skewers

1 **Marinate the beef**
Cut the flank steak across the grain into slices ¼ inch (6 mm) thick. In a shallow glass or ceramic dish, stir together the sake, soy sauce, vinegar, honey, sesame oil, ginger, garlic, red pepper flakes, and coriander. Add the flank steak and stir to coat thoroughly. Cover and let stand for 30 minutes at room temperature or up to 4 hours in the refrigerator.

2 **Prepare the skewers and grill**
Meanwhile soak 12 bamboo skewers in cold water for at least 30 minutes. Prepare a gas or charcoal grill for direct-heat grilling over high heat and oil the grill rack. Or, preheat a broiler (grill).

3 **Cook the beef**
Remove the meat from the marinade and discard the marinade. Thread the beef slices onto the skewers. Place the skewers on the grill rack, or put them on a rimmed baking sheet and place under the broiler. Cook, turning once or twice, until seared, 3–4 minutes total for medium-rare, or until done to your liking. Arrange on plates and serve. »

Flank steak, 1½ lb (750 g)

Sake, dry sherry, or mirin, ⅓ cup (3 fl oz/ 80 ml)

Soy sauce, ¼ cup (2 fl oz/60 ml)

Rice vinegar, ¼ cup (2 fl oz/ 60 ml)

Honey, 1 tablespoon

Asian sesame oil, 1 tablespoon

Fresh ginger, 2 tablespoons finely chopped

Garlic, 3 cloves, minced

Red pepper flakes, 1 teaspoon

Ground coriander, ½ teaspoon

MAKES 4 SERVINGS

cook's tip

For a complete meal, serve the skewers over scallion rice. Cook the rice according to the package directions. Before serving, stir in ¼ cup (1 oz/30 g) thinly sliced green (spring) onions and 1 tablespoon toasted sesame seeds.

beef sukiyaki with noodles

1 Make the braising liquid
In a bowl, combine ½ cup (2 fl oz/ 60 ml) water and the soy sauce, mirin, sake, and sugar and stir well.

2 Stir-fry the vegetables
Heat a wok or large frying pan over high heat until very hot and add the oil. Add the yellow onion and stir-fry just until tender, about 3 minutes. Add the mushrooms and stir-fry for 1 minute. Add the cabbage and stir-fry just until the cabbage wilts and the mushrooms have softened, about 2 minutes.

3 Braise the vegetables and beef
Reduce the heat to medium, pour the braising liquid over the vegetables, and bring to a low simmer. Stir in the noodles and beef, and simmer for about 3 minutes. Serve garnished with the green onions.

> **cook's tip** The meat must be very thinly sliced for this dish. Ask your butcher to slice it for you with a slicing machine. Or, put the whole sirloin in the freezer for at least 30 minutes or up to 1 hour and then slice it yourself with a very sharp knife.

Soy sauce, 1 cup (8 fl oz/250 ml)

Mirin, ½ cup (4 fl oz/ 125 ml)

Sake, ½ cup (4 fl oz/ 125 ml)

Sugar, 2 tablespoons

Canola or peanut oil, 2 tablespoons

Yellow onion, 1, thinly sliced

Shiitake mushrooms, ½ lb (8 oz/250 g), stems discarded and caps thinly sliced

Napa cabbage, ½ large head, shredded

Cellophane noodles, 6 oz (185 g), soaked in hot water to cover for 15 minutes and drained

Beef sirloin, 1 lb (500 g), very thinly sliced across the grain

Green (spring) onions, 2, white and pale green parts, thinly sliced

MAKES 4 SERVINGS

braised brisket

Flour, ¼ cup (1½ oz/45 g) plus 2 tablespoons

Salt and freshly ground black pepper

Beef brisket, 3½–4 lb (1.75–2 kg), trimmed of excess fat

Olive oil, ¼ cup (2 fl oz/60 ml)

Yellow onions, 2, thinly sliced

Garlic, 2 cloves, minced

Cayenne pepper, 1 teaspoon

Beef broth, 1 cup (8 fl oz/ 250 ml)

Red wine vinegar, ½ cup (4 fl oz/125 ml)

Sugar, ⅓ cup (3 oz/90 g)

Tomato paste, 2 tablespoons

MAKES 6–8 SERVINGS

1 Brown the brisket

On a large plate, combine the ¼ cup flour, 1 teaspoon salt, and ½ teaspoon black pepper. Coat the brisket with the flour mixture, shaking off the excess. In a large frying pan over high heat, warm the oil. Add the brisket, fattier side down, and cook until browned on both sides, about 14 minutes total. Transfer, fat side up, to a Dutch oven or slow cooker.

2 Sauté the vegetables

Pour off all but 1 tablespoon fat from the frying pan and return to medium-high heat. Add the onions, garlic, and cayenne and sauté for 2–3 minutes. Stir in the 2 tablespoons flour and cook for 1 minute. Pour in the broth and vinegar. Bring to a boil, stirring to scrape up the browned bits on the pan bottom. Stir in the sugar and tomato paste. Pour over the brisket.

3 Cook the brisket

If using a Dutch oven, preheat the oven to 375°F (190°C). Cover and cook in the oven until the meat is tender, about 3 hours. (If using a slow cooker, cook on the high-heat setting for 3–4 hours or the low-heat setting for 6–8 hours.) Skim off the excess fat, transfer the meat to a cutting board, and let rest for 10 minutes. Slice the meat across the grain and serve with the braising liquid.

shepherd's pie

1 Cook the potatoes

In a large saucepan, combine the potatoes, water to cover, and a generous pinch of salt. Bring to a boil over high heat, reduce the heat to medium, and cook until tender, 12–15 minutes. Drain well. Pass the potatoes through a ricer into a bowl, or mash with a potato masher in a bowl. Add the milk and 1 tablespoon of the butter and beat with a wooden spoon or with a handheld mixer on medium speed until smooth and fluffy. Season with ½ teaspoon salt and ¼ teaspoon pepper.

2 Simmer the filling

In a large saucepan over medium heat, melt the remaining 1 tablespoon butter. Add the onion and carrots and sauté until softened, about 5 minutes. Stir in the brisket, braising liquid, peas, and thyme. Bring to a simmer and cook, stirring occasionally, until heated through, 7–10 minutes.

3 Assemble and cook

Preheat the broiler (grill). Spoon the hot filling into a shallow 9-inch (23-cm) square baking dish. Spread the potatoes evenly over the filling. Place under the broiler and broil (grill) until the potatoes are tinged with brown, about 1 minute. Serve directly from the baking dish.

Russet potatoes, 2 lb (1 kg), peeled and cut into chunks

Salt and freshly ground pepper

Milk or half-and-half (half cream), ¾ cup (6 fl oz/180 ml)

Unsalted butter, 2 tablespoons

Yellow onion, 1 small, finely chopped

Carrots, 2, finely chopped

Braised Brisket (page 320), 3 cups (18 oz/560 g) shredded meat

Braising liquid from Braised Brisket (page 320), 2 cups (16 fl oz/ 500 ml), or 1 cup (8 fl oz/ 250 ml) beef broth

Frozen petite peas, 1 cup (5 oz/155 g), thawed

Fresh thyme, 1 tablespoon minced

MAKES 4 SERVINGS

bbq brisket sandwiches

Barbecue sauce, ½ cup (4 fl oz/125 ml)

Braised Brisket (page 320), 2 cups (12 oz/375 g) sliced or shredded meat

Crusty sandwich rolls, 4, split

MAKES 4 SERVINGS

1 Warm the brisket
In a frying pan over medium heat, warm the barbecue sauce. Add the brisket and turn in the sauce until heated through.

2 Assemble the sandwiches
Lightly toast the rolls. Place the open rolls on plates. Spoon the brisket on the bottom halves and moisten the meat with some of the sauce. Set the top halves in place and serve.

cook's tip If you would rather have a less saucy sandwich, instead of immersing the meat in the sauce when warming it, pour the sauce into a small bowl and use a basting brush to smear it on the meat.

braised short ribs

1 Brown the ribs
Preheat the oven to 325°F (165°C). Season the ribs with salt and pepper. In a Dutch oven or large ovenproof frying pan over high heat, warm the oil. Working in batches if necessary, add the ribs, and cook, turning once, until browned, 8–10 minutes. Transfer to a plate.

2 Braise the ribs
Add the onion to the pot and sauté until softened, 2–3 minutes. Add the wine and Port and cook, stirring to scrape up the browned bits on the pan bottom, 2–3 minutes. Return the ribs and any juices from the plate to the pot, and add enough broth so that it comes one-third of the way up the ribs. Bring to a boil and remove from the heat. Cover the pot tightly with aluminum foil, place the lid on the pot, and braise in the oven until the meat is fork-tender, 1½–2 hours. Add the potatoes and carrots and cook, covered, until the vegetables are tender, about 30 minutes.

3 Finish the dish
Using a slotted spoon, divide the ribs and vegetables among shallow bowls. Skim the fat from the sauce. Spoon some of the sauce over the ribs, garnish with the parsley, and serve.

Beef short ribs, 4–5 lb (2–2.5 kg) total weight, cut into 3-inch (7.5-cm) pieces

Salt and freshly ground pepper

Olive oil, 3 tablespoons

Yellow onion, 1, finely chopped

Dry red wine, 2 cups (16 fl oz/500 ml)

Port or brandy, 1 cup (8 fl oz/250 ml)

Chicken broth or stock, 2 cups (16 fl oz/500 ml), homemade (page 29) or purchased

Boiling potatoes, 1 lb (500 g), quartered

Carrots, 2, cut into large chunks

Fresh flat-leaf (Italian) parsley, 2 tablespoons minced

MAKES 4–6 SERVINGS

beef with ginger & caramelized onions

Beef tenderloin or sirloin, 1½ lb (750 g), cut across the grain into thin strips

Soy sauce, 5 tablespoons (2½ fl oz/75 ml)

Rice wine or dry sherry, 2 tablespoons

Worcestershire sauce, 2 tablespoons

Asian sesame oil, 2 teaspoons

Freshly ground pepper

Sugar, ½ teaspoon

Cornstarch (cornflour), ½ teaspoon

Canola or peanut oil, 2 tablespoons

Yellow onion, 1 large, thinly sliced

Fresh ginger, 1 tablespoon grated

Red pepper flakes (optional)

Steamed rice, for serving

MAKES 4 SERVINGS

1 Marinate the beef
In a large bowl, combine the beef, 1 tablespoon of the soy sauce, and the wine and toss to coat the beef evenly. Set aside for 10 minutes.

2 Make the sauce
In a bowl, combine 4 tablespoons (2 fl oz/60 ml) water, the remaining 4 tablespoons soy sauce, Worcestershire sauce, sesame oil, 1 teaspoon pepper, sugar, and cornstarch. Stir to dissolve the sugar and cornstarch.

3 Stir-fry the vegetables
Heat a wok or large frying pan over high heat until very hot and add 1 tablespoon of the canola oil. Add the onion and stir-fry until caramelized, about 10 minutes. Using a slotted spoon, transfer the onion mixture to a plate. Return the pan to high heat and add the remaining 1 tablespoon canola oil. Add the ginger and stir-fry until fragrant, about 10 seconds. Add the beef with its marinade and stir-fry just until it begins to brown but is still rare in the center, about 1 minute. Return the onion mixture to the pan. Give the sauce a quick stir, add to the pan, and stir until the sauce thickens slightly, about 10 seconds. Sprinkle with red pepper flakes to taste, if desired. Serve with the rice.

veal chops with tomato vinaigrette

1 Prepare the grill
Prepare a gas or charcoal grill for direct-heat grilling over high heat. If using a gas grill, turn one burner on low and the other burner(s) on high. If using a charcoal grill, spread the coals into a slope.

2 Grill the veal and tomatoes
Season the veal with 1 teaspoon salt and ½ teaspoon pepper. Lightly oil the grill rack. Place the veal chops and tomatoes over the hottest area of the grill and cover. Cook the chops until the undersides are seared with grill marks, about 2 minutes. Turn and cook the second sides, about 2 minutes longer. Cook the tomatoes for the same total time, turning occasionally, until the skins are lightly charred. Transfer the tomatoes to a plate. Move the veal to the cooler area of the grill, cover, and cook for about 5 minutes longer for medium, or until cooked to your liking. Transfer to plates.

3 Make the tomato vinaigrette
Remove and discard the tomato skins. In a blender or food processor, combine the tomatoes and vinegar and process until puréed. With the machine running, add the oil. Add the tarragon, ¼ teaspoon salt, and ⅛ teaspoon pepper and pulse to combine. Drizzle the veal chops with the vinaigrette and serve. »

Veal rib chops, 4, each 1 inch (2.5 cm) thick

Salt and freshly ground pepper

Plum (Roma) tomatoes, 2 large

Red wine vinegar, 2 tablespoons

Olive oil, ½ cup (4 fl oz/125 ml)

Fresh tarragon, 2 teaspoons chopped

MAKES 4 SERVINGS

cook's tip

This is a perfect dish for the summertime, when tomatoes are in season. Experiment with different varieties depending on which ones look the freshest at the market. You can also grill extra tomatoes and serve them whole, sprinkled with coarse salt and pepper.

veal piccata

1 Cook the veal
Season the veal with salt and pepper. In a large frying pan over medium-high heat, melt 1½ tablespoons of the butter. Add half of the veal and cook, turning once, until browned, about 2 minutes total. Transfer to a plate. Repeat, using 1½ tablespoons of butter and the remaining veal. Do not overcook.

2 Make the sauce
Add the remaining 1 tablespoon butter to the pan and melt over medium-high heat. Add the garlic and sauté until fragrant, about 30 seconds. Add the broth and wine and cook, stirring to scrape up the browned bits on the pan bottom, until the sauce is reduced by about one-fourth, 2–3 minutes. Stir in the capers and simmer for 1 minute. Season to taste with salt and pepper and add the parsley. Return the veal and any juices on the plate to the pan and cook until heated through, about 2 minutes. Divide the veal among plates, spoon the sauce over the veal, and serve.

Veal scallops, 8, about 1½ lb (750 g) total weight, pounded to about ¼ inch (6 mm) thickness

Salt and freshly ground pepper

Unsalted butter, 4 tablespoons (2 oz/60 g)

Garlic, 2 large cloves, minced

Chicken broth, ½ cup (4 fl oz/125 ml)

Dry white wine, ½ cup (4 fl oz/125 ml)

Capers, 2 tablespoons

Fresh flat-leaf (Italian) parsley or chervil, 2 tablespoons chopped

MAKES 4 SERVINGS

cook's tip You can substitute 4 skinless, boneless chicken breast halves for the veal. Pound each breast half with a meat pounder until it is ¼ inch (6 mm) thick.

baked ham
with green beans

Smoked ham on the bone, 3½ lb (1.75 kg), fat trimmed and meat scored in a diamond pattern

Orange juice, ½ cup (4 fl oz/125 ml)

Green beans, 2 lb (1 kg), trimmed

Shallots, 2, minced

Salt and freshly ground pepper

MAKES 6–8 SERVINGS

1 **Bake the ham**
Preheat the oven to 325°F (165°C). Place the ham in a large roasting pan and pour the orange juice into the pan. Cover the pan tightly with aluminum foil and bake for 1 hour. Remove the foil and continue to roast until the ham is completely heated through, about 1 hour longer. Baste the ham occasionally during the last hour of cooking. Bake until an instant-read thermometer inserted into the thickest part of the ham away from the bone reads 160°F (71°C). Transfer to a carving board and let rest for 20 minutes.

2 **Prepare the green beans**
While the ham is resting, pour off all but 2 tablespoons fat from the roasting pan. Add the green beans and shallots, season with salt and pepper, and toss to combine. Return the pan to the oven and roast, stirring occasionally, until the green beans are tender-crisp, about 15 minutes. Slice the ham and arrange on individual plates with the green beans.

storage tip Leftover ham can be cooled, wrapped in plastic wrap, and stored in the refrigerator for up to 1 week, then used in the recipes on pages 133 and 329.

baked croque monsieurs

1 Make the sauce

Preheat the oven to 400°F (200°C). In a saucepan over low heat, melt the butter. Add the flour and whisk until smooth. Cook, whisking constantly, for 1 minute. Slowly whisk in the warmed milk, raise the heat to medium, and bring to a simmer. Simmer, whisking often, until thickened, about 5 minutes. Remove from the heat, stir in ½ cup (2 oz/60 g) of the cheese, and season with salt and pepper. Let stand, stirring often, until cooled.

2 Toast the bread

Arrange the bread slices on a large baking sheet lined with parchment (baking) paper. Toast the bread, turning once, until golden, about 10 minutes total. Remove from the oven.

3 Bake the sandwiches

Preheat the broiler (grill). Spread 4 bread slices with the mustard. Top each with 1 slice of ham and 1 tablespoon of the sauce, and then with the remaining bread slices. Spread the remaining sauce on the tops of the sandwiches, being sure to cover the edges. Sprinkle with the remaining ¼ cup (1 oz/30 g) cheese. Broil (grill) until the cheese is melted and golden brown, about 2 minutes. Transfer to plates and serve.

Unsalted butter, 2 tablespoons

Flour, 2 tablespoons

Milk, 1 cup (8 fl oz/ 250 ml), warmed

Gruyère cheese, ¾ cup (3 oz/90 g) shredded

Salt and freshly ground pepper

Country-style white sandwich bread, 8 slices

Dijon mustard, 4 tablespoons

Baked Ham (page 328) or purchased cooked ham, 4 slices

MAKES 4 SERVINGS

pork schnitzel with arugula

Lemons, 2

Coarse fresh bread crumbs, 1½ cups (3 oz/90 g) (see tip, page 214)

Flour, ⅓ cup (1½ oz/45 g)

Salt and freshly ground pepper

Egg, 1

Pork cutlets, 4, 1½ lb (750 g) total weight, pounded to about ½ inch (12 mm) thick

Olive oil, 4 tablespoons (2 fl oz/60 ml)

Shallot, 1, minced

Arugula (rocket) or frisée, 6 cups (6 oz/ 185 g), tough stems removed

MAKES 4 SERVINGS

1 **Bread the pork**
Finely grate 2 teaspoons zest and squeeze 2 tablespoons juice from 1 lemon. Cut the second lemon into 8 wedges. Spread the bread crumbs on a plate. On another plate, stir together the flour, lemon zest, ½ teaspoon salt, and ¼ teaspoon pepper. In a shallow bowl, beat the egg with 1½ tablespoons water. One at a time dip both sides of a cutlet in the flour mixture, shaking off the excess. Dip it in the egg, letting the excess drip back into the bowl, and finally dip it in the bread crumbs, patting them on firmly.

2 **Cook the pork**
In a large frying pan over medium-high heat, warm 2 tablespoons of the oil. Add the cutlets and cook, turning once, until golden brown on both sides and barely pink in the center, 4–6 minutes total. Transfer to a plate.

3 **Make the salad**
Add the remaining 2 tablespoons oil to the pan over medium heat. Add the shallot and sauté until softened, about 1 minute. Stir in the lemon juice, scraping up the browned bits on the pan bottom. Remove from the heat, add the arugula, and toss briefly to coat. Place the cutlets on plates, top with the arugula, garnish with the lemon wedges, and serve.

chile verde

1 Cook the stew
Place the chiles and their liquid in a Dutch oven or slow cooker, tearing the chiles into coarse strips. Stir in the pork, broth, garlic, oregano, 1½ teaspoons salt, and ½ teaspoon white pepper. If using a Dutch oven, bring to a boil over high heat, reduce the heat to low, partially cover, and cook until the pork is very tender and the sauce has thickened, 2–3 hours. (If using a slow cooker, cover and cook on the high-heat setting for 4 hours or the low-heat setting for 8 hours.)

2 Serve and garnish the stew
Taste and adjust the seasonings. Ladle the stew into bowls over steamed rice and serve garnished with sour cream and cilantro. Pass flour tortillas at the table, if desired.

Canned roasted whole green chiles, 1 cup (8 oz/250 g) with liquid

Boneless pork shoulder, 3 lb (1.5 kg), cut into 1-inch (2.5-cm) cubes

Chicken broth or stock, 2 cups (16 fl oz/500 ml), homemade (page 29) or purchased

Garlic, 4 cloves, minced

Dried oregano, 1 teaspoon

Salt and freshly ground white pepper

Steamed white rice, for serving

Sour cream, ¾ cup (6 oz/185 g)

Fresh cilantro (fresh coriander), ½ cup (¾ oz/20 g) chopped

Warmed flour tortillas, for serving (optional)

MAKES 6–8 SERVINGS

pulled pork sandwiches

Canola or peanut oil,
3 tablespoons

Boneless pork shoulder,
4 lb (2 kg), cut into
3 equal pieces

Yellow onion, 1, finely
chopped

Cider vinegar, ¾ cup
(6 fl oz/180 ml)

Ketchup, ¾ cup
(6 fl oz/185 ml)

Brown sugar, ⅓ cup
(2½ oz/75 g) firmly
packed

Light molasses, ¼ cup
(2½ oz/75 g)

Worcestershire sauce,
1 tablespoon

Red pepper flakes,
2 teaspoons

Dry mustard, 1 teaspoon

Salt and freshly ground
pepper

Soft sandwich rolls, split
and toasted

MAKES 6–8 SERVINGS

1 Brown the pork
In a large frying pan over medium-high heat, warm the oil. Add the pork and brown on all sides, about 12 minutes total. Transfer to a Dutch oven or slow cooker.

2 Make the sauce and cook the pork
Pour off all but about 1 tablespoon fat from the pan and return to medium-high heat. Add the onion and sauté until golden, about 5 minutes. Add the vinegar and stir to scrape up the browned bits on the pan bottom. Stir in the ketchup, brown sugar, molasses, Worcestershire sauce, red pepper flakes, mustard, and 1 teaspoon each salt and pepper. Cook, stirring, just until the mixture begins to bubble. Pour over the pork. If using a Dutch oven, cover and cook over medium heat, turning occasionally, until tender, about 2 hours. (If using a slow cooker, cover and cook on the high-heat setting for 4–5 hours or the low-heat setting for 8–10 hours.)

3 Shred the pork and serve
Transfer the pork to a platter. Using 2 forks, pull the pork into shreds, discarding any large pieces of fat. Skim the fat from the sauce. Return the pork to the sauce and stir to combine. Serve the pork and sauce with the toasted rolls and let diners assemble their own sandwiches.

roast pork loin
with pan sauce

1 Roast the pork
Preheat the oven to 450°F (230°C). Rub the pork all over with the cut sides of the garlic clove. Sprinkle with 1 teaspoon each salt and pepper. Place the pork, fat side up, on a rack in a shallow roasting pan. Roast for 15 minutes. Reduce the temperature to 400°F (200°C) and roast until an instant-read thermometer inserted into the center registers 145°–150°F (63°–65°C) and the pork is barely pink in the center, about 1 hour. Transfer to a carving board and let stand for 10 minutes.

2 Prepare the pan sauce and serve
Remove the rack from the roasting pan and place the pan over medium heat. Add the butter and stir with a whisk to scrape up the browned bits on the pan bottom. Sprinkle in the flour and cook, stirring, for about 2 minutes. Add the wine and broth and stir until smooth and thick. Snip the strings and slice the pork. Serve drizzled with the pan sauce. »

storage tip You can double this recipe and use the leftovers for another recipe (see pages 336 and 337). Let the extra pork loin cool, then wrap tightly in plastic wrap and refrigerate for up to 4 days.

Boneless pork loin, 2 lb (1 kg), rolled and tied

Garlic, 1 clove, halved

Salt and freshly ground pepper

Butter, 3 tablespoons

Flour, 1 tablespoon

Dry white wine, ¼ cup (2 fl oz/60 ml)

Chicken broth, ¼ cup (2 fl oz/60 ml)

MAKES 4–6 SERVINGS

roast pork loin with pan sauce

continued

cook's tip

Serve this hearty pork dish with the same wine that you use to make it. A good guideline is to always choose a wine for cooking that you also enjoy drinking. Also, avoid cooking with liquid labeled "cooking wine," or the overall flavor of your dish will suffer.

quick choucroute

1 **Cook the sausages**
In a large frying pan over medium-high heat, warm the oil. Add the sausages, cut side down, and cook until browned, 3–4 minutes. Turn the sausages, add the onion, and cook, stirring occasionally, until the onion is softened, 4–5 minutes. Add the apple and cook, stirring occasionally, until the apple is softened and the onion is golden, about 3 minutes.

2 **Simmer the dish**
Stir in the sauerkraut, bay leaf, caraway seeds, juniper berries, and wine. Add the pork chops in a single layer. Bring to a simmer over medium-high heat, reduce the heat to medium-low, cover, and cook for 10–12 minutes to blend the flavors. Remove and discard the bay leaf. Season to taste with pepper. Transfer the choucroute to plates and serve.

cook's tip In its traditional form, Alsatian *choucroute garnie* calls for serving sauerkraut with a variety of fresh and cured meats. In this easy version, smoked pork chops and sausages top the sauerkraut. Round out the meal with a salad of sturdy greens with blue cheese, hearty bread, and boiled potatoes.

Olive oil, 3 tablespoons

Kielbasa, bratwurst, or knockwurst, or a combination, ¾ lb (375 g), cut in half lengthwise

Yellow onion, 1, sliced

Tart apple such as Granny Smith, 1, peeled, halved, cored, and sliced

Sauerkraut, 1 lb (500 g), well drained

Bay leaf, 1

Caraway seeds, 2 teaspoons

Dried juniper berries, 1 teaspoon, lightly crushed

Dry white wine, 1 cup (8 fl oz/250 ml)

Smoked pork chops, 4, each 4–6 oz (125–185 g)

Freshly ground pepper

MAKES 4 SERVINGS

cuban pork sandwiches

Crusty rolls such as
Portuguese rolls, 4, split

Dijon mustard,
4 teaspoons

Roast Pork Loin
(page 333), 12 slices

Smoked ham or Genoa
salami, 1 lb (500 g),
thinly sliced

Swiss cheese, ½ lb
(250 g), thinly sliced

Dill pickle slices, ½ cup
(2 oz/60 g)

Unsalted butter,
2 tablespoons, melted

MAKES 4 SERVINGS

1 **Assemble the sandwiches**
Preheat a heavy frying pan or ridged
grill pan over medium-high heat. Spread
the bottom of each roll with mustard.
Layer the pork, ham, cheese, and pickles
on the rolls, dividing evenly. Set the top
roll halves in place and press gently. Brush
the tops of the rolls with the melted butter.

2 **Grill the sandwiches**
Place the sandwiches in the heated
pan and weight with a second pan. Grill
until the undersides are golden, about
2½ minutes. Turn the sandwiches, weight
again, and cook until the other sides are
golden and the cheese is melted, about
2½ minutes longer. Serve warm.

cook's tip The sandwiches can
also be made on a split baguette
or split large rustic loaf such as
ciabatta. After layering the
ingredients in the baguette or loaf,
cut the large sandwich into four
individual sandwiches, and serve.

chipotle pork tacos

1 Heat the pork
In a large frying pan over medium-high heat, warm 2 tablespoons of the oil. Add the pork, season with salt and pepper, and cook until heated through, about 2 minutes.

2 Assemble the tacos
In a blender, purée the chipotle chiles in adobo, the remaining 1 tablespoon oil, and the lime juice. Divide the pork evenly among the tortillas. Drizzle with the chipotle salsa and top with the avocado. Garnish with cilantro, onion, and *queso fresco*, and serve.

cook's tip The versatile chipotle salsa can be made up to 1 week in advance and stored in an airtight container. Serve as a condiment for grilled chicken or to top scrambled eggs on toasted country bread.

Olive oil, 3 tablespoons

Roast Pork Loin (page 333), 3 cups (1½ lb/750 g) thin strips or shredded meat

Salt and freshly ground pepper

Chipotle chiles in adobo sauce, 1 can (7 oz/220 g)

Lime juice, from 1 lime

Corn tortillas, 8, warmed

Hass avocado, 1, halved, pitted, peeled, and thinly sliced

Fresh cilantro (fresh coriander) leaves, ½ cup (½ oz/15 g)

Red onion, ¼, minced

Queso fresco, ½ cup (2½ oz/75 g) crumbled

MAKES 4 SERVINGS

pork chops with apple-sage stuffing

Unsalted butter,
2 tablespoons

Shallots, 2 tablespoons
minced

**Fresh coarse bread
crumbs,** 1 cup (2 oz/60 g)
(see tip page 214)

Dried apples, ½ cup
(1½ oz/45 g) coarsely
chopped

Fresh sage,
2 tablespoons minced

Ground fennel seeds,
¼ teaspoon

Hard cider, ⅓ cup
(3 fl oz/80 ml)

**Salt and freshly ground
pepper**

**Bone-in, center-cut pork
loin chops,** 4, each
1½ inches (4 cm) thick

MAKES 4 SERVINGS

1 **Prepare the grill**
Prepare a gas or charcoal grill for
direct-heat grilling over high heat. If using
a gas grill, turn one burner on medium
and the other burner(s) on high. If using a
charcoal grill, spread the coals across the
fire bed into a slope.

2 **Stuff the pork chops**
In a frying pan over medium heat,
melt the butter. Add the shallots and sauté
for 2 minutes. Stir in the bread crumbs,
dried apples, sage, fennel seeds, and
cider. Season with salt and pepper and
remove from the heat. Cut a deep
horizontal slit into the center of each chop,
starting from the meatier side, and use a
small spoon to fill the slit with the stuffing.
Close the slits with toothpicks. Season the
chops with salt and pepper.

3 **Grill the pork chops**
Lightly oil the grill rack. Grill the
pork chops over the hottest area of the
grill until seared with grill marks, about
2 minutes. Turn and grill for 2 minutes
longer. Move the chops to the cooler area
of the grill and cover. Grill until the chops
feel firm and spring back when pressed
in the center, about 16 minutes longer.
Transfer the pork to a platter and serve.

mu shu pork stir-fry

1 Marinate the pork
Preheat the oven to 400°F (200°C). In a large bowl, stir together the ⅓ cup hoisin sauce and the soy sauce. Add the pork, stir to coat, and set aside.

2 Cook the vegetables
In a large wok or frying pan over high heat, warm the oil. Add the mushrooms, cabbage, green onions, carrots, and water chestnuts and stir-fry until the vegetables are tender, 4–5 minutes. Add the ginger and stir-fry for 30 seconds. Add the pork strips and any remaining marinade and stir-fry until lightly browned, 2–3 minutes. Give the cornstarch mixture a stir, add it to the pan, and cook, stirring often, until the sauce is thickened and the pork is opaque throughout, 2–3 minutes. Transfer to a shallow dish and serve, passing the tortillas and hoisin sauce at the table.

cook's tip Make a vegetarian version of this dish by omitting the pork and adding vegetables such as shredded red cabbage and thinly sliced celery or cubed tofu. Cook with the other vegetables in Step 2.

Hoisin sauce, ⅓ cup (3 fl oz/80 ml), plus more for serving

Soy sauce, 2 tablespoons

Boneless pork loin chops, 1 lb (500 g), cut into thin strips

Canola oil, 2 tablespoons

Shiitake mushrooms, 6 oz (185 g), stems discarded and caps thinly sliced

Savoy cabbage, 1 small head, halved, cored, and thinly sliced crosswise

Green (spring) onions, 4, white and pale green parts, thinly sliced

Carrots, 3, coarsely grated

Water chestnuts, 1 can (8 oz/250 g), sliced

Fresh ginger, 2 tablespoons minced

Cornstarch (cornflour), 2 tablespoons, mixed with 2–3 tablespoons water

Flour tortillas, 8, each 8 inches (20 cm) in diameter, warmed

MAKES 4–6 SERVINGS

asian roast pork & squash

Boneless pork loin roast, 2–2½ lb (1–1.25 kg)

Salt and freshly ground pepper

Hoisin sauce, 2 tablespoons

Soy sauce, 2 tablespoons

Asian sesame oil, 1½ teaspoons

Acorn squash, 1 small, halved, seeded, and cut into wedges

Red onion, 1, halved and cut into wedges

MAKES 4–6 SERVINGS

1 Roast the pork
Preheat the oven to 450°F (230°C). Season the pork with salt and pepper. Place the pork, fat side up, in a roasting pan. Pour 1–2 tablespoons of water around the pork and roast for 25 minutes. If the pan becomes dry during roasting, add another 1 tablespoon water.

2 Season the vegetables
Meanwhile, in a bowl, stir together the hoisin sauce, soy sauce, and sesame oil. Add the squash and onion and toss well to coat.

3 Finish the pork
Reduce the oven temperature to 325°F (165°C). Baste the pork with the pan drippings and arrange the vegetables around the pork. Continue to roast until an instant-read thermometer inserted into the center of the pork registers 145°–150°F (63°–65°C) and the pork is barely pink in the center, 45–50 minutes longer. Transfer the pork to a carving board and let rest for 10 minutes. Slice the pork and serve with the vegetables.

braised pork chops with cherry sauce

1 Brown the pork chops
Sprinkle the pork chops with salt, pepper, and the rosemary, patting the seasonings firmly to adhere to the meat. In a large frying pan over medium-high heat, melt 2 tablespoons of the butter. Add the pork chops and cook, turning once, until golden on both sides, about 6 minutes total. Transfer to a plate.

2 Make the sauce
Melt the remaining 1 tablespoon butter in the pan over medium heat. Add the leeks and sauté until softened, 3–4 minutes. Add the broth and cook, stirring to scrape up the browned bits on the pan bottom, for 1 minute. Stir in the Port, vinegar, and cherries.

3 Finish the dish
Return the pork chops and any juices from the plate to the pan and spoon the liquid over them. Cover, reduce the heat to medium-low, and simmer until the pork is tender and barely pink in the center, about 15 minutes. Transfer to plates, top with the sauce, and serve. »

Bone-in, center-cut pork loin chops, 4, each ¾ inch (2 cm) thick

Salt and freshly ground pepper

Fresh rosemary, 1 tablespoon minced

Unsalted butter, 3 tablespoons

Leeks, 2, white and pale green parts, halved, rinsed, and thinly sliced

Chicken broth, 1 cup (8 fl oz/250 ml)

Port wine, ¼ cup (2 fl oz/60 ml)

Balsamic vinegar, 2 tablespoons

Dried cherries, ½ cup (2 oz/60 g)

MAKES 4 SERVINGS

braised pork chops with cherry sauce

continued

cook's tip

If fresh cherries are in season, they can easily be substituted for the dried cherries in this recipe. Increase the amount to 1 cup (6 oz/ 185 g). Cut them in half, remove the pits, and add to the pan along with the leeks in Step 2.

sausages with white beans

1 **Cook the sausages**
Prick the sausages in a few places with a fork and place them in a large frying pan with a lid. Add ½ cup (4 fl oz/125 ml) of the wine. Bring to a boil over medium-high heat, cover, reduce the heat to medium-low, and simmer for 5 minutes. Uncover the pan, raise the heat to medium-high, and cook the sausages, turning occasionally, until well browned, 8–10 minutes. Transfer to a plate.

2 **Cook the vegetables**
Meanwhile, in another large frying pan over medium-high heat, warm the oil. Add the onion and bell pepper and cook, stirring occasionally, until softened and beginning to brown, about 5 minutes. Add the garlic and cook, stirring constantly, for 30 seconds. Add the beans, oregano, remaining ½ cup wine, and broth. Bring to a boil, reduce the heat to medium, and simmer, uncovered, until the liquid is reduced by half, 4–5 minutes.

3 **Finish the dish**
Add the sausages to the beans and simmer for about 1 minute to warm through. Season to taste with salt and pepper. Arrange the sausages, beans, and arugula on plates, drizzle with any liquid left in the pan, and serve.

Hot or sweet Italian sausages, 8 small or 4 large, 1½ lb (750 g) total weight

Dry white wine, 1 cup (8 fl oz/250 ml)

Olive oil, 2 tablespoons

Yellow onion, 1, finely chopped

Red bell pepper (capsicum), 1 large, seeded and chopped

Garlic, 2 cloves, minced

White Beans (page 36) or canned white beans, 2 cups (14 oz/440 g)

Fresh oregano, 2 tablespoons minced

Chicken broth, ¾ cup (6 fl oz/180 ml)

Salt and freshly ground pepper

Arugula (rocket), 2–3 cups (2–3 oz/ 60–90 g)

MAKES 4 SERVINGS

asian-style barbecued ribs

Canola oil, 1 tablespoon

Fresh ginger,
2 tablespoons grated

Garlic, 1 clove, minced

Green (spring) onion,
1 large, white and pale
green parts, minced

Ketchup, ⅔ cup (5 fl oz/
160 ml)

Hoisin sauce, ⅓ cup
(3 fl oz/80 ml)

Dry sherry,
2 tablespoons

Pork baby back ribs,
4 lb (2 kg)

**Salt and freshly ground
pepper**

MAKES 4–6 SERVINGS

1 Make the hoisin glaze
Prepare a gas or charcoal grill for direct-heat grilling over medium-high heat. In a saucepan over medium-high heat, warm the oil. Add the ginger and garlic and sauté for about 30 seconds. Add the green onion and cook until wilted, about 1 minute. Stir in the ketchup, hoisin sauce, and sherry and bring to a simmer. Reduce the heat to low and cook, stirring often, for about 5 minutes. Set aside.

2 Grill the ribs
Cut the ribs into 4 equal portions. Season on both sides with salt and pepper. Wrap each slab in a double thickness of heavy-duty aluminum foil. Place on the grill rack, cover, and cook, turning the ribs occasionally and taking care not to pierce the foil, for 45 minutes. Open the foil and pierce the ribs with the tip of a knife; they should be barely tender. If not yet tender, rewrap and cook for 5–10 minutes longer. Remove the packets and unwrap the ribs, discarding the foil and juices. Add more coals to the charcoal fire if the coals have burned down. Oil the grill rack. Put the ribs on the grill and cook, turning occasionally, until lightly browned, about 5 minutes. Brush with the hoisin glaze and grill for 5 minutes longer. Cut into individual ribs and serve.

chile-rubbed pork with corn salsa

1 Roast the pork
Preheat the oven to 425°F (230°C). Rub the pork with 1 tablespoon of the oil, then season with salt, pepper, and the chile powder. In a large frying pan over medium-high heat, warm the remaining 1 tablespoon oil. Add the pork and brown on all sides, about 5 minutes total. Transfer the pork to a shallow roasting pan. Reserve the frying pan and drippings. Roast the pork until an instant-read thermometer inserted into the center registers 145°–150°F (63°–65°C) and the meat is barely pink in the center, 15–20 minutes. Transfer the pork to a carving board, tent with aluminum foil, and let stand for 10 minutes.

2 Make the salsa
While the pork rests, add the corn and cumin to the drippings in the frying pan and place over medium-high heat. Cook, stirring, until the corn is lightly browned, 3–4 minutes. Remove from the heat and stir in the onion, tomato, lime juice, and cilantro. Season to taste with salt and pepper. Cut the pork into thin slices and serve with the warm salsa.

Pork tenderloins, 2,
1½ lb (750 g) total weight

Olive oil, 2 tablespoons

Salt and freshly ground pepper

Ancho chile powder,
2 teaspoons

Fresh or thawed frozen corn kernels, 1 cup
(6 oz/185 g)

Ground cumin,
¾ teaspoon

Yellow onion, 1 small,
finely chopped

Tomato, 1 large, seeded
and finely chopped

Lime juice, from 1 lime

**Fresh cilantro
(fresh coriander),**
¼ cup (⅓ oz/10 g)
chopped

MAKES 4–6 SERVINGS

grilled pork chops with romesco

Boneless, center-cut pork chops, 4, each 1 inch (3 cm) thick

Salt and freshly ground pepper

Romesco Sauce (page 35), ½ cup (4 fl oz/125 ml)

Olive oil, 6 tablespoons (3 fl oz/90 ml)

Yukon gold potatoes, 1½ lb (750 g)

Sherry vinegar, 1 tablespoon

Green (spring) onions, 3, chopped

MAKES 4 SERVINGS

1 Marinate the pork chops
Season the pork chops with salt. In a shallow glass or ceramic dish, whisk the romesco with 1 tablespoon of the oil. Add the chops, turn to coat, and let stand at room temperature for up to 1 hour.

2 Make the potato salad
Meanwhile, bring a saucepan of water to a boil over high heat. Add 1 tablespoon salt and the potatoes. Cook until the potatoes are tender, about 25 minutes. Drain, rinse under cold running water, and let cool slightly. In a large bowl, whisk together the remaining 5 tablespoons (2½ fl oz/75 ml) oil and the vinegar. Slice the potatoes and transfer to the bowl. Add the green onions and mix gently. Season with salt and pepper.

3 Grill the pork chops
Prepare a gas or charcoal grill for indirect-heat grilling over high heat. If using a gas grill, preheat using all of the burners, then turn off the burner directly below where the chops will sit. For a charcoal grill, arrange the hot coals on either side of the grill. Lightly oil the grill rack. Place the chops on the cooler area of the grill, cover, and cook for 5 minutes. Turn and cook until the chops feel firm when pressed, about 5 minutes longer. Serve with the potato salad.

quick cassoulet

1 **Cook the sausages**
Slit each sausage diagonally several times on both sides. In a frying pan over medium heat, warm the oil. Add the sausages and cook, turning once, until browned on the outside and cooked through, about 10 minutes total.

2 **Prepare the beans**
In another large frying pan over medium heat, sauté the bacon until it starts to brown, 5–7 minutes. Drain off all but 2 tablespoons of the bacon drippings. Stir in the beans, thyme, tomatoes, and sugar. Bring to a simmer and cook, stirring frequently, until the beans are heated through, about 5 minutes. Season to taste with salt and pepper.

3 **Bake the cassoulet**
Cut the sausages crosswise into bite-sized pieces. Butter a 3-qt (3-l) ovenproof pan or gratin dish and distribute the sausages evenly in the pan. Spoon the bean mixture over the sausages, discarding the thyme sprig. Spread the bread crumbs on top and drizzle with the melted butter. Bake until the beans are bubbly and the crumb topping is golden brown, about 20 minutes. Transfer to a rack, let cool slightly, and serve.

Pork sausages, 1½ lb (750 g)

Olive oil, 1 tablespoon

Thick-cut bacon, 5 slices, chopped

White Beans (page 36), 4 cups (1¾ lb/875 g)

Fresh thyme, 1 sprig

Diced plum (Roma) tomatoes, 1 can (14½ oz/455 g)

Sugar, 1½ teaspoons

Salt and freshly ground pepper

Fresh bread crumbs, 1 cup (2 oz/60 g) (see tip, page 214)

Unsalted butter, 4 tablespoons (2 oz/60 g), melted

MAKES 4–6 SERVINGS

sichuan braised pork with eggplant

Canola or peanut oil,
4 tablespoons
(2 fl oz/60 ml)

Boneless pork shoulder,
1½ lb (750 g), cut into
large cubes

Soy sauce, ⅓ cup
(3 fl oz/80 ml)

Rice wine or dry sherry,
¼ cup (2 fl oz/60 ml)

Brown sugar,
2 tablespoons firmly
packed

**Chinese five-spice
powder,** 1 teaspoon

Cornstarch (cornflour),
½ teaspoon

**Asian eggplants
(slender aubergines),**
½ lb (250 g), cut into
cubes

Fresh ginger, 4 thin slices

Green (spring) onions,
2, white and pale green
parts, thinly sliced

Garlic, 4 cloves, minced

Steamed rice, for serving

MAKES 4 SERVINGS

1 **Sear the pork**
Heat a Dutch oven or large, deep frying pan over high heat until hot and add 2 tablespoons of the oil. Add the pork in a single layer and cook, turning once, until golden brown, 8–10 minutes. Using a slotted spoon, transfer to a plate.

2 **Cook the eggplant**
In a bowl, stir together 2 cups (16 fl oz/500 ml) water and the soy sauce, wine, brown sugar, five-spice powder, and cornstarch. Return the pot to high heat and add the remaining 2 tablespoons oil. Add the eggplants and sauté until lightly browned and just beginning to soften, about 5 minutes. Using the slotted spoon, transfer the eggplant to a bowl.

3 **Braise the pork**
Return the pot to medium heat, add the ginger, 3 tablespoons of the green onions, and the garlic, and sauté until fragrant, about 10 seconds. Pour in the soy sauce mixture, bring to a boil, and stir in the seared pork. Cover, reduce the heat to low, and cook until the pork is tender, 60–70 minutes. Uncover, add the reserved eggplant, and simmer until the eggplant is tender and the flavors are blended, 10–15 minutes. Transfer to a serving bowl, garnish with the remaining green onions, and serve with the steamed rice.

pork chops with cider

1 **Brown the pork chops**
Season the pork chops with salt and pepper. In a large frying pan over medium-high heat, warm the oil. Add the chops and cook, turning once, until golden brown, about 5 minutes total. Transfer to a plate.

2 **Cook the cabbage**
Add the cabbage to the pan and cook, stirring, until softened, 3–4 minutes. Raise the heat to high, add the apple cider and vinegar, and boil until the liquid is reduced to about 1 cup (8 fl oz/250 ml), 8–10 minutes. Stir in the thyme.

3 **Finish the pork**
Return the pork chops and any juices from the plate to the pan and spoon the sauce and cabbage over them. Cover, reduce the heat to medium-low, and simmer until the pork is tender and barely pink inside, about 5 minutes. Arrange the cabbage and pork on a platter, top with the sauce, and serve. »

Bone-in, center-cut pork loin chops, 4, each about ¾ inch (2 cm) thick

Salt and freshly ground pepper

Olive oil, 2 tablespoons

Red cabbage, 1 head, halved, cored, and thinly sliced crosswise

Apple cider or apple juice, 2½ cups (20 fl oz/625 ml)

Apple cider vinegar, 1 tablespoon

Fresh thyme leaves, 1 tablespoon

MAKES 4 SERVINGS

cook's tip

Roasted chunks of potatoes, root vegetables, or winter squash are the perfect accompaniment for pork chops. Toss the vegetable chunks with olive oil, salt, and pepper, then roast in a 425°F (220°C) oven, stirring often, until tender, about 25 minutes.

lamb tagine with apricots & almonds

1 **Prepare the lemon zest and juice**
Using a vegetable peeler, remove the zest in long wide strips from the lemon and then squeeze 1½ tablespoons juice. Reserve the zest and juice.

2 **Brown the lamb**
Season the lamb with salt and pepper. In a Dutch oven or deep, heavy frying pan over medium-high heat, warm the oil. Working in batches if necessary, add the lamb and cook, turning, until browned, 6–8 minutes total. Using a slotted spoon, transfer the lamb to a plate. Add the onion and garlic to the pot, reduce the heat to medium, and sauté until the onion is softened, 4–5 minutes. Stir in the coriander, cumin, and cinnamon. Return the lamb and any juices from the plate to the pot and stir to coat. Stir in the broth and bring to a simmer.

3 **Braise the tagine**
Cover, reduce the heat to low, and cook for 1 hour. Uncover, stir in the apricots, almonds, and lemon zest and juice and simmer, uncovered, until the lamb is very tender and the liquid has slightly thickened, about 20 minutes longer. Discard the lemon zest. Season to taste with salt and pepper. Transfer to plates and serve.

Lemon, 1 large

Boneless lamb from leg, 2 lb (1 kg), cut into 2-inch (5-cm) chunks

Salt and freshly ground pepper

Olive oil, 3 tablespoons

Yellow onion, 1 large, chopped

Garlic, 3 large cloves, minced

Ground coriander, 1½ teaspoons

Ground cumin, 1½ teaspoons

Ground cinnamon, 1 teaspoon

Chicken broth or stock, 2 cups (16 fl oz/500 ml), homemade (page 29) or purchased

Dried apricots or pitted dates, or a mixture, ¾ cup (4 oz/125 g) coarsely chopped

Slivered almonds, ½ cup, toasted

MAKES 6 SERVINGS

lamb chops with garlic & rosemary

Lemons, 3

Olive oil, ¼ cup
(2 fl oz/60 ml)

Anchovy fillets,
5 (optional)

Fresh rosemary,
1 tablespoon minced

Garlic, 4 cloves, minced

Lamb loin chops, 8,
each 6 oz (185 g) and
1 inch (2.5 cm) thick

Freshly ground pepper

White Beans (page 36),
2 cups (14 oz/440 g)

MAKES 4 SERVINGS

1 Marinate the lamb
Grate 2 teaspoons zest from the lemons and squeeze ½ cup (4 fl oz/125 ml) juice. In a shallow glass or ceramic dish just large enough to hold the lamb in a single layer, combine the oil and the anchovies, if using, and mash with a spoon to form a paste. Stir in the lemon zest and juice, rosemary, and garlic. Season the lamb chops with pepper. Place in the marinade and turn to coat. Let stand at room temperature for 10 minutes, or cover and refrigerate up to overnight.

2 Warm the beans
In a saucepan over medium heat, warm the beans, stirring frequently, until heated through, about 2 minutes.

3 Cook the lamb
Meanwhile, prepare a gas or charcoal grill for direct-heat grilling over high heat and oil the grill rack. Or, preheat a broiler (grill). Remove the lamb from the marinade, discarding the marinade. Place the chops on the grill rack, or put them on a baking sheet and place under the broiler. Cook, turning once, for about 10 minutes total for medium-rare, or until done to your liking. Transfer the beans and chops to plates and serve.

greek lamb kebabs

1 Marinate the lamb
Place 8 bamboo skewers in cold water to soak. Grate 3 teaspoons zest from the lemons and squeeze 5 tablespoons (2½ fl oz/75 ml) juice. In a shallow glass or ceramic dish, combine 2 teaspoons of the lemon zest, 3 tablespoons of the lemon juice, the oregano, half each of the onions and garlic, and the oil. Season the lamb with salt and pepper. Add to the marinade and turn to coat. Let stand for 15 minutes at room temperature.

2 Make the yogurt sauce
Meanwhile, in a bowl, stir together the yogurt, the cucumber, the remaining 1 teaspoon lemon zest and 2 tablespoons juice, and the remaining onions and garlic. Season with salt and pepper. Cover and refrigerate while you cook the lamb.

3 Cook the lamb
Prepare a gas or charcoal grill for direct-heat grilling over high heat and oil the grill rack. Or, preheat a broiler (grill). Remove the lamb from the marinade, discarding the marinade. Thread the lamb onto the skewers. Place on the grill rack, or put on a baking sheet and place under the broiler. Cook, turning once, for 6–7 minutes for medium-rare, or until done to your liking. Serve with the yogurt sauce.

Lemons, 2 large

Fresh oregano,
2 tablespoons minced

Green (spring) onions,
5, white and pale green parts, thinly sliced

Garlic, 5 cloves, minced

Olive oil, ¼ cup
(2 fl oz/60 ml)

Boneless lamb from leg,
1½ lb (750 g), cut into
2-inch (5-cm) cubes

Salt and freshly ground pepper

Plain yogurt, 1 cup
(8 oz/250 g)

Cucumber, 1 small, peeled, seeded, and chopped

MAKES 4 SERVINGS

moroccan lamb burgers

Lean ground (minced) lamb, 1½ lb (750 g)

Fresh mint, 5 tablespoons (½ oz/15 g) minced

Fresh Italian (flat-leaf) parsley, 5 tablespoons (½ oz/15 g) minced

Yellow onion, 1 small, finely chopped

Ground cumin, 1¼ teaspoons

Ground cinnamon, ½ teaspoon

Salt

Cayenne pepper

Plain yogurt, ½ cup (4 oz/125 g)

Plum (Roma) tomatoes, ¾ cup (4 oz/125 g) diced

Cucumber, 1 large, halved lengthwise, seeded, and thinly sliced crosswise

Pita breads, 4, cut into wedges

MAKES 4 SERVINGS

1 Make the lamb patties

Prepare a gas or charcoal grill for direct-heat grilling over high heat or have ready a frying pan. In a bowl, using your hands, mix together the lamb, 4 tablespoons each of the mint and parsley, the onion, 1 teaspoon of the cumin, the cinnamon, ½ teaspoon salt, and a pinch of cayenne. Form the lamb mixture into 4 oval patties.

2 Prepare the minted yogurt sauce

In a small bowl, stir together the yogurt, the remaining 1 tablespoon mint and 1 tablespoon parsley, and the remaining ¼ teaspoon cumin. Season to taste with salt and cayenne. Set aside.

3 Cook the lamb patties

Oil the grill rack. Grill the lamb patties, turning once, for about 10 minutes total for medium, or until done to your liking. (Or, cook the patties on the stove top in a lightly oiled, heavy frying pan over medium-high heat, turning once, for about 10 minutes total for medium.) Transfer the lamb burgers to plates, then top with some of the yogurt sauce, sprinkle with the tomatoes, and accompany with the cucumber slices. Serve, passing the remaining yogurt sauce and the pita wedges at the table.

meat made easy

A wide array of beef, veal, pork, and lamb cuts are available, and the choices can often seem overwhelming. But if you put together a weekly meal plan and vary the cuts and cooking techniques you use, you'll find that choosing and cooking meat can be surprisingly simple.

CHOOSING MEAT

Beef & veal Marbling refers to the little streaks of fat running through the meat. The more marbling, the more tender and juicy the meat will be. Look for meat with an even red color as well as nice white fat running throughout. Avoid dark and brownish meat with grayish fat. Press the meat (even through plastic) to make sure it is firm.

Pork Fresh pork should have a clean smell, white fat, and dark pink or rosy pink flesh, depending on the cut. Mass-produced hams are sold either fully or partially cooked, and are available with or without the bone (bone-in hams generally have more flavor).

Lamb Fresh, young lamb will have red, fine-grained flesh and firm, white fat.

Meat styles Many butcher shops carry locally sourced, organic, and/or pasture-raised meats. Taste and compare what is offered to discover which type you prefer.

cooking meat

Safety Before and after you handle raw meat, especially pork, wash your hands thoroughly with warm water and lots of soap. Be sure to thoroughly wash any cutting surfaces, dishware, and kitchen tools that come in contact with the raw meat.

Checking for doneness Use a thermometer and your senses to avoid overcooking meat. Remember that the internal temperature of meat rises 5°F to 10°F (3°C to 6°C) after it is removed from the heat source and allowed to rest for 5 or 10 minutes. The figures below reflect the temperatures that meats need to reach prior to the resting period.

DONENESS TEMPERATURES AND CUES

Ground (minced) meat	
160°F (71°C) for medium	Meat in center no longer pink.
Beef, veal, and lamb	
120–125°F (49–52°C) for rare	Texture is soft when pressed. Interior red and shiny.
125–130°F (52–54°C) for medium-rare	Meat has give when pressed. Interior rosy pink and juicy.
135–140°F (57–60°C) for medium	Meat has slight give when pressed. Pink only at center.
150°F (65°C) for well done	Meat feels firm to the touch. Interior is evenly brown, no traces of red or pink. Moist but no juices.
Pork	
140–150°F (60–65°C) for medium	Meat has slight give when pressed. Pink only at center. Pale pink juices.
160°F (71°C) for well done	Evenly brown throughout, no traces of red or pink. Moist but no juices.

SAMPLE MEALS

Here are some ideas for creating meals that center on meat. "In Minutes" meals include easy recipes and accompaniments that can be put together quickly. "Fit for Company" meals are tailored for stress-free get-togethers, complete with a wine suggestion.

IN MINUTES	FIT FOR COMPANY
Steaks with Herb Butter (page 303) twice-baked potatoes grilled zucchini (courgettes) and portobello mushrooms	**Chimichurri Steak (page 304)** corn on the cob with chile butter grilled cherry tomatoes crusty bread Cabernet Sauvignon
Thai Red Curry Beef (page 311) steamed jasmine rice cucumber, cilantro (fresh coriander), and red onion salad	**Braised Short Ribs (page 323)** celery root and potato purée mixed greens salad with red wine vinaigrette Merlot or Bordeaux
Veal Piccata (page 327) warmed ciabatta bread sautéed summer squash	**Roast Pork Loin with Pan Sauce (page 333)** roasted potatoes sautéed Brussels sprouts with pancetta Sauvignon Blanc or Malbec
Quick Choucroute (page 335) boiled potatoes baby spinach salad with blue cheese pumpernickel bread	**Lamb Chops with Garlic & Rosemary (page 352)** grilled radicchio sliced fresh tomatoes with feta cheese and thyme Barolo or Syrah
Braised Pork Chops with Cherry Sauce (page 341) mashed potatoes sautéed spinach	

STORING MEAT

Below are general tips for storing meat. See page 419 for a full list of meat storage times.

In the refrigerator Store meat in its wrapper and in the coldest part of the refrigerator, usually at the back of the bottom shelf or in a meat drawer. If any juices are seeping from the packaging, wrap the package in a layer of plastic wrap. Do not unwrap meat until just before cooking; unnecessary exposure to air can add to deterioration.

In the freezer Trim any excess fat from steaks, chops, and roasts, wrap the meat in freezer-weight plastic wrap or put it into a resealable plastic freezer bag, and freeze. Ground (minced) beef freezes best if divided into small portions. Discard any beef that develops an "off" smell.

Thawing meat Frozen meat should be thawed in the refrigerator. If you are short on time, you can put frozen meat in a resealable plastic bag and immerse it in a large container of cold water. This will cut the thawing time by about one-third, but the food will be drier when cooked. Never thaw meat in warm water.

desserts

nectarine-raspberry cobbler

1 Mix the filling

Preheat the oven to 375°F (190°C). Have ready an 8-inch (20-cm) square baking dish. In a large bowl, gently stir together the nectarines, raspberries, and 3 tablespoons of the sugar. Pour into the baking dish, spreading evenly.

2 Mix the topping

In a small bowl, whisk together the buttermilk and vanilla. In a large bowl, mix together the flour, ¼ cup (2 oz/60 g) of the sugar, the baking powder, the baking soda, and the salt. Using a pastry blender or 2 knives, cut in the cold butter until the mixture forms coarse crumbs. Add the buttermilk mixture and stir gently until a soft dough forms. Drop the dough by heaping spoonfuls onto the fruit, spacing it evenly. Brush the dough lightly with the melted butter, then sprinkle with the remaining 1 tablespoon sugar.

3 Bake the cobbler

Bake until the filling is bubbling, the topping is browned, and a toothpick inserted into the center of the topping comes out clean, about 35 minutes. Let cool for 15 minutes on a wire rack. Serve warm with vanilla ice cream, if desired.

Nectarines, 1½ lb
(750 g), pitted and sliced

Raspberries, 1 cup
(4 oz/125 g)

Sugar, ½ cup (4 oz/125 g)

Buttermilk, ¾ cup
(6 fl oz/180 ml)

Pure vanilla extract,
1 teaspoon

Flour, ¾ cup (4 oz/125 g)

Baking powder,
1 teaspoon

**Baking soda
(bicarbonate of soda),**
1 teaspoon

Salt, ½ teaspoon

Unsalted butter,
6 tablespoons (3 oz/90 g)
cold, cut into ½-inch
(12-mm) pieces, plus
1 tablespoon, melted

Vanilla ice cream, for
serving (optional)

MAKES 8 SERVINGS

apricot clafoutis

Apricots, 1 lb (500 g),
quartered and pitted

Brandy or Cognac,
2 teaspoons (optional)

Eggs, 2

Milk, ¾ cup (6 fl oz/
180 ml), plus
2 tablespoons

Granulated sugar,
6 tablespoons (3 oz/90 g)

Lemon zest, 1 teaspoon
finely grated

Pure vanilla extract,
1 teaspoon

Salt, 1 pinch

Flour, ⅓ cup (2 oz/60 g)

Powdered (icing) sugar,
2 tablespoons

MAKES 4 SERVINGS

1 Prepare the baking dishes
Preheat the oven to 350°F (180°C).
Butter four 1-cup (8–fl oz/250-ml) ramekins
or ovenproof custard cups and place on
a rimmed baking sheet. Place the apricots
in the bottom of the dishes, dividing them
evenly, and sprinkle the apricots with
the brandy, if using.

2 Mix the batter
In a blender, combine the eggs, milk,
granulated sugar, lemon zest, vanilla, salt,
and flour. Process until smooth. Pour the
batter over the apricots, dividing it evenly
among the dishes.

3 Bake the clafoutis
Bake until each clafouti is puffed and
golden brown, 23–25 minutes. Transfer to
a wire rack to cool slightly. Dust the tops
with powdered sugar and serve.

strawberries with lemon & mint

1 Prepare the strawberries
In a large bowl, toss together the strawberries, lemon zest, mint, and sugar to taste. Let stand at room temperature for 15 minutes. Spoon the strawberries into bowls and serve.

cook's tip For an added touch, serve this dish over vanilla ice cream. Or, make a quick strawberry purée to serve with a chocolate cake or pound cake. Combine all of the ingredients in a food processor and process until a smooth purée forms, about 1 minute. Strain through a fine-mesh sieve and serve.

Strawberries, 1 lb (500 g), hulled and sliced

Lemon zest, from 1 lemon, finely grated

Fresh mint, 2 tablespoons minced

Sugar, 2–4 tablespoons

MAKES 4–6 SERVINGS

lemon-buttermilk bars

Unsalted butter,
6 tablespoons (3 oz/90 g),
at room temperature

Granulated sugar, ¼ cup
(2 oz/60 g), plus ⅔ cup
(5 oz/155 g)

Flour, ⅔ cup (3 oz/90 g),
plus 2 tablespoons

Salt, ⅛ teaspoon

Eggs, 2

Lemon zest,
1 tablespoon finely
grated

Lemon juice, ⅓ cup
(3 fl oz/80 ml)

Buttermilk, ½ cup
(4 fl oz/125 ml)

Powdered (icing) sugar,
for dusting

MAKES 8 BARS

1 Make the crust
Preheat the oven to 350°F (180°C).
Butter the bottom and sides of an 8-inch
(20-cm) square baking pan. In a large
bowl, using an electric mixer on medium
speed, beat together the butter and ¼ cup
granulated sugar until creamy. Add the
⅔ cup flour and the salt and mix on low
speed until blended. Transfer the dough
to the prepared pan and press evenly into
the pan bottom. Bake until the crust is
golden, 15–18 minutes.

2 Make the filling
Meanwhile, in a bowl, using the electric
mixer on medium speed, beat the eggs
and the remaining ⅔ cup granulated
sugar until blended. Add the remaining
2 tablespoons flour, the lemon zest and
juice, and the buttermilk and beat until
smooth. Pour the filling over the crust.

3 Bake the bars
Bake until the top of the filling is
set and barely browned at the edges,
20–25 minutes. Let cool completely in
the pan on a wire rack. Cut into 8 bars,
dust with powdered sugar, and serve.

strawberry shortcakes

1 Prepare the strawberries
In a bowl, combine the strawberries with 2 tablespoons of the sugar. Preheat the oven to 425°F (220°C). Line a baking sheet with parchment (baking) paper.

2 Make the shortcakes
In a bowl, stir together the flour, the remaining 3 tablespoons sugar, the baking powder, and the salt. Using a pastry blender or 2 knives, cut in the butter until the mixture forms coarse crumbs. Add the heavy cream and mix just until evenly moistened. The dough should be soft; if the dough seems dry, mix in 1–2 tablespoons more cream. Divide the dough into 4 equal portions and shape each portion into a disk about ¾ inch (2 cm) thick. Place the dough disks on the prepared sheet, spacing them at least 3 inches (7.5 cm) apart. Bake the shortcakes until golden, 12–15 minutes. Transfer the shortcakes to a wire rack and let cool slightly.

3 Fill the shortcakes
Split the shortcakes horizontally and place the bottoms on plates. Top with the strawberries and whipped cream, then the shortcake tops, and serve. »

Strawberries, 3 cups (12 oz/375 g) hulled and sliced

Sugar, 5 tablespoons (2½ oz/75 g)

Flour, 1 cup (5 oz/155 g)

Baking powder, 1½ teaspoons

Salt, ¼ teaspoon

Unsalted butter, 4 tablespoons (2 oz/60 g) cold, cut into cubes

Heavy (double) cream, ⅓ cup (3 fl oz/80 ml), or more if needed

Whipped cream (page 362), for serving

MAKES 4 SERVINGS

cook's tip

To make whipped cream, in a large bowl, combine
1 cup (8 fl oz/250 ml) well-chilled heavy (double) cream,
1 teaspoon pure vanilla extract, and 2 tablespoons
sugar. Using an electric mixer on medium-high speed,
beat the cream until soft peaks form, about 2 minutes.
Cover and refrigerate until ready to serve or for up to
2 hours. Makes about 2 cups (16 fl oz/500 ml).

blackberry fool

1 Purée the blackberries
In a food processor, purée 1 cup (4 oz/125 g) of the blackberries. Using a rubber spatula, press the purée through a fine-mesh sieve into a small bowl. Discard the seeds.

2 Whip the cream
In a large bowl, using an electric mixer on medium-high speed, beat together the cream, sugar, brandy, if using, and vanilla until firm peaks form.

3 Finish the fool
Using a rubber spatula, gently fold the blackberry purée and the remaining whole blackberries into the whipped cream. Spoon into footed parfait glasses or small bowls and serve.

Blackberries, 2¼ cups (9 oz/280 g)

Heavy (double) cream, 2 cups (16 fl oz/500 ml), chilled

Powdered (icing) sugar, ¼ cup (1 oz/30 g)

Brandy, preferably blackberry, 1 tablespoon (optional)

Pure vanilla extract, 1 teaspoon

MAKES 8 SERVINGS

cook's tip If you do not whip the cream well, it will lose its volume when you fold in the purée and whole berries. To test if the peaks are firm enough, lift the beater; the peaks should stand almost straight with just minimal droop at the tips. But, be careful not to overwhip the cream or you will end up with butter.

caramelized
bananas with coconut

Sweetened flaked or shredded dried coconut, ⅓ cup (1¼ oz/35 g)

Unsalted butter, 2 tablespoons

Light brown sugar, ½ cup (3½ oz/105 g) firmly packed

Dark rum or water, 2 tablespoons

Salt, 1 pinch

Bananas, 4, peeled and quartered crosswise and lengthwise

Vanilla or coconut ice cream, for serving

MAKES 4 SERVINGS

1 Toast the coconut
Preheat the oven to 350°F (180°C). Spread the coconut on a rimmed baking sheet and toast in the oven, stirring occasionally, until lightly golden, about 5 minutes. Set aside.

2 Caramelize the bananas
In a frying pan over medium heat, melt the butter. Add the brown sugar and stir to moisten with the butter. Add the rum and salt and stir to mix. Add the banana quarters, cut side down. Reduce the heat to medium-low and cook, turning once, until just tender and golden, about 5 minutes total.

3 Finish the dessert
Transfer the caramelized bananas and sauce to plates. Place a scoop of ice cream on each plate, sprinkle with the toasted coconut, and serve.

brown sugar blondies

1 Mix the batter
Preheat the oven to 350°F (180°C). Butter an 8-inch (20-cm) square baking pan. In a bowl, stir together the flour, baking powder, baking soda, and salt. In a large bowl, using an electric mixer on medium speed, beat together the butter and sugar until creamy. Add the eggs and vanilla and beat until smooth. Add the dry ingredients to the wet ingredients and mix on low speed just until blended. Spread the batter in the prepared pan. Sprinkle evenly with the almonds.

2 Bake the blondies
Bake until golden brown and a toothpick inserted into the center comes out almost clean, about 30 minutes. Let cool in the pan on a wire rack. Using a sharp knife, cut into 16 squares and serve. »

Flour, 1¼ cups (6½ oz/ 200 g)

Baking powder, 1 teaspoon

Baking soda (bicarbonate of soda), ½ teaspoon

Salt, ¼ teaspoon

Unsalted butter, ¾ cup (5 oz/155 g), at room temperature

Light or dark brown sugar, 1 cup (7 oz/220 g) firmly packed

Eggs, 2

Pure vanilla extract, 1 teaspoon

Sliced (flaked) almonds, ⅔ cup (2½ oz/75 g)

MAKES 16 BLONDIES

cook's tip

For rich blondie sundaes, put squares of blondies into individual bowls, top each with a scoop of vanilla or coffee ice cream, or Toasted Almond Gelato, page 401, and drizzle with bittersweet chocolate sauce.

chocolate-raspberry brownies

1 Melt the butter and chocolate
Preheat the oven to 325°F (165°C). Butter a 9-inch (23-cm) square baking pan. In a small, heavy saucepan over low heat, combine the butter and chocolate and heat, stirring often, just until melted. Remove from the heat and let cool slightly.

2 Mix the batter
In a large bowl, whisk together the eggs, sugar, salt, and vanilla until blended. Whisk in the chocolate mixture until well combined. Add the flour and whisk just to incorporate. Spread the batter in the prepared pan. Spoon the raspberry jam in dollops over the batter, then run a knife through the batter a few times to create a marbled effect.

3 Bake the brownies
Bake until a toothpick inserted into the center of the brownies comes out with a few moist crumbs still clinging to it, about 30 minutes. Let cool completely in the pan on a wire rack. Using a sharp knife, cut into squares and serve.

cook's tip To add variety to your brownies, try swirling peanut butter or sweetened cream cheese into the batter in place of the jam in Step 2.

Unsalted butter, ½ cup (4 oz/125 g)

Unsweetened chocolate, 4 oz (125 g), finely chopped

Eggs, 3

Sugar, 1½ cups (12 oz/375 g)

Salt, ¼ teaspoon

Pure vanilla extract, 1 teaspoon

Flour, ¾ cup (4 oz/125 g)

Seedless raspberry jam or preserves, ½ cup (5 oz/155 g)

MAKES 16 BROWNIES

chocolate star cookies

Chocolate Cookie Dough (page 43), 1 disk, at cool room temperature

Coarse sugar, about 4 tablespoons, for sprinkling

MAKES ABOUT 40 COOKIES

1 Roll out and cut the dough
Preheat the oven to 350°F (180°C). Line 2 rimless baking sheets with parchment (baking) paper. Place the dough between 2 sheets of plastic wrap and roll out until ⅛ inch (3 mm) thick. Using a 2-inch (5-cm) star-shaped (or other shape) cookie cutter, cut out as many cookies as you can. Transfer them to the prepared sheets, spacing them 1½ inches (4 cm) apart. Gather the dough scraps, reroll, and cut out more cookies. Sprinkle the cookies with the sugar.

2 Bake the cookies
Bake until the edges of the cookies are crisp, 8–10 minutes. Let cool briefly on the sheets, then transfer to wire racks to cool completely.

ice cream sandwiches

1 Roll out and cut the dough
Preheat the oven to 350°F (180°C). Line 2 rimless baking sheets with parchment (baking) paper. Place the dough disk between 2 sheets of plastic wrap and roll out until ¼ inch (6 mm) thick. Using a 3-inch (7.5-cm) round cookie cutter, cut out as many cookies as you can. Transfer the cookies to the prepared baking sheets, spacing them 2 inches (5 cm) apart. Gather the scraps, reroll, and cut out more cookies. You will need 16 cookies total.

2 Bake the cookies
Bake until the edges of the cookies are crisp, 8–10 minutes. Let cool on the sheets on wire racks for 2 minutes, then transfer the cookies to the wire racks to cool completely.

3 Make the sandwiches
Place 8 of the cookies, bottom side up, on a work surface. Place a scoop of the ice cream on each cookie. Top with the remaining 8 cookies, bottom side down, and gently press each sandwich together to flatten the ice cream evenly. Place the sandwiches on a baking sheet, cover with plastic wrap, and freeze for at least 1 hour. To store the sandwiches longer, place them in heavy-duty resealable plastic bags and store in the freezer for up to 3 weeks.

Chocolate Cookie Dough (page 43), 1 disk, at cool room temperature

Ice cream, 1½ pt (24 fl oz/750 ml) flavor of your choice, slightly softened

MAKES 8 SANDWICHES

mocha sandwich cookies

Chocolate Cookie Dough (page 43), 1 disk, at cool room temperature

Unsalted butter, 1½ tablespoons, at room temperature

Powdered (icing) sugar, ½ cup (2 oz/60 g)

Unsweetened cocoa powder, 2 teaspoons

Brewed double-strength coffee or espresso, 1 tablespoon

MAKES ABOUT 20 COOKIES

1 **Roll out and cut the dough**
Preheat the oven to 350°F (180°C). Line 2 rimless baking sheets with parchment (baking) paper. Shape the dough into a log about 2 inches (5 cm) in diameter. Using a sharp knife, cut the log into slices ⅛ inch (3 mm) thick. Transfer the slices to the prepared sheets, spacing them 1½ inches (4 cm) apart.

2 **Bake the cookies**
Bake until the edges of the cookies are crisp, 8–10 minutes. Let cool on the sheets on wire racks for 2 minutes, then transfer the cookies to the wire racks to cool completely.

3 **Fill the cookies**
In a small bowl, mix the butter with a fork until light and fluffy. Sprinkle the sugar and cocoa over the butter and stir until blended. Stir in the coffee until smooth. Place half of the cookies, bottom side up, on a work surface. Using a spatula, spread the frosting evenly on the cookies. Top with the remaining cookies, bottom side down. Let stand at room temperature until the filling is set, about 1 hour, and serve.

chocolate-dipped butter cookies

1 **Roll out and cut the dough**
Preheat the oven to 350°F (180°C). Line 2 rimless baking sheets with parchment (baking) paper. Place the dough between 2 sheets of plastic wrap and roll out until ¼ inch (6 mm) inch thick. Using a 2-inch (5-cm) round cookie cutter, cut out as many of the cookies as you can. Transfer the cookies to the prepared sheets, spacing them 1 inch (2.5-cm) apart.

2 **Bake and dip the cookies**
Bake until the cookies are golden, about 15 minutes. Transfer to a rack to cool. Meanwhile, in a saucepan over low heat, melt the chocolate chips until smooth. (Or, melt the chocolate chips in the microwave at 10-second intervals until smooth, stirring often.) Dip one half of each cookie into the melted chocolate and return to the rack. Let stand until the chocolate is set.

Butter Cookie Dough (page 44), 1 disk, at cool room temperature

Semisweet (plain) chocolate chips, 8 oz (250 g)

MAKES ABOUT 30 COOKIES

ginger-molasses cookies

Unsalted butter, ¾ cup (6 oz/185 g), at room temperature

Light brown sugar, 1 cup (7 oz/220 g) firmly packed

Egg, 1

Light molasses, ⅓ cup (3½ oz/105 g)

Flour, 2 cups (10 oz/ 315 g)

Baking soda (bicarbonate of soda), 1½ teaspoons

Salt, ¼ teaspoon

Ground ginger, 1 teaspoon

Ground cinnamon, 1 teaspoon

Ground allspice, ½ teaspoon

MAKES ABOUT 40 COOKIES

1 Prepare the baking sheets
Preheat the oven to 350°F (180°C). Line 2 rimless baking sheets with parchment (baking) paper.

2 Mix the dough
In a large bowl, using an electric mixer on medium speed, beat the butter and sugar until creamy. Add the egg and molasses and beat until smooth. In another bowl, stir together the flour, baking soda, salt, ginger, cinnamon, and allspice. Add the dry ingredients to the wet ingredients and mix on low speed until blended.

3 Bake the cookies
Drop level tablespoonfuls of the dough onto the prepared sheets, spacing them 2 inches (5 cm) apart. Bake until the cookies are browned and firm to the touch, 10–12 minutes. Let the cookies cool on the baking sheets on wire racks for 5 minutes, then transfer the cookies to the wire racks to cool completely.

> **cook's tip** Parchment (baking) paper has a nonstick surface that can withstand the intense heat of the oven. Do not substitute waxed paper. If you don't have parchment, grease baking sheets with butter.

pound cake

1 **Sift the dry ingredients**
Preheat the oven to 325°F (165°C). Butter a 9-by-5-inch (23-by-13-cm) loaf pan and line with buttered parchment (baking) paper. Sift together the flour, baking powder, and salt into a bowl.

2 **Make the batter**
In a large bowl, using an electric mixer on medium speed, beat together the butter and granulated sugar until fluffy and lightened in color, about 2 minutes. Add the eggs two at a time, beating well after each addition. Mix in the vanilla. Add half of the flour mixture and mix on low speed until incorporated. Mix in the cream until blended. Add the remaining flour mixture and mix just until smooth. Pour the batter into the prepared pan.

3 **Bake the cake**
Bake until the top of the cake is golden and a toothpick inserted into the center comes out clean, about 1 hour. Let cool in the pan on a wire rack for about 20 minutes. Remove the cake from the pan and let cool completely. Dust the top with powdered sugar. Cut into slices to serve.

Flour, 2 cups (10 oz/ 315 g)

Baking powder, ½ teaspoon

Salt, ¼ teaspoon

Unsalted butter, ½ cup (8 oz/250 g), at room temperature

Granulated sugar, 1½ cups (12 oz/375 g)

Eggs, 4, lightly beaten

Pure vanilla extract, 1 teaspoon

Heavy (double) cream, ¼ cup (2 fl oz/60 ml)

Powdered (icing) sugar, for dusting

MAKES ONE 9-BY-5-INCH (23-BY-13-CM) LOAF CAKE

cherry trifle

Jarred, pitted sour cherries, 2 cups (12 oz/ 375 g) drained

Kirsch, 5 tablespoons (2½ fl oz/75 ml)

Granulated sugar, 1 tablespoon

Heavy (double) cream, 2 cups (16 fl oz/500 ml)

Powdered (icing) sugar, ¼ cup (1 oz/30 g)

Pure vanilla extract, 1 teaspoon

Pound Cake (page 379) or purchased pound cake, 1 loaf

MAKES 10 SERVINGS

1 Prepare the cherries
In a bowl, gently stir together the cherries, 4 tablespoons (2 fl oz/60 ml) of the kirsch, and the granulated sugar. Let stand for 10–15 minutes. Drain the cherries through a fine-mesh sieve placed over a bowl to capture the liquid. Reserve the cherries and liquid separately.

2 Whip the cream
In a large bowl, using an electric mixer on medium-high speed, beat together the cream, powdered sugar, remaining 1 tablespoon kirsch, and vanilla just until firm peaks form.

3 Assemble the trifle
Trim off the ends of the cake and cut the cake into chunks. Line the bottom of a 2½–3-qt (2.5–3-l) clear glass bowl with about one-third of the cake. Brush with one-third of the reserved cherry liquid. Spoon one-third of the cherries over the cake and spread one-third of the whipped cream over the cherries. Repeat the layers two more times, ending with whipped cream. Cover and refrigerate for at least 3 hours or up to overnight before serving.

mixed berry–cream cake

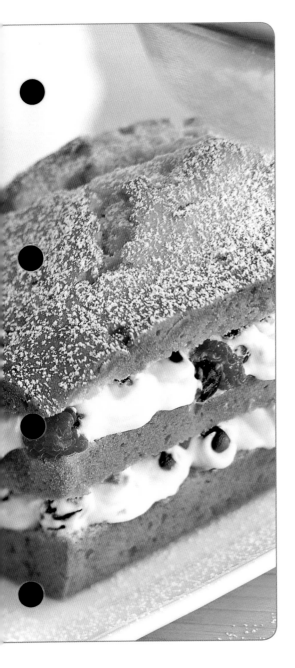

1 **Make the filling**
In a large bowl, using an electric mixer on medium-high speed, beat together the cream, the ¼ cup powdered sugar, liqueur, and vanilla until stiff peaks form. Using a rubber spatula, gently fold in the raspberries and blueberries.

2 **Assemble the cake**
Using a serrated knife, cut the pound cake horizontally into 3 equal layers. Place the bottom cake layer on a serving plate and, using a spatula, spread with half of the whipped cream–berry mixture. Place the middle cake layer on top, and spread with the remaining whipped cream–berry mixture. Top with the final cake layer. Refrigerate for at least 2 hours or up to 5 hours. Just before serving, dust the top of the cake with powdered sugar. Cut into slices and serve.

> **cook's tip** Any combination of berries will work for this cake, such as blackberries and strawberries or boysenberries and raspberries. You will need about 2 cups (8 oz/250 g) mixed berries total.

Heavy (double) cream, 1 cup (8 fl oz/250 ml), chilled

Powdered (icing) sugar, ¼ cup (1 oz/30 g), plus more for dusting

Raspberry liqueur, 1 tablespoon

Pure vanilla extract, 1 teaspoon

Raspberries, 1 cup (4 oz/125 g)

Blueberries, 1 cup (4 oz/125 g)

Pound Cake (page 379) or purchased pound cake, 1 loaf

MAKES 8 SERVINGS

almond pound cake

Slivered almonds, 1 cup (4½ oz/140 g), toasted

Unsalted butter, 1 cup (8 oz/250 g), at room temperature

Granulated sugar, 2 cups (1 lb/500 g)

Eggs, 6

Pure vanilla extract, 1½ teaspoons

Pure almond extract, ½ teaspoon

Flour, 3 cups (15 oz/ 470 g)

Baking soda (bicarbonate of soda), ¼ teaspoon

Salt, ¼ teaspoon

Sour cream, 1 cup (8 oz/250 g)

Powdered (icing) sugar, for dusting

MAKES ONE 10-INCH (25-CM) CAKE

1 Prepare the pan
Preheat the oven to 350°F (180°C). Butter a 10-inch (25-cm) Bundt pan. Sprinkle with flour and tap out the excess. In a food processor, process the almonds just until finely ground.

2 Prepare the batter
In a large bowl, using an electric mixer on medium speed, beat together the butter and granulated sugar until creamy. Add the eggs one at a time, beating well after each addition. Stir in the vanilla and almond extracts. In another bowl, stir together the flour, baking soda, and salt. With the mixer on low speed, mix the dry ingredients into the butter mixture in 2 additions, alternating with the sour cream, beating until smooth after each addition. Stir in the almonds. Spread the batter evenly in the prepared pan.

3 Bake the cake
Bake until the cake is golden and a toothpick inserted into the center comes out clean, 1–1¼ hours. Let cool in the pan on a wire rack for 10 minutes. Invert the cake onto the rack. Let the cake cool completely. Dust the top with powdered sugar, slice, and serve.

cinnamon-walnut coffee cake

1 **Mix the batter**
Preheat the oven to 350°F (180°C). Butter a 9-inch (23-cm) square baking pan. In a bowl, stir together the flour, baking powder, baking soda, and salt. In another large bowl, using an electric mixer on medium speed, beat together the butter, sour cream, eggs, orange zest, ¾ cup (6 oz/180 g) of the sugar, and the vanilla until blended. Add the dry ingredients to the wet ingredients and beat on low speed until smooth.

2 **Fill the pan**
In a bowl, stir together the remaining ¼ cup (2 oz/60 g) sugar, the cinnamon, and the walnuts. Spread half of the batter evenly in the prepared pan and sprinkle with half of the walnut mixture. Top with the remaining batter and sprinkle with the remaining walnut mixture.

3 **Bake the cake**
Bake until the cake is golden brown and a toothpick inserted into the center comes out clean, 25–30 minutes. Let cool slightly in the pan on a wire rack. Cut into squares and serve warm.

Flour, 2 cups (10 oz/ 315 g)

Baking powder, 1½ teaspoons

Baking soda (bicarbonate of soda), ½ teaspoon

Salt, ¼ teaspoon

Unsalted butter, ½ cup (4 oz/125 g), at room temperature

Sour cream, ¾ cup (6 oz/185 g)

Eggs, 2

Orange zest, 1 tablespoon finely grated

Sugar, 1 cup (8 oz/240 g)

Pure vanilla extract, 1 teaspoon

Ground cinnamon, 2 teaspoons

Walnuts, 1 cup (4 oz/ 125 g) toasted and chopped

MAKES ONE 9-INCH (23-CM) SQUARE CAKE

cranberry upside-down cake

Unsalted butter,
4 tablespoons (2 oz/60 g)

Light brown sugar,
¾ cup (6 oz/185 g) firmly packed

Fresh or thawed frozen cranberries, 2 cups
(8 oz/250 g)

Flour, 1¼ cups (6½ oz/
200 g)

Baking powder,
½ teaspoon

**Baking soda
(bicarbonate of soda),**
¼ teaspoon

Salt, ¼ teaspoon

Egg, 1

Granulated sugar, 1 cup
(8 oz/250 g)

Canola oil, ½ cup
(4 fl oz/125 ml)

Pure vanilla extract,
1 teaspoon

Sour cream, ½ cup
(4 oz/125 g)

**MAKES ONE 9-INCH
(23 CM) ROUND CAKE**

1 Prepare the glaze

Preheat the oven to 350°F (180°C). Butter a 9-inch (23-cm) round cake pan. Line the bottom with parchment (baking) paper and butter the paper. In a saucepan over medium-low heat, melt together the butter and brown sugar, stirring until smooth. Transfer to the prepared pan, tilting the pan to spread the glaze evenly. Arrange the cranberries over the glaze.

2 Make the batter

Sift together the flour, baking powder, baking soda, and salt into a bowl. In a large bowl, using an electric mixer on medium speed, beat together the egg and granulated sugar until fluffy, about 2 minutes. On low speed, slowly add the oil and vanilla and beat until blended. Mix in the sour cream just until no white streaks remain. Mix in the flour mixture until incorporated. Spread the batter over the cranberries.

3 Bake the cake

Bake until a toothpick inserted into the center of the cake comes out clean, about 45 minutes. Let cool in the pan on a wire rack for 10 minutes. Run a thin-bladed knife around the edge of the pan and invert the cake onto a serving plate. Lift off the pan and peel off the parchment paper. Cut into wedges and serve warm.

dark chocolate cake

1 Prepare the cake pan

Preheat the oven to 350°F (180°C). Line the bottom of a 9-inch (23-cm) springform pan with parchment (baking) paper. Or, butter the pan, sprinkle with flour, and tap out the excess.

2 Mix the batter

In a small saucepan over medium-low heat, melt the butter and the bittersweet and unsweetened chocolates, stirring to blend. Remove from the heat. In a large bowl, using an electric mixer on high speed, beat the eggs with the salt until thick and pale in color. Gradually beat in the granulated and brown sugars until the mixture is light and doubled in volume, about 5 minutes. Beat in the Cognac. Using a rubber spatula, stir in the melted chocolate mixture and then the flour. Pour the batter into the prepared pan.

3 Bake the cake

Bake the cake until the top is set and a toothpick inserted into the center of the cake comes out clean, 30–35 minutes. Let cool in the pan on a wire rack for about 10 minutes. Remove the pan sides and let the cake cool to room temperature. Dust the top with powdered sugar, cut into wedges, and serve. »

Unsalted butter, ¾ cup (6 oz/185 g)

Bittersweet or semisweet (plain) chocolate, 8 oz (250 g), chopped

Unsweetened chocolate, 1 oz (30 g), chopped

Eggs, 6

Salt, ⅛ teaspoon

Granulated sugar, ½ cup (4 oz/125 g)

Light brown sugar, ½ cup (3½ oz/105 g) firmly packed

Cognac, rum, or brewed double-strength coffee, 2 tablespoons

Flour, ⅓ cup (2 oz/60 g), sifted

Powdered (icing) sugar, 2 tablespoons

MAKES ONE 9-INCH (23-CM) ROUND CAKE

cook's tip

To turn this simple cake into an impressive dinner-party dessert, add a drizzle of raspberry coulis. To make the coulis, purée 2 cups (8 oz/250 g) raspberries in a blender or food processor and strain through a fine-mesh sieve into a bowl. Add sugar and fresh lemon juice to taste.

rhubarb pie

1 **Roll out the dough**

Preheat the oven to 400°F (200°C). On a lightly floured work surface, roll out the dough into a 12-inch (30-cm) round. Fit into a 9-inch (23-cm) pie dish and trim the dough to allow a 1-inch (2.5-cm) overhang. Fold the overhang under itself and crimp to make a decorative edge.

2 **Prepare the filling and streusel**

In a small bowl, dissolve the cornstarch in 1 tablespoon water. In a large bowl, use a fork to lightly toss the rhubarb with the granulated sugar. Stir in the cornstarch mixture. Spoon the filling into the dough-lined dish. In another bowl, stir together the flour and the brown sugar. Using a pastry blender or 2 knives, cut in the butter until the mixture is crumbly. Sprinkle over the filling.

3 **Bake the pie**

Bake until the juices are bubbling and the crust is golden brown, 40–45 minutes. Let cool briefly on a wire rack. Cut into wedges, top with ice cream or whipped cream, if desired, and serve warm.

Flaky Pastry Dough (page 38), 1 disk, at cool room temperature

Cornstarch (cornflour), 3 tablespoons

Rhubarb, 1 lb (500 g), trimmed and chopped (about 5 cups/12 oz/ 375 g)

Granulated sugar, 1½ cups (12 oz/375 g)

Flour, ⅔ cup (4 oz/120 g)

Light brown sugar, ⅔ cup (5 oz/155 g) firmly packed

Unsalted butter, ½ cup (4 oz/125 g), cold, cut into pieces

Vanilla ice cream or whipped cream (page 362), for serving (optional)

MAKES ONE 9-INCH (23-CM) PIE

pumpkin pie

Flaky Pastry Dough (page 38), 1 disk, at cool room temperature

Eggs, 3

Light brown sugar, ¾ cup (6 oz/185 g) firmly packed

Ground cinnamon, ½ teaspoon

Ground ginger, ½ teaspoon

Ground allspice, ¼ teaspoon

Salt, ½ teaspoon

Pumpkin purée, 1 can (15 oz/470 g)

Half-and-half (half cream) or milk, 1½ cups (12 fl oz/375 ml)

Whipped cream (page 362), for serving (optional)

MAKES ONE 9-INCH (23-CM) PIE

1 Partially bake the pastry shell
Preheat the oven to 425°F (220°C). On a lightly floured work surface, roll out the dough into a 12-inch (30-cm) round. Fit into a 9-inch (23-cm) pie pan and trim the dough to allow a 1-inch (2.5-cm) overhang. Fold the overhang under itself and crimp to make a high edge on the rim of the pan. Using a fork, make a decorative edge around the outside of the crust, and then prick the bottom of the dough a few times. Freeze for 5 minutes. Blind bake the pastry shell (see page 409) until lightly golden, about 10 minutes. Let cool completely on a wire rack. Reduce the oven temperature to 375°F (190°C).

2 Prepare the filling
In a large bowl, whisk the eggs until blended. Add the sugar, cinnamon, ginger, allspice, and salt and mix well. Mix in the pumpkin purée and half-and-half until well blended. Pour into the pastry shell.

3 Bake the pie
Bake until the filling is set and the crust is golden brown, 35–40 minutes. Let cool briefly on a wire rack. Cut into wedges, top with whipped cream, if desired, and serve warm.

apple crumble

1 Prepare the apples
Preheat the oven to 375°F (190°C). Butter a 10-inch (25-cm) pie dish or 9-inch (23-cm) square baking pan or dish. Peel and core the apples, then slice them into a bowl. Add the lemon juice and granulated sugar and toss to coat. Place the apples in the prepared dish and pat them level.

2 Mix the topping
In a bowl, stir together the oats, brown sugar, flour, cinnamon, salt, and walnuts, if using. Drizzle the melted butter over the oat mixture and toss with a fork until evenly moistened. Cover the apples evenly with the topping.

3 Bake the crumble
Bake until the apples are tender and the topping is browned, 35–45 minutes. Let cool slightly in the pan on a wire rack. Spoon the crumble into bowls, top each with a dollop of whipped cream or a scoop of ice cream, if desired, and serve warm.

cook's tip Keep an eye on the crumble as it bakes. If the topping begins to brown before the apples are fully cooked, cover the pan with aluminum foil and reduce the oven temperature to 350°F (180°C).

Large tart apples such as Granny Smith, about 2 lb (1 kg)

Lemon juice, 1 tablespoon

Granulated sugar, 2 tablespoons

Old-fashioned rolled oats, ¾ cup (2½ oz/75 g)

Light brown sugar, ½ cup (3½ oz/105 g) firmly packed

Flour, ⅓ cup (2 oz/60 g)

Ground cinnamon, 1 teaspoon

Salt, 1 pinch

Walnuts, ½ cup (2 oz/ 60 g) chopped (optional)

Unsalted butter, 6 tablespoons (3 oz/90 g), melted

Whipped cream (page 362) or vanilla ice cream, for serving (optional)

MAKES 6 SERVINGS

pecan tart

Sweet Tart Dough (page 39), 1 disk, at cool room temperature

Eggs, 3

Light brown sugar, ½ cup (3½ oz/105 g) firmly packed

Dark corn syrup, 1 cup (10 fl oz/315 ml)

Pure vanilla extract, 1 teaspoon

Unsalted butter, 4 tablespoons (2 oz/60 g), melted

Pecan halves, 1½ cups (6 oz/185 g)

Whipped cream (page 362), for serving (optional)

MAKES ONE 9½-INCH (24-CM) TART

1 Partially bake the tart shell
Preheat the oven to 425°F (220°C). On a lightly floured work surface, roll out the dough into a 10½-inch (26-cm) round. Fit into a 9½-inch (24-cm) tart pan with a removable bottom. Fold the overhang over itself and press into the sides of the pan to make a sturdy rim. Freeze for 5 minutes. Blind bake the tart shell (see page 409) until lightly golden, about 10 minutes. Let cool on a wire rack.

2 Prepare the filling
In a large bowl, whisk together the eggs, sugar, corn syrup, and vanilla until blended. Whisk in the butter. Stir in the pecans. Pour the filling into the tart shell.

3 Bake the tart
Bake until the filling is set but is still slightly soft in the center, 40–45 minutes. Let cool slightly in the pan on a wire rack. Remove the pan rim. Cut the tart into wedges, top with whipped cream, if desired, and serve warm.

> **cook's tip** For a Chocolate-Pecan Tart, add 1 cup (6 oz/185 g) semisweet (plain) or bittersweet chocolate chips to the filling along with the pecans. Bake as directed.

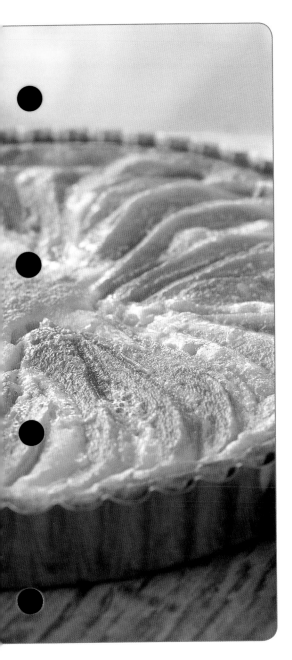

pear custard tart

1 Partially bake the tart shell
Preheat the oven to 425°F (220°C). On a lightly floured work surface, roll out the dough into a 10½-inch (26-cm) round. Fit into a 9½-inch (24-cm) tart pan with a removable bottom. Fold the overhang over itself and press into the sides of the pan to make a sturdy rim. Freeze for 5 minutes. Blind bake the tart shell (see page 409) until lightly golden, about 10 minutes. Let cool on a wire rack.

2 Make the filling
Arrange the pear slices in the cooled tart shell. In a bowl, using an electric mixer on medium speed, beat the eggs until thick and pale in color. Beat in the sugar. Add the butter, cream, lemon zest, flour, and vanilla and mix well. Pour the mixture evenly over the pears.

3 Bake the tart
Bake the tart for 15 minutes. Reduce the oven temperature to 400°F (200°C) and bake until the filling is set and the crust is golden brown, about 25 minutes longer. Let cool slightly in the pan on a wire rack. Remove the pan rim. Cut the tart into wedges and serve warm.

Sweet Tart Dough (page 39), 1 disk, at cool room temperature

Pears such as Bartlett, Anjou, or Bosc, 4, peeled, halved, cored, and thinly sliced

Eggs, 2

Sugar, ⅔ cup (5 oz/155 g)

Unsalted butter, 2 tablespoons, melted

Heavy (double) cream, 2 tablespoons

Lemon zest, 1 teaspoon finely grated

Flour, 3 tablespoons

Pure vanilla extract, 1 teaspoon

MAKES ONE 9½-INCH (24-CM) TART

apple tart

Frozen puff pastry,
1 sheet, thawed overnight
in the refrigerator

Granny Smith apples, 2

Sugar, ¼ cup (2 oz/60 g)

MAKES 6–8 SERVINGS

1 Roll out the puff pastry
Preheat the oven to 425°F (200°C).
Line a rimmed baking sheet with parchment
(baking) paper. Lay the sheet of puff
pastry on a very lightly floured work
surface, and gently rub the top with a bit
of flour. With a rolling pin, roll out the
dough into a 10-by-15-inch (25-by-38-cm)
rectangle ⅛ inch (3 mm) thick. Place the
pastry rectangle on the prepared baking
sheet and freeze for 5 minutes.

2 Assemble the tart
Core the apples, halve them
lengthwise, and slice into very thin half
moons. With a sharp paring knife, cut a
1-inch (2.5-cm) border along the edges of
the puff pastry, being careful not to cut
more than halfway through the pastry. With
a fork, prick the puff pastry all over inside
the border. Sprinkle with 2 tablespoons of
the sugar. Arrange the apple slices, slightly
overlapping, inside the border and sprinkle
with the remaining 2 tablespoons sugar.

3 Bake the tart
Bake until the pastry is golden brown
and the apples are tender, 15–20 minutes.
Cut into pieces and serve warm or at
room temperature.

cherry turnovers

1 Roll out the puff pastry
Preheat the oven to 425°F (220°C).
Line a baking sheet with parchment
(baking) paper. Place the puff pastry sheet
on a lightly floured work surface and roll
out into a 10-by-15-inch (25-by-38-cm)
rectangle. Cut in half lengthwise and then
cut each half crosswise into 3 squares
to make a total of 6 squares. Place the
squares on the prepared baking sheet,
spacing them evenly.

2 Prepare the cherry filling
Place the cherries in a bowl and
sprinkle with the brandy, if using. Add
the granulated sugar and flour and toss.

3 Fill and bake the turnovers
In a small bowl, whisk together the
egg and milk. Brush a ½-inch (12-mm)
border of the egg mixture around
2 adjacent sides of each square. Spoon
about 3 tablespoons of the cherry filling
almost in the middle of each square. Fold
the pastry over the filling to make a triangle
and press the free edges with a fork to
seal. Brush the tops with the remaining
egg mixture and sprinkle with the coarse
sugar. Bake until the turnovers are puffed
and golden brown, 15–18 minutes. Let
cool slightly on the baking sheet on a wire
rack. Serve warm. »

Frozen puff pastry,
1 sheet, thawed overnight
in the refrigerator

**Pitted sour or sweet
cherries,** 1 jar (28 oz/
875 g), drained

Brandy or Cognac,
1 teaspoon (optional)

Granulated sugar, ¼ cup
(2 oz/60 g)

Flour, 1 tablespoon

Egg, 1

Milk, 1 tablespoon

**Coarse sugar such as
turbinado,** for sprinkling

MAKES 6 TURNOVERS

turnover variation

cook's tip

The turnovers can also be filled with other seasonal fruits. In summer, peel, pit, and cut 2 peaches into slices ½ inch (12 mm) thick. In winter, peel and core 2 pears such as Anjou or Bosc and cut into slices ½ inch (12 mm) thick.

chocolate-raspberry tartlets

1 **Partially bake the tartlet shells**
Preheat the oven to 425°F (220°C).
Divide the dough disk into 4 equal
portions. Pat each piece evenly into the
bottom and up the sides of a 4½-inch
(11.5-cm) tartlet pan with a removable
bottom. Freeze for 5 minutes. Place the
tartlet pans on a rimmed baking sheet
and blind bake (see page 409) until lightly
golden, about 5 minutes. Let cool on the
baking sheet on a wire rack. Reduce
the oven temperature to 375°F (190°C).

2 **Prepare the filling**
In a saucepan over low heat, combine
the butter, chocolate, and coffee and heat,
stirring occasionally, until melted and
thoroughly blended, about 3 minutes. In
a bowl, whisk the eggs until combined.
Gradually whisk in the granulated sugar.
Stir in the chocolate mixture and vanilla.
Pour the filling evenly into the tartlet shells.

3 **Bake the tartlets**
Bake until the filling is set, about
15 minutes. Transfer the tartlets to a wire
rack and let cool. Arrange the raspberries
on top of the filling. Dust lightly with
powdered sugar. Remove the pan rims,
slide the tartlets from the pan bottoms
onto plates, and serve.

**Sweet Tart Dough
(page 39),** 1 disk, at cool
room temperature

Unsalted butter,
4 tablespoons (2 oz/60 g)

Bittersweet chocolate,
6 oz (185 g), finely
chopped

**Brewed double-strength
coffee or espresso,**
1 teaspoon

Eggs, 3

Granulated sugar, ⅔ cup
(5 oz/155 g)

Pure vanilla extract,
1 teaspoon

Raspberries, 1⅓ cups
(5½ oz/170 g)

Powdered (icing) sugar,
for dusting

MAKES 4 TARTLETS

key lime tart

**Butter Cookie Dough
(page 44),** 1 disk, at cool
room temperature

Eggs, 2

Sugar, 1½ cups (12 oz/
375 g)

**Lime zest, preferably
from Key limes,**
1 teaspoon finely grated

**Fresh lime juice,
preferably from Key
limes,** ½ cup (4 fl oz/
125 ml), from 7 or 8 limes

Flour, ¼ cup (1½ oz/45 g)

Heavy (double) cream,
¼ cup (2 fl oz/60 ml)

**Whipped cream
(page 362),** for serving
(optional)

**MAKES ONE 10½-INCH
(26-CM) TART**

1 **Partially bake the crust**
Place the dough between 2 large sheets of parchment (baking) paper and roll out into a 12-inch (30-cm) round. Fit into a 10½-inch (26-cm) tart pan with a removable bottom and trim the dough to allow a ½-inch (12-mm) overhang. Fold the overhang over itself and press into the sides of the pan. Freeze for at least 30 minutes or up to overnight. Preheat the oven to 375°F (190°C). Place the pan on a baking sheet and blind bake the crust (see page 409) for 10 minutes. Remove the foil and weights and bake until the crust is lightly golden, about 5 minutes longer. Transfer to a wire rack and reduce the oven temperature to 350°F (180°C).

2 **Fill and bake the tart**
In a large bowl, whisk together the eggs, sugar, and lime zest and juice until smooth, about 1 minute. Whisk in the flour and then the cream until blended. Pour the filling into the partially baked crust. Bake until the filling is set when you gently shake the pan, about 30 minutes. Transfer to a wire rack and let stand until the top feels cool to the touch, about 1 hour. Remove the tart from the pan. Cover and refrigerate for at least 3 hours or up to overnight. To serve, cut the tart into wedges and serve with whipped cream, if desired.

berry galette

1 Roll out the dough
Preheat the oven to 425°F (220°C). Line a baking sheet with parchment (baking) paper. On a lightly floured surface, roll out the dough into a 13-inch (33-cm) round. Transfer the dough to the prepared sheet.

2 Fill and bake the galette
In a bowl, lightly toss together the berries, lemon juice, sugar, and flour. Spoon the filling onto the dough, leaving a 2-inch (5-cm) border uncovered around the edge. Fold the edge up and over the filling, crimping to form loose pleats. Bake until the pastry is golden brown and the filling is bubbling, about 25 minutes. Transfer the galette to a wire rack and let cool slightly. Cut into wedges and serve warm. Top with whipped cream, if desired.

Flaky Pastry Dough (page 38), 1 disk, at cool room temperature

Blackberries, blueberries, or a mixture, 4 cups (1 lb/500 g)

Lemon juice, 2 tablespoons

Sugar, ¼ cup (2 oz/60 g)

Flour, 3 tablespoons

Whipped cream (page 362), for serving (optional)

MAKES ONE 9-INCH (23-CM) GALETTE

strawberry–
cream cheese tart

Sweet Tart Dough (page 39), 1 disk, at cool room temperature

Cream cheese, 6 oz (185 g), at room temperature

Heavy (double) cream, ¾ cup (6 fl oz/180 ml)

Powdered (icing) sugar, ¼ cup (1 oz/30 g)

Pure vanilla extract, 1 teaspoon

Strawberries, 2 cups (8 oz/250 g), hulled and halved lengthwise

MAKES ONE 9½-INCH (24-CM) TART

1 Bake the tart shell
Preheat the oven to 425°F (220°C). On a lightly floured work surface, roll out the dough into a 10½-inch (26-cm) round. Fit into a 9½-inch (24-cm) tart pan with a removable bottom. Fold the overhang over itself and press into the sides of the pan to make a sturdy rim. Freeze for 5 minutes. Blind bake the tart shell (see page 409) until golden brown, 15–18 minutes. Let cool on a wire rack.

2 Finish the tart
In a large bowl, using an electric mixer on medium speed, beat the cream cheese until light and fluffy. Add the cream, sugar, and vanilla and beat until very smooth, 2–3 minutes. Spread the filling in the cooled tart shell. Place the berries, cut side down, on top of the filling. Cover and refrigerate for about 2 hours. Remove the pan rim. Cut the tart into wedges and serve.

lemon tart
with raspberries

1 Partially bake the crust

Place the dough between 2 large sheets of parchment (baking) paper and roll out into a 12-inch (30-cm) round. Fit into a 10½-inch (26-cm) tart pan with a removable bottom and trim the dough to allow a ½-inch (12-mm) overhang. Fold the overhang over itself and press into the sides of the pan. Freeze for at least 30 minutes or up to overnight. Preheat the oven to 375°F (190°C). Place the pan on a baking sheet and blind bake the crust (see page 409) for 10 minutes. Remove the foil and weights and bake until golden, about 5 minutes longer. Transfer to a wire rack to cool and reduce the oven temperature to 350°F (180°C).

2 Fill and bake the tart

In a food processor, process the eggs and sugar until smooth, about 1 minute. Add the cream cheese, pulse briefly, and then process until smooth. Add the sour cream, lemon zest and juice, flour, and vanilla and process until smooth, about 20 seconds. Pour the filling into the baked crust. Bake until the filling is set when you gently shake the pan, about 35 minutes. Transfer to a wire rack to cool. Remove the tart from the pan. Cover and refrigerate for at least 3 hours or up to overnight. Just before serving, top with the raspberries and cut into wedges.

Butter Cookie Dough, (page 44), 1 disk, at cool room temperature

Eggs, 2

Sugar, ⅔ cup (5 oz/155 g)

Cream cheese, 12 oz (375 g), at room temperature

Sour cream, ½ cup (4 oz/125 g)

Lemon zest, 2 teaspoons finely grated

Lemon juice, from 1 lemon

Flour, 2 tablespoons

Pure vanilla extract, 1 teaspoon

Raspberries, 1½ cups (6 oz/185 g)

MAKES ONE 10½-INCH (26-CM) TART

coconut rice pudding

Eggs, 4

Milk, 1⅔ cups
(13 fl oz/410 ml)

Light brown sugar,
½ cup (3½ oz/105 g)
firmly packed

Ground cinnamon,
1 teaspoon

Salt, ⅛ teaspoon

Pure vanilla extract,
1 teaspoon

Long-grain white rice,
1½ cups (10½ oz/330 g)

**Sweetened shredded
dried coconut,** ⅔ cup
(2½ oz/75 g), plus toasted
coconut (see page 366)
for serving (optional)

Mango, 1 large, peeled,
pitted, and sliced
(page 100)

MAKES 8 SERVINGS

1 Combine the ingredients
Preheat the oven to 325°F (165°C).
Butter a 2-qt (2-l) baking dish. In a large
bowl, whisk together the eggs, milk, sugar,
cinnamon, salt, and vanilla. Stir in the rice
and the ⅔ cup coconut. Pour the mixture
into the prepared dish.

2 Bake the pudding
Bake until the pudding is set and
lightly browned, 45–50 minutes. Transfer
to a wire rack and let cool completely.
Serve at room temperature or refrigerate
to chill slightly. Spoon into bowls,
accompany with the sliced mango, and
sprinkle with toasted coconut, if using.

toasted almond gelato

1 Infuse the milk and cream
In a heavy saucepan over medium heat, warm the milk, cream, and almonds until a few bubbles appear along the edge of the pan. Remove from the heat and set aside to steep for at least 15 minutes. Pour through a fine-mesh sieve into a liquid measuring cup.

2 Prepare the custard
In a large bowl, whisk together the egg yolks and granulated and brown sugars until fluffy and lightened in color. Whisking constantly, pour the warm milk mixture into the egg yolk mixture. Transfer the mixture to the saucepan over medium-low heat and cook, stirring constantly, until the custard thickens slightly and reaches 170°F (77°C) on an instant-read thermometer, about 5 minutes. Do not let the custard boil. Pour into a bowl, let cool, cover, and refrigerate until very cold, at least 5 hours or up to overnight.

3 Process and freeze the ice cream
Transfer the custard to an ice cream maker and process according to the manufacturer's directions. Transfer the ice cream to an airtight container, press a layer of plastic wrap onto the surface, and freeze until firm, at least 2 hours. Let soften slightly before serving. »

Milk, 1½ cups
(12 fl oz/375 ml)

Heavy (double) cream,
1½ cups (12 fl oz/375 ml)

Slivered almonds, 2 cups
(9 oz/280 g), toasted

Egg yolks, 5

Granulated sugar, ⅓ cup
(3 oz/90 g)

Light brown sugar,
⅓ cup (2½ oz/75 g) firmly packed

**MAKES ABOUT 1 QUART
(32 FL OZ/1 L)**

cook's tip

For a late summer or early fall treat, top servings of this gelato with sliced fresh figs. Look for ripe figs with skins free of bruises and any sign of mold. Add a drizzle of good-quality honey, if desired.

frozen chai

1 **Make the chai**
In a saucepan over medium-high heat, warm the milk just until steam begins to rise. Remove from the heat and add the tea bags, peppercorns, ginger, and sugar. Stir briefly to dissolve the sugar. Let cool to room temperature, then transfer to an airtight container and chill for at least 2 hours or up to overnight.

2 **Blend the chai and ice cream**
Pour the chai mixture through a fine-mesh sieve into a blender. Add the ice cream and process until smooth. Pour into tall glasses. Top with whipped cream and cinnamon, if using, and serve.

cook's tip To chill the chai tea mixture quickly, place it in a small bowl or measuring cup and nest it inside a larger bowl filled with ice. Stir the mixture occasionally to hasten the cooling.

Milk, 4 cups (32 fl oz/1 l)

Chai tea, 4 tea bags

Peppercorns, 10

Fresh ginger, 3 slices

Sugar, 2 tablespoons

Vanilla ice cream, 1 pint (16 fl oz/500 ml), softened

Whipped cream (page 362), for serving (optional)

Ground cinnamon, for garnish (optional)

MAKES 4 SERVINGS

melon granita

Sugar, ½ cup (4 oz/125 g)

Ice cubes, 10

Cantaloupe, 1, peeled, seeded, and cut into pieces (about 4 cups/ 1½ lb/750 g)

Fresh lemon juice, 3 tablespoons

MAKES 8 SERVINGS

1 Make the sugar syrup
In a small, heavy saucepan over medium-high heat, combine the sugar with ½ cup (4 fl oz/125 ml) water and heat, stirring occasionally, until the sugar dissolves, about 3 minutes. Remove from the heat, pour into a heatproof bowl, and stir in the ice cubes. Continue stirring until the sugar syrup is cold, about 1 minute. Discard any unmelted ice. You will have about 1¼ cups (10 fl oz/310 ml) syrup.

2 Make the granita base
In a food processor, combine the cantaloupe, lemon juice, and sugar syrup. Pulse a few times until the cantaloupe is broken up, and then process until a smooth purée forms, about 1 minute.

3 Freeze the granita
Pour the cantaloupe mixture into a 9-inch (23-cm) square stainless-steel pan or heavy glass dish. Freeze until the mixture is just frozen, about 1 hour. Using a fork, stir and scrape the granita to break up the ice crystals into clumps with a slushy texture. Return to the freezer and freeze until firm, but not solid, up to 1 hour. Spoon into glasses or bowls and serve.

plum sorbet

1 Make the sugar syrup
In a saucepan over medium heat, combine ¾ cup (6 fl oz/180 ml) water and the sugar and heat, stirring occasionally, until the sugar dissolves and the syrup just comes to a boil. Pour into a small bowl, cover, and refrigerate until well chilled, at least 3 hours.

2 Prepare the sorbet mixture
In a food processor, combine the sugar syrup, plums, lemon juice, and brandy and process until a smooth purée forms, about 1 minute. Strain through a fine-mesh sieve into a bowl. Transfer to an ice cream maker and process according to the manufacturer's directions.

3 Freeze the sorbet
Transfer the sorbet to an airtight container, press a layer of plastic wrap onto the surface, and freeze until firm, at least 2 hours or up to 5 days. Let soften at room temperature for about 10 minutes before serving.

Sugar, 1 cup (8 oz/250 g)

Ripe plums, 2 lb (1 kg), halved and pitted

Fresh lemon juice, ¼ cup (2 fl oz/60 ml)

Brandy, preferably plum, ¼ cup (2 fl oz/ 60 ml)

MAKES ABOUT 1 QUART (32 FL OZ/1L)

italian affogato

Toasted Almond Gelato (page 401), or vanilla ice cream, 1 pint (16 fl oz/500 ml)

Bittersweet or semisweet (plain) chocolate bar, 1

Freshly brewed espresso or strong coffee, 1 cup (8 fl oz/ 250 ml)

MAKES 4 SERVINGS

1 Scoop the ice cream
Put a large scoop of gelato or ice cream in each serving bowl. Using a vegetable peeler, shave bits of the chocolate over the gelato.

2 Finish the dessert
Pour the hot espresso into espresso cups. Serve alongside the bowls of gelato, inviting diners to pour the espresso over their servings.

cook's tip Toasted almond ice cream is available at many supermarkets, which is a great time-saver. Experiment with other flavors of ice cream or gelato such as chocolate or *dulce de leche*.

chocolate pudding

1 Warm the milk
In a heavy saucepan over medium heat, warm the milk until a few bubbles appear along the edge of the pan. Remove from the heat.

2 Cook the pudding base
In a bowl, whisk together the egg yolks and sugar until smooth. Sift the flour and cocoa powder over the yolk mixture and whisk until smooth. Whisking constantly, slowly pour in the hot milk. Return the mixture to the pan and cook over medium heat, stirring constantly with a wooden spoon, until the mixture comes to a boil and thickens, about 4 minutes. Reduce the heat to low and cook, stirring constantly, for 1 minute.

3 Finish the pudding
Pour the pudding base through a fine-mesh sieve into a bowl. Immediately add the semisweet and unsweetened chocolates and stir until melted. Stir in the vanilla. Pour into serving bowls or glasses. Refrigerate until cold, about 2 hours. Serve with whipped cream, if desired.

Milk, 2 cups (16 fl oz/500 ml)

Egg yolks, 6

Sugar, ¾ cup (6 oz/185 g)

Flour, 3 tablespoons

Unsweetened cocoa powder, 2 tablespoons

Semisweet (plain) chocolate, 6 oz (185 g), finely chopped

Unsweetened chocolate, 2 oz (30 g), finely chopped

Pure vanilla extract, 1 teaspoon

Whipped cream (page 362), for serving (optional)

MAKES 6 SERVINGS

mocha
chocolate mousse

Semisweet (plain) chocolate, 10 oz (315 g), finely chopped

Heavy (double) cream, 1½ cups (12 fl oz/375 ml), chilled

Powdered (icing) sugar, ⅔ cup (2½ oz/75 g)

Instant coffee powder, 1 tablespoon

Pure vanilla extract, 1 teaspoon

MAKES 6 SERVINGS

1 Melt the chocolate
Put the chocolate in the top of a double boiler and place it over (not touching) barely simmering water. Heat, stirring often, until the chocolate melts. Scrape the melted chocolate into a large bowl and set aside.

2 Whip the cream
In another large bowl, using an electric mixer on medium-high speed, beat together the cream, powdered sugar, instant coffee powder, and vanilla until firm peaks form.

3 Finish the mousse
Beat about one-third of the whipped cream mixture into the chocolate until smooth. Using a rubber spatula, fold the remaining whipped cream into the chocolate mixture. Transfer the mousse to footed goblets or bowls. Cover and refrigerate for at least 2 hours or up to overnight. Serve chilled.

desserts made easy

A delicious dessert is the perfect ending to nearly every meal, but many people don't think they have the time to prepare one from scratch. Most of the sweet treats in these pages come together quickly, some requiring just 15 minutes or less of hands-on time.

TESTING DONENESS

Cakes and quick breads The center of the cake or bread should spring back when pressed lightly with a fingertip, and the edges should have pulled away from the sides of the pan. A wooden toothpick inserted into the center should come out clean.

Pies and tarts The crust should be golden brown. Fruit fillings should be bubbly and juicy, and custard fillings should be set.

Cookies Cookies should generally be firm and lightly browned around the edges.

BLIND BAKING

To bake a tart or pie shell evenly before adding the filling, line it with aluminum foil and fill with pie weights or dried beans. Follow the recipe's instructions for baking, then remove the weights and foil and continue as directed.

baking techniques

The recipes in this book can be easily mastered even by novice bakers. If you haven't done a lot of baking, familiarize yourself with some common techniques that you'll need to know before you start.

Beating Mixing ingredients together vigorously until they are smooth and thoroughly amalgamated is called beating. It's also the term used for whipping air into heavy (double) cream or egg whites. Egg whites and cream can be beaten with a whisk, a handheld electric mixer, or the whip attachment on a stand mixer.

Creaming Beating softened butter with sugar or other ingredients is called creaming. This process mixes air into the butter, which helps the mixture rise when baked. It also blends the sugar into the butter, forming a smooth mixture. Beat the butter with a wooden spoon, a handheld mixer, or the paddle attachment of a stand mixer for several minutes, until creamy. Gradually add the sugar and beat with the butter for a few minutes, until the mixture is fluffy.

Cutting in Recipes for biscuits, scones, and pastry dough often call for cutting chilled butter into the flour mixture. If making the dough by hand, cut the butter into the flour using a pastry blender or two table knives. The resulting mixture should be coarse with pea-sized pieces of butter. If using a food processor, pulse the cold butter into the flour in short bursts, just until the same consistency is reached.

Folding Delicate ingredients, such as beaten egg whites, should always be folded, rather than stirred, into heavier mixtures. This keeps the air bubbles intact, helping the baked item rise in the oven. With a rubber spatula, scoop the lighter ingredient on top of the heavier one. Then, using a U-shaped motion, gently draw the spatula down through the center of the bowl and up the side of the bowl. Continue, rotating the bowl as you fold, until the mixture is nearly uniform.

baking tools, pans & dishes

You don't need a lot of fancy gadgets to be a good baker, but you want to have on hand some basic tools specifically used for baking, such as baking sheets and pans. Although you can always improvise, you'll save time and energy by having the right equipment, and you'll be happier with the results.

TOOLS

Bowls A set of nesting bowls is used for holding ingredients and mixing batters and doughs.

Food processor A food processor makes quick work of chopping nuts and is a great time-saving choice for making pastry dough.

Measuring cups & spoons Use clear glass or plastic pitchers with measurements marked on the side for liquid ingredients, and use a set of metal or plastic cups in graduated sizes for measuring dry ingredients.

Mixer A handheld mixer with detachable beaters works well for creaming butter, whipping egg whites and cream, and mixing batters. A stand mixer, usually with three attachments—paddle, whip, and dough hook—can accommodate larger amounts of batter and leave your hands free for adding ingredients.

Rasp grater A flat grater with a handle is the most efficient tool for zesting citrus fruits.

Rolling pin Usually made of wood, these heavy cylinders are used for rolling out pastry and cookie doughs. Pins with handles are the easiest to use.

Spoons, rubber spatulas & whisks Wooden spoons are ideal for mixing batters. Rubber spatulas are used for scraping bowls and folding in delicate ingredients. Whisks—particularly balloon whisks—are handy for creating smooth mixtures and for whipping cream and egg whites.

PANS & DISHES

Baking dishes & pans These are usually made of tempered glass or heavy-gauge aluminum. For this book, you'll need 8-inch (20-cm) and 9-inch (23-cm) square pans, a 9-by-13-inch (23-by-33-cm) pan, and a 9-by-5-inch (23-cm-by-33-cm) loaf pan.

Baking sheets Sometimes called cookie sheets, these large rectangular metal pans have a shallow rim, or they are rimless, making it easier to slide cookies onto cooling racks. It's handy to have two sheets, so you can work with one sheet while the other one is in the oven.

Cake pans These round pans are generally 2 inches (5 cm) deep and 8 or 9 inches (20 or 23 cm) in diameter. Specialized cake pans you may need are a Bundt or tube pan (with a hollow, cylindrical stem in the middle) and a springform pan, whose hinged rim makes for easy unmolding.

Pie pans & dishes These round pans and dishes are made of metal, tempered glass, or ceramic and have gently sloping sides that make them perfect for pies and quiches. Glass pie dishes have the advantage of allowing you to see if the bottom crust is browned.

Ramekins These single-serving, ovenproof dishes are useful for making individual desserts.

Tart pans Available in many sizes and shapes, shallow metal tart pans usually have fluted edges and a removable bottom for easy unmolding.

Using fresh seasonal ingredients is an easy way to ensure great flavor and to match what you bake with the mood and weather of the moment. Below is a general guide to year-round baking.

Spring Celebrate the return of the warm weather and the start of the growing season by showcasing early spring produce such as ripe strawberries, rhubarb, and fragrant fresh mint in pies and crumbles.

Summer Shortcakes, pies, crisps, and cobblers are particularly well suited to the season's abundance of sweet berries and juicy stone fruits. Use the summertime bounty of melons to make light, simple, appealing desserts.

Autumn Warm up with spicy treats scented with cinnamon, ginger, and nutmeg and packed with apples, cranberries, nuts, pears, and pumpkin.

Winter Holiday festivities mean dinner parties, cookie exchanges, and long, lazy brunches. Indulge in chocolate cakes and cookies. Bake with year-round staples such as dried fruits, maple syrup, and fruit jams.

quick & easy desserts

Making a dessert does not have to take hours in the kitchen. Speed and ease characterize all of these desserts, any one of which would be welcome on a weeknight menu when you're short on time.

- CHOCOLATE-TOPPED SWEETS Drizzle melted chocolate over coffee or vanilla ice cream. Or, to make chocolate-dipped strawberries, leaving the stems intact, dip each berry into the melted chocolate, coating three-fourths of the fruit. Place on parchment (baking) paper to set and then serve. To melt chocolate, chop it into small chunks and place it in the top pan of a double boiler or a heatproof bowl set over barely simmering water. Make sure the water does not touch the bottom of the top pan, and do not let the water boil. As it melts, stir the chocolate with a wooden spoon. (Or, to melt chocolate in a microwave, place the chunks in a microwave-safe dish and heat on low. Stir it after 1 minute and check it every 30 or 40 seconds thereafter to avoid scorching it.)

- ICE CREAM SANDWICHES Make quick ice cream sandwiches with purchased cookies and a complementary ice cream, such as chocolate wafers with mint-chip ice cream or gingersnaps with vanilla gelato. Let the ice cream soften, spread a thick layer on the bottom side of half of the cookies, top with the remaining cookies, and wrap with plastic wrap. Freeze for at least 1 hour to firm.

- ROASTED OR GRILLED STONE FRUIT Halve and pit nectarines or peaches and brush with honey or sprinkle with brown sugar. Roast in a hot oven or on a grill until browned and caramelized. Serve with vanilla ice cream or crème fraîche.

- SAUTÉED AUTUMN FRUIT Sauté sliced pears and apples in a little unsalted butter and brown sugar until they start to caramelize. Mix in a generous handful of toasted chopped walnuts and raisins. Add a dash of cinnamon, if desired. Serve with a dollop of crème fraîche or whipped cream (page 362).

- SUMMERTIME MIXED-BERRY COMPOTE Simmer raspberries or mixed berries, either fresh or frozen, with a cinnamon stick, or a split vanilla bean, and sugar to taste. Cook gently until syrupy, about 15 minutes. Add a little fresh lemon juice. Serve over purchased pound cake or vanilla ice cream.

storing desserts

Most baked goods can be stored at room temperature in airtight containers or wrapped in plastic wrap for a couple of days. Some items require refrigeration, however, or can be frozen for longer storage. Desserts such as tarts and pies can be made in advance and refrigerated; bring them to room temperature before serving. See the storage chart on page 418 for a list of storage times.

Quick breads & cookies To store cookies and quick breads such as muffins for more than a couple of days, freeze them: Let them cool completely after baking, then wrap tightly in aluminum foil, plastic wrap, or freezer paper. Store small items in resealable plastic freezer bags, expelling as much air as possible from the bag before sealing. Thaw at room temperature or in the refrigerator.

Tart & pastry dough Store unbaked dough, tightly wrapped or in a resealable plastic bag, in the refrigerator for 2 to 3 days. To freeze dough, unbaked pie or tart shells, and filled unbaked fruit pies, wrap in aluminum foil, plastic wrap, or freezer paper. Frozen pie and tart shells can go directly from the freezer to the oven without thawing. Frozen unbaked fruit pies can also be baked without thawing.

Pies, tarts & cakes In general, pies and tarts with custard-based fillings, such as pumpkin pie, do not freeze well. Store them in the refrigerator, unless they will be eaten within a few hours of baking. Remove from the refrigerator about 30 minutes before serving. Refrigerate cakes with whipped cream frostings immediately and those with butter frostings within 2 hours.

Ice cream, sorbet & gelato Generally, freshly made ice cream, gelato, and sorbet should be put in the freezer for at least 2 hours, or until firm, before serving. Place in an airtight container and press plastic wrap directly onto the surface of the ice cream, gelato, or sorbet. Store in the freezer for up to 5 days, and let soften at room temperature for about 10 minutes before serving.

Puff pastry Frozen commercial puff pastry is an excellent alternative to making the pastry yourself. Thaw the frozen puff pastry in the refrigerator according to the package instructions and keep it chilled until ready to use.

SWEET CONCLUSIONS

EASY FRUIT DESSERTS
- Strawberries with Lemon & Mint (page 359)
- Blackberry Fool (page 365)
- Caramelized Bananas with Coconut (page 366)

FROZEN TREATS
- Toasted Almond Gelato (page 401)
- Melon Granita (page 404)
- Plum Sorbet (page 405)

ELEGANT ENDINGS
- Roasted Plums with Ginger & Cream (page 364)
- Lemon Tart with Raspberries (page 399)
- Italian Affogato (page 406)

QUICK & SIMPLE
- Oatmeal–Chocolate Chip Cookies (page 375)
- Pound Cake (page 379)
- Apple Tart (page 392)

CHOCOLATE DECADENCE
- Chocolate-Raspberry Brownies (page 369)
- Dark Chocolate Cake (page 385)
- Chocolate Pudding (page 407)

KID FRIENDLY
- Brown Sugar Blondies (page 367)
- Ice Cream Sandwiches (page 371)
- Cherry Turnovers (page 393)

reference

measuring ingredients

While the recipes in this book provide metric conversions for liquid and solid ingredients and for temperature, these general guidelines for common conversions are handy at a moment's notice.

volume

Teaspoons	Tablespoons	Fluid Ounces	Milliliters	Cups	Pints	Quarts	Gallons
3 teaspoons	1 tablespoon	½ fluid ounce	15 ml				
	2 tablespoons	1 fluid ounce	30 ml				
	4 tablespoons	2 fluid ounces	60 ml	¼ cup			
	8 tablespoons	4 fluid ounces	125 ml	½ cup			
	16 tablespoons	8 fluid ounces	250 ml	1 cup			
		16 fluid ounces	500 ml	2 cups	1 pint		
		32 fluid ounces	1 liter	4 cups	2 pints	1 quart	
		128 fluid ounces	4 liters	16 cups	8 pints	4 quarts	1 gallon

weight

Ounces	Grams	Pounds
¼ oz	7 g	
½ oz	15 g	
1 oz	30 g	
2 oz	60 g	
3 oz	90 g	
4 oz	125 g	¼ lb
5 oz	155 g	⅓ lb
6 oz	185 g	
8 oz	250 g	½ lb
10 oz	315 g	
12 oz	375 g	¾ lb

Ounces	Grams	Pounds
14 oz	440 g	
16 oz	500 g	1 lb
18 oz	560 g	
20 oz	625 g	1¼ lb
22 oz	690 g	
24 oz	750 g	1½ lb
26 oz	815 g	
28 oz	875 g	1¾ lb
30 oz	940 g	
32 oz	1 kg	2 lb
64 oz	2 kg	4 lb

temperature

Fahrenheit	Celsius
100°	38°
200°	95°
250°	120°
300°	150°
325°	165°
350°	180°
375°	190°
400°	200°
425°	220°
450°	230°
475°	245°

yields & equivalents

Each recipe in this book provides specific ingredient measurements, but when you are at the market or prepping ingredients it's helpful to know the quantity of juice in an average lemon or the approximate volume of chopped or sliced produce yielded by the purchased items.

Fruit

Apples	3 medium = 1 lb = 3 cups sliced
Apricots	8–12 medium = 1 lb = 2 cups sliced
Bananas	3 medium = 1 lb = 2 cups sliced
Blueberries	4 oz = 1 cup
Cranberries	4 oz = 1 cup
Grapefruit	1 medium = ¾ cup juice or 1½ cups segments
Grapes	1 lb = 3 cups
Lemon	1 medium = 2–3 tablespoons juice and 1½–2 teaspoons zest
Lime	1 medium = 1–2 tablespoons juice and 1–1½ teaspoons zest
Mango	1 medium = ¾ cup cubed
Orange	1 medium = ⅓–½ cup juice and 1–2 tablespoons zest
Peaches	2–3 medium = 1 lb = 2¾ cups sliced
Pears	3 medium = 1 lb = 3 cups sliced
Plums	3–4 medium = 1 lb = 2½ cups sliced
Pomegranate	1 medium = 1–1½ cups seeds
Strawberries	1 pint = 2 cups hulled and sliced

Nuts

Almonds	5 oz = 1 cup chopped
Peanuts	5 oz = 1 cup whole
Walnuts	4 oz = 1 cup chopped

Vegetables

Asparagus	16–20 medium spears = 1 lb
Avocado	1 medium = 1 cup diced
Broccoli	1 lb = 2 cups florets
Carrots	1½ medium = 1 cup shredded
Cauliflower	1 lb = 2 cups florets
Corn	2 medium ears = 1 cup kernels
Cucumber	1 medium = 1½ cups chopped
Eggplant (aubergine)	1 medium = 1½ lb = 3 cups diced
Garlic	2 medium cloves = 1 teaspoon minced
Onion	1 medium = ⅔ cup chopped
Potatoes	2 medium = 1 lb = 2½ cups sliced
Salad greens	½ lb = 8 cups
Shallot	1 medium = 2 tablespoons minced
Tomatoes	3 medium = 1 lb = 2 cups chopped
Zucchini (courgettes)	3–4 medium = 1 lb = 3 cups sliced

Dairy

Butter	½ stick = 4 Tbsp = ¼ cup = 2 oz
	1 stick = 8 Tbsp = ½ cup = 4 oz
	2 sticks = 1 cup = 8 oz
Cheese	4 oz Cheddar = 1 cup grated
	5 oz feta = 1 cup crumbled
	8 oz ricotta = 1 cup

ingredient substitutions

Despite your best efforts to stock your kitchen and to shop for your weekly meals, you may start to make a recipe and realize that you are missing a crucial ingredient. Yogurt can stand in for sour cream, for example; lemon juice for vinegar; and dried herbs for fresh.

FOOD	AMOUNT	SUBSTITUTION
Baking powder	1 teaspoon	½ teaspoon cream of tartar plus ¼ teaspoon baking soda (bicarbonate of soda)
Baking soda (bicarbonate of soda)	1 teaspoon	4 teaspoons double-acting baking powder
Bread crumbs, dry	1 cup	1⅓ cups fresh bread crumbs
Butter, unsalted	1 cup	1 cup salted butter (decrease the salt in the recipe by ½ teaspoon)
Buttermilk	1 cup	1 tablespoon fresh lemon juice or vinegar plus enough milk to make 1 cup
		1 cup plain yogurt or sour cream
Cardamom, ground	1 teaspoon	¾ teaspoon ground cinnamon plus ¼ teaspoon freshly grated lemon zest
Cheese, mascarpone	1 cup	¾ cup cream cheese beaten with ¼ cup heavy (double) cream
Cheese, ricotta	1 cup	1 cup cottage cheese, puréed
Chocolate, bittersweet or semisweet (plain)	1 oz	½ oz unsweetened chocolate plus 1–1½ tablespoons granulated sugar
Chocolate, semisweet (plain) chips	1 cup	6 oz semisweet baking chocolate, chopped
Chocolate, unsweetened	1 oz	3 tablespoons unsweetened cocoa powder plus 1 tablespoon unsalted butter or shortening
		1⅔ oz bittersweet or semisweet chocolate (reduce the sugar in the recipe by 4 tablespoons)
Cocoa, unsweetened	3 tablespoons	1 oz unsweetened chocolate (reduce the fat in the recipe by 1 tablespoon)
Cornstarch (cornflour)	1 tablespoon	2 tablespoons all-purpose flour

ingredient substitutions continued

FOOD	AMOUNT	SUBSTITUTION
Corn syrup	light – 1 cup	1 cup sugar plus ¼ cup water
	dark – 1 cup	¾ cup light corn syrup plus ¼ cup molasses or maple syrup
Cream, half-and-half (half cream)	1 cup	½ cup partly skimmed milk plus ½ cup heavy (double) cream
		⅞ cup whole milk plus 2 tablespoons unsalted butter
Cream of tartar	¼ teaspoon	⅛–¼ teaspoon white vinegar
Cream, sour	1 cup	1 cup plain yogurt
Crème fraîche	1 cup	1 cup sour cream
		½ cup sour cream plus ½ cup heavy (double) cream
Ginger, minced fresh	2 teaspoons	1½ teaspoons dried ginger plus ½ teaspoon fresh lemon juice
Herbs, chopped fresh	1 tablespoon	¾–1 teaspoon dried herbs
Honey	1 cup	¾ cup light molasses, dark corn syrup, or maple syrup, plus ½ cup granulated sugar
Leeks, sliced	½ cup	½ cup sliced shallots or green (spring) onions
Lemongrass	2 stalks, minced	Finely grated zest and juice of 1 lemon
Lemon juice, fresh	2 tablespoons	1½ tablespoons fresh lime juice
Lemon zest, grated	2 teaspoons	2 teaspoons orange or lime zest
Lime juice, fresh	2 tablespoons	2½ tablespoons fresh lemon juice
Lime zest, grated	2 teaspoons	2 teaspoons lemon or orange zest
Pure vanilla extract	1 teaspoon	1-inch piece vanilla bean, halved and scraped
Sugar, brown	1 cup	1 cup granulated sugar combined with 2 tablespoons molasses
Vinegar, white	¼ cup	⅓ cup lemon juice
		¼ cup apple cider vinegar or Champagne vinegar
Wine, red (for deglazing)	1 cup	1 cup beef broth or stock
Wine, white (for deglazing)	1 cup	1 cup chicken broth or stock

storing fruits & vegetables

FOOD	REFRIGERATE FOR UP TO	FREEZE FOR UP TO
Fruits		
Apples	1–3 weeks	8–12 months
Apricots	1 week	8–12 months
Avocados	3–5 days	
Bananas	1–2 days, unpeeled	4–6 months
Berries and cherries	1–2 days	8–12 months
Citrus fruits	3 weeks	4–6 months
Grapes, peaches, pears, plums, and rhubarb	3–5 days	8–12 months
Melons	1 week	
Vegetables		
Asparagus	2–3 days	8–12 months (blanched)
Beans, green or wax	3–5 days	8–12 months (blanched)
Beets, cabbage, carrots, and turnips	1–2 weeks	
Broccoli, cauliflower	1 week	8–12 months (blanched)
Brussels sprouts	1 week	
Celery	1 week	
Corn, in husks	1–2 days	
Cucumbers	1 week	
Lettuce, other salad greens	1 week	
Mushrooms	1–2 days	
Peas and lima beans, unshelled	3–5 days (store unshelled in refrigerator until use)	8–12 months (blanched)
Peppers, bell (capsicums)	1 week	8–12 months (blanched)
Radishes	1–2 weeks	
Tomatoes	5–6 days	
Zucchini (courgettes)	1 week	

storing dairy & baked goods

FOOD	REFRIGERATE FOR UP TO	FREEZE FOR UP TO
Dairy		
Butter	1–2 months	6–9 months
Buttermilk	1–2 weeks	
Cheese, cottage and ricotta	5–7 days	
Cheese, cream	2 weeks	
Cheese, firm or soft	2–3 weeks	6–8 months
Cheese, hard: Parmesan, romano (grated)	6 months	6–8 months
Cream, heavy (double)	1 week	
Cream, light, or half-and-half (half cream)	1 week	3–4 months
Cream, sour	2–3 weeks	
Milk, whole or low-fat	1–2 weeks	1–3 months
Yogurt	1–2 weeks	
Eggs		
Eggs in shell, fresh	3 weeks	
Eggs in shell, hard cooked	1 week	
Egg-based dishes	1–2 days	
Breads and baked goods		
Breads, baked	1–2 weeks	2–3 months
Cakes, baked frosted	1–2 days	1–2 months
Cakes, baked unfrosted		2–4 months
Cookie/tart dough, unbaked	3 days	1–2 months
Cookies, baked	1 week	2–3 months
Fruit pies, baked	2–3 days	6–8 months
Muffins, baked		6–12 months
Quick breads, baked		2 months
Yeast dough, unbaked	3–4 days	2 months

storing meats

FOOD	REFRIGERATE FOR UP TO	FREEZE FOR UP TO
Fresh Meats		
Chops: lamb	3–5 days	6–9 months
Chops: pork and veal	2–3 days	4–6 months
Ground (minced) beef, lamb, pork, and veal	1–2 days	3–4 months
Roasts: beef	3–5 days	6–9 months
Roasts: lamb	3–5 days	6–9 months
Roasts: pork and veal	3–5 days	4–8 months
Sausage: fresh pork and beef	1–2 days	1–2 months
Sausage: precooked	5–7 days	2–3 months
Steaks: beef	3–5 days	6–9 months
Stew meat: beef, lamb, pork, and veal	1–2 days	3–4 months
Cooked Meats		
Cooked meat and meat dishes	3–4 days	2–3 months
Gravy	1–2 days	2–3 months
Meat broth	1–2 days	2–3 months
Cured Meats		
Bacon	7 days (once vacuum seal package is opened)	1 month
Cold cuts, opened	3–7 days	1–2 months
Frankfurters	7 days (once vacuum seal package is opened)	1–2 months (frozen cured meats lose quality rapidly; use as soon as possible)
Ham: half (cooked)	3–5 days	1–2 months
Ham: whole (cooked)	7 days	1–2 months
Sausage, smoked	7 days	1–2 months
Salami, dry and semi-dry	2–3 weeks	1–2 months

storing poultry, seafood & misc.

FOOD	REFRIGERATE FOR UP TO	FREEZE FOR UP TO
Poultry		
Chicken and turkey: ground (minced)	1–2 days	3–4 months
Chicken and turkey: whole	1–2 days	12 months
Chicken: pieces	1–2 days	9 months
Turkey: pieces	1–2 days	6 months
Turkey: smoked or cured sliced breast	3–7 days	1–2 months
Cooked chicken pieces	3–4 days	1 month
Cooked poultry dishes	3–4 days	4–6 months
Seafood		
Crab	1–2 days	2 months
Fish, fatty (mullet, salmon, striped bass, and tuna)	1–2 days	2–3 months
Fish, freshwater (cleaned)	1–2 days	6–9 months
Fish, lean (cod, flounder, haddock, halibut, and trout)	1–2 days	4–6 months
Lobster (shelled or not)	1–2 days	3–6 months
Scallops	2–3 days	3 months
Shellfish (clams, mussels, and oysters), live	1–2 days (store in coldest part of refrigerator)	
Shrimp (prawns)	1–2 days	3–6 months
Cooked fish	2–3 days	1 month
Smoked fish	1–2 weeks	4–5 weeks (vacuum-sealed)
Miscellaneous		
Ground spices		6–12 months
Salad dressings, bottled (opened)	6 months	
Soups, stews	2–3 days	4–6 months

index

Oxmoor
House®

OXMOOR HOUSE

Oxmoor House books are
distributed by Time Inc. Home Entertainment
135 West 50th Street, New York, NY 10020

VP and Associate Publisher Jim Childs
Director of Marketing Sydney Webber
Brand Manager Victoria Alfonso

WILLIAMS-SONOMA, INC.

Founder & Vice-Chairman Chuck Williams

THE WEEKNIGHT COOK

Conceived and produced by Weldon Owen Inc.
415 Jackson Street, San Francisco, CA 94111
Tel: 415-291-0100 Fax: 415-291-8841
www.weldonowen.com

In Collaboration with Williams-Sonoma, Inc.
3250 Van Ness Avenue, San Francisco, CA 94109

A Weldon Owen Production
Copyright © 2009 Weldon Owen Inc.
and Williams-Sonoma, Inc.

First printed in 2009
10 9 8 7 6 5 4 3 2 1

ISBN-13: 978-0-8487-3293-6
ISBN-10: 0-8487-3293-6

Printed in China by SNP-Leefung

WELDON OWEN INC.

Group Publisher, Bonnier Publishing Group John Owen
CEO and President Terry Newell
Senior VP, International Sales Stuart Laurence
VP, Sales and New Business Development Amy Kaneko
Director of Finance Mark Perrigo

VP and Publisher Hannah Rahill
Executive Editor Kim Laidlaw
Assistant Editor Julia Nelson

VP and Creative Director Gaye Allen
Associate Creative Director Emma Boys
Art Director Kara Church
Designer Joey Christensen

Production Director Chris Hemesath
Production Manager Michelle Duggan
Color Manager Teri Bell

Authors Melanie Barnard, Brigit Binns,
Georgeanne Brennan, Carolynn Carreño,
Julia Della Croce, Jay Harlow, Dana Jacobi,
Elinor Klivans, Norman Kolpas, Rick Rodgers,
Lou Seibert Pappas, and Farina Wong Kingsley

Photographers Bill Bettencourt and Tucker + Hossler

Food Stylists Kevin Crafts and Jennifer Straus

Prop Stylists Leigh Nöe and Robin Turk

Weldon Owen gratefully acknowledges editorial
and design assistance from: Judith Dunham,
Leslie Evans, Ashley Martinez, Jennifer Newens,
Elizabeth Parson, and Sarah Putman Clegg.